The Selling Sound

REFIGURING AMERICAN MUSIC

A series edited by Charles McGovern & Ronald Radano

The Selling Sound

THE RISE OF THE COUNTRY MUSIC INDUSTRY

Diane Pecknold

DUKE UNIVERSITY PRESS

Durham & London   2007

© 2007 Duke University Press

All rights reserved

Printed in the United States of America

on acid-free paper ∞

Designed by C. H. Westmoreland

Typeset in Warnock Pro by Keystone Typesetting, Inc.

Library of Congress Cataloging-in-Publication data ap-

pear on the last printed page of this book.

Contents

Acknowledgments

I started this project in 1997, while working for the Billions Corporation. In some measure, it was an effort both to redeem my own relentless music fandom and to recuperate the experiences of dozens of "noncreative" people I knew from the image of corporate evil that attaches to the very name "music business." Though he will undoubtedly disagree with just about every philosophical viewpoint expressed here (if only out of the habit of disagreeing with me), Boche Billions has served as an inspiration throughout. I am particularly grateful that he forgave me for quitting so I could write this.

My emotional attachment to this work stems from my non-academic experience, but my intellectual approach to it was shaped by the faculty of Indiana University's Department of History, who served as role models, mentors, and advisors. Michael McGerr provided personal, professional, and scholarly guidance throughout the evolution of this project. He gave me the confidence and direction that made it possible to complete an otherwise overwhelming task. I am also grateful to my dissertation committee members—John Bodnar, Wendy Gamber, Glenn Gass, and Jeffrey Wasserstrom—for offering perceptive feedback and suggestions for future research directions. The department also offered a grant-in-aid of research as I was formulating the project, and I was especially honored to receive the Wiseman Family Fellowship in support of research on rural life and culture.

Several colleagues outside the department also took the time to read all or part of the manuscript and to provide comments and criticism that greatly improved the final result. I am grateful to James Akenson, Kristine McCusker, and Pamela Robertson Wojcik for their generosity and their keen insights on early drafts. I am especially indebted to the readers for Duke University Press, David Sanjek and Aaron Fox. Their comments on the initial manuscript were invaluable in transforming it into a book. Both have gone well beyond the call of duty by reading additional revisions on an informal basis and offering feedback and ideas in personal conversation. They turned what is usually an anonymous and therefore impersonal role into an opportunity to mentor a much less experienced writer, and I am eternally grateful for their support. Thanks also to the participants in the 2005 Word on Music conference at Duke University, who gave me a fresh perspective on what I was doing when I really needed it.

I could not have dreamed of a better publishing experience than the one I have had at Duke University Press. Ken Wissoker and Courtney Berger guided me through an unfamiliar review and editing process, shared their wisdom and long experience, offered timely reassurances, and rescued me from many flaws in framing and style. They endured several years of questions and delays without ever giving the impression of being importuned even a little bit. I feel tremendously fortunate to have worked with them.

Before this was a book manuscript, however, it was a sprawling and intimidating research project and would probably have remained so without the generous help I received at various research sites. I owe a special debt of gratitude to Dr. John Rumble at the Country Music Hall of Fame and Museum. Without his research expertise and extensive knowledge of the country industry and its key figures, I would never have found the sources that are the foundation of this story. Other staff members at the museum also graciously offered their time, skills, and expertise. Ronnie Pugh, Lauren Bufferd, and Dawn Oberg were especially helpful in the process of locating materials. Lee Rowe tolerated an intolerably complex request for photos with great patience. Michael Gray encouraged this and a number of other projects and always made me feel especially welcome at the archive. Kevin Parks at SOUNDIES was good-hearted enough to share his impressive personal collection of country music materials with an unknown researcher and to allow the reproduction of images from that collection for the book.

I also could not have finished my research without the assistance of a number of fans and professionals who shared their time, enthusiasm, and wisdom. Thanks to Linda Kay at the National Association of Fan Clubs, whose willingness to dig through dusty boxes to oblige a total stranger epitomizes the spirit of generosity that makes fan club work so rewarding for so many people. Joe Allison, Jo Walker-Meador, and Loudilla Johnson entertained hours of questions with patience and kindness. Bill Anderson responded to a number of e-mail queries in spite of his busy schedule. If the final product does not always reflect their own views, I hope it at least celebrates their efforts and achievements.

I'm still astonished at how much time it takes (for me) to write a book, and I'm grateful to a number of employers who allowed me the time and flexibility to keep working at it. At the University of Illinois at Chicago, Nina Shepherd was almost as fiercely determined that I should finish as I was. I wish she had seen the book reach publication. John Wanat, Uday Sukhatme, and Clark Hulse were similarly understanding about part-time schedules and conference leave. The wonderful staff at the Study Abroad Office took up the slack when I was otherwise occupied; thanks to Irina Krymova, Nicole Seidlitz, and Lexy Sobel especially.

At the University of Louisville, where I have since found a congenial and stimulating home, I am grateful to Thomas Byers, J. Blaine Hudson, Nancy Theriot, and Elaine Wise for their support and encouragement, and to Natalie Polzer for her companionship. Thanks, too, to the faculty and staff of the Department of Women's and Gender Studies and the Division of Humanities, as well as the Feminist Theory Reading Group, for providing moral support and a welcome relief from the isolation of research and writing. Special thanks are also due James Hensley, whose timely intervention averted the loss of every file related to the project just a few weeks before the final manuscript was submitted.

I have had the good fortune to be surrounded by wonderful friends, family, and colleagues throughout the decade-plus it has taken to complete this work. David Thelen, Susan Armeny, Patrick Ettinger, Julie Plaut, Paul Schadewald, Scott Stephan and the staff at the *Journal of American History* made my experience there the most important and pleasurable of graduate school. They taught me that no single-authored work is ever really the work of a single author, and they showed me how important it is to focus my attention on real people, especially when discussing things, like popular culture, that can so easily become unmoored from the lives that produce them.

A lot happens in ten years—two children, three moves, four jobs—and my family made it possible to survive it all. My love and gratitude go to Kathleen Holden, David Pecknold, Kathryn Courtney, and Julie and Richard Johnson for cheerfully toting the barge in so many ways.

Most of all, though, this book was made possible by the support, infinite patience, and plain old hard work of Clark Johnson. Clark taught me to love country music, and then tenaciously endured the lasting consequences of that terrible mistake. Lilian and Lucy have made innumerable sacrifices in seeing this work to its conclusion. I love you. Thanks for putting up with the obsession.

Introduction

"There's money in the new songs if you are willing to put on a hillbilly outfit and stand up to the mike and do what Rufus tells you," observes Danny MacGregor, the narrator and protagonist of *The Big Ballad Jamboree*. Written in the 1950s by the agrarian poet Donald Davidson, the novel explores the themes of commercialism and tradition in the country music business. Danny is a guitarist with the Turkey Hollow Boys, a hillbilly band in the golden age of barn dance radio, and the novel traces his internal struggle to reconcile the cultural traditions of his rural community with the commercial demands of his career as a musician. At times Danny chafes at the emphasis on profit, as when he gives in to his impulse to play an old mountain ballad rather than a modern hillbilly song during a Turkey Hollow Boys broadcast. "To begin with, the commercial set my teeth on edge," he grumbles to the reader by way of explanation. "Start the day with Kurly Krisps! Kurly, Kurly, Kurly Krisps! Sweet and crunchy! Good and munchy!" When he finishes his unauthorized indulgence in traditional folk balladry, he faces the wrath of Rufus, his bandleader, and the station manager. "Cut out that long-hair stuff!" the manager tells him, "We want real hillbilly music."[1]

But when the Turkey Hollow Boys play at a local high school gymnasium, Danny is transported by the excitement and pleasure he shares with the audience, no matter how carefully staged or slickly planned the act.

> There was something about it that always made the hairs on the back of my neck stand up and thrill. . . . Maybe it was just partly the excitement of the crowd that I could hear rustling and stirring and even yelping a little on the other side of the stage. . . . Some would call it almost too slick. . . . Some would even say "trashy," but when the fiddles are bowing fast and full, with the strong beat of the guitars and bass bearing them up, and the voices coming in, it goes right to the marrow of the bone, it just gathers you up, and I don't see how any man or woman can stand out against it.

While the tension he feels between commerce and authenticity is never resolved, Danny's occasional dissatisfaction with the profit-obsessed production system of hillbilly is ultimately immaterial to the experiential power of listening to and playing his music.[2]

Few expressions of popular culture have been shaped as strongly by the relationship between commercialism and authenticity as country music. Though its apparent realism, sincerity, and frank depictions of everyday life are its most obvious stylistic hallmarks, it has always been defined as a genre by its relationship to business. In the 1920s and 1930s, upper-class folk preservationists distinguished hillbilly from folk music not so much by instrumentation or formal structure as by the fact that the former was performed for money while the latter was presented as a philanthropic exercise in cultural uplift. In the 1950s, country music remained distinct from rockabilly in large part by virtue of its different location within the production system of the music industry. In the 1960s, the renewal of the music's commercial popularity after a period of decline prompted concern about whether it could persist as an independent genre.

Although the importance of commercialism in shaping the artistic development of country music has long been recognized, it has usually been treated as a transparent concept: the falsehood to authenticity's truth, the fabrication to authenticity's spontaneity. Frequently, commercialism is understood simply as the shameful secret that country music's pretensions to authenticity must labor to obscure. "Success in Nashville has always been about the twin pursuits of myth and money," writes one journalist in his account of the contemporary country industry. Celebrations of everyday life, imbued with mythical status by the words and imagery of country music, he says, "provide a homey distraction from the turning wheels of the machine that is the business of country." While authenticity signifies, commercialism just is.[3]

But just how distracting is the constructed naturalness of country music to its listeners? Whatever else they may hear in a favorite voice or song, do they not also hear the wheels of the business machine turning? Certainly midcentury social critics thought not. When Vance Packard testified before Congress in 1958 that radio broadcasters were manipulating the public taste to create an unnatural demand for rock and roll and country music, he relied on the assumption that audiences took what they got and learned to like it, an assumption that has characterized a good deal of scholarship on popular music. In this formulation, consumers of industrially produced culture are "oblivious targets of an industrial system that perceives them as nothing more than customers." Listeners fail to recognize the power relationships inherent in the production of industrial cultural texts and absorb uncritically the dominant values reflected there, particularly the values of capitalism and commercialism.[4]

A 2002 feature article in the *New York Times* lamenting the state of contemporary country radio demonstrated the persistence of this collection of assumptions about country music and commercialism: that the financial economy of popular music goes unnoticed by its audience; that that economy controls and distorts audience tastes; and that it makes for aesthetically bad music. Responding to the critical and commercial success of the soundtrack for the film *O Brother Where Art Thou?*—an album that featured traditional country, bluegrass, and "roots" music and won a Grammy for Album of the Year but was not played on country radio—the article argued that the legends and traditions of country were being tossed aside for hunks in hats singing love songs to suburban housewives in the interest of peddling personal care products. "If there's one culprit in the current state of country music, it may be Crest Whitestrips," the article's author asserted. "Because when you point a finger at Crest Whitestrips, you're pointing at Procter & Gamble, the product's maker and one of the largest purchasers of radio advertising time. And the major advertisers are the people who really control what you hear on the radio." This corporate control distorts the tastes of country listeners, who, the article averred, "have much broader taste than radio programmers, advertisers, and record-label executives tend to believe." Given that country was then the most popular radio format in America, a reader could only conclude that advertisers had successfully duped insouciant listeners into uncritically accepting not only bad music but also the products advertised, and indeed the whole nefarious complex of commercialism and consumer culture. In essence, the article concluded, "More than any other genre, country is a fine-tuned jingle."[5]

A great deal of evidence, however, suggests that as the country genre took shape in the twentieth century, listeners could indeed hear the wheels of commerce turning. From early fan magazines that explained the economics of radio broadcasting to more recent best-sellers that trace the inner workings of Nashville for their readers, the workings of the country business have been a central element of the music's image. Rather than seeing that commercial machinery as a filter through which listeners approached a song or performance, however, the narrative presented in this book treats commercialism as a cultural text in its own right. Our understanding of how country (and popular music more generally) is produced and received can be enriched by exploring how commercialism itself may become a way of expressing deeper emotions and hopes harbored by many listeners. The fact of country's commercial popularity or lack of it—the music's status as a consumer product—was an issue to which many listeners, fans and critics alike, attached meaning and importance, even when these did not affect their direct experience of listening to country music. When country fans complained in the mid-1950s about elite control of mass media or when they expressed their gratitude that the Country Music Hall of Fame served as a physical symbol of the industry's commercial power, they engaged directly with the commercial apparatus surrounding country music, not with the texts it produced.

This is not to suggest that the cultural meanings attached to commercialism by country listeners were always unambiguously celebratory. Gary Cross has written that in twentieth-century America, "Consumerism succeeded where other ideologies failed because it concretely expressed the cardinal political ideals of the century—liberty and democracy—and with relatively little self-destructive behavior or personal humiliation." Popular magazines aimed at country fans, and reader responses to them, certainly invoked the popularity of country music as a symbol of consumer democracy. Resentment of the perceived cultural elitism in attitudes toward country music prefigured in quite specific ways the anti-liberal politics of the New Right. But the same writings and declarations also evinced a sophisticated understanding of cultural authority and power and expressed a clear critique of both. There remained in them broader misgivings about the pitfalls of consumer capitalism and the boundaries of class. These sentiments suggest that many country music listeners found themselves caught somewhere between the anti–mass media suspicions of the old left and the joyful populist consumer democracy of Richard Nixon.[6]

If scholars and journalists have tended to portray audiences as oblivious to the workings of country music's financial economies, they have generally imagined the producers of country—artists; record producers, artist-and-repertoire managers, label executives; and broadcasters—to be so obsessed with the pursuit of profit that cultural meaning and cultural value simply do not exist within the economy of the music industry. While a host of studies have examined the culturally productive activities of readers, listeners, and watchers of popular culture, the circulation of contested cultural meanings within the commercial institutions that make up the culture industries has remained largely unexamined. But the shibboleth that "people are in it for the money" is, as David Sanjek and Keith Negus have suggested, only a partial truth. Throughout the history of country music, the entrepreneurs and artists of the business have been as concerned as their audiences with the genre's cultural status and its aesthetic and social values. Their decisions about how to present themselves and their music were based not only on their imaginings of how best to make a profit but also on the same kinds of personal desires—for dignity, for identification, for recognition—that animate much of American consumerism. Thus, the history of the field's most important trade organization, the Country Music Association, is as indicative of the aspirations and insecurities of its members as it is of their pursuit of financial success.[7]

The history of country's relationship to the larger music industry also demonstrates the importance of the cultural economy that circulates through the businesses of popular culture. The critics and businessmen of Tin Pan Alley were so scornful of hillbilly in its early days in large part because they hoped to maintain their monopoly on American popular music and to minimize the threat that hillbilly musicians posed to the control of the entrenched financial economy of popular music. The publishers and labor leaders of the music industries enlisted a set of cultural meanings already circulating around the idea of the "hillbilly" to bolster their economic prerogatives. By defining hillbilly music as culturally bad, they justified a series of institutional exclusions whose effect was to make hillbilly music economically cheap for radio broadcasters and advertisers. In turn, that economic cheapness helped to reshape the cultural meaning of hillbilly.[8]

During the 1950s, the same interests again worked to minimize the cultural value of country and other commercialized vernacular forms in order to protect their control of licensing profits. In hearings before Congress, supporters of the Tin Pan Alley system mobilized the negative associations academic and popular critics had elaborated around the idea of the cultural commodity, suggesting that the popularity of country and rock and roll was a result of manipulation by unscrupulous entrepreneurs whose practices threatened both cultural standards and basic liberty and should therefore be limited. This bid to re-establish Tin Pan Alley's monopoly over licensing failed in large part because representatives of the country field successfully defended their economic rights through an impassioned defense of the cultural value of their music. Throughout the conflict over popular music licensing, conscious intervention in the cultural economy profoundly affected the structure of the music business's financial economy.

Conversely, and perhaps most unexpectedly, the concerted and largely successful effort to recast country music as an art form worthy of intellectual study was made possible only by the commercial power of the country industry, focused through the Country Music Association. Committed journalists and folklorists struggled against official cultural hierarchies that denigrated commercial country music throughout the 1950s and 1960s, publishing the landmark "hillbilly issue" of the *Journal of American Folklore* and organizing the John Edwards Memorial Foundation to promote serious study of the music. But the incorporation of country music into the American cultural canon as a form that could be compared to the poetry of Walt Whitman and Ralph Waldo Emerson was ultimately accomplished not within the academy but through the Country Music Hall of Fame and Museum. While motivated in part by a strictly preservationist spirit, the museum was also manifestly an effort to reach out to the lucrative folk market and to defend marketing and production boundaries, and it was initially funded overwhelmingly by commercial record sales. Here again, the cultural and financial values of country were inextricably connected.[9]

The failure to imagine the audience as active, critical participants in the culture industries and the concomitant neglect of the ways cultural meanings are contested within and help to structure the music's financial economy have distorted traditional assessments of country music. In his important exploration of the cultural construction of authenticity as a shifting synthesis of old and new, for example, Richard Peterson presents stylistic innovation in the 1930s and 1940s as the result of changing industrial conditions, almost without reference to an audience. When the audience does appear, the nature of its preferences and power is speculative and unclear. Peterson explains that Depression-era radio artists adopted "open, down-home, and utterly conventional" personas because advertisers and broadcasters demanded them, but he seems unwilling to accept the notion that audiences might have consciously, and rationally, embraced the "conventional bourgeois morality" that advertisers and broadcasters sought to impose on the working-class audience they imagined for hillbilly broadcasts. Dismissing the possibility that audiences might have embraced such ideologies for their own purposes, he renders the age of barn dance and barnstorming country radio simply as a mechanistic adaptation to technological and economic forces.[10]

Interpretations of the commercialization associated with the Nashville Sound of the late 1950s and early 1960s reflect the same shortcomings. Even when they seem ultimately sympathetic to the desire of Nashville Sound–era producers and businessmen to broaden country's appeal, historians tend to view the period's stylistic changes and marketing strategies as a cynical hoax perpetrated against an unsuspecting audience. Joli Jensen, for instance, perceptively argues that the truth or untruth of charges that country music "sold out" are less important than the role the debate itself plays in helping us to recognize the irresolvable dilemmas of modern life: the payoffs and losses associated with waged work, cheap consumer goods, and intense individualism. But she also describes the Nashville Sound first as an economic strategy and only secondarily as a meaningful expression of aesthetic or social values. Country's smoother sounds, she argues, were a set of "economically based changes" that had to be retrospectively "justified as necessary and, ultimately, worthwhile." The notion that audiences might have found the changes worthwhile precisely because of the commercialism they represented remains unexamined.[11]

Commercialism is a complex social construction. Its meanings and rhetorical uses have changed over time. Throughout the twentieth century, both consumers and producers of country music were engaged in ongoing debates about the importance of commercialism and the impact of specific commercial structures on their music. Meanings circulated in the cultural economy have legitimized or challenged the way country was produced and valued within the financial economy, and country's financial economy itself has become a critical component of its meaning in the cultural economies of critics, scholars, and policymakers as well as those of "conventional" consumers. Like Danny MacGregor, those audiences have recognized the flaws and inequalities of commercial cultural production systems but embraced their fruits all the same. In the process, they have found meaning not only in the emotional and social power of the music itself but also in the cultural texts of commercialism. This book attempts to trace both the vital cultural economy embedded within the industry and the changing cultural meanings of the country business.

Chapter 1 begins by situating country music as a product of the modernizing forces that changed the nature of the popular music industry in the 1920s and 1930s. The advent of country music as a commercial style was rooted partly in the social dislocations associated with urbanization. But equally important were changes in the technology and institutions of the popular music industry that made it possible, even necessary, to profit from rural vernacular styles. I thus begin by examining how the early business arrangements surrounding the production of country music—especially its particularly close alliance with broadcasting and broadcast advertising—affected perceptions of the genre's cultural value.

The second part of the chapter examines the changing contours of the country music audience during the same years, roughly 1920 to 1947. Here and throughout, the concept of "audience" is understood to include not only listeners who enjoyed country music but also nonlisteners for whom country music carried material or symbolic importance: intellectuals and academics; professional critics and others who viewed themselves as arbiters of taste; and fans of other kinds of music who defined themselves in contradistinction to country and country listeners. This section seeks to illustrate how a new, more class-based understanding of the genre was forged from above and from below. Changing local performance contexts and audience experiences shaped a more aggressive, distinct sound based on southern vernacular styles. Early audience research and other cultural-political forces also helped to narrow the image of the country audience during the Depression and war. Country listeners, meanwhile, constructed symbolic personal relationships with favored stars and used country music to reinforce social relationships in their own communities. They began to develop ways of understanding the meaning of commercialism and the relationship between older systems of producing popular music and newer, more commercial ones.

Chapter 2 sketches the dramatic changes in the culture industries in the wake of the Second World War and examines how those changes both created a full-fledged country music industry and threw it into crisis. The rise to power of the record industry and the proliferation of independent radio stations during the late 1940s resulted in a dramatic increase in country's popularity and ultimately in the birth of rock. The same circumstances also produced an organized, self-aware cadre of country music professionals with an interest in protecting the boundaries of the genre and the profits that resulted from it. These entrepreneurs and artists undertook the work of channeling a hodgepodge of regional and commercial styles into a single genre with a focused, managed, and marketable image, and they came to preside over an increasingly centralized system of production located in Nashville. This chapter traces their initial efforts to define and defend an autonomous country music industry.

Chapter 3 focuses on the place of country music in what Michael Kammen calls the "Great Debate" over cultural power and cultural authority that accompanied the postwar reconfiguration of the mass media and culture industries. The congressional anti-monopoly hearings that produced a now-famous collection of vituperations against rock and youth culture initially directed an equal amount of scorn and dismay at country music. The ways that different audiences separated country music from rock and other genres by the race, age, and, most importantly, class of its listeners spoke to the importance of country music as a means of establishing both the respectability and the power of its audience. These divisions also presaged the extremely successful marketing strategy of the Country Music Association. At the same time, the battle over the economic spoils of country music exposed increasing uncertainties about the definition of cultural value, as commercial popularity vied with the opinion of educated critics as a legitimate criterion by which to measure aesthetic quality. Country listeners' perceptions of the mass media and their suspicion of the cultural elite they felt controlled the media revealed significant continuities with leftist critiques of the media and signaled important fissures in the white middle class.

Chapter 4 returns to Nashville in 1958 to trace the formation and mission of the Country Music Association (CMA), the trade group that organized the various sectors of the country industry in support of a unified marketing strategy. During the 1960s, the CMA developed a sophisticated campaign to polish the image not only of country music but of its blue-collar audience as well. For those in Nashville's country business, commercialism became a language for expressing the dignity of both its producers and its audience. In the process, the CMA became one avenue for mediating knowledge about class difference in the southern white migration. At the same time, the development of format country radio helped to define a historical canon for the genre while eliminating remaining regional variations and made country music a truly national style.

Chapter 5 looks again to the country audience, particularly its response to the more sophisticated, uptown Nashville Sound that had become the dominant style within the genre. By the 1960s, many of the local performance contexts that had once influenced country music had disappeared, changing the cultural meaning of country and fans' relationship to it. Listener responses to changes in country music evinced uncertainty about the effects of postwar abundance and the consequences of absorption into the suburban middle class. Though many were ambivalent about the embrace of commercialism in country music and elsewhere in American culture, most country fans appear to have accepted and even endorsed the economic aspirations of the industry. This viewpoint was encouraged by the new history-making institutions of the Country Music Association, which fused cultural power and cultural authority to create a popular historical narrative that celebrated commercial success as part of the country tradition.

Finally, chapter 6 examines how the country audience, at last fully defined as a commodity with specific socio-cultural features, was mobilized as both a market and a metaphor during the late 1960s and early 1970s. After years of participating directly in the financial economy of the business, many fans resisted the reduction of the audience to a market and the concomitant imposition of a strict distinction between producers and consumers. The creation of Fan Fair and the accompanying controversy over the articulation between fan clubs and the industry helped to institutionalize the fan culture that remains one of the most remarkable features of the country industry. At the same time, the country audience as a marketing demographic received new, more politically charged attention. Critics on both the left and right recapitulated the marketing assumptions of the CMA and broadcasters as they searched for "Silent America." And, as it had during the 1950s, country continued to serve as a metaphor for the impact of commercialism and popular culture on American life, a metaphor enshrined most powerfully through Robert Altman's *Nashville*.

Most investigations of cultural production and consumption have taken as their subject contemporary manifestations of popular culture and rely heavily on ethnographic methods. The historical approach taken here offers a clearer notion of change in popular understandings of commercial culture over time, and therefore of the effect of different institutional arrangements on those understandings. But it also poses evidentiary difficulties that ethnographers do not face. Because their activities and responses were long thought to be uncritical and simplistic, little historical material created by country listeners survives. What is available has usually been filtered by the industry in some way, either by the editors of commercial magazines to which listeners wrote, or by selective retention in radio station and artist files designed to demonstrate the nature and loyalty of the audience. Fan letters are often somewhat elliptical, as well, assuming that editors and readers understand the full context and the specific artists and styles to which the writer refers. And, of course, the number of fans who did not leave a record of their thoughts outweighs by hundreds of thousands the number who did write about their experiences. The stories of fans presented here are not meant to be characterizations of the whole country music audience, a polyglot formation that defies generalizations. Instead, I have invoked the voices of listeners and fans in an effort to explore some of the possibilities they identified in their listening and fan activities.

Fans of country music in particular will be struck by the extent to which this book is expressly not about the music itself. I do not discuss individual artists or songs except insofar as they help to illuminate professional, popular, and fan discourses about the meaning of country as a genre and an industry. I have chosen to ignore the traditional texts of country music studies for a number of reasons. A host of insightful studies have detailed the musical development of country's many and varied subgenres, and there seems little point in reiterating them here. Moreover, because of its richness and variety, there are few generalizations that can be extended to country as a whole, yet the genre itself clearly carries relatively unified meanings that transcend individual song texts. I am interested here not in the possible political, cultural, and social expressions offered by specific country music songs but rather in what the genre has been made to represent in American culture at large, both by those who are intimately familiar with its songs and by those who are not. Most importantly, I avoid the music itself in order to emphasize the cultural meanings attached to the system that produces it.

It was back in 1924 that the barn dance moved down out of the hay-mow into the living room of the American home. Close on its heels followed the vogue for mountain music. Out from the latter cycle strode Ezra K. Hillbilly to become the core of an industry which rings the cash registers of radio and entertainment to the tune of $25,000,000 a year. And that's important money in any business.—HARRY STEELE, "The Inside Story of the Hillbilly Business"

1

Commercialism and the Cultural Value of Country Music, 1920–1947

On Saturday nights during the 1920s, thousands of listeners turned on their radio sets to be "hypnotized by the yellow eye of the dial." The technology of broadcasting seemed almost disquieting in its novelty— one fanzine later referred to "the days when hillbilly radio entertaining was just a futuristic dream." As they peered at their sets, listeners could imagine that "the delicate mechanism of the radio . . . caught and brought to the ears of us earth dwellers the noises that roar in the space between the worlds." Like the airplanes she sometimes saw fly overhead as she worked the cotton fields, radio was an emissary of the wider world to Florence Ward Ausburn. The daughter of Georgia sharecroppers, Ausburn marveled at her landlord's battery-operated radio and the changes it augured, even though the music she heard every Saturday night when he tuned in the Grand Ole Opry for his tenants was reassuringly familiar. The old-time fiddlers, ancient ballads, and well-worn popular tunes she enjoyed were wrapped in a veneer of unmistakable modernity, delivered from the ether amid the advertising messages of a new consumer order that was reshaping the countryside.[1]

Given country music's association with rusticity and nostalgia, it is sometimes difficult to imagine that its earliest audiences and critics approached the genre through a veil of modernity and commercialism. Early hillbilly traded on the emotional associations, visual imagery, and performance styles of the past, but its structural connections to new technologies and to the early-twentieth-century extension of consumer capitalism into the hinterland positioned it as an exponent of the contemporary world and complicated, maybe even necessitated, its pretensions to simplicity and timelessness. Commercial hillbilly music was embraced as a marketing vehicle by the emerging broadcast advertising industry, rejected as a cynical corruption of tradition by folklorists and preservationists, cited as an example of the deleterious potential of mass media by radio reformers, and rebuffed as a cultural irritant that symbolized the problematic nature of Southern migrants in the minds of established residents of the urban north and west. Paradoxically, in spite of being patently pastoral, hillbilly music often represented unsettling forces of technological, industrial, and class change between 1920 and 1940. Indeed, the specific forms hillbilly's invented authenticity assumed —traditional, rough-hewn, rural—constituted a mirror image of the discourses about modernity that some anxious outsiders imposed on it—a glossy, cheap confection of modern radio; a harbinger of culture's subservience to commerce in a mass media regime; and a product of the disruptions of urban migration.

Richard Peterson and others have shown that hillbilly was enmeshed in conspicuously modern commercial relationships—in new conceptions of intellectual property expressed in copyright law and in the growing cash nexus that made farmers new consumers to the life insurance industry— but fewer chroniclers of the genre's history have recognized that contemporary observers, no less than current scholars, perceived it that way. In contrast to its aesthetic, hillbilly's economic position represented the confluence of technological advances and the maturing power of commercial culture, and critics and fans responded to it as they responded to the possibilities of industrial mass consumerism itself, with a mixture of fascination, unease, and excitement. Those responses, which were often meant to guard or extend specific economic and social privileges, helped to determine hillbilly's cultural and class meaning. Listeners, critics, and entrepreneurs all made sense of the new genre and fixed its cultural significance as much through their understandings of its commercialism as through their readings of its visual and musical substance.[2]

Commercialism and Country Music

Hillbilly music was above all a creature of radio. Although the earliest indications of the genre's commercial potential were the recordings of artists like Vernon Dalhart, it was broadcasting rather than publishing or recording that provided the lasting foundation for the country music industry. From the mid-1920s through the end of the Depression, radio remained the cornerstone of the hillbilly economy. Few performers survived on the wages they earned from the stations, and fewer still from the royalties generated by publishing or record sales, but a radio show served as a means of advertising the products that did support artists: the live shows that were the mainstay of every hillbilly musician's livelihood, the photographs and self-published song folios that they sold by direct inquiry, and, less importantly, the recordings marketed by the music industry.[3]

The first barn dance show, an hour-and-a-half program of square dance and fiddle music, was broadcast over WBAP in Fort Worth, Texas, in 1923. In those early days of radio, the station's signal could be heard as far away as Haiti, so there is some possibility that the WBAP square dances served as a model for the barn dance format. More likely, though, is the explanation offered by Edgar L. Bill, station manager for the Sears-Roebuck station in Chicago, which in 1924 inaugurated the most important and oft-replicated model for the hillbilly barn dance, the WLS *National Barn Dance*. According to Bill, the station's programmers, like most of their peers in the fledgling industry, "would try anything once," broadcasting classical music, dance bands, choral music, and whatever else could be arranged. Bill's later account attributed the decision to broadcast a fiddler and a square-dance caller one Saturday night to a spirit of reasoned experimentation. "When it came to Saturday night," he said, "it was quite natural to book old-time music, including old-time fiddling, banjo and guitar music and cowboy songs. We leaned toward the homey, old-time familiar tunes because we were a farm station."[4]

As Bill's description of his programming aims suggest, what is now called country music was not constituted as a single recognizable genre during these years. Variously designating it as hillbilly, old-time music, folk, or in one particularly loquacious formulation, "mountain, barn and hillbilly music," programmers, audiences, and the press were likely to lump it together with other "light" music, ethnic fare, and hymns until the mid-1940s. The elasticity of the radio barn dance encouraged this conjoining of diverse styles. The typical barn dance was a stylized rendition of the tradition of old-fashioned "country 'sociables,'" consisting of a series of musical and comedy selections introduced by a master of ceremonies who was also frequently the advertisers' spokesman. Comedians and musicians alike developed theatrical stock characters that drew on a variety of rural and regional stereotypes. These personalities were usually designed to accord with the act's specialized performance style: Victorian ladies and small-town sweethearts sang old-time sentimental pop, string bands and rube comedians wore overalls and toted jugs, and clean-scrubbed mountain balladeers reaffirmed valued folkways. The characters, and frequently the personnel as well, came straight from the vaudeville stage. Even the Grand Ole Opry, the most emphatically hillbilly of the major barn dances, started out with an astonishingly diverse assortment of music that included jazz, Dixieland, string bands, military bands, and gospel and barbershop quartets along with old popular standards. Well into the 1930s, the show featured vaudeville performers passing through Nashville and pop-influenced stars like the vocal harmony trio the Vagabonds.[5]

Once developed, the form of the barn dance remained relatively constant, though its content and imagery underwent significant change. This continuity was due in large part to the regular exchange of musical and managerial personnel from station to station. In the Midwest and South, the diffusion of staff from the WLS *National Barn Dance* to a number of smaller regional shows is easily traced. The most important spinoff of the *National Barn Dance*, the Grand Ole Opry, was created by George D. Hay, who had developed his "Solemn Old Judge" character at WLS before moving to WSM in 1926. Lowell Blanchard and Richard Westergaard, creators of Knoxville's WNOX *Midday Merry Go-Round* and *Tennessee Barn Dance*, had previously worked together in Des Moines, home of WHO's *Iowa Barn Dance Frolic*, which had been founded by Joe Maland, a former WLS programmer. By the late 1930s, Cincinnati's WLW aired two major barn dance shows in addition to a host of less-well-known hillbilly offerings. John Lair, who had enjoyed many years of success as a performer on the *National Barn Dance*, started his own show, the *Renfro Valley Barn Dance*, in 1937. The following year the *Boone County Jamboree*, produced by the former WLS program manager George Biggar and the WLS talent bureau agent Bill McKluskey, went on the air.[6]

Though the structure was formulaic, the barn dance allowed for a great deal of regional diversity. As the shows proliferated in the 1930s, originality within the standard format became an important commodity for sponsors. When John Lair left WLS to create the *Renfro Valley Barn Dance*, he and his advertising representative, Freeman Keyes, shared a concern for establishing an "individuality that will satisfy the sponsor" and strove to lend the show "a different atmosphere" that would "still keep it in the barn loft." As a result, Lair emphasized rural humor, folk traditionalism, and old-time songs to a greater degree than many contemporaries, though he still made room for more current pop numbers. WNOX in Knoxville also developed a signature style within the constraints of the barn dance formula. In addition to the standard fiddle tunes and rube comedy routines, WNOX broadcasts featured a more polished, country-jazz sound rendered by the Stringdusters and the Dixieland Swingsters, whose personnel included the comedy duo Homer and Jethro and the guitarist Chet Atkins. Regional variation, rooted in the various folk forms from which hillbilly developed and fostered under the umbrella of the barn dance format, persisted for decades and strongly shaped the listening preferences of audiences. One Southern California deejay later commented that, even into the 1950s, he could easily identify where the listeners making song requests came from by the artists and styles requested.[7]

One of the most important features of the barn dance, and other hillbilly radio, was its close association, both institutionally and stylistically, with the advent of broadcast advertising. Indeed, in spite of several years of strong record sales in the 1920s, hillbilly can reasonably be interpreted more as an adjunct of radio broadcast advertising than as a part of the music industry until after World War II. Barn dance shows (and all other forms of hillbilly broadcasting) originated almost exclusively at independent stations or those, like WLS and WSM, which continued to produce their own programming even after affiliating with the networks. Most independents were small stations with low signal strength, but several had nearly national coverage. WNAX in Yankton, South Dakota, went on the air with a fiddle contest in 1927 and received 8,700 telegrams from all over the forty-eight states. More notorious was KFKB in Milford, Kansas, whose owner, chief sponsor, and greatest spokesman, Dr. John Romulus Brinkley, used the station to promote his line of goat-gland extracts. Between Dr. Brinkley's helpful diagnoses, the station aired a steady stream of evangelical shows, fiddle music, and cowboy singers.[8]

The music's over-representation on independents was complemented by its under-representation on the urban network stations that set the standard for genteel broadcasting. NBC's programming statistics for the years 1927 to 1932 show that hillbilly accounted for less than 10 percent of sponsored network time, while popular and variety music accounted for nearly half of the network's sponsored time by 1932. NBC affiliates, however, were more likely to carry a network broadcast of hillbilly music than a similar show featuring pop fare. There are a number of possible explanations for this difference. Since the key stations that originated network programming were all urban, they may have been reluctant to program hillbilly for fear of alienating local audiences. Thus, when the network picked up the feed of a hillbilly show originated by a regional station, key urban broadcasters might have substituted their own pop programming. On NBC's Boston key station WBZ, for example, hillbilly accounted for just 2.5 percent of programming time. Conversely, affiliates may have not only picked up network hillbilly shows but supplemented them with additional home-grown "folk and ballad" shows—at the expense of the network's pop feed—with a more rural audience in mind. Or affiliates may simply have been more interested in the relatively fewer hillbilly shows because they could be counted on to deliver large audiences of listeners who had nowhere else to hear their favorites. Whatever the reason, hillbilly music was, literally, a break from more respectable network programming.[9]

The independent and semi-autonomous stations where hillbilly originated were characterized by their vanguard role in promoting direct advertising and, by extension, for supporting the growth of commercial broadcasting. "Farmer" stations such as Shenandoah, Iowa's KFNF engaged in direct advertising even in the mid-1920s, when most stations still hesitated to annoy radio listeners with commercial appeals. KFNF's owner, Henry Field, insisted that his audience "want to hear prices named," preferring "frank speaking and direct methods better than any polite evasions." One listener supported this assertion and linked it to both independent broadcasters and hillbilly music when she wrote to *Radio Digest* that "We want direct advertising. . . . We don't want to hear the chain stations. If anybody wants to hear WEAF, they can tune in direct. We don't want WEAF all over the dial. . . . We want old-time music. We understand it and like it."[10]

Not only was hillbilly linked more closely with advertising than other genres; it was linked with the cheapest kind of advertising. In addition to luring sponsors whose constituency was primarily rural, such as Sears, hillbilly attracted sponsors from high-risk, low-profit industries such as food staples producers and medicinal companies. For sponsors like Crazy Water Crystals, Texas Crystals, JFG Coffee, and others who paid their hillbilly musicians directly, the cost of production for a hillbilly show was a mere pittance compared to what a successful pop show might cost. And since many advertisers used hillbilly as part of a coordinated regional campaign strategy, hillbilly sponsors could attain broad regional or national coverage at local and independent rates. The advertising time slots that hillbilly was likely to fill were also less expensive than the time usually devoted to pop. While the most popular barn dance shows were broadcast on Saturday night, the majority of hillbilly was programmed in the early morning and at the noon hour; inexpensive time designed to fit the farmer's schedule.[11]

The independent status of the majority of stations programming hillbilly and the decentralized nature of the profession opened the way to a continued, if tenuous, regional diversity within radio's mass reach, and to grassroots-level audience influence. At the same time, though, hillbilly was identified as a product of the most heavily commercialized branch of radio broadcasting, and it was widely interpreted as a successful genre whose genesis lay outside the established popular music industry. As a result, it became for many a troublesome emblem of commercialism's effects on American culture.

The structure of the radio barn dance during the first several decades of hillbilly broadcasting reflected the music's status as an agglomeration of regional vernaculars and old-time tunes based on nineteenth-century vaudeville numbers. As one might imagine of such a hodgepodge, hillbilly music attracted fans from a variety of backgrounds. While we have come to think of country as the music of the white working class, the genre's initial appeal and image was much broader. Hillbilly's first successful entrepreneurs imagined an audience that included as many middle-class as working-class listeners, and the middle-class respectability promoted by early barn dances became an important feature of the genre for many fans.

Edgar Bill consciously targeted a middle-class audience. In the mid-1920s, migration to Chicago had already produced a few recognizable enclaves of white Southerners, but the great bulk of white migration had yet to arrive. Though the migrants would eventually be well represented among the show's listeners, Bill aired it primarily because it seemed like a "natural" for the rural audience, the prosperous and pious farmers of the Midwest who typified the ideal Sears catalogue customer. Martin L. Davey—a "tree surgeon" whose sponsorship of the old-time *Davey Tree Hour* contributed to both a personal fortune and a political career that culminated in the governorship of Ohio—told potential broadcast sponsors that, in devising the show, his staff "carefully avoided everything that is vulgar and everything that would be objectionable to people of refined taste." Davey advocated cleaving to the middle and suggested that programmers "maintain an atmosphere of respect and dignity without being highbrow. . . . The only fair way to build a program is to base it on average tastes and conditions of the average homes. Those average homes are neither lowbrow nor highbrow, but they have the elements of culture, either in the matter of education or else in their instincts." Davey also considered race in his effort to appease the sensitivities of his imagined audience. He classified "folk songs . . . including English, Irish, Welsh, etc., as well as many of the old American songs and those with a distinctly southern flavor," as being simple music of "good racial origin," presumably in contrast to the questionable racial origin of the jazz and urban blues that he excluded from the programming list.[12]

Old-time music seemed like the natural offering for these listeners in part because the farm population was aging, but also because of the broader associations attached to it. By the early 1920s, nineteenth-century parlor ballads and heart songs were popularly identified as an aural counterweight to the raucous modernity of ragtime and jazz, within the music industry and among the audience. A survey of phonograph owners conducted by Thomas A. Edison, Inc. uncovered a dedicated audience for old familiar ballads and revealed the depth of emotion that listeners attached to the tunes. According to the handwritten comments on the surveys, old-time music evoked "memories of home," "Grandfather days," and "the days of childhood." Frequently the tunes recalled distant or departed loved ones. These sentimental tunes—what one observer uncharitably called the "sob songs of several generations ago"—were the basis of much of the early hillbilly repertoire, especially on the Midwestern shows that were the genre's first national successes. The comfort and continuity of hearth and family evoked by the pop forerunners of hillbilly offered a stark opposite to the pell-mell bustle and mobility of the jazz age, even as their availability on the radio and on record firmly identified them as products of the modern industrial order.[13]

Though the *National Barn Dance* was conceived by Edgar Bill, it was

Burridge D. Butler who shepherded the show to its greatest national prominence during the 1930s, first on WLS's own fifty-thousand-watt clear channel and then as a feature on the NBC Blue Network. Butler, a farm publisher and rural reformer who bought WLS from Sears, Roebuck in 1928, insistently intervened to maintain the respectable image he thought was appropriate for the *National Barn Dance*. The music and personalities on the show, he felt, should reflect the popular, homespun traditions of the rural Midwest rather than "the toothy, slicked-up aura which characterized many hillbilly bands of the tavern trade." Butler's cast also worked to support the *Barn Dance*'s middle-class image. The balladeer John Lair mobilized a number of middle-class images to establish an aura of dignity and tradition for the show. Both Lair and his fellow cast member, Bradley Kincaid, presented themselves as genteel folk revivalists, explicitly rejecting the hillbilly image of benightedness and poverty. In the third volume of his popular songbook series, *Favorite Old-Time Songs and Mountain Ballads,* Bradley Kincaid wrote to his audience that he hoped the book would help them "distinguish between these fine old folk songs, and the so-called Hilly Billy songs" being issued by record companies. Lair presented himself as a collector of original folk tunes, and he used his "Notes from the Music Library" column in the station's weekly newsletter, *Stand By!* as a forum to discuss the distinction between hillbilly and folk music. Through management of the identities of female artists like Linda Parker, the "Sunbonnet Girl," Lair also invoked images of Victorian purity and motherhood that resonated with middle-class gender ideology.[14]

Station management was often at pains to reassure fans of the educated and respectable backgrounds of *Barn Dance* cast members in real life, as well. One promotional souvenir booklet featured cast members at Chicago's 1933 "Century of Progress" fair. Photo layouts were accompanied by brief biographical descriptions of the performers that deliberately contrasted their personal histories with the image of the uneducated hillbilly. The caption under the picture of the popular singing sweetheart Lulu Belle emphasized to readers that, in spite of her spunky onstage performance, she was in fact "a gentle and thoroughly civilized young lady." Her duet partner and future husband, Skyland Scotty Wiseman, was similarly portrayed as belonging to the middle class: "[Scotty] possesses a college degree, and is highly qualified for the teaching of literature." Even in an article that otherwise indulged every possible opportunity to poke fun at impoverished and ignorant hillbillies, Cum-

1 WLS *National Barn Dance* cast members Lulu Belle and Red Foley visit the Century of Progress fair in Chicago, 1933. The station's souvenir program for the fair depicted WLS stars in regular street clothes and emphasized their middle-class lives offstage. *Photo courtesy of SOUNDIES Archive, Chicago.*

berland Ridge Runner Hartford Taylor managed to convey a sense of respectability, if only for a moment. Back home in Kentucky, he told his interviewer, "I was a banker and made $25 a week. . . . That $25 I was getting was tops for a hill man, but now that we're up here making that much a day, it certainly makes things different. Now we got cars and a lot of clothes and most of the boys have even got bank accounts."[15]

The producers and artists of the *National Barn Dance* worked to make the show appealing to the middle-class listeners of the rural Midwest. At the same time, an atmosphere of plain-folks simplicity was a central element of hillbilly's audience appeal, and its selling power. No matter how often broadcasters made reference to the respectability of hillbilly performers and audiences, the genre's studied lack of sophistication, its disadvantaged position in the economic structure of the broadcasting industry, and its lack of appeal to the highest-income audiences branded it as lowbrow entertainment. Observers of the nascent music industry and broadcast advertising business occasionally reminded sponsors and record executives that hillbilly commanded a significant middle-class audience, but their protestations served primarily to reveal a widespread assumption among urban executives that hillbilly listeners came from the ranks of the less educated and prosperous.

A bemused record retailer wrote in one of the day's most prominent music magazines that the maudlin appeal of hillbilly discs seemed to transcend class lines. "What could be more absurd than this [hillbilly music]?" he asked his readers. "Only one thing—the existence of hundreds of thousands of native Americans who love and buy [it]." The music's audience was as mystifying as its allure. He reported with wonderment that he sold hillbilly records "daily to farmers, laborers and mechanics, to young and old, rich and poor—yes, even to bankers, contractors, salesmen and merchants." Identifying a similar middle-class constituency for hillbilly, an early study of broadcast advertising reminded sponsors not to overlook well-to-do rural listeners by quoting a "distinguished judge" from the Midwest: "Many of my acquaintances of the same age as myself like Hillbilly music . . . we went to parties when we were young where Hillbilly music was played. We courted to those melodies. . . . I listen regularly to opera myself. But many an evening I like to slip away to the study, turn on my own radio, put on my slippers or sit in my stocking feet, and wriggle my toes to the tunes to which I danced when I was young." But even the judge seemed to realize that his weakness for hillbilly would strike others as incongruous. By the early 1940s, assumptions about the hillbilly audience promulgated in trade papers and advertising literature influenced marketing, distribution, and programming in ways that sharpened distinctions between different kinds of potential consumers and distanced hillbilly from other genres.[16]

CULTURE AND COMMERCE:
FIXING THE SOCIAL MEANING OF HILLBILLY

A number of social, political, and cultural factors helped to fix the meaning of hillbilly music in the popular imagination. Existing holders of cultural power and authority had many reasons to view hillbilly and other vernacular music brought into the commercial realm by radio as threatening and undesirable. Hillbilly was perceived by many such observers as being outside, and even antithetical to, older cultural hierarchies. Segments of the established music industry, preservationist guardians of middle-class cultural values, and communications researchers and policy makers all contributed to the class redefinition of hillbilly as a by-product of their responses to changing structures of cultural power. By virtue of its association with commercial broadcasting, hillbilly served as a portent of modernization even as it nostalgically invoked the rural past, and its association with commercialism's disturbing encroachment on American life helped to fix its lowly position on the new cultural hierarchy.

Prior to the advent of radio, the production and distribution of commercial music was controlled almost exclusively by a handful of publishing houses in New York City which were known collectively as Tin Pan Alley, a term that evoked the cacophony produced by the dozens of pianos upon which songwriters and publishers laboriously pitched their latest tunes. The music of Tin Pan Alley was delivered to the American public by scores of vaudevillians, musical comedy casts, and touring bands, most of them under the control of a handful of booking and management agencies who engineered the choice of songs. The troupes and their management syndicates shopped for their repertoires among New York's publishing houses and then scattered across the country, carrying Tin Pan Alley's compositional and lyrical wares to the remotest hamlet, where they were purchased in the form of sheet music. As the most widely available technology for delivering reproduced music of acceptable listening quality, the piano still dominated the music industry, and Tin Pan Alley focused on a relatively narrow spectrum of popular song: tunes that could become popular with a wide audience of amateur pianists. Music that did not interest New York's publishers—such as improvisation-based fiddle music—remained in the folk tradition, played and enjoyed by thousands of Americans but systematically excluded from the highly consolidated machinery of commercial song publishing and promotion.[17]

Tin Pan Alley publishers and recording executives were among the first to identify hillbilly as a genre, and their response was typical in the way they mobilized cultural condescension to protect their own prerogative in the face of economic and social change. Industry observers briefly hailed the popularity of recorded hillbilly in the early 1920s as marking "the initial move in the passing of jazz." With evident relief, *Talking Machine World* suggested that the hillbilly trend argued for "more simplification of our popular renditions" and offered some refuge from the unrelenting popularity of dance bands and their "over-arranged jazz offerings." Listener interest in sentimental ballads, the magazine hopefully mused, "does show that the great American public is returning to songs and after all 'the song is the thing.'" All the same, the editors could not help but remark in passing on the inferior quality of hillbilly songs, finding it "questionable that music lovers will accept the situation as an improvement," no matter how tired of jazz they might be.[18]

Though relieved that the jazz craze showed signs of slowing, music professionals' distaste for country was nonetheless immediate and palpable. In his contribution to *Variety*'s 1926 annual retrospective, the music editor Abel Green commented on the mysterious explosion in the genre's popularity and offered a famously derogatory definition for those unfamiliar with the term "hillbilly," characterizing hillbillies as "illiterate and ignorant, with the intelligence of morons" and supporting this assertion with the apparently damning fact that "the sing-song, nasal-twanging vocalizing of a Vernon Dalhart or a Carson Robison [two of the earliest hillbilly songsters on Tin Pan Alley] . . . intrigues their interest." Professional composers and publishers were eager to distance themselves from a field characterized by its novelty and semi-professional status. In spite of its self-proclaimed position as the traditional center of American music production, the Tin Pan Alley system was itself only a few decades old. It had emerged as something of a parvenu around the turn of the century, when it too had been much castigated for not being "serious" enough by the already entrenched publishers of classical and parlor music. Now its established impresarios found themselves just barely on the other side of respectability, a position they fervently hoped to preserve. One wag unwittingly exposed vaudevillians' desire to distance themselves from the lowbrow reputation of hillbilly, and the spitefulness of their insecurities, when he noted that Carson Robison worked "within a stone's throw of Tin Pan Alley (and many would like to measure it that way for themselves)."[19]

The aesthetic and economic values that Tin Pan Alley assigned to hillbilly were closely interconnected. Pop songwriters viewed their hillbilly counterparts as unprofessional and possessed of poor taste. More importantly, though, hillbilly songwriters posed a threat to the compensation structure of the music business. As late as 1943, *Time* summed up the sentiments of the pop music business. "Almost any simple soul might write hillbilly words and the composition of hillbilly music has always been viewed by Tin Pan Alley as a variety of unskilled labor." Their fears were not entirely misplaced, for, like its alliance with radio, hillbilly's publishing arrangements were decidedly untraditional. When Ralph

Peer established Southern Publishing Company, he engineered a new understanding of the profit potential in copyright law. Peer foresaw that his publishing concern could prosper exclusively on the mechanical royalties generated by record sales, and he created Southern as a holding company for intellectual property rights rather than as a distributor of any manufactured product such as sheet music or records. Peer's prolific hillbilly artists wrote new tunes, modified traditional songs in the public domain to create new compositions that could be copyrighted, or appropriated original songs from less canny amateurs, all without the benefit of Tin Pan Alley's imprimatur, and without the need of directly handling any physical product.[20]

But even Peer, who ultimately enjoyed greater success in the field than any of his competitors, would later complain that he spent most of his career "trying to get away from hillbilly and into the legitimate publishing field." Like that of other music professionals, Peer's reticence was both economic and cultural. Although they sold records and generated mechanical royalties, hillbilly and race music were all but excluded from the emerging wellspring of profit for the popular music industry: the performance royalties that guaranteed the copyright holder a fee for every public, for-profit performance of his song. Though performance royalties were available to any songwriter in theory, in practice the negotiation and collection of fees required a complex group strategy. In order to collect on the performance royalty interest as an individual or single firm, a composer or publisher would have to approach nightclubs, dancehalls, vaudeville theaters, and other venues, negotiate a fee with each, and monitor each one for performances of his work. A venue owner who found one composer's performance royalty too onerous could simply cease performance of a song and use material by another composer or publisher. The performance royalty, then, could only be lucrative if a blanket fee contract and group monitoring system could be implemented that could control access to a significant portion of the nation's popular music. In 1914, the publishers and composers of Tin Pan Alley created the American Society of Composers and Publishers (ASCAP) to do just that.

Until the 1940s, ASCAP was the only major organization devoted to collecting and distributing performance rights fees. As important as this economic role was, though, ASCAP was equally powerful as an insular cultural fraternity. Its membership was limited to the men who had engineered the rise of commercial music industry at the turn of the century and to those who followed in their footsteps. ASCAP admitted only publishers with "not less than one year of regular engagement in the music publishing industry," and composers with not less than five songs "regularly published," which in practice meant published by ASCAP firms. Applicants were also required to have the sponsorship of at least two members of the society's board and the approval of the membership committee. The membership rules created an effective Catch-22, particularly after 1929, when record sales dropped precipitously. Few publishers could survive exclusively on the profits from hillbilly music, and Tin Pan Alley publishers were loath to associate themselves with such low-grade music. Even those composers and publishers, like Gene Autry, whose overwhelming success finally gained them admittance to the society shared little or not at all in ASCAP's profits because of a sampling and distribution system that favored long-established members over newcomers. Hillbilly, though highly profitable for a few, was consigned to underclass status, and the disparaging attitude of ASCAP and its members would rankle for decades, helping to foster a sense of wounded pride and defensiveness that shaped the development of the industry into the 1960s.[21]

The denizens of Tin Pan Alley also viewed hillbilly as a menacing example of radio's potential impact on the economics of publishing. Tension between publishers and broadcasters dated from radio's inception. Metropolitan publishing houses had realized early on that radio could be a significant avenue of exposure for new tunes and made every effort to place songs with radio artists. But the entrenched music publishing interests represented by ASCAP also viewed radio with some suspicion, and the new medium quickly proved to be serious competition for the traditional source of music in the home, the amateur pianists who purchased sheet music. Moreover, broadcasters and publishers predictably disagreed over performance royalties. ASCAP reasoned that station owners, like nightclub and restaurant owners, should be forced to pay performance royalties for the entertainment from which they profited. Broadcasters argued that the exposure gained by radio airplay earned the publishers enough profit, and that attempts to obtain performance royalties on top of increased sales were nothing short of extortion. The situation worsened dramatically with the onset of the Depression, as sheet music sales tumbled into sharp and irrevocable decline, making performance royalties from radio the most important component of publishing revenues. What had once been an insignificant element in publishing profits now determined the fortunes of Tin Pan Alley professionals, who, like everyone else, were struggling to make ends meet. The popularity of non-ASCAP hillbilly music served as a stark reminder of the dangers that lay in store if broadcasters were able to circumvent Tin Pan Alley's monopoly on popular music.[22]

Hillbilly musicians fared no better than the genre's songwriters and publishers. Most hillbilly musicians were not formally trained in the sightreading of music and were therefore ineligible to join musicians' unions. Semi-professional performers gave way to fully professionalized casts on almost all of the radio barn dances over a period of relatively few years. But most of the hillbilly artists who appeared on shorter sponsored shows at independent stations remained semi-professional, and certainly non-union, through the Depression. Excluded from the central economic structures of the industry, partly for aesthetic and partly for economic reasons, hillbilly musicians and compositions were indeed far less expensive than their pop peers for broadcasters to use. Especially during the Depression, radio stations were eager to cut costs by using hillbilly. One station manager pointed out that during those years hillbilly was cheaper even than recorded pop music. "We had more hillbillies than we had records," he told an interviewer.[23]

Established producers of commercial popular music were not alone in their concern about how hillbilly and the technological changes that produced it would affect cultural hierarchies and values. The patrons of the folk preservation movement and the Victorian middle class they represented assimilated commercial hillbilly into a more encompassing philosophy of anti-modernism that militated against the influences of mass media and industrialization. Policy makers and intellectuals sought to defend the expansion of mass communication by portraying it as a source of cultural uplift rather than degradation, and they were troubled by the popularity of lowbrow fare such as hillbilly. By dismissing it as anomalous, restricted in its appeal to an unimportant lower-class or geographic minority, those who had traditionally wielded cultural power and authority were able to contain, albeit temporarily, the threats that hillbilly and the new commercial media represented.

Middle-class rural and cultural reformers became interested in the folk music upon which commercial hillbilly was partially based because they viewed it as "real American music," an expression of the Anglo-Saxon values that had built the nation and that the preservationists themselves also represented. Their attraction to folk reflected deeper uncertainties about the nation's economic and political future as it drifted far from its mythical yeoman-farmer moorings (however unrealistic that image might have been). Somewhat paradoxically, it was also born of a desire to show that American culture, like American industry, had produced works to rival the greatest achievements of Europe.[24]

The romantic nationalist interest in the folk antecedents of hillbilly had found first expression through Teddy Roosevelt, who lamented the fact that American composers had yet to find a musical idiom that reflected the nation's character rather than parroting the fashions of Europe. In 1904, this concern was echoed by Emma Bell Miles in an article in *Harper's Magazine* titled "Some Real American Music." The article began by dismissing composers' efforts to work with "negro themes" and "aboriginal Indian music" because these could be "no expression of American life and character." But the ballads of Appalachia's mountaineers, Miles suggested, might "one day give birth to a music that shall take a high place among the world's great schools of expression." The mountaineers themselves she described as "primitives." Though they might unconsciously produce the purest musical reflection of the national spirit, Miles implied, they could not understand or appreciate its aesthetic value in the same way that an educated, urbane middle-class listener would.[25]

This distinction between the treasured musical heritage that folk represented and the crudeness of those who most often played it and listened to it remained a defining characteristic of folk preservation through the rise of Popular Front cultural initiatives in the mid-1930s and, some would argue, even beyond. The dichotomy deepened as the commercial influences that had always been present in vernacular music became more apparent to preservationists, who viewed commercialism and the popular media as the chief threats to their work. The conundrum was perhaps nowhere better demonstrated than in the writings and experience of Annabel Morris Buchanan, who founded Virginia's White Top Folk Festival in 1931. Buchanan hoped that White Top would bring attention, sympathy, and money to the impoverished residents of the mountains of Virginia. She continually struggled with the mountain's chief landowner to keep him from using the festival as a vehicle for profit, not only because she felt commercial music was antithetical to the concept of folk tradition but also because one of his standard techniques for minimizing costs was exploiting the performers. But Buchanan was also quite sure that her own assessment of aesthetic value was superior to that of the musicians with whom she worked, and she saw little irony in the idea of charging a forty-cent admission to the festival during the height of the Depression, a decision that in itself helped to distinguish her folk music from the cheaply available hillbilly music against which she defined folk. Her efforts to preserve mountain music were a revolt against urban culture, but the economic and social context ensured that the only mountaineers in attendance would be onstage; "high standards cannot walk hand in hand with simon-pure democracy," she wrote. She struggled with the moral and aesthetic consequences of commercialism, but Buchanan's White Top Festival was nonetheless commercial in its own right.[26]

Buchanan also worked to distinguish folk stylistically from hillbilly. She deplored what she viewed as the adulteration of folk music by "crude modern . . . productions with cheap tunes based on ancient Broadway hits" and actively shaped the repertoires and styles of the artists who appeared at the festival so they would accord with her own understanding of "native material." Just as semi-professional and professional artists quickly learned the preferences of broadcasters, the amateurs who competed at White Top and other festivals learned what their social superiors considered worthwhile, or they did not compete. One observer reported that, while the first festival had produced only a few "reluctant" ballad singers, the fourth presented twenty-two of them. At the same time, organizers eliminated at least twenty string bands in 1934 "by reason of their evident leaning toward what radio listeners now know as 'hill-billy.'" Musicians and local residents of the mountains were not permitted to judge the contestants; that task was performed by "qualified" judges. As David Whisnant has written, for preservationists, the "risk of celebrating folk culture in public was . . . that the folk, if left to themselves, might celebrate the wrong thing." By carefully controlling the development of folk, preservationists elaborated a largely false distinction between their own activities and those of commercial entrepreneurs and assigned the latter a lower cultural value.[27]

A second manifestation of cultural reform also sharpened the class meanings surrounding hillbilly. Animated by many of the same concerns about cultural uplift that underpinned the folk preservation movement, radio audience research came into its own during the mid-1930s and focused attention immediately upon the importance of class in listening habits. The impetus behind radio research derived from a number of curiosities, the most basic of which was to regain a feel for the identity

Commercialism and Country Music

and interests of listeners that had been lost because the audience was no longer physically present. The introduction of live studio audiences was one way of imagining the kinds of people who might be listening, but advertisers especially wanted a better idea of the whole audience, not just those with the time, money, and proximity to attend a broadcast. As broadcast advertising became a more common practice, it cultivated a thriving industry of audience surveying and rating services. Basic rating services were the first to appear: the Cooperative Analysis of Broadcasting was established in 1929 to measure audience volume by phoning urban homes and asking who in the household had listened to what shows during the preceding twenty-four hours. In 1934, CAB was joined by Crossley-Hooper, Inc., a firm that offered much the same information, except that their survey method asked what telephone respondents were listening to at that very moment. Neither service offered analysis beyond whole numbers, but within a few years NBC began to employ its own statisticians to analyze ratings data figures for class preferences.[28]

Radio research also derived from the constellation of politicians and cultural critics who hoped that the medium could be more than a vehicle for entertainment and profit. Instead, they imagined radio as an avenue of education and cultural uplift for the masses that had theretofore been unreachable. Some elements of this group, including many rural reformers, opposed the commercial networks because they viewed the system as monopolistic and corrosive of the very cultural standards they thought radio should support. During the latter half of the 1920s, rural anti-monopolists repeatedly complained that government regulations unfairly privileged network stations, whose programming originated almost exclusively in New York and Chicago, over independent rural stations. Testifying in government hearings held in 1930 to determine whether the independent station WLS would have to share its clear-channel broadcasting frequency, Burridge D. Butler argued that the station provided a respite from the dominance of urban culture. "Is there a place on the air for the voice of the country—for the songs of the prairies and hills, for the barn dance fiddlers, for the homely virtues of the everyday folks who have made America?," he asked. "We believe that there should be. . . . It is not our fight but the fight of agriculture."[29]

Between the advertisers and broadcasters who sought to perfect radio's commercial potential and the reformers who hoped to harness the power of radio to cultural uplift—and sometimes emerging as partisans for one side or the other—stood the social scientists who sought to analyze the impact of radio. Most received their funding from both sources at one time or another. Paul Lazarsfeld, for example, performed much of his early research with funding from the Rockefeller Foundation, but he also worked for the National Association of Broadcasters to develop the sampling method that Broadcast Music, Inc. (BMI) used to calculate performance royalty distributions. Similarly, data for many of the early studies by Lazarsfeld's Office of Radio Research were drawn from CAB ratings and subsequent analyses performed by H. M. Beville for NBC. Like Lazarsfeld, most social scientists who worked in the field ultimately found themselves in the difficult position of arguing for the educational potential of radio in spite of a growing body of criticism—to which they often contributed—that attacked the mass media as vapid at best and dangerous at worst.

These conflicting motives, however, both pointed in the same direction with regard to hillbilly music. The pro–mass media forces and anti–mass media forces each had their own interests in emphasizing the inferiority of hillbilly and in portraying its audience as backward. As resistance to commercial broadcasting and network expansion grew, broadcasters increasingly portrayed network radio as the only cost-effective way of providing "urban, 'quality' programs to rural hicks." In the mid-1930s, for example, NBC spent three pages of an elaborate public relations release stridently refusing to apologize for broadcasting hillbilly and other "light" entertainment because, the company argued, audiences lured to radio by such fare could then be exposed to a better class of music. For reformers, the argument that radio needed to be regulated depended on showing that it reached people of a "lower cultural level," and that commercial interests, if left to themselves, would simply pander to the lowest common denominator to attract listeners, programming hillbilly and other poor quality music. The belief that "cultural level" and listening preferences corresponded with socioeconomic status was central to all involved.[30]

Audience research both measured and reinforced the swing toward a class-based definition of hillbilly music. One of the earliest works on radio and education offered a few generalizations about the medium's audience but did not make any connection between barn dance music and class. "Simple music and homely drama [are] more popular in rural districts," the report concluded. "Old-fashioned melodies, news reports, religious services, and women's programs [are] more popular in small towns than in cities"; and "laboring groups [had] marked preference for

Commercialism and Country Music

TABLE Average Proportion of Radio Owners Listening during Winter Season on Different Cultural Levels

Name of program	Cultural level (percent)			
	A (high)	B	C	D* (low)
Metropolitan Opera	19.7	17.4	11.9	
Ford Hour	20.3	17.0	13.7	
General Motors Symphony	16.6	14.1	10.4	
NBC Symphony	10.4	9.1	7.2	
Today's Children	4.8	8.4	11.1	
Amos 'n' Andy	6.8	11.1	15.7	
Lum and Abner	5.0	7.5	10.7	
Major Bowes	11.4	21.1	27.7	
National Barn Dance	4.3	9.9	14.2	
Pick and Pat	6.3	11.2	14.5	
First Nighter	8.0	12.9	18.0	
Gangbusters	7.5	12.5	16.3	

Source: Paul F. Lazarsfeld, *Radio and the Printed Page: An Introduction to the Study of Radio and Its Role in the Communication of Ideas* (New York: Duell, Sloan, and Pearce, 1940), 22.
* For the D column (low), there are no reliable data from telephone surveys.

news and popular music and a distaste for classical music and sports." By 1938, hillbilly was beginning to appear as the opposite of classical music on the scale of "seriousness." In the first major publication of the Office of Radio Research, Paul Lazarsfeld correlated "cultural level," which in this case simply meant income level, with 1937 CAB ratings for a number of programs and presented a chart of the generally popular programs that showed the greatest disparity of listeners across social categories.[31]

The *National Barn Dance* was the only musical program to appear in the lower category of this analysis. But the main difference between it and the Metropolitan Opera was not that lower-class people liked hillbilly a great deal more than classical but rather that upper-class people—who represented only the seven top percentile points of interviewees—liked it a great deal less. In the middle-class "B" category, the NBC Symphony and the *National Barn Dance* were rated almost identically. Nonetheless, Lazarsfeld concluded that hillbilly was the socioeconomic opposite of classical music.

There is probably no question pertaining to radio listening which . . . is so sensitive to social differences as listening to serious music . . . a recent study is reported from Washington, D. C., in which the question "Do you like hillbilly music?" was asked. Sixty-two percent of the lower income groups said "Yes," as against only 29 percent of the higher income groups.[32]

Lazarsfeld further developed this cultural opposition in his next monograph, *The People Look at Radio*, published in 1946. This data was more systematic and inclusive than that which formed the foundation of the earlier report, but it failed to turn up such a clear-cut distinction in the "cultural level" of hillbilly listeners. In fact, equal numbers of listeners at all educational levels listed "old familiar music" as a programming preference. Lazarsfeld commented that the term probably "means a great variety of different things depending on the listener's interpretation. . . . Thus, it is understandable that no clear-cut audience listener differences can be found in such a heterogeneous category." This was undoubtedly true, but most barn dance shows, at least through the Depression, included a variety of styles precisely in order to appeal to listeners of different backgrounds with different interpretations of how traditional rural music should sound.[33]

Two years later, Lazarsfeld conducted another, nearly identical study. In general, the second study concluded that tastes had changed little in the two-year period separating it from its predecessor. In this study, which Lazarsfeld described as a "look at listeners themselves," social differences in listening habits were assumed from the outset and then explained. This second survey also differed from the first in the term it used to refer to the music that one might hear on a barn dance. This time, listeners were asked for their preferences about "hillbilly and western music" rather than "old familiar music." A number of possible reasons for the change present themselves: the narrowing of the genre in programming practice, the increased representation of Southern styles on national broadcasts, and the more consistent use of hillbilly and western as labels in the music trade press. Whatever the reason for the change in terminology, it had a profound effect on the results of the study, which now showed dramatic differences in listener preferences according to education. Lazarsfeld summarized with a small chart that showed the overlap between preferences for different kinds of music. With the least overlap between classical music and hillbilly, the latter came to symbolize the lowest point on the cultural spectrum.[34]

It is unlikely that audience survey research had a direct effect on listener preferences, and it would be unfair to argue that radio research created the class divisions that became so central to hillbilly's image over the next decade. But broadcasters and advertisers, ever sensitive to the accumulation of data that would help them predict the responses of their audience, were certainly aware of the content of such studies. The definition of the hillbilly audience as lower class was prevalent enough among them by the late 1940s that their assumptions about the kind of audience they were addressing with hillbilly programming affected the styles they sought, script content, and advertising. The narrowing of the hillbilly format was, however, a slow process. Throughout the Depression, just as preservationists had feared, radio exposed listeners and future performers to a broad array of music that diversified the tastes of previously isolated local markets. After World War II, listeners who wanted to hear old familiar tunes would surely have found the increasingly specialized sound of hillbilly radio shows less welcoming. But while hillbilly shifted away from the eclecticism that had initially given it broad appeal, it was a long way from delivering a standard product that aimed to please all of its diverse audience segments at once. Not until the late 1950s did the centralization of production in Nashville begin to minimize sensitivity to local audiences and their varied preferences.[35]

THE HILLBILLY BUSINESS AS POPULAR ENTERTAINMENT

Preservationists and intellectuals rejected the commercialism of hillbilly music, but the emergent fan culture fostered by broadcasters and artists portrayed commercialism as a cultural validation of an underappreciated folk tradition. The harmony between commercialization and folk production was made possible in part by the relatively low functional barriers between audience and artist, and by the continuity that fans themselves created between older forms of community cultural activity and newer mass entertainment. It also depended on a frank display of the theatricality and fabrication of the hillbilly image. Broadcasters and artists were not anxious to inform listeners about the economic structures of their business, but they did not often try to conceal the staging and artifice involved in barn dance radio. At the same time, the nascent hillbilly fan press began to elaborate a sense of distinction between hillbilly and other genres, and between its listeners and other audiences.

This construction of the audience drew on the rural-urban dichotomy that animated the rural reform and populism of figures like Burridge Butler. The early hillbilly fan press thus extended elements of romantic agrarian thought into the modern media age, creating the basis for a feeling of cultural separateness that would become one of the chief characteristics of country fan culture by midcentury.

Radio listeners seemed to have little difficulty reconciling commercialism with folk production. The local nature of most hillbilly broadcasting helped make the dividing line between audience and artist, amateur and professional, relatively permeable, as the unease of Tin Pan Alley's denizens suggested. The field diary of the folklorist and music educator Margaret Valiant offers one account of the ways radio and commercialization affected understandings of the relationship between audiences and artists. Valiant was employed by Charles Seeger to run a music program for Cherry Lake Farms, a New Deal Resettlement Administration community in northern Florida. In keeping with the "New Frontier" philosophy from which the settlement sprang, Seeger and Valiant wanted community participation in the production of folk music "to restore a sense of confidence in the people at the time who were very frightened by changes that they did not anticipate" and to foster "a sense of confidence in the old pioneer spirit of exploring and learning."[36]

Valiant's first discovery about the social function of music in Cherry Lake Farms was that both commercialism and modern tastes would be unavoidable. As soon as she arrived, she was made painfully aware of the local cultural opposition between jazz and hillbilly. Her first letter to Seeger reported with chagrin that "the going [would] be slow and rough" in her efforts to create a folk music program because of "a cheaply sophisticated group of young people . . . who scorn folk dancing and singing as 'countrified,' preferring their 'hot' dance music." She observed that the jazz faction and the old-time faction did share one thing in common, though. Neither group was willing "to perform for the sake of performing." Instead, they expected performers to be paid for their work and viewed musicianship as an economic opportunity. Music in the hinterlands of north Florida had already become a thoroughly commercial affair, a fact that Valiant attributed to the influence of the popular amateur radio contest, *Major Bowes' Hour*.[37]

Though they were reluctant to see music simply as an enjoyable creative activity, the residents of Cherry Lake Farms did not imagine a vast gulf between their own roles as consumers of music and the role of the professional musicians. In fact, Valiant soon found that she could take advantage of her pupils' fascination with radio by suggesting to her faltering string orchestra that they might be able to perform on a local broadcast if they "worked up a programme." The prospect of becoming radio performers induced some local residents to participate in the music program, and Valiant soon encouraged more participation by enlisting the help of the fiddler in "the local hillbilly band . . . [which] played customarily for money in honky-tonks in the hot joints between Jacksonville and Tallahassee." The fiddler became the popular feature attraction at several Resettlement Administration–sponsored barn dances and the mainstay of the new community string band; Valiant interceded with the community manager to get him a homestead.[38]

Within a few months, somewhat to Valiant's surprise, the community music project had become a semi-professional hillbilly orchestra. Whatever her initial intentions, Valiant was quick to realize that her pupils drew a close connection between the commercial value and the aesthetic value of the music they played. She embraced commercial opportunities with gusto. Charles Seeger later recounted to a colleague that the local baseball league had approached Valiant to have the string band play at a team exhibition fundraiser. The band would play, Valiant told him, but only for a "divvy at the gate." The event was a great success and the county superintendent of education was even persuaded "to do his 'break down' to the tune of 'Chicken Reel' for the WPA cameras." Valiant herself obviously took pride in the band's transformation from amateur to semi-professional. She reported her triumph to Seeger in May, five months after her first report. "Enthusiasm was so high" after the band's first radio broadcast, she wrote, that "we began planning immediately for another appearance within two weeks on a sustaining hour." There was even some possibility of obtaining a regular live engagement. "We stopped by our favorite honky-tonk for a sandwich and a glass of beer," she told Seeger, "put on a performance and were immediately offered an opportunity to perform there every Saturday evening." The distance between audience and performer, amateur and professional, may have been clear on the major barn dances, but the line between production and consumption was permeable elsewhere. For music lovers at Cherry Lake Farms, hillbilly functioned simultaneously as a symbol of rural backwardness and, through its connection to radio and musical commerce, as a portent of the modernization of rural life. Its popularity in this local context depended on its ability to embody dimensions of both tradition and modernity.[39]

The folklorists Charles Todd and Robert Sonkin discovered a similar phenomenon on their WPA-sponsored trip to the Farm Security Administration camps in California during the early 1940s. Though Todd and Sonkin presented themselves as folk collectors, the songs that migrants offered up were frequently contemporary commercial hits. These amateur musicians had absorbed not only the songs but also the performance techniques of radio broadcasting; one introduced himself for the tape recorder as "Homer Pierce, the singin' cowboy from way down in Missouri." Aspirations of fame as hillbilly stars were widespread enough that one woman commented of her first husband, "like most 'Okies' he was a musician." Radio clearly was influencing the styles and preferences of amateur performers and audience members, as Annabel Morris Buchanan and others feared, but the relationship between radio artist and broadcast listener had not become a one-way, passive encounter.[40]

Hillbilly listeners created cultural practices that synthesized modernity and rusticity in other ways as well. At least through the Depression, radio listeners used their mutual interest in old-time music to build audience communities. These early audience communities reinforced local ties and perpetuated many of the socializing functions of folk music. Business owners played barn dance shows on their radios, neighbors gathered at each other's sets, and barn dance broadcasts enlivened community and family work. Radio listener Delores Saeger's description of the Fort Dodge, Iowa, Old Timers Club demonstrated how the barn dance extended existing patterns of rural sociability while at the same time providing an opportunity for listeners to participate in the stylized performance of a nostalgic rural past. "Two months ago we started a club in town. It's been a grand success," she wrote to nearby station WHO. "Every Saturday night a group of people . . . come dressed in overalls, straw hats, farm aprons, etc., and carrying everything from a milk stool to a pitchfork . . . and all their dancing is done to [WHO's] Sunset Corners Frolic." In response to Delores's letter, the editors of *Rural Radio* encouraged other listeners to form their own "Saturday Night Barn Dance Club[s]" and promised to notify the barn dances of each club's existence so they could be greeted over the air. Another reader, from rural Ontario, told the editors that he had "seen as many as twenty or thirty gathered in our home on Saturday night to enjoy the Saturday Night Barn Dance."[41]

Commercialism and Country Music

While radio listeners assimilated the new medium to older cultural practices, they were not likely to imagine them as being the same, and audience practices that reinforced local community ties were quickly joined by others that exploited radio's ability to transcend time and space in order to create a national sense of rural cultural identity. Beginning with its first broadcasts, the *National Barn Dance* regularly received hundreds of telegrams during the show, and hundreds more letters and postcards during the week. Such audience response, including frequent requests for photos and song folios, encouraged stations and stars to develop new ways to communicate with fans.

By the mid-1930s, broadcasting magazines like *Stand By!* (published by the owners of WLS) and *Rural Radio* offered listeners an array of additional materials with which to construct symbolic personal relationships to the music and its stars. In addition to publishing mail from listeners, the magazines offered feature articles on stars, question-and-answer columns, song lyrics, and information about where to hear favorite artists. Stations promoted their stars through photo albums, by-request mailings, advertising promotions, and essay contests. These efforts demonstrated the size of the listening audience and helped to create the emotional bonds broadcasters hoped would foster loyalty to program and sponsor alike. Regular listeners contributed to the emergence of hillbilly fan culture by creating fan-run clubs. Jimmie Rodgers, unquestionably the biggest recording success in hillbilly prior to the Depression, became the honoree of the Jimmie Rodgers Social Club in 1933. Lulu Belle and Skyland Scotty Wiseman were honorees of a fan club in the late 1930s, as were fellow *Barn Dance* castmembers Patsy Montana, her fiddler Tex Atchison, and Arkie the Arkansas Woodchopper. Still, as names like the Jimmie Rodgers Social Club, the Gene Autry Friendship Club, and the Atchison Loyalty Club suggested, the concept of the fan club and its functions were still being defined.[42]

Social clubs surrounding country music programs and stars drew on the patterns set by movie fan clubs, which enjoyed a tradition of rural participation several decades old by the time the first hillbilly fan clubs appeared. As Kathryn Fuller has demonstrated, movie fan culture began as a sexually undifferentiated activity that encompassed a variety of ways of interacting with the new post-nickelodeon film industry. Early movie fan magazines encouraged an interest in the modern technologies of film recording and projection, offered an outlet for the creative literary impulses of amateur script and scenario writers, and provided fodder for the communal fantasy that almost anyone could attain film stardom. Hillbilly radio magazines, too, indulged readers' interests in the mechanics of radio reception and the politics of radio broadcasting and offered speculation on how radio might modernize all kinds of aspects of rural life. They encouraged a sense of personal connection to stars through familial imagery but also fostered a more pragmatic form of identification through the promise that, as cultural producers, amateurs and professionals were not so far removed from each other.[43]

One of the earliest hillbilly clubs, the Song Exchange Club, was founded by John Lair in 1937 as an extension of his folksong column in *Stand By!* The club's official newsletter, *Song Exchange News,* carried fan club announcements, reviewed song folios, and published lyrics to traditional, popular, and hillbilly songs. Much of the newsletter consisted of announcements for personal appearances and song folio publications that would have helped fans follow the careers of hillbilly favorites. A significant number of the articles and advertisements, though, were written especially with the amateur songwriter in mind and advanced a somewhat schizophrenic view of commercialization. *Song Exchange News* promoted songwriting and song exchange simply as a pleasurable hobby, but it also clearly encouraged the notion that almost anyone who could pen a quaint turn of phrase could embark on a lucrative career as a professional songwriter. In doing so, it reinforced the permeability of the boundary between amateur and professional, vernacular and commercial. It also provided a forum through which a stable nationwide fan community could emerge. A number of the club's members went on to populate the ranks of fan club presidents in the 1940s, and several became regular contributors to *National Hillbilly News,* one of the first hillbilly fan papers to define itself in explicitly genre-based terms, rather than by reference to a particular artist or as an extension of songwriting or radio broadcasting.

As the mix of fandom, amateurism, and professionalism in *Song Exchange News* suggests, the commercial discourse of early country music encouraged aficionados to imagine themselves as part of a relatively undifferentiated musical practice that encompassed both commercial and vernacular manifestations. Similarly, while the conventions of barn dance radio invoked the immediacy of family and community, the developing fan press also emphasized to readers the difference between this intimate imagery and the reality of professional performance and theatricality. The contrast between the two modes made for a welter of different signals that opened space for different audience interpretations of the genre. On the one hand, artists frequently addressed their listeners in personal terms, as friends and neighbors, and encouraged those in the radio audience to imagine that every word was directed to them. Listeners participated actively in creating this illusion of intimacy. A woman from Missouri wrote to one early magazine about her own way of bringing broadcasts to life. "I paste each picture or group of pictures on great big cardboard, then tack the cardboard over my radio so I can see them. When you hear them over the radio it seems like you are in the crowd watching them." Another woman maintained her own family album that included photos she had taken of herself with *National Barn Dance* stars on a trip to Chicago, baby pictures of the stars' children, and pictures of her own family. Fan letters to *Stand By!* were often addressed to "Dear Radio Friend" or "our old pals and new." When a *National Barn Dance* cast member died suddenly, listeners offered condolences and shared their own sorrow. One wrote, "Our entire house is filled with sorrow, in fact as much as at the passing of a dear friend, because that is the place she always held in our home."[44]

Even as they promoted an image of sincerity and intimacy, however, broadcasters and fan magazines explicitly drew attention to the difference between the actors and artists who played barn dance characters and the characters themselves. When *Rural Radio* started a column titled "Family Gossip" to answer requests for personal information about the stars, the editor was compelled to remind readers that they must identify the station where they had heard the personality they wanted to know more about. Listeners could not assume, the editor explained, that the hillbilly field really was like one big family where everyone knew everyone else. WLS's "Century of Progress" souvenir booklet showed *Barn Dance* cast members in regular street clothes rather than in character costume, thereby elaborating its stars' images as performers and underlining the artifice of their onstage personas. When *Rural Radio* featured a column by the Grand Ole Opry's master of ceremonies, George D. Hay, the photo it ran was not of the Solemn Old Judge the announcer played on the air but one of Hay as a serious editorialist in a suit. The magazine's feature article on Phillips H. Lord, the comic actor who played the hayseed Seth Parker on an NBC rural comedy, pictured Lord first as a professional actor in regular dress, then in costume for the studio performance of the show, and finally in an elaborate outdoor set of the fictive Parker farm over the caption, "The camera man catches

PHILLIPS H. LORD as . . .   . . . the beloved SETH PARKER

2   The radio actor Phillips H. Lord in street clothes and in
costume for his role as the hayseed Seth Parker. Early radio
fan magazines frequently distinguished between actors and
the characters they played, drawing listeners' attention to the
artifice involved in creating broadcast images of down-home
sincerity. *Photo courtesy of Country Music Hall of Fame and
Museum.*

Seth and Ma Parker at their home at Jonesport, Maine." Listeners participated actively in the theatrical burlesque of hillbilly, too, as when the
members of the Fort Dodge Old Timers Club convened dressed in overalls and aprons. Barn dance listeners embraced the nostalgic images of
rural community that hillbilly radio offered, but they were well aware
that the image was an artifice manufactured for their entertainment.[45]

The early hillbilly fan press presented barn dance broadcasting as an
easily accessible part of the modern entertainment industry, but it also
cultivated readers' sense of separateness from urban-dominated commercial culture. In 1938, *Rural Radio* offered a prize to the readers who
wrote in with the best pro and con answers to the question of whether
rural listeners wanted different kinds of programming than their urban
counterparts. Reader responses indicated how alienated many rural people felt by urban-controlled national commercial culture, and the extent
to which hillbilly radio was perceived as the one form of entertainment

designed for them. Even the winning letter that advanced the argument in favor of the similarities between urban and rural audiences began by noting their differences. "City people may prefer the classic in music, but when it comes to news, general interest and heart appeal . . . town folks and country folk are one." The winning letter on the opposing side was written by a woman from Marion, Michigan, who viewed the cultural differences between urban and rural audiences as an extension of different ways of life.

> City folks have a different attitude toward entertainment, because they have the opportunity to see and hear the features in the auditorium itself. They become used to higher class entertainment, and thus appreciate concerts, operas, orchestra, etc. These features are enjoyed by the city dweller, but have no place in the heart of a farmer. The farmer lives simply, and works close to nature. He needs recreation, and the radio is the best means within easy reach. So tune in to the guitars and banjos, with all the happy voices that go with them, and really enjoy yourself!

Other readers echoed this distinction. A woman from Elberton, Georgia, who described herself as "very fond of string music like nearly all other country people," thanked the editors for putting out a magazine that didn't "contain so much Hollywood and big network stuff. That is all you find in other radio magazines and nothing about programs that come from individual stations." Mrs. Ruth Williams of Crossville, Alabama, struck a similar note when she urged the editors to "Keep *Rural Radio* going by *not* going Hollywood."[46]

Ultimately, *Rural Radio*'s own editorial stance promoted the division between rural and urban cultural systems. A November 1938 section called "Cracker Barrel" noted that while brass instrument sales were on the rise in cities and stringed instruments were becoming less popular, the very opposite was true in rural areas. "Folks still like the fiddle and guitar" in the countryside, the editors opined, "And we agree with them when they say they don't want swing." On the occasion of its first publication anniversary, the magazine ran an open letter from the publishers reaffirming their commitment to provide the same coverage of rural and independent entertainment that other magazines provided for the stars of Hollywood and Broadway. "As we saw it, and as we still see it, the 48 per cent of America's population that lives in rural communities represents both the backbone and the breastbone of the nation," they wrote.[47]

Hillbilly and rural radio fan publications signaled a distinctively rural position on middle-class consumer culture during the 1930s. Though inspired in part by the popularity and practices of movie fan culture, rural radio magazines and hillbilly fan publications during the 1930s differed from the movie fan press in their failure to promote a middle-class culture of consumerism. As early as the 1920s, movie magazines used film fandom as a vehicle for promoting a complete consumer lifestyle, especially to young women. More explicitly than the films they covered, movie magazines encouraged young women to emulate their favorite stars by purchasing a vast array of beauty products, clothing, soft drinks, and candies. Hillbilly music magazines, by contrast, featured very little advertising beyond announcements related directly to the consumption and production of the music itself. *Song Exchange News* might feature ads for publishers, song-poem services, and guides on composing, but it did not carry the kind of star endorsements that filled the pages of a movie magazine such as *Photoplay*. Even rural radio magazines, designed to reinforce listeners' "friendly" feelings for radio advertisers, emphasized the most practical of product categories—no-nonsense items such as steel fence, agricultural loans, and fire insurance—and employed a correspondingly straightforward style of advertising. Few features or ads in such magazines suggested that consumerism might be an avenue to emotional fulfillment or an entrée to a glamorous lifestyle.[48]

Hillbilly radio's first listeners were profoundly influenced by the new medium, but they incorporated broadcast music into existing cultural practices in ways that minimized the impact of the transition from folk-produced culture to industrially produced culture. Unlike the preservationists of the middle class, hillbilly fans did not perceive commercialism and authenticity as mutually exclusive. Indeed, commercialism functioned for some as one way of assigning social and aesthetic value to cultural creations that were often disdained by the urban cultural elite. Barn dance audiences, at least those who also read the publications of the nascent hillbilly fan press, were well aware of the artifice involved in producing their favorite shows. Yet they were still able to use these images to construct an imagined rural community—often one in opposition to urban-dominated mainstream culture—on a national scale. This oppositional cultural stance would be elaborated and refined during the 1950s as a critique of cultural authority and the power relations of mass media, transmuting rural populism into one element of urban white working-class identity.

Although hillbilly began by attracting an array of regionally and socially diverse audiences as a result of its eclecticism, by the end of the 1940s it had been fully defined as a class-oriented style. A listener survey conducted in 1948, one of the first national studies to identify hillbilly as its own category, offers some notion of the change in the genre's class valence. In contrast to later surveys that showed a universal decline in the popularity of hillbilly among listeners over fifty, this survey showed that the genre was actually more popular in one group of listeners as age increased—those with a college education. Among college-educated listeners, the popularity of hillbilly dropped precipitously from those over fifty to those between thirty and forty-nine years of age, a point roughly corresponding with the advent of radio. For listeners over fifty, who had grown up listening to the sentimental balladry of the late nineteenth and early twentieth centuries, the old-time components of hillbilly figured as part of the middle-class culture of their youth. Younger listeners from the same class, whose tastes were shaped by radio and the dance craze of the 1920s, found little in their own experience to give meaningful social context to the music. The class meaning of hillbilly for listeners of this generation was instead open to determination by the position the genre occupied in the media and in the marketing structure of the music industry.[49]

The economics of the music business and radio broadcasting played a significant role in defining hillbilly's social location, but the most important factor shaping evolving popular perceptions of hillbilly was the dramatic shift of populations that took place between 1920 and 1960. During these years, rural counties in the South and Midwest became the points of origin for the largest internal migrations the nation has ever experienced, and many of them suffered net population losses for the three-decade period. The Dust Bowl exodus flooded Southern California with displaced Plains farm families, while cities like Cincinnati, Detroit, and Chicago absorbed the youth of the mid-South and the Midwest into the industrial workforce. Like the working-class ethnic and racial communities whose music also infused the airwaves and occupied phonograph turntables during the 1920s, white rural-to-urban migrant communities fashioned an urban, working-class identity in part on the basis of their encounters with hillbilly music and other forms of popular culture. The music also shaped outside perceptions of the migrants. Remarking the "indiscriminate application of the term [hillbilly] to all southern white laborers" in the late 1940s, one sociologist thought the most likely explanation for the widespread use of the term was "the influence of 'hillbilly music', heard on radio programs featuring southern white performers and in taverns frequented by southern white migrants." Fear of migrant communities also shaped perceptions of hillbilly music. Honky-tonks and hillbilly taverns became symbols of the poverty-stricken urban ports of entry to which rural-to-urban migrants flocked during and after the war. Hillbilly music and its live performance contexts thus gave diverse groups of migrants an opportunity to develop a shared culture but also became an audible marker of inferior class status.[50]

The cultural politics of hillbilly music can be traced in the everyday conflicts that surrounded it. One such set of conflicts surrounded the social differences between audiences and radio programmers, and it often fell to hillbilly artists to mediate between dramatically differing expectations. As with all radio performance of the day, audience response in the form of cards, letters, and telegrams was critical in establishing a hillbilly artist's listenership for potential sponsors. But local audiences also played a much more significant role in the livelihood of hillbilly musicians than in that of pop artists. In the absence of salaries or significant publishing and record royalties, hillbilly artists relied almost exclusively on personal appearances and direct sales of song folios to earn their living. By the 1930s, most stations had set up artist bureaus to help their musicians book shows in their broadcast areas. In the case of WLS, this arrangement was part of a deliberate effort to use mass media to support rural social life, but the majority of stations simply sought to satisfy listener demand and help artists supplement their radio earnings. Most artists traveled from station to station, playing live shows in the surrounding countryside until they were no longer novel enough to pull a sizeable audience, then moving on. Under these circumstances, maintaining cordial relations with fans was absolutely essential.[51]

A particularly compelling exchange of letters between Emma Riley Akeman of Hamilton, Ohio, and the *National Barn Dance* star Bradley Kincaid demonstrates the gap between programmers and audiences. Akeman wrote to Kincaid in April 1931 to complain about the singer's recent performance in Hamilton, at which he appeared in standard rustic barn dance costume rather than a suit. Akeman accused Kincaid of betraying "the very thing we [Kentuckians] stand for aristocratsy [*sic*], dignity, honesty" and of perpetuating negative hillbilly stereotypes. The complaint might have seemed abstract to Kincaid, but it was connected to very concrete concerns for Akeman. As one sociologist later discovered, native residents of Hamilton viewed Southern migrants—or "Briars" as they were labeled locally—as dirty, lazy, illiterate, and, perhaps most salient of all, as having been employed by local manufacturers at the expense of Hamiltonians during the Depression. Akeman was not idly complaining when she worried that the *Barn Dance* show had intensified already ingrained local prejudices. "Hamiltonians," she wrote, "hate Kentuckians the worse."[52]

Kincaid's response was as telling of the circumstances in which he worked as Akeman's complaint was of the burdens of regional prejudice. "I . . . hasten to tell you how very very sorry I am that I have made the wrong impression on my Kentucky friends," he wrote before offering an explanation for his attire. "The theatre people everywhere demand that you wear the costume in keeping with the type of program you give. The costume that I wore is their conception of what the average mountain boy would look like. Personally, I would have preferred to come out on the stage in a nice new suit, but they would not let me."[53]

Kincaid may have exaggerated the influence of others on his professional presentation. The owner of WLS, Burridge D. Butler, expressly controlled the appearance of his performers, but Kincaid had left the *Barn Dance* in 1929 for Cincinnati station WLW. Nonetheless, Kincaid's self-created image as the Kentucky Mountain Boy was meant to express the dignity and tradition of mountain folk music. Obviously, though, Kincaid's idea of rural respectability differed from Akeman's. The exchange, and the assumptions behind it, demonstrated how intense listeners' expectations of hillbilly music could be and how far afield of those expectations the genre sometimes fell.[54]

The desires of migrants to the textile towns of the Carolina Piedmont were similar to those expressed by Emma Akeman, though they appear to have been in perfect accord with the preferences of radio programmers there. By the early 1930s, residents of the Piedmont had been experiencing intense industrialization and expansion of the textile industry for several decades. In the process, rural migrants were uprooted from traditional social contexts and transplanted into an environment in which older signs of respectability and status were no longer available. Without the financial resources to present themselves as members of the "respectable" classes, impoverished migrants to the textile mills turned to their cultural traditions, including hillbilly music, to establish a measure of dignity in their lives. For the artists who played Charlotte's WBT *Crazy Barn Dance*, sponsored by Crazy Water Crystals, the demands of this audience were well understood and very important. Bill Bolick, later of the Blue Sky Boys, recalled allowing the *Crazy* programmer, J. W. Fincher, to dictate his wardrobe and band name, but that repertoires were influenced solely by the musicians' own preferences and by audience response. As elsewhere, *Crazy Barn Dance* artists relied on live performances for the bulk of their livelihood. These performances were usually at community events, and organizers wanted such events to reflect the moral tone that helped them establish personal dignity. To please their constituency, artists added gospel tunes to their repertoires on and off the air and worked to maintain a clean public image. As one performer recalled, "Word gets around, and it didn't take but one word that didn't sound right, and brother, you was in bad shape. They always looked at you up there as a bunch of nice people, you see." Like Emma Akeman, working-class residents of the Piedmont in the 1930s clearly felt that hillbilly musicians were a part of their community, subject to the same rules of behavior and censure, and representative of the community's moral standards.[55]

Audience concerns about the perceived respectability of hillbilly music and musicians were well founded, particularly as the numbers of rural-to-urban migrants swelled in the late 1930s and early 1940s. In many communities that received an influx of migrants, dislike of hillbilly music and hostility toward its audience were conflated and mutually reinforcing. A 1938 survey of Modesto Junior College students on the subject of their attitudes toward the residents of the area known as "Little Oklahoma" revealed the usual litany of charges that the Dust Bowl migrants were "illiterate," "scum," "lazy," and "dirty" but also elicited responses such as "See cheap shows. Listen to cowboy music on the radio." Modesto natives regarded migrants as invaders of their physical and cultural space as well as burdens on the relief system. The junior college students reported that the migrants had "ruined" a local park, and residents complained that radio stations had begun to cater too much to the migrants' (bad) taste. One grumbled to an interviewer that "all you hear on the air today are these [expletive] hill-billy songs and Kentucky wisecracks!" Another wrote a letter of protest to the editor of the *Modesto Bee*.

Commercialism and Country Music

I wonder how long the public must listen to the so called cowboys on the radio? . . . I am young and I love music of any kind, even cowboy tunes, but I love to hear them played and sung by people who can play and sing at least as well as the average person. . . . The other day I turned on the radio and one . . . of the cowboys was saying: "Aw rite, folks, now we will try to git" so and so "to play a little ole tune that they played when we was actin with Gene Autry down in Hollywood. Aw rite, boys, burn it up." A few whoops and blood curdling yells and they play. Boy was it terrible! May I say, too, that the fact that they played with Gene Autry does not make them musicians. Who, besides a few Texans and Oklahomans, thinks he can sing?

The sound of rural and regional accents on hillbilly radio may have provided comfort to the migrant audiences of Southern California, but to hostile natives these voices signified yet another arena in which their dominion was being challenged.[56]

The same animosity surfaced with regard to one of hillbilly's emerging performance contexts—the honky-tonk. The term "honky-tonk" had been in circulation as part of regional Southern vernaculars since before the turn of the century, but the rural roadside bars boomed along with the economy of the Texas oil fields after the repeal of Prohibition in 1933. The term, and its smoke-filled beer-joint image, entered the universal hillbilly vocabulary with Al Dexter's 1937 recording "Honky Tonk Blues," and by 1938 Roy Acuff was singing about honky-tonk woes on his way to the Grand Ole Opry. If the passage of time had mellowed the connotations of unsavory behavior that sometimes accompanied traditional hillbilly events and turned them into glowing memories of Victorian sing-songs, the honky-tonk encapsulated the worst stereotypes about rowdy, uncontrollable backwoodsmen and updated them for an undeniably contemporary context. As honky-tonks sprang up in Southern California, in Northern urban centers like Detroit and Chicago, and near burgeoning military bases throughout the South and West in the 1940s, they contributed to an increasingly seedy image for country music. The honky-tonk not only attached to hillbilly an association with drinking and violence; it also altered the content of the music. Few bar patrons wanted to hear about the Church in the Wildwood over their beer, and songs recorded with the tavern jukebox in mind were considerably more secular and sinful than pop- and gospel-influenced radio repertoires.[57]

The influence of changing live performance contexts was particularly evident in Chicago, home of the *National Barn Dance*. In a study of Chicago's West Side just after World War II, the sociologist Lewis Killian found a thriving community of white Southerners along West Madison Street, an area that was soon known as the "Tennessee Valley" in popular parlance. Most of the migrants had arrived in the late 1930s and early 1940s, following jobs created by the war boom. By 1937, the area was an obvious enough port of entry for Southern migrants that the cousin of a *National Barn Dance* performer thought it would be a good place to open a hillbilly bar. As the migration intensified, the number of bars featuring hillbilly music multiplied. One police officer told Killian, "When I came to this district in 1941 that was the only hillbilly tavern on Madison Street . . . but now you'll find them from 1700 west to 3200 west on Madison." A bar owner named his tavern the Southern Inn and hung a sign advertising it as a "Hillbilly Hangout"; others advertised their hillbilly bent with Western names like the Dome Stables or the Wagon Wheel. Area residents were quick to point out that the taverns were not part of Southern culture as it existed in the South but rather an out-growth of urban living. Killian agreed, but he argued that the bars played an important role in the urban culture the migrants developed. The "hillbilly tavern," he wrote, was "in several respects the institution which is of the most significance for the great body of the southern white migrants in this area" because it offered a physical space for migrants to meet and share a public culture.[58]

While the area was home to all kinds of taverns, the distinguishing feature of the dozen or so hillbilly taverns was the music played there, sometimes on jukebox but especially by live bands. Bar owners who featured live hillbilly music consciously catered to white Southerners. One told Killian that 75 or 80 percent of his trade was transplanted Southerners; another replied to questions about whether the Southern crowd kept others away by remarking simply, "To hell with the other people. . . . We cater to the southern people—we have this hillbilly band. The other people don't like that kind of music." Still another made the slightly more conciliatory remark, "Of course, some people don't like the music we have, but we make a lot of converts! We get a lot of these city slickers to liking hillbilly music!" The same was apparently true of hill-billy bars in other Northern cities. One migrant to Detroit emphasized the variety of backgrounds represented at the tavern he frequented: "they had just as many if not more from the North that went to the country music bars. . . . You've got a lot of people in Michigan, New York state and all up through there that was raised up on country music."[59]

To most Northerners, though, the hillbilly bars along Madison Street, and later in Uptown on the city's north side, were associated mainly with fighting and drunkenness. When the Grand Ole Opry star Goldie Hill opened her nightclub, the Hillbilly Hayloft, on the strip, the city's jazz magazine, *Down Beat,* reported that the club itself was well appointed in campy hillbilly style, with "potato sack table cloths and bartenders in blue jeans and country cartoons on the walls." But the editors also noted that Hill had undertaken "a real man sized job," by opening on the near west side: "The location isn't the most to be desired, being located on Chicago's famed or ill-famed Madison Street." The reputation of the area was a fact of which many Southerners were painfully aware. "Everybody around here knows what goes on over there," one Southern woman told Killian, "they give all the other southern people a bad name."[60]

The image projected by this new center of hillbilly activity was in marked contrast to the plain-folks, family image that the *National Barn Dance* continued to cultivate a few miles away in its Eighth Street theater, and the predominating styles played in the two contexts differed as well. Glenn Snyder, station manager of WLS, upheld the Burridge Butler philosophy by banning the use of the word "hillbilly," which appeared so frequently in the advertising of the Madison Street bars. Snyder also eschewed what he called "hungry hillbilly," with its honky-tonk twang and nasal sound. The policy set him squarely against the dominant trends in the business. Although it would continue to be heard locally for another decade, the *Barn Dance* was clearly on the decline by the opening years of the 1950s. In Chicago, Detroit, and Southern California, as well as Nashville, modernized versions of the Southern styles most commonly associated with the hillbilly label now predominated. The sharpening of the style, as the residents of Modesto suggested, alienated many who had been attracted to barn dance music in its "old familiar tunes" incarnation. But hillbilly broadcasts and bars contributed to the formation of a new class culture, bringing together white rural-to-urban migrants who often shared little more in common than their experience as new members of the urban working class.[61]

By the early 1940s, the hillbilly field had already undergone several stages of development as a commercial genre. What began as a novelty recording market had developed into a significant segment of the broadcast advertising industry and had nurtured a new cadre of professional artists. Shows like the Grand Ole Opry and the *National Barn Dance* had attained national reach, but local and regional cultures continued to dominate the different sounds of hillbilly music shows across the country. The hillbilly business as a professional community also remained diffuse and polyglot as a result of variations in broadcasting environments and economies. But as World War II threatened to engulf the United States, the commercial machinery for exploiting publishing rights on new compositions was poised to transform the burgeoning field into a fully developed component of the popular music industry and stimulate the process of centralization in Nashville.

The social dynamics of hillbilly had also changed. Although many of its entrepreneurs and artists tried to locate hillbilly within the social and cultural values of the middle class, even the formative hillbilly press soon began to emphasize the differences between its audience and aficionados of Tin Pan Alley pop. This sense of difference was initially based less in class antagonism than in the alienation many rural dwellers felt from a national commercial culture that originated almost exclusively in urban centers. Listeners to barn dance radio were aware of artists' dual identities as professionals and theatrical characters. They seem to have been unconcerned about the commercial nature of hillbilly, even eager to embrace the technological and cultural changes that radio delivered to their homes along with hillbilly music. They tended to view hillbilly broadcasting and songwriting in realistic terms, as a business and an opportunity for economic advancement. In fact, hillbilly's position as modern entertainment produced outside Hollywood and key network-originating stations accounted for much of its audience appeal. In time, the rural populism that underpinned this appeal, cultivated by the hillbilly fan press, would become part of the working-class identity of thousands of migrants to urban centers.

2

Country Music

Becomes Mass Culture, 1940–1958

By the end of World War II hillbilly music could be heard on radio stations all over the country. Honky-tonks, dance halls, and a burgeoning business in outdoor "hillbilly parks" provided multiple live performance contexts. Daily live radio broadcasts and a brief revitalization of the barn dance formula in the shape of shows like the *Louisiana Hayride* and the *Ozark Jubilee* still nurtured a sizeable group of professional performers. The spread of country music in the wake of rural-to-urban migrants displaced by economic and ecological upheavals from the Dust Bowl to World War II had established country as a commercial genre identified with the native white working class. Already Nashville had begun to emerge as a center of production around the artists and businessmen of the Grand Ole Opry, the WSM Artists Bureau, and Acuff-Rose Publications. The city was increasingly the target of scrutiny by the music industry at large, whose executives were eager to collect the profits from the new genres exploited by BMI. The royalties collected by BMI supported a growing community of artists and made country music important to those outside the field.

Nonetheless, it was not until the postwar period that country music consolidated as a unified field and a fully developed branch of the popular music industry. This unification was accomplished first at the level of language and concept. After rebelling against the derogatory "hillbilly" label, disassociating itself from the left-sounding (and middle-class—sounding as well) "folk" tag, and rejecting the regionally limited connotations of "western music," the national and commercial identity of the genre was finally accurately reflected in the moniker "country." The coalescence of country music was a matter of institutionalization as well as one of semantics. Throughout the early 1950s, various elements of the industry were coming together as a self-aware whole that included broadcasting, publishing, recording, booking, and management. At the same time, changes in broadcasting and recording fundamentally altered the economic and geographical structure of the music business in such a way that centralization in a single city, Nashville, became not only possible but sensible. This institutionalization and the articulation between country and the larger pop industry, first evident in the career of Hank Williams, helped to make the rockabilly revolution possible. But it also created a crisis in the new industry as a national network of talent and professionals collapsed into the Nashville nucleus. Artists and businessmen struggled over the impact that specific forms of commercialism would have on the production of country music even as they began to develop a new understanding of the field based on commercial success.[1]

OPPORTUNITY KNOCKS: BMI VS. ASCAP

As the nation inched toward war, hillbilly remained a marginal element of the music business. Its incarnations as radio vaudeville and celluloid horse opera had proved popular with audiences throughout the country, and especially in the Southeast, but its artists were aggressively excluded from the unions, licensing societies, and social formations that constituted the music business. Certainly the war itself helped to expand hillbilly's popularity and profitability. Southerners in search of war work packed their fiddles and guitars along with their other belongings as they headed for urban centers such as Chicago and Detroit, while young men from the Northeast and West learned to appreciate hillbilly music in the barracks of Southern training camps and in the honky-tonks that surrounded them. But these internal migrations alone do not explain the transformation of the hillbilly business between 1940 and 1953, nor do they illuminate the dramatic consolidation of the industry in Nashville after 1953.

Perhaps no single event in its history had more impact on hillbilly music than the clash between publishers and broadcasters that resulted in the formation of Broadcast Music, Inc. and the temporary boycott of ASCAP music on the air. Nearly twenty years later, many hillbilly artists remembered this as the watershed between subsisting on the margins of popular music and becoming a full-fledged music industry in their own right. The influence of radio and broadcast advertisers had helped to make hillbilly widely accessible in spite of the music industry's reticence, but it had also ensured that, with few exceptions, hillbilly artists were excluded from the main profit-making machinery of that industry. By independently providing a system for monitoring airplay and collecting performance royalties, the formation of BMI paved the way not only for the creation of a single identifiable field of country music, distinct from pop or jazz or blues, but also for the development of a distinct industry infrastructure. While the new institutions were distinct, though, they were also parallel to those of the pop music industry and would ultimately be subject to the centralizing forces that had always characterized the Tin Pan Alley system.[2]

Throughout the 1930s, ASCAP and the National Association of Broadcasters (NAB) had engaged in a bitter struggle over what constituted fair performance licensing fees. As they had from radio's inception, ASCAP argued that broadcasters profited from the use of music they did not own, while broadcasters complained that they did publishers a service by popularizing songs free of charge. On December 30, 1940, the contractual agreements that had produced a tenuous truce between the two sides were set to expire. As the date approached, each side prepared for a confrontation, and at the national NAB convention in October the group chartered its own licensing society, Broadcast Music, Inc. The brainchild of a CBS attorney, Sidney Kaye, BMI was established with a $1.5 million investment gathered from NAB members and was wholly owned by the broadcasters. Though the government would eventually charge that BMI was a monopoly even more insidious than ASCAP, the new society was faced at the outset with the task of breaking ASCAP's nearly complete control of popular music licensing and promotion. Its first move was to sign contracts with publishers not already affiliated with ASCAP. Not surprisingly, houses that handled hillbilly music were well represented in this group. One of BMI's first affiliates was the M. M. Cole Company of Chicago, which had long been a publisher of folios for WLS *National Barn Dance* stars. Similarly, one of the first defectors from ASCAP was Ralph Peer, whose repeated requests for a more profitable membership classification in the society had been denied because performances of the race, hillbilly, and Latin American popular music that formed his catalogue were undercounted in the society's sampling methods.[3]

The moment of truth in the great battle between broadcasters and publishers finally arrived on December 31, 1940, when nearly all broadcasters put into effect a complete ban on the use of ASCAP-licensed music. Listeners may have been "driven almost frantic by endless repetitions" of familiar favorites in the public domain and the few popular tunes over which BMI had been able to gain control, but their public silence during the ban was deafening. After ten months of standoff and the issue of a federal consent decree, the broadcasters' solidarity crumbled when the Mutual Network signed the first major new contract with ASCAP. CBS and NBC followed suit, and ASCAP music returned to the airwaves. But the establishment of BMI, and its broadened commercial exploitation of previously marginalized artists and sounds, would have a revolutionary impact on the structure of the popular music industry.[4]

Like the advent of radio itself, the formation of BMI undermined the centralization of popular music production in New York and Los Angeles. BMI's sampling methods, developed by Paul Lazarsfeld, were much more favorable to hillbilly and race music than those used by ASCAP. Based on logs supplied by a number of licensed stations—independent and network, urban and rural—the BMI system not only provided better representation of different kinds of broadcasters but also counted transcription and recorded performances in addition to live renditions. Unlike ASCAP, the distribution principles for songwriters whose compositions were published directly by BMI included no seniority provision, so newcomers to the field enjoyed a much higher return on their work than they could hope for from ASCAP. And in its first years BMI also supported fledgling publishers by offering guaranteed annual payment rather than an unpredictable percentage of the corporation's receipts. For many new publishers, this guarantee provided vital start-up capital and a reservoir from which to make advances to songwriters. The availability of BMI capital spurred the professionalization of hillbilly songwriters and composers just as radio had helped to professionalize hillbilly performers. In a few short years, the different institutions and profit systems of pop and hillbilly, as well as the race field, would be reduced to a set of parallel structures, all functioning according to the same rules of economics and popularization.[5]

Just as a confluence of diverse economic, technological, and social forces was required to prompt the development of commercial hillbilly in the mid-1920s, so a variety of forces was necessary to move hillbilly from the margins of the popular music industry to its center. The formation of BMI was just one of these forces, but its impact can be judged by its role in the formation of the first major Nashville publishing house, Acuff-Rose Publications. The idea to form the company came from Grand Ole Opry star Roy Acuff, one of the first generation of artists whose professional aspirations and musical styles had developed under the influence of an already commercialized hillbilly field. Acuff's musical career had begun in 1932 with a medicine-show tour of the Tennessee mountains, and by 1942 he led the hillbilly field with a headline spot on the NBC Prince Albert segment of the Grand Ole Opry, film appearances, and a bustling business in self-published song folios.[6]

Acuff and his peers benefited from the changes wrought by BMI, but the singer's savvy as a businessman was also one of the characteristics that set this new generation of hillbillies apart from their forebears. By the early 1940s—with network barn dances multiplying and the hillbilly recording industry in the full flush of revitalization after the devastation of the Depression—New York and Chicago firms that might once have dismissed the hillbilly songwriter with contempt were now offering Acuff as much as $2,000 for a single composition. Given his own experience with sales of his folios, Acuff recognized that this offer was only a fraction of the long-term value of his songs, so he approached the songwriter and pianist Fred Rose with the idea of creating their own publishing firm. Rose himself was a member of ASCAP and had produced pop hits as well as a string of musical numbers for Gene Autry's cowboy pictures. Indeed, once Acuff-Rose was established in October 1942, Rose first tried to affiliate the new firm with ASCAP, whose membership requirements had become less strict as a result of the 1941 consent decree. However, John Paine, the society's general manager, advised Rose that he would do better to license his country compositions through BMI. BMI offered the new firm advance capital of $2,500, an advance that made it possible to leave Roy Acuff's initial investment untouched. In the coming years, royalties collected by BMI and distributed through

Acuff-Rose served to bankroll the development of an independent hill-billy industry in Nashville.[7]

MAKING SENSE OF COUNTRY MUSIC

David Brackett has argued that until World War II, "the New York-centered music industry literally could not *perceive* the popularity of 'hillbilly' music," because it "was set up to produce, promote, distribute, and above all *recognize the importance of* one kind of music only—the music centered around Tin Pan Alley." The pop industry's attention to hillbilly as the 1940s opened resulted from the fait accompli of the genre's accession to the music industry as a component of the BMI catalogue. Far from being a response to grassroots popularity or listener demand for something new, the trade's sudden desire to understand hillbilly emerged from the internal dynamics of the economic conflict over publishing royalties. The formation of BMI, and the systematic exploitation of hillbilly and race music that came with it, drew attention to these fields in a way that the pop industry could, even had to, begin to understand.[8]

Sponsor and *Broadcasting*, the trades for the radio business, had been covering barn dance radio as an advertising vehicle since the early 1930s, but when *Billboard* began to try to interpret hillbilly and other vernacular styles for the popular music industry, the results revealed the music trade's general confusion. The paper inaugurated its first regular country review column in 1941 under the banner "Hillbilly & Foreign Record Hits of the Month"—a title that might be understood in light of the defining influence of the barn dance formula, where Lulu Belle and Scotty were comfortably joined by Olaf the Swede, and also in terms of the primary strengths of BMI. The next choice of title for the column, "Western and Race," which appeared in January 1942, was even more indicative of the pop industry's conventional logic about hillbilly, since the two styles were linked mainly by the fact that they had been excluded from the profit structures of the mainstream music business. Later that month, the column was retitled again, this time as the ultimate grab-bag of non–Tin Pan Alley material: "Western, Race, Polkas." By February 1942 the editors finally hit on a designation that gave some cohesion to the field as it might have been perceived by its audience and producers, and the column appeared under the title "American Folk Records: Cowboy Songs, Hillbilly Tunes, Spirituals, Etc."[9]

In other incarnations, this wrangling over terminology was a battle for respect on the part of the country field and its audience. But the early confusion in *Billboard* reflected instead the music industry's struggle to grasp the meaning and magnitude of country's potential popularity. The two issues intersected at the marketing department, where the question of whether the genre should be viewed as kitsch, nostalgia, or a contemporary style that its audience accepted quite seriously took on a measure of real importance. Fuzziness about the content and importance of hillbilly also reflected a more general disorientation in the music business, as the variety of delivery mechanisms and products mushroomed beyond the ability of executives in any one field to effectively monitor.

Although it settled earlier on a name and qualitative definition for the music, it was not until 1944 that *Billboard* added the element that was really needed for the larger industry to make sense of hillbilly music: popularity charts. The addition was prompted in part, no doubt, by the surprise success of Al Dexter's single "Pistol Packin' Mama," which became a million-selling hit before it was included in the Lucky Strike Hit Parade. The first *Billboard* country charts were based on jukebox play, where Dexter's hit had first broken, but an area that had been something of an afterthought for pop charts. Four years later, the paper added a retail sales chart and a news column called "Folk Talent and Tunes" edited by Johnny Sippel and presented the whole package as the "Folk Record Section." In 1949, the section title was amended again to "Folk (Country & Western)," and the first country radio airplay charts appeared. By the opening of the 1950s, the charts offered executives outside the country field a well-rounded way of understanding both exposure and success within the field. The system was perfected when *Billboard* decided to make success in the various fields intelligible in relation to each other by modifying the pop, country, and R&B charts so that their relative lengths reflected their relative popularity in the industry as a whole.[10]

But even as they began to recognize country music as a coherent field that might be made to operate according to rules everyone could understand, the trade papers presented a bifurcated image of the genre, as David Brackett has argued. Since the end of World War II, they had been remarking that businessmen in the country field had become the equals

of their pop counterparts, but the tone of shock and dismay that characterized such stories continued to make the field seem backward. A 1946
Billboard article on the country business, for example, reported that
Northern recording companies were lamenting the passing of "the gullible zekes" who, as a result of the war, had "picked up enough metropolitan savvy to hoist their market value and asking price." A year later
the magazine wrote that the "trend prompted one major disk exec to
remark painfully that 'I expect in a short time to give *The Billboard* a
story on how the country bumpkins are putting things over on us." Such
denigrating portrayals generally appeared in the feature sections of the
paper, while more serious coverage was relegated to the back sections.
Charts helped pop executives understand the market value of country
music, but there obviously remained a great deal of work to be done in
translating the aesthetic appeal of the music and the market approach of
its entrepreneurs into Tin Pan Alley terms.[11]

Roy Acuff's publishing partner, Fred Rose, was uniquely suited for this
job of transposing the content of hillbilly music into an idiom that New
York and Hollywood could understand. Rose's musical career began in
Chicago, where he worked as a pop performer and songwriter on WLS
and WBBM. By the time he arrived in Nashville in 1933, he was already a
successful member of ASCAP, familiar with the practices and preferences of Tin Pan Alley. His involvement with country music was somewhat fortuitous, a result of his work as a pop performer on WSM and his
friendship with the pop-influenced Vagabonds, whom he had known in
Chicago and who probably assisted him in finding a job at WSM. With
several decades of experience to his credit by the time he arrived in
Nashville, Rose approached songwriting as a craft. His ability to reshape
hillbilly styles according to standard pop conventions was perfected in
his work with Gene Autry during the 1930s. Pop had always influenced
hillbilly music; Rose's accomplishment was in selling country music back
to Tin Pan Alley and Hollywood.[12]

This interpretive effort was carried out at several levels—legitimation,
song structure, and business practices—and Rose was involved in all
three. Almost as soon as he began to work as a country songwriter, he
joined a growing group of figures in the music industry—including Columbia's Art Satherly and, later, *Billboard* editor Paul Ackerman—who
tried, during the 1940s, to effect a reevaluation of country music. Several
authors, including Richard Peterson and Bill Malone, have suggested
that the singing cowboy was the country industry's response to denigrat-

ing hillbilly stereotypes. But it is equally worth noting that the industry campaign for respectability emerged in the immediate wake of the first stages of the urban intellectual folk revival and demonstrated significant continuities with that movement. As they had for John Lair and for Bradley Kincaid, the folk roots of commercial hillbilly became for the second generation of country entrepreneurs a context through which to explain country music as something more than poorly executed vaudeville heart songs.

Like Kincaid, Lair, and the rural reformers of the 1920s, music executives such as Rose and Satherly harked back to sturdy pioneers, simple values, and a producerist cultural democracy to make country music respectable. In an open letter to the trade that he published in *Billboard* in 1946, Fred Rose rehearsed the basic tropes that would become the music industry standard for explaining the value of country music by the early 1950s. Drawing on the highbrow appeal of the concept of "folklore," Rose pointed out that while intellectuals embraced the folklore of Europe ("we call it 'opera' and 'music appreciation'"), they dismissed American folklore as "'hillbilly' music, and sometimes [they're] ashamed to call it music." Country music, Rose argued, was the folklore of America, a reflection of the compassion, simplicity, and purity of the "good American folks." Satherly argued that country music was a reflection of the nation's agrarian past, "native folk music" to which Americans would respond no matter how far removed from their rural roots their adult lives became. He encouraged artists with whom he worked to "make it an all-out effort . . . to remind one and all that we [don't] consider ourselves to be 'hillbillies,'" and to use "folk music," "mountain music," or "country music" instead.[13]

Satherly, with his British accent and patrician bearing, was easily portrayed as something along the lines of a commercial folk preservationist, seeking "emotional depth," "sincerity," and, above all, "an indigenous genuineness of dialect and twang" as he traveled from backwater to backwater with his portable recording equipment. Rose, on the other hand, could not be mistaken for anything but the modern professional that he was, and his defense of country music anticipated a newer mode of argument about the democratization of culture that relied on consumerism rather than citizenship. In closing his *Billboard* disquisition on the folk music of America, Rose gently noted that "75 per cent of all the people in the United States like and love simple things and simple music (folklore), and all of them are potential buyers of your product."[14]

Fred Rose embodied the growing articulation between the popular and country fields, and his willingness to defend the legitimacy of country music was critical in establishing an aesthetic justification for the genre among music industry peers. But he translated the country field into standard pop idioms in a more literal sense as well. Moving back and forth between Nashville, New York, and Hollywood, Rose was one of few composers in the late 1930s and early 1940s who could write country and western songs made to order for the singing cowboy film stars. When he struck up his partnership with Roy Acuff, he put the same skills to work. Throughout the 1930s he developed a network of acquaintances in the film and music businesses and an understanding of the pop industry that proved critical to his success as a country publisher. For Hank Williams and others, Rose took country material and brought it into line with standard pop conventions. His ability to regularize meters, polish lyrics, and simplify melodies was employed over and over as he worked with a wide variety of songwriters to improve their craft. Even more important, though, was his ability to work with the pop industry and pop A&R (artist and repertoire) men to secure performances of Acuff-Rose compositions by mainstream pop stars.[15]

There are a number of interpretations of the origins of Rose's relationship with pop executives, especially Mitch Miller of Columbia Records. As Fred's son, Wesley Rose, told it, he was sent to New York to try to place Hank Williams's tune "Cold, Cold Heart" for a pop version, and was told by every producer in town that it was "a hillbilly song" before finally overcoming Mitch Miller's resistance and convincing him to record it with Tony Bennett. Miller contends that he had been working with the Roses as early as the late 1940s when he was at Mercury Records. Fred Rose's history as a pop songwriter and several successes in placing songs with pop singers at Capitol and London suggest that the relationship with Miller was the result of an incremental strategy rather than a heroic breakthrough. Whatever its origins, after the success of the pop cover of "Cold, Cold Heart," Miller and the Roses maintained a mutual agreement whereby Miller was given a pre-release demo of any song Rose thought had pop appeal so that he could line up a singer and have a pop version ready if the country version proved a hit. In exchange, Miller agreed to hold up release of the pop cover until the country version had charted.[16]

In addition to proving lucrative for his composers, Fred Rose's business practices, influenced by his understanding of the workings of the popular music trade, provided a basis upon which country music could emerge as a consolidated national industry. Rose's work transcended the traditional role of the publisher. He took on many of the responsibilities that were, in the pop field, becoming the province of record company promotional departments: coordinating retail and radio exposure in connection with personal appearances, calling on distributors to make sure that recordings of Acuff-Rose songs were being offered to retailers, and ensuring that promotional copies of new records were being sent to the appropriate deejays. In the absence of a country music trade press, Rose served as a conduit for information about the field generally. He traveled and corresponded with disc jockeys around the country, relaying information about promising records, even those of songs by competitors, and offering programming advice. He and his promotional staff consistently figured as important shapers of the field in *Billboard* polls. In a 1951 poll, the former Mercury executive and then-current Acuff-Rose representative Murray Nash actually won out over the *Billboard* charts as the most important source of radio programming ideas among country disc jockeys. By becoming involved in so many phases of production and distribution, Acuff-Rose served informally as a trade infrastructure for the field as it became integrated into the popular music business.[17]

THE CONTEXT DISSOLVES

That the most powerful institutional force shaping the country music industry in the late 1940s and early 1950s was a publishing firm is all the more remarkable in light of the fact that the role of the publisher in popular music was in irrevocable decline. As Joli Jensen has argued, the transformation of country music in the 1950s was just one phase of a larger upheaval in the culture industries. Even without the demographic changes that created the youth revolution, uncertainty about the role of records, the impact of television, and the future of radio made the music business particularly unpredictable in the wake of World War II. In the space of little more than a decade, radio broadcasting was completely transformed twice: first when deejays and recorded music replaced live broadcasting, and again when sales charts replaced deejay opinion as the primary source of programming selections. Network television, meanwhile, took over the position network radio had once occupied: variety entertainment aimed at the broadest possible audience. And within the popular music business itself, the long-delayed primacy of the recording sector permanently reconfigured the industry's economy.[18]

Hampered at first by the Depression, then by wartime shellac shortages and a recording ban by the American Federation of Musicians, the record industry in the postwar period became the lynchpin of the music business. In 1945, retail sales of records totaled approximately $109 million; in 1946, the total came to nearly $218 million. Total sales figures fluctuated somewhat over the next ten years—including a notable dip in 1948 and 1949 that threw the trade into a panic—but they never again dropped below $170 million, more than double the average sales figures for the boom of the 1920s and nearly twenty times those of the Depression. At the same time, as a result of changes in FCC policy, the number of small independent radio stations increased dramatically—from around 200 in 1946 to more than 1,000 in 1951. These small stations relied heavily on records and transcriptions as an inexpensive source of programming material. Pre-recorded music soon became the most important means of exposure. Country stars continued to earn the bulk of their living from live appearances, but the fee they commanded relied, as it had for three decades, on the amount of radio exposure they could garner, which now depended in turn on promotion of their records.[19]

These developments accompanied and contributed to the vitiation of the power of publishing houses. Performance royalties, which had been the industry's second most important source of income after concert fees throughout the Depression, shifted into third place behind record sales for gross income. Nor was this reordering a matter of economics alone, for it was accompanied by an even more influential conceptual transformation. After a brief transitional period in which multiple versions of a single song might be cut by different artists on different labels for different markets, the unique recorded performance replaced the song as the organizing unit of measure for the industry. The publisher's song-plugger metamorphosed into the record label's A&R representative, whose job it was to produce not just hits but recognizable stars with unique styles whose recordings would have the potential appeal and consistency of a brand name. The importance of the publisher was reduced even further by the continued decline of sheet music sales. In the absence of sheet music, publishers became holding companies for performance rights rather than producers of a physical product, a concept originally pioneered by Ralph Peer. Every artist, label executive, or manager in the business could now serve as his own publishing firm if he could influence song selection at a recording session. Acuff-Rose successfully shaped radio airplay as late as 1954, but the promotional apparatus now belonged to the record companies, whose interests lay in the configuration over which the label exercised control: the recording.[20]

As had happened thirty years earlier with the advent of radio, changes in technology had far-reaching effects for the relative importance of different sectors of the music business, and ultimately for the ways that popular music was marketed and consumed. Television had replaced radio as the family entertainment medium, and listening audiences fragmented as portable transistors and car radios became personalized devices. Changes in record speeds and player marketing similarly produced multiple markets within the family: mom and dad's handsome, furniture-like console lent itself to long-playing records, while the portable 45 rpm player dominated marketing to teens. The effects of this fragmentation on country broadcasting, which had traditionally been aimed at the family audience, were particularly discomfiting.

The supremacy of the record also transformed radio from a locus of production to a locus of consumption and distinguished the deejay from the announcers, emcees, and bandleader hosts who had preceded him. Before the advent of record airplay, radio personalities had been performers as musicians, actors, or members of an ensemble cast. To be sure, deejays continued to construct theatrical personalities, and in the case of country music they were often singers as well, but the core of the deejay's role was no longer to create a performance. Instead, he functioned as chief fan, expert consumer, and independent critic. The primary factor in determining the deejay's worth remained the size and demography of his listenership, but this now rested in turn upon the ratification of his tastes by the record-buying public, that is, his ability to identify and associate himself with hits. Deejays had an interest in promoting the music industry as a whole, for the value of their expertise and on-air personalities depended on the success of the artists with whom they were associated. This new loyalty was strengthened by the fact that deejays relied on record labels for the promotional copies of records that made up the raw material for their shows.[21]

The general confusion and sense of retrenchment within the music industry were apparent in the proliferation of organizations designed to defend the interests of various sectors of the business from other sectors. The National Record Retailers Federation was formed in 1947, the Record Industry Association of America in 1951. The American Federation of Musicians engaged in a series of job actions in the late 1940s and early 1950s that were aimed at protecting the country's legions of live radio performers from the predations of the turntable but which could not hope to staunch the steady erosion of staff musician slots. The deejays organized in their turn, founding the National Association of Disk Jockeys in 1947. And, as we have seen, all sectors turned to the increasingly complex popularity charts to try to make sense of the welter of information and interests that now constituted the music industry.[22]

(THE) COUNTRY BEGINS TO CONVERGE

It was in the midst of this reshuffling of the established order that the country music business emerged. That it developed in Nashville was a natural outgrowth of the musical and managerial talent that converged around WSM and the Grand Ole Opry, but this was not the only probable outcome. Many scholars have pointed out that several other cities, including Chicago and Cincinnati, were equally well placed at the end of World War II to become Music City USA. And even this observation obscures what appears to have been the most likely alternative given the circumstances at the time: that country music, like the revitalized popular field in the wake of rock, would develop as a truly national practice, drawing on a number of regional styles to create a flexible, shifting synthesis of local cultures. Instead, perhaps because it emerged on the cusp of the transition, the Nashville system became the closest equivalent to Tin Pan Alley to survive the midcentury passage to fully realized mass culture. And while much of the rest of American culture became increasingly locked into national networks of television channels, retail chains, and advertising campaigns, the centralization of country music in Nashville represented an anomalous re-assertion of regionalism.

To an observer in 1950, the country business, finally recognizable as a coherent field, would still have appeared a far-flung confederation. Disc jockeys like Randy Blake at WJJD in Chicago, Nelson King at WCKY in Cincinnati, Connie B. Gay at WNBW in Washington, D.C., and Rosalie Allen at WOV in New York were becoming nationally known, and they were frequently involved in other phases of the industry such as concert promotion, production companies, or record labels. *Billboard* estimated that about 1,400 deejay shows aired each week across the United States and figured the average broadcast time of the country deejay to be eleven hours a week. As their numbers and importance increased, the deejays developed informal networks to share ideas and problems. Biff Collie, an announcer who grew up in east Texas and worked at Houston's KNUZ and as an emcee for the Philip Morris package show before moving to KFOX in Long Beach, California, recalls that the conduit for early organization was Johnny Sippel's weekly "Folk Talent and Tunes" column in *Billboard*.[23]

> That column was as big a factor as anything else I know. That's how we guys started getting common ground and became acquainted with each other's names, then began corresponding through the mail and sometimes by phone. Finally there was an agreement that we would get together in Nashville in November of 1950 and go to the Opry and sit around and talk about country music and radio.[24]

One announcer's recollection that the leading country deejays "felt like brothers" captures the sense of common purpose and professionalism that characterized the growing cadre. Just as the barn dances of the pre-war era had been dominated by a rotating and expanding group of personnel based initially at the WLS *Barn Dance*, the deejays of the postwar period moved from station to station, working with each other and sharing programming ideas. Biff Collie, for instance, worked with deejay Joe Allison at KMAC in San Antonio, Texas, during Collie's first announcing stint in 1943. They remained in touch throughout the 1950s and by 1959 they ended up together again at Pasadena station KFOX— one of the pioneers of all-country broadcasting—along with an all-star cast that included Dick Haynes, "Squeakin'" Deacon Moore, Cliffie Stone, and Hugh Cherry, who had earlier replaced Allison at Nashville's WMAK when the latter had moved to WSM. In addition to the constant mixing of talent as they moved from staff to staff, deejays like Nelson King and Eddie Hill who worked at 50,000-watt stations had a wide enough listening area that their colleagues at smaller stations could easily tune in. Both kinds of interaction helped to establish common practices and a sense of professional identity.[25]

By 1950, "Folk Talent and Tunes" had expanded its deejay coverage to a section titled "Disk Jockey Doings," in order to distinguish it from news about artists and releases. The column frequently included personal announcements in addition to suggestions for mail-pull contests or reports on artists doing particularly well in a local market. Rosalie Allen used the column to announce the birth of her child in 1948 and, two years later, the marriage of her sister as well. Items such as Tom Moore's suggest the extent of the informal networking among hillbilly deejays: "Uncle Tom (Moore), at WNOX, Knoxville, started his vacation last week, motoring with his family thru Kentucky, Illinois, Michigan, and Pennsylvania. Tom intends to visit plenty of his h.b. [hillbilly] and Western buddies."[26]

The deejays were on the front lines of the industry; only the artists were likely to have a similar level of interaction with the audience. *Billboard* noted the particular importance of the relationship between country deejays and their fans, which reflected "a mutual understanding and respect for one another." It was the deejays who were responsible for creating the "loyal segment of a highly music conscious public" that country fans comprised, the article contended. The deejays also felt their direct connection with country fans to be one of their chief strengths. "The Country Disc Jockey," wrote Joe Allison, "is a man respected in his community and his profession—and through his own initiative and promotional ability is crusading day and night to sell rural songs . . . as a real form of true American entertainment. [He] is doing this because he believes it himself."[27]

It was the general sense of bonhomie and innovation that characterized the new profession, rather than an explicit agenda, that provided the original impetus for a meeting in Nashville. "Nobody had any thoughts of doing anything other than socializing and getting drunk in the fall," Joe Allison later recalled. Allison credited Dal Stallard, a deejay at Kansas City's KCMO and a regular contributor to Sippel's column, with the organizational effort that made the early meetings a success. "We had never met each other, but we all knew each other by reputation," according to Allison. "We wrote back and forth . . . about 35 of us decided we would come to Nashville one fall and just meet each other and put a face to the name and have a good time." The deejays agreed to meet again in 1951 and by 1952, in Biff Collie's words, "there were around seventy of us and WSM claimed they sponsored us. That was the beginning of the 'Grand Ole Opry' celebration."[28]

In retrospect, many deejays, including Allison and Collie, harbored ill will over WSM's control of this event after 1952, when it became the WSM Disc Jockey Festival. The resentment was inflamed, no doubt, by the fact that the deejays lost out in the ensuing free-for-all to control the image of the country field within the popular music business. The hard feelings also reflected the position of the country deejay in the industry. No matter how popular he became, in the final analysis, the deejay was just an employee, and he had to answer to the very same kinds of station managers who were now stepping in to capture the glory for the development of the country industry. This can only have been exacerbated by the fact that WSM management at the time, like that of most radio stations, was not uniformly enthusiastic about country music. Even as late as 1966, the station manager, Ott Devine, told the *Saturday Evening Post*, "Except for the Opry and a few record shows we're a *good* music station."[29]

Prior to the involvement of WSM, though, the gathering had been based exclusively on personal relationships and had not even garnered a mention in *Billboard*. The station brought to the event its public relations acumen, prestige, and a systematic organizational structure that moved the annual meeting from an informal caucus to a national convention. Still, it seems clear that if WSM wasn't aware of the fall meetings, the station was at least catching up with developments already underway within the structure of the industry as a whole. Deejays had been the cornerstone of Capitol Records' much-imitated promotional strategy for almost ten years; the National Association of Disk Jockeys was five years old; and *Billboard* had already written of the particular importance of deejays to the country field, which had relatively fewer reliable avenues of exposure than pop. The idea to host the deejays was thus a combination of epiphany and opportunity, as Bill McDaniel, then the station's director of public relations, remembered it a decade later.

> We were sitting around one day throwing around ideas on what to do to celebrate the Grand Ole Opry's 27th birthday. . . . Although we were aware of the importance of the disk jockeys in the promotion of the Opry, we had never really gone out of our way to encourage their effect on the music. We had recently learned that we could obtain a fairly reliable list of the nation's disk jockeys so the idea was conceived to entertain them at the party on the night of the anniversary performance of the Grand Ole Opry.[30]

WSM had long prided itself on being at the vanguard of radio broadcasting. Indeed, it was this ambition that prompted the station's founders to lure the most popular radio announcer in America, George D. Hay, away from WLS when WSM first went on the air. Now that Acuff-Rose had defined and described a nationwide structure for the field through its promotional roster (the list to which McDaniel referred), WSM was again presented with an opportunity to be a national leader in broadcasting. The station sent out engraved invitations to deejays around the country, though McDaniel later estimated that the announcers would have had only two weeks notice by the time they received the invitations. In spite of the short notice, on November 22, 1952, nearly one hundred of them attended the Opry and a small party at the Andrew Jackson Hotel. The meeting was informal, but it augured the future of the business.[31]

OVER THE TOP: 1953

When Hank Williams was found dead on the morning of January 1, 1953, many in the industry assumed that his passing marked the end of a career whose hurried decline had been as notable as its meteoric ascent. Williams had been a big star and, thanks to the tutelage of Fred Rose, an even bigger songwriter, but he had hardly dominated the field in the minds of either deejays or fans; he was consistently bested by the likes of Hank Snow and Eddy Arnold in opinion polls of both groups. Observers were thus understandably shocked when his funeral on January 4 drew more than 20,000 people to Montgomery, Alabama. Requests for photographs grew from a handful each week to 300 in three days following his death. Retailers sold out of Williams records, and MGM delayed new releases and added a shift at their pressing plant to try to keep abreast of the demand. Acuff-Rose reported that deejays were programming blocks of up to two hours of Hank Williams songs. In death, even more than he had been in life, Hank Williams was a bonanza for the country music business.[32]

Outpourings of grief at the death of country stars were not uncommon and followed naturally from the familial images upon which the genre had long traded. When WLS's "Sunbonnet Girl," Linda Parker, died suddenly of a burst appendix in 1935, the station received thousands of letters mourning her loss, and when the issue of *Stand By!* featuring her obituary biography sold out, the station had so many outstanding requests for the number that they printed up a special one-sheet obituary and photo to send out in its stead. But no public mourning for a star until that time nearly approached the audience response in the months following Hank Williams's death. Grief over the death of Jimmie Rodgers—the best-known star before Williams to die relatively close to the pinnacle of his popularity—occasioned a tearful reception

Country Music Becomes Mass Culture

and front-page headlines in his hometown when his body was returned from New York. For the most part, though, Rodgers's death was re- marked and then passed over by both the trade and popular press. Cer- tainly the news of Rodgers's death was overshadowed by the turmoil of the Depression and the specter of war in Europe, but the greatest gulf between the two events was in the state of country music itself. Between 1933 and 1953, the business had developed a publicity structure capable of recognizing, absorbing, and promulgating the spontaneous expres- sion of emotion.[33]

Williams's death was the first of a series of events that combined to propel the country music industry into the biggest promotional windfall it had experienced in its short history. The timing was largely fortuitous; WSM had already held its first deejay meeting, and Ernest Tubb had been laying plans for almost two years for a memorial celebration and monument in Meridian, Mississippi, to honor Jimmie Rodgers. But the three events together created a sustained media event in the mainstream press and pop music trade papers that far exceeded the sum of its con- stituent parts and stimulated a dramatic wave of organization in the country business. At the beginning of 1953, the country field had a solid history of commercial success and a chart in the back reaches of *Bill- board*. By the end of the year, the industry had its first independent trade paper; an industry-wide convention, complete with awards ceremonies; its first national professional organization; an annual feature section in *Billboard* that proclaimed it to be America's "native art" derived "from the heart of a country"; and a congressional proposal for a day of national observance.[34]

As attention to the field grew, those in the country business continued to stake their claim to respectability within the popular music industry, and the effects of that campaign were evident in the Jimmie Rodgers Memorial Day celebration. Ernest Tubb and Hank Snow had begun arranging for the dedication of a monument to Jimmie Rodgers in 1951, though they did not originally conceive it as the enormous event it finally became. Given the circumstances, both must have felt pressured to make the unveiling ceremony an homage on par with the unplanned tribute to Hank Williams that had just taken place. Few knew of the plans before the winter of 1953, but by February 1953 Tubb had in mind a day-long celebration culminating in a concert spectacular to include Roy Acuff, Red Foley, Jimmie Davis, and Webb Pierce. Tubb encouraged *Billboard* to advertise the ceremony, which the paper did with a feature, unusual for the time, on country music and Rodgers's influence. Included in the spread was a note from Tubb and Snow themselves which, like Fred Rose's appeal to the popular music business in 1946, suggested a new basis for hillbilly's claim to respectability. To Tubb and Snow, Rodgers deserved recognition not only because of his musical talent but even more importantly because he "made the value of country songs and records into a commercial product that since then has been recognized as an important part of the music industry."[35]

Tubb and Snow also lobbied Representative William Arthur Winstead of Mississippi to introduce a resolution in Congress declaring the day of the dedication a national observance. Tubb, who had been instrumental in eliminating the term "hillbilly" from the Decca catalogue, could not have been pleased to learn that Winstead proposed the honorific day under the title "National Hillbilly Music Day," but the congressman clearly was not familiar enough with the genre to know better. In an interview on the *Old Dominion Barn Dance*, Winstead told the audience he had introduced the resolution in order to recognize the artistic contributions to American life made by those who wrote and sang "what we have come to think of as hillbilly music, supper music, folk music, cowboy ballads and what not." Obviously the campaign for a uniform nomenclature had yet to reach the capitol.[36]

In spite of the poorly chosen name (which was never actually endorsed by the House), the celebration was a success, and the presence of a number of politicians—including Tennessee governor Frank Clement, Mississippi governor Hugh White, and former Louisiana governor Jimmie Davis—helped to promote an image of reverence and respectability for country music. The festivities were attended by some 25,000 fans, who filled up every hotel room within a seventy-five-mile radius of Meridian. Even *Newsweek* reported on the event, and although the article referred exclusively to "hillbilly music," the haybale hilarity that usually characterized popular press coverage of country music was entirely absent. The Jimmie Rodgers Day celebration demonstrated that the frenzy over Hank Williams's death was not just a morbid anomaly, and it served as a ritual emblem of the legitimacy and sense of tradition that people like Tubb, Fred Rose, and Art Satherly had been working to develop. But it did not fundamentally alter the pop trade's analysis of its country cousin. The crowd was enormous and enthusiastic, but the loyalty of the country audience had long been recognized as one of the market's chief strengths. Indeed, the turnout only confirmed existing understandings

3 Justin Tubb and Hank Snow dedicate the memorial statue of Jimmie Rodgers at the first Jimmie Rodgers Memorial Day celebration. The celebration was one of several events that converged in 1953 to demonstrate to the music industry the popularity of country music, and it soon became a part of Nashville's struggle to define and control the genre's national image. *Photo courtesy of Country Music Hall of Fame and Museum.*

of the field, for the festival might as easily have been an overblown holdover from the medicine show tradition as a manifestation of a new branch of the popular music business. The exaggerated profitability of the personal appearance sector was perceived by the pop industry as one of the characteristics that set the country field apart from the regular order of business. If anything, the success of the Jimmie Rodgers Day celebration confirmed the stereotype of country music as a regional phenomenon that did not function according to the normal rules of the industry.[37]

The event that did change such preconceptions was the 1953 WSM Disc Jockey Festival, which immediately became a catalyst, not only for organizing the country field but also for focusing the attention of professionals in the larger popular music industry on country's development, especially in Nashville. *Billboard* had been offering its readers a somewhat schizophrenic view of the field, part slighting commentary about "ridge-runners and stump-jumpers," and part serious coverage of stars and record sales. If the scale of Hank Williams's funeral and the turnout for the Jimmie Rodgers Memorial Day had demonstrated that country fandom was deeper than had been realized, the proportions of the 1953 Disc Jockey Festival proved conclusively that country music was a business, not a novelty. In the interim between its first and second years, wsm's birthday celebration had metamorphosed from an oversized party into a two-day convention that included hospitality suites and receptions sponsored by RCA Victor and Capitol, among others, and award ceremonies by *Down Beat, Billboard,* and *Country Song Roundup.* The meeting was attended by more than five hundred people, four hundred of them deejays. BMI president Carl Haverlin declared at the licensing company's award ceremony that country music was "the voice of America," while ASCAP was, as *Billboard* noted, "conspicuous by its absence." The wsm festival captured the attention of the trade press as no other event had and triggered a reorientation of industry wisdom about recent developments in the country field.[38]

For *Billboard,* the broader lesson of the convention was country's establishment as a national pop music category. "It will be virtually impossible for advertisers and their agencies to overlook the promotional implications of . . . country music," wrote Paul Ackerman, "To consider it a local manifestation when some 400 disc jockeys pay their way to attend the festival is obvious blindness." Clearly persuaded by its own argument, the magazine premiered in its next issue the first annual spotlight on country and western. The lead editorial reverently described country music as "one of the bright ornaments of America's musical heritage," a field characterized by artists and businessmen who "let their inspiration spring from the heart of a nation." Even *Down Beat,* a trade paper generally devoted to jazz and other "longhair" music, expanded its tentative efforts at covering the field by running feature articles aimed at interpreting country for its decidedly highbrow audience. Articles by the deejay Cliffie Stone and the western swing bandleader Hank Thompson sought to explain the affinity between country and improvisational jazz by emphasizing the professionalism of country musicians and the artistry involved in playing exclusively from informal "head arrangements" rather than written music. For the country field, the attention garnered by the convention was a powerful object lesson in how the industry's image could be cultivated and managed through the activities of its businessmen as well as its artists.[39]

As public relations extravaganzas go, the 1953 Disc Jockey Festival was an unparalleled success. It was also an opportunity to give coherence to a field that, for the rest of the year, was still geographically and organizationally scattered. This systematizing function was accomplished through the physical substantiation of a network of professionals that was otherwise (literally) ethereal. But the festival also prompted the first attempt to formally organize the country music field as an independent industry: the Country Music Disc Jockey Association (CMDJA). As it would throughout its brief history, the CMDJA reflected in its goals and concerns the unease created by the expansion of the country market and the increasing complexity of the music business. The organizers of the CMDJA were clearly concerned about the corrupting influences of the music industry and hoped to set themselves apart as disinterested arbiters of taste for the field. *Down Beat* reported that the group's members had agreed that "no outside aid from any source would be accepted," and the organization would rely solely on membership dues for support. The newsletter the association planned to publish would accept no advertising and the association would not align itself with any artist, record company, or publisher. Newly elected president Nelson King of WCKY in Cincinnati was also careful to point out that the association was not a union and would neither engage in the settlement of employment disputes nor function as a placement service. Instead, its aims would be "the furtherance of public acceptance of Country Music and the betterment of Country Music disc jockey shows," and it took as its slogan "the Voice of America's Music."[40]

The congruence between the concerns expressed by the CMDJA and those that dominated the pages of Nashville's first trade paper was striking. In the early months of 1953, the editors of *Pickin' and Singin' News* rolled out the first issue of their paper—complete with a prominent message headed "In Memoriam (Stars Who Have Gone on Ahead)," which listed Hank Williams at the top of a roster filled out by Jimmie Rodgers and Uncle Dave Macon. Earlier magazines such as *Stand By!*, *Rural Radio*, *National Hillbilly News,* and *Country Song Roundup* had been targeted at fans, but *Pickin' and Singin' News* was the first to carry information of interest to professionals from disc jockeys to talent agents. Although the paper described its publisher, Charles G. Neese, as a "country lawyer" from Paris, Tennessee, the staff obviously had an understanding of its audience that betrayed attempts at rusticity. The "Audition Issue" reported that the publisher had consulted "top-placed executives in the Country Music world" before taking on the task of serving the country industry. Early issues featured letters of support from industry leaders such as Capitol's Ken Nelson, Mercury's D Kilpatrick, and Miami deejay Cracker Jim Brooker, all of whom would later be influential in the Country Music Association (CMA). Writers indulged in *Variety*-style lingo like "pubberies" and "cleffers" and covered the comings-and-goings of record executives and producers as well as stars. The paper featured a deejay column called "Tune Twisters" and deejays, Joe Allison among them, responded by writing in.[41]

Like the CMDJA, *Pickin' and Singin' News* spoke to the tensions and concerns that suffused the country business as it developed institutions parallel to those of the established music industry. The editors argued that the growing economic power of the country industry entitled it to a higher cultural status than it had traditionally been assigned, but they also expressed concern that the new complex of institutions responsible for the industry's growth might prove deleterious in the long run. The paper trumpeted Nashville's success and independence from the traditional centers of production in New York and Los Angeles, but it simultaneously warned against excessive centralization and cynical manipulation of the genre and fans by those in search of profits alone. Ironically, ambivalence about industry development was nowhere better expressed than in the paper's coverage of the CMDJA. While the editors conceded that "there is strength in unity and a great deal of good could be accomplished for all concerned," they also sounded an ominous note of warning alongside the good wishes and congratulations. "Many benefits could come from the successful operation of such an association. On the other hand some unwholesome effects could result. . . . [I]f developments are witnessed which this paper considers to be against the best interests of any segment of Country Music—including its millions of fans—this newspaper will . . . sound the warning." Like the CMDJA, the paper sought a position as external critic and safeguard against the dilution of country's essence.[42]

From its very first issue, the paper claimed Nashville as the core of the new industry. "Time was when almost anybody who was ambitious to go to the top in the music world had to go to New York or one of the other big cities," but Nashville's "Tin-Pan Valley" had proved otherwise. The editors rejected not only New York's position as the center of the music industry and final measure of good taste but also the business workings of the popular music industry itself. In a move that presaged later struggles, the paper announced that it would not publish popularity charts. "While we cannot ignore . . . record sales and . . . jukebox selection polls, PICKIN' & SINGIN' NEWS believes a better system of rating talent and tunes can be found than has yet been hit upon by the trade journals." In the meantime, the paper would list top talent in alphabetical order and top songs in general groups, regardless of which recording of a particular tune was then favored. The paper could hardly have chosen a system more thoroughly in line with the older, publishing-dominated system or more completely out of step with the emerging order based on recordings. "No popularity poll has yet been devised which is foolproof," the editors steadfastly averred. "Polls are merely samples, and not proof of the situation."[43]

Pickin' and Singin' News also argued for a strategy of success that looked to the health of the entire country industry rather than one based on individual profit. "Stars have not been made in Country Music by being placed in starring positions; they have risen, as all the ranks of Country Music came together and, in the concentration, pushed some to the top of the heap." Their warnings, the editors were quick to point out, were not intended to ward off changes in the music, though. "Change is the one thing we can be certain of . . . and Country Music must be ready to change to keep in step with progress," but simplicity and naturalness should not be sacrificed on the basis of short-term market calculations.

Beyond evincing uncertainty about the effects of entering a mass market, as opposed to the traditional agglomeration of local and regional markets, the arguments in *Pickin' and Singin' News* spoke to a concerted strategy of independence from the larger music industry. The editors, like writers in the mainstream trade press, viewed the authenticity and believability of country music as a folk genre as its greatest strength; they championed the music's down-home virtues not simply out of respect for tradition but because they understood those virtues to be its chief market appeal. Safeguarding that appeal meant holding country apart from the popular music industry, whose commitment to the genre was limited. This opinion was evident in the paper's response to a proposal that country and pop stars should be packaged together for personal appearances. Advising artists to "proceed with extreme caution," the editors warned that diluting country music through association with pop could "kill the goose that laid the golden egg," while serving only outside interests that sought to profit unfairly from country's success.

The reason the promoters now suggest combining the two forms of amusement is that they wish to make more money. . . . Making money is a worthy motive, provided basic long-range values are not destroyed for the sake of making a few extra dollars. . . . One of the things that has made Country Music great is the naturalness of the artists. . . . Country Music certainly does not want to lose the natural touch. Neither does it want to be absorbed by the professionals.[44]

A DIFFICULT ACCOMMODATION

The standing mythology of country music describes the rise of commercialism in the late 1950s as a response to the overwhelming competition from rock and roll, but the turmoil over charts and pop influence that characterized the reportage of *Pickin' and Singin' News* long preceded rock's immense popularity. Later complaints about the need to separate pop and country charts more thoroughly were aimed specifically at protecting country music's avenues of exposure to the rest of the industry from being dominated by rock artists. But concern about the use of charts in 1953 was a more general criticism of the ways the pop industry sized up its audience and assessed value, of how the mass market worked. The concerns of the CMDJA and the tensions revealed in *Pickin' and Singin' News* represented a nebulous anxiety about the direction the business would take as it made the transition from a structure based on a diffuse network of broadcasting and live performance venues to a centralized, recording-based industry anchored in Music Row. This crisis of accommodation with the pop music industry, and the conflict over Nashville's dominance that accompanied it, began well before rock and Top 40 formatting nearly eliminated country music from radio airplay. As Joe Allison wrote at the time, "Country music is no longer a baby but a great big ol' overgrown youngun with growing pains. He needs the proper nourishment and the correct attention to bring him into proper manhood."[45]

The coming of age was an arduous process. The first indication of the trouble that lay ahead surfaced at the disastrous 1954 Jimmie Rodgers Memorial Day Festival. The immediate debacle was precipitated by the way that politics and country music came together at the observance, or more precisely, the way they came apart. For decades, Southern politicians like Tom Watson, Lee O'Daniel, and Huey Long had used associations with hillbilly music to establish their populist credentials. As one

Country Music Becomes Mass Culture

Texan wrote of O'Daniel in 1938, although the governor-elect was really "a modern, up-to-now, wide awake business man," he identified himself with hillbilly music "to convey the idea that he is for the 'hillbilly' folks." And after years of the grinding hardships of the Depression, she noted, "Any change is welcome to us." It was in keeping with this tradition, if not its specific partisan leanings, that Ernest Tubb and Hank Snow had initially made the Jimmie Rodgers festival palatable to the civic leaders of Meridian by suggesting that it could also serve as a celebration of the city's railroad workers. Like Rodgers himself, Meridian had once enjoyed an image of modernity and progress for the working man by its association with the railroads that dominated the city. The city fathers no doubt hoped to suggest a symbolic link between Meridian's role in the great industry of the past and its nurture of the founder of an unexpectedly influential modern industry.[46]

The second memorial observance, like the first, incorporated unionism and politics into the festivities, but this time with far less felicitous results. Democratic presidential hopeful Adlai Stevenson was invited to speak, and unlike the more experienced Southern politicians who were accustomed to husbanding the delicate congress of popular culture and politics, he did not confine himself to a brief populist paean to the folk and their music. Instead, he delivered a lengthy speech in which he excoriated the Republican Party for sanctioning the McCarthy-Army hearings and emphasized the Democratic Party's support for the working man through stronger unionism. The New York Times reported that the forty-five-minute oration drew laughter and cheers from the crowd, but the industry took a dim view of the festival's political bent, in part because of the Republican affiliations of prominent country stars like Roy Acuff, who decried the show's politics when he followed Stevenson on the stage. Billboard reported that the Stevenson speech "rankled both performers and audience" and warned of "grim rumblings" among the crowd that many would not attend the festival again.[47]

The Stevenson incident attracted sharp criticism for several years and hinted at the failure of the Democratic intelligentsia to grasp the meaning of working-class popular culture as a political force. The avatar of staid, noblesse-oblige Northern liberalism, Stevenson had chosen Meridian to reach out to the Southern wing of an increasingly divided party and, no doubt, to temper his egghead image. (Two years later, during a losing primary battle to a coonskincap-wearing senator Estes Kefauver of Tennessee, Stevenson's handlers used country music again to try to create an earthier persona for their candidate, sending him on a swing through Florida behind "the musical automobile of Cowboy Brown," whose "car equipped with amplifiers and an endless supply of hillbilly records" led the Stevenson motorcade.) The reaction against Stevenson's appearance at Meridian summarized a host of political and commercial considerations. Stevenson's vocal condemnation of the McCarthy-Army hearings could well have raised the specter of reprisal, even in the final days of McCarthy's power; country artists and entrepreneurs had worked assiduously to avoid the fate of the urban folk movement, which had been decimated by persecution from the House Un-American Activities Committee. More likely, though, the industry's response hinged on what it perceived as a general sense of cultural arrogance and shameless appropriation on the part of powerful outsiders. *Billboard* opined that Stevenson had reduced country's biggest annual event to little more than the "all-too-incidental locale of a major political address" and clearly chafed at the elitism of "the politicos and labor leaders who descended on this city en masse," heralded by "screaming police sirens . . . at all hours of the day and night." In the end, the 1954 Jimmie Rodgers Memorial served as an object lesson about the potential dangers of seeking publicity and respectability through association with "national names" who might turn the music to their own ends.[48]

But what most plagued the festival, and the industry, for the remainder of the decade was the intractable struggle to locate and control the image of a nationalized country music. A spirit of competition grew up almost immediately around the location of the Rodgers festivities. After the first commemoration, Roy Acuff and Tennessee's governor Frank Clement had each expressed their hopes that the celebration might be moved to Nashville. Then, just before the 1954 event, Congressman Howard Baker of Tennessee introduced a resolution for a week-long national celebration of country music in the first week of July, a suggestion that would neatly disconnect the observance from the Rodgers memorial in Mississippi. The rivalry can only have been exacerbated when, in 1954, *Billboard* decided to move its annual country music issue, which had first appeared in conjunction with the WSM Disc Jockey Festival, to coincide instead with the Jimmie Rodgers celebration, which it now rechristened the "2nd Annual National Country Music Jubilee." National ownership of the festival was probably an unreasonable expectation for an observance that began essentially as a personal act of devotion on the part of Ernest Tubb. But such an explanation did little to assuage the anger of *Louisiana Hayride* cast members who arrived in Meridian—perhaps remembering the informal jam-session atmosphere of the first celebration—to find that they could not have a place on the program because the headlining show was already filled with Grand Ole Opry performers.[49]

Attendance at the third celebration in 1955 suffered as a result of the conflicting purposes with which the festival was burdened. The railroad men's barbecue again preceded the memorial, but organizers were careful to note in the trade press that the union activities would not be an integral part of the observance. And this year, organizers made room for the *Louisiana Hayride*, a fact that KWKH, the *Hayride*'s originating station, highlighted by buying a full-page ad in *Billboard* to announce its sponsorship of the event and to welcome all in attendance. (This was supplemented by a separate quarter-column ad bearing Elvis Presley's "Howdy to all my friends at the Jimmie Rodgers Memorial.") Aside from Tubb and Snow, however, the biggest attractions from the Opry did not appear. It is difficult to know whether the paucity of Opry stars resulted from factional conflicts between station executives, or from the more specific fear that Presley might overshadow the Opry's biggest names, and possibly even ignite another riot, as he had in Jacksonville a few weeks earlier. Whatever the precise motive, the composition of the celebration demonstrated the difficulties that beset the industry as it tried to establish a unified tradition and a national appeal.[50]

As a result of such squabbling, the 1955 festival ended with an impromptu protest meeting organized by Biff Collie. Collie and other deejays—irked that they had not been offered an official place on the agenda—gathered to criticize "so-called memorial celebrations honoring certain late country & western music stars," referring to Rodgers and Hank Williams, in whose name another annual memorial festival was being observed. Such events, the deejays argued, should be replaced by some sort of "national" observance "to which all c&w talent, all radio and TV jamboree units, and all related facets of the trade would be invited to participate." A proper national observance would move from city to city to represent the different regions (and different deejay markets) from which country music drew its popularity. Ernest Tubb—responding to the suggestion that all sectors of the business should be represented, though not to the idea of regional inclusiveness—suggested that the following year's celebration be planned by a committee "consisting of two members of each segment of the industry" that would report on plans at the fall Disc Jockey Festival. No such committee appears to have been formed, but Tubb's proposal closely paralleled the structure and intent of the Country Music Association that was formed three years later. The timing of the idea—some six months before Elvis Presley signed his contract with RCA, and only a few weeks after the riot in Jacksonville—suggests that the pressures of integration into a national constellation of mass culture, not the popularity of rock, propelled the initial impulse to centralize the management of country's image.[51]

No doubt because they were themselves widely dispersed, the deejays, more than any other group, continued to forward proposals that would reflect country music's diverse regional cultures. At the fall WSM Disc Jockey Festival, the CMDJA announced plans for its own national cele- bration. Observing that the existing festivals were "local rather than national in character," CMDJA president Nelson King announced that the group would sponsor its own celebration on a geographically rotat- ing basis, with the first event to be offered to WSM for May 1956. Public relations director Bill McDaniel declined to discuss whether the station would accept such an offer. Meanwhile, both the CMDJA and WSM announced their tentative, and independent, plans for a country music hall of fame. To some degree, the competition over who would control the canonization of country music was simply self-aggrandizement. A number of contemporaries later observed that the CMDJA seemed ul- timately to become a promotional vehicle for Nelson King and other members of the board, and WSM's hard-nosed pursuit of the publicity and profits to be gleaned from country music certainly earned the sta- tion a number of enemies during the period. But there was also clearly a deeper disagreement about what was to be sanctified and by whom.[52]

This conflict over who should serve as arbiter of taste for the industry was equally evident in the disc jockeys' conflicts with the record labels. In spite of Tom Moore's plea to his colleagues at the 1954 Disc Jockey Festival to "consider themselves as part of the entire music-radio indus- try," many deejays felt they were "bound primarily to [their] audience" and had a duty to safeguard the audience's interests by curbing the excesses of the industry. This included policing their own ranks for opportunists who secretly disdained country music and played it only for a profit, and monitoring new releases for "objectionable" material. The CMDJA even suggested that it should determine who was or was not a real country deejay. In an extended argument over the major labels' distribution of promotional records, the organization argued that its

Country Music Becomes Mass Culture

members, by virtue of their commitment to the field as demonstrated through their membership, should automatically receive free records, while deejays less devoted to the cause could be eliminated from promotional lists. When one deejay complained about the major labels—"They ask us to play their records; they give us whiskey to get us drunk; then they don't give us the records"—he unwittingly hit on the fact that the deejay was becoming as much a target market as an integral part of the music business's promotional machinery. Increasingly, record companies could determine, through promotion within the industry, which records a deejay had to have—whether he had to pay for them or not.[53]

By 1956, the power of the deejays was already waning, heading ineluctably toward the final deluge of the 1960 payola hearings. Todd Storz had already introduced the endless rotations of the Top 40 format in the pop market, and uncertainty about just who was in charge of record selection for airplay was pervasive. In a poll for the 1956 *Billboard* radio programming issue, 94 percent of deejays reported that they chose their own music, and that they did so not primarily by reference to trade charts but on the basis of listener requests and their own opinions about the records. But in a simultaneous poll, station managers reported that they expressly controlled their deejays' selections and that the chief consideration in programming was the rankings in trade popularity charts. Country music had not yet undergone the transformation to a tight hit-rotation format, but the impact of the development in the pop field on country deejays was even worse than on their pop counterparts. A formula based on popularity alone discriminated, of necessity, against specialized genres in favor of mass-appeal hybrids, and the shift to Top 40 essentially eliminated country programming in many areas.[54]

The CMDJA's decision to directly confront the rest of the country industry in 1956 was thus particularly ill timed. In February, Nelson King announced that the celebration the group had decided on the previous fall would not only take place in the same month as the Jimmie Rodgers celebration in Meridian but on the very same day. WSM declined to host the event because of the schedule conflict, and the deejays ultimately tied their first celebration to RadioOzark's June "Ozark Square Dance Jubilee" in Springfield, Missouri, but not before the affront had been duly noted by the trades. The lead editorial for *Billboard*'s country and western issue, which now appeared in March (notably divorced from any of the contending festivals), called for all in the country field to "drop petty bickering" and "pull together." Deejays were singled out for criticism, both on account of the festival conflict and because of their continued refusal to play rockabilly or pop-influenced records. The conflict actually seemed to work to the benefit of the Jimmie Rodgers Memorial Day celebration. With 30,000 in attendance at the final concert, the festival seemed to recover, if only fleetingly, from the ill will generated by the Stevenson address of 1954.[55]

The CMDJA, meanwhile, withdrew further and further from the rest of the industry. The June meeting attracted representatives from WSM, RCA, and most of the other major institutions in the field, but the event was poorly organized, and the benefit concert that concluded it drew only about a thousand people, netting the organization a mere $1,200 for its treasury. The deejays announced that the event was meant primarily for the broader public in any case, again reinforcing its stance that the tastes of the audience, not the industry, should determine the genre's course of development. The real indicator of the CMDJA's fate, though, was the "highly secretive" meeting convened to formulate the following year's event, and the directors' refusal to reveal the outcome of the meeting "for fear that the idea might be lifted." In November 1956, the CMDJA voted to separate its annual meeting from the WSM Disc Jockey Festival. "We know that we're now strong enough to exist without the help of any established country music functions," Nelson King told trade reporters. In truth, membership stood at only about two hundred, well under half the annual deejay attendance at the Disc Jockey Festival. Several proposed newsletters failed to materialize, and the association had yet to publish its bylaws, which had been ratified, in theory, at the first full membership meeting in 1954. The June 1957 meeting in Kansas City drew a scant forty registrants, and ticket sales for the concert spectacular that was to have been nationally televised, before negotiations fell through, were optimistically described as "fair." At the following year's June meeting in Miami, the board of directors unanimously voted to disband the CMDJA and form a new organization that would represent all sectors of the country industry, the Country Music Association (CMA). In February 1959, the remainder of the CMDJA's treasury, about $1,200, was transferred to the CMA.[56]

The collective memory of the country music business, even among deejays, has generally condemned the CMDJA. Looking back on its history, Joe Allison remarked with some frustration that the CMDJA "didn't plan one thing. . . . It looked like that they didn't know how even if they wanted to," a fact that Allison and others attributed to the scattered, self-aggrandizing agendas of the association's leadership. By the time it was disbanded, the group's defensiveness and secretive posture encouraged rumors of embezzlement and conspiracy. But the causes of the CMDJA's failure extended beyond the personal shortcomings of the organization's leadership. The deejays possessed neither the financial nor the political capital to lead the industry, particularly as their programming power was progressively undermined by reliance on the trade charts. Only a hand-ful made more than a basic living wage, and their positions were always tenuous, subject to the whim of the audience and station management. They certainly couldn't afford to subsidize their organization in the same way that publishers and record labels were ultimately willing to do in order to perpetuate the CMA and gain the ear of station managers.[57]

The deejays also sounded an unwelcome note of discord in the rising chorus of voices that proclaimed country music's ascent to the pantheon of commercial genres that could be marketed to a mass audience. As a group, the deejays were hindmost in the economic chain of the business, closest to their audience in socioeconomic terms, and were thus most likely to experience firsthand the class politics of playing and listening to country music. Perhaps as a result of that experience, they seem to have been most acutely concerned with preserving the respectability, integ-rity, and ultimately commercial and symbolic control of the music by keeping it distinct from the pop field. For many deejays, its location in the grid of class and cultural hierarchies remained the defining feature of country music. To them, the most important part of the deejays' duty lay in "taking pride in our work, holding our profession to the highest es-teem, [educating] those who do not understand us, and above all, [say-ing], 'I'm proud to be a Hillbilly!'"[58]

AN EXCESS OF SUCCESS—
COUNTRY, ROCK AND ROLL, AND MASS CULTURE

Concerns about what the rise of mass culture might mean for country music and its audience began to engross the industry as soon as the genre achieved national success. Suspicion of popularity charts, strug-gles over creating a national definition and image for the music, and conflict over who could best determine the preferences of the country audience all preceded the rise of rock and roll, and indeed sprang from the same reorganization of the music industry that produced rock. But the advent of the new sound crystallized opinions about absorption into a mass market and polarized an already divided country industry.

The traditional mythos of the rise of rock is a heroic narrative in which a revolutionary, integrative sound overcame institutional barriers and corporate prudes to give a soul-starved audience the emotional intensity and sonic innovation it craved. The parallel popular narrative of country music during the period contends that "rock nearly killed country," ultimately forcing the stylistic innovations that produced the Nashville Sound as the industry frantically worked to broaden country's appeal to counter the rock threat. Both stories share the basic assumptions that the divide between rock and country was considerable and immediately apparent and that the response of "the industry," whether pop or country, was monolithic and based on prejudice or snobbery. Neither of these assumptions withstands closer scrutiny, nor do the narratives as a whole. At least until its popularity exceeded the ability of the country field's institutions to control it, rockabilly, as its suffix suggests, was perceived as country music. And if one defines "the industry" as major labels, record executives, and publishers, then the music business embraced rock and roll even before the immensity of its commercial potential was entirely clear. In the country field, the most intense industry resistance to the new trend came from the same source that had most invoked concerns over the effects of a national mass market in the first place: the deejays.[59]

There is no doubt that racism underlay much of the country industry's response to the growing influence of R&B, but the cultural politics of country music, more complicated than mere bigotry, worked into a twisted and tightening knot of race, class, and sex. From the perspective of the deejays, the dividing lines between white country and black R&B were already tenuous. Country and R&B occupied the same marginal spaces with respect to the pop mainstream, a fact that Nelson King recognized when he railed against the fickleness of pop A&R men who were free to choose "favored darlings" as the opportunity arose. The genres' positions in broadcasting were also similar, for country and R&B frequently coexisted on separate shows on the same stations. Chicago station WJJD, for example, was host to Randy Blake's extremely successful country show *Suppertime Frolic* during the same years that it featured Al Benson, the first black deejay in the Chicago market to play urban blues and address his audience with a Mississippi accent and black slang. The same, of course, was true of record labels. Though he was an

Country Music Becomes Mass Culture

outspoken critic of blues lyrics—which he associated with the influence of R&B in spite of country's own rich history of risqué songs—Nelson King was himself a producer for Syd Nathan's King Records. Like Sun Records in Memphis, King Records released tunes by both R&B and hillbilly artists, and artists in each field were encouraged to cover hits from the other.[60]

Both black and white deejays of the older generation shared anxieties about the implications of the sexualized lyrics and dance styles that rock and roll popularized. Jack Cooper, a pioneering black deejay and broadcaster in Chicago, voiced the same concerns about risqué lyrics as Nelson King and scrupulously maintained an ambiance in his broadcasts that reflected the middle-class gentility of his primarily black audience. Within a few years, Nat D. Williams of Memphis station WDIA would express as much dismay over the spectacle of respectable young black women screaming for Elvis Presley as White Citizen's Council secretary Robert Patterson did at the sight of middle-class white women screaming for Louis Armstrong. Indeed, some of the most explicit and open discussion of fears about combining country and R&B appeared in *Down Beat*, which devoted more space and critical thought to black music and musicians than any other trade paper. For blacks and whites alike, the libidinous spirit of rhythm and blues and rockabilly challenged the hierarchies of class, race, and gender they felt established respectability for them and their audiences.[61]

The intense class politics that went along with playing country records also helps to account for country deejays' opposition to rock and roll. Record executives and music trade papers complained continually about the deejays' refusal to play R&B and pop-influenced songs, and in this regard Eddy Arnold's re-recording of "Cattle Call," with a string-laden sweet pop arrangement by Hugo Winterhalter that anticipated the Nashville Sound, was as likely to face resistance as a rockabilly hit. "It's . . . about as far uptown as we want to go," remarked one unenthused deejay. The populist, anti-corporate logic that connected these repudiations to the larger constellation of suspicions deejays expressed about mass markets was revealed clearly in a two-part article in *Down Beat* by Nelson King. King began by clearly distinguishing between the interests of those "connected with country and western music in the field of radio" and the industry that produced the music, anyone "connected with C&W music (publisher, artist, A&R, etc.)." King blamed the latter for the decline in country record sales and the burgeoning popularity of R&B.

While the article evinced the same kind of thinly veiled racial antagonism that would soon characterize many public responses to rock, King's real target was "the A&R boys and the dyed-in-the-wool, nothing-is-good-but-Gershwin pop advocates." The immediate cause of country's decline was the incorporation of too many R&B elements and a failure to write quality songs, King argued. But both phenomena stemmed from a single weakness: the country industry's willingness to be influenced by charts and the tastes of New York and Los Angeles record executives. The true cause of country's decline, according to King, lay in the production of "Country music for pop's sake; not country music for country music's sake."[62]

From a different perspective, though, the emergence of Elvis Presley and the popularity of rockabilly were viewed as the ultimate triumph of the country industry, and of the vast, disparaged hinterland over the tyranny of the bicoastal popular music empire. Presley certainly incorporated a heavier R&B influence than previous country musicians had generally been willing to do, but his style was not without precedent in the field. Western swing had long capitalized on the same hybridization of urban black and rural white music; the Maddox Brothers and Rose, the Delmore Brothers, Moon Mullican, and Hardrock Gunter all prefigured Presley's style. Bill Haley, whose title track for the film *Blackboard Jungle*, "Rock Around the Clock," signaled the advent of rock and roll hysteria (and, for some critics, the co-optation and death of real rock and roll), had also begun as a country artist and in the mid-1940s had appeared regularly on WOWO's *Hoosier Hop* barn dance as a member of the Down Homers.[63]

In addition to the obvious continuities between his style and that of other country artists, Presley was very clearly a product of the field's new intra-industry promotional structures. Chip Crumpacker, director of promotions for RCA's country division, convinced Steve Sholes, the division's head, to pursue Presley's contract on the basis of the singer's showstopping 1955 performance at what had become the country field's most important showcase concert, the Jimmie Rodgers Day celebration. And when negotiations for the unprecedented $35,000 deal were at their most delicate, Colonel Tom Parker relied on the fall WSM Disc Jockey Festival to generate promotional momentum for his client. Peter Guralnick has written that "the Colonel was simply counting on RCA's increasing commitment to the *idea* of the deal to carry them through the unpleasant financial details." But he did all he could to make the idea an attractive one by timing RCA's decision deadline to coincide with the announcement at the WSM convention that Presley had won the *Country & Western Jamboree* reader's poll for "New Star of the Year," and that both *Cashbox* and *Billboard* surveys had identified him as the most promising country and western artist. It was a skilled use of the country field's commercial clout to overcome the misgivings of RCA's New York offices and general skepticism in the pop trade.[64]

And, as his sweep of the country polls in 1955 indicates, Presley was at first popularly received as a country artist, for good or ill, in spite of the resistance he encountered among many in the country business. When the Sun single of "That's All Right" was released, a Knoxville record retailer explained to his RCA distributor that something "really weird" was happening: the single was selling to country fans, not on the basis of the flip-side cover of Bill Monroe's "Blue Moon of Kentucky," but on the R&B-influenced sound of the A side. His point was confirmed when an elderly man, "an obvious country fan," walked up to the counter and demanded a copy of "That's All Right," which the retailer was playing in the store at that moment. *Country Song Roundup* introduced Presley to its readers in 1955 as the "Folk Music Fireball." That the magazine's editors placed him among the breed of newcomers who "every so often . . . stirs up a fuss with a different kind of record, an unusual singing style, or a 'gimmick' of one sort or another" testified to the novelty of his sound, but also to the fact that it appeared to be simply one of many passing variations on the country music theme. And when teen pop icon Pat Boone, who had grown up in Nashville and married Red Foley's daughter, appeared with Presley the following month, he was moved to wonder "how in the world a hillbilly could be the next big thing." Presley's uncertainty about how to negotiate the transition was evident to Boone when, after an enthusiastic response to his first song, Presley "opened his mouth and said something . . . so hillbilly that he lost the crowd."[65]

Certainly the pop industry interpreted the rockabilly craze as evidence of country's popularity and ability to influence the pop field. In 1953, country music had hit the peak of its popularity in record sales and crossover success on the pop charts. That year, a country song was twice as likely as a rhythm and blues song to achieve success on the pop charts; in 1954, the figures were exactly reversed. Part of what distinguished rockabilly from pop in 1955, then, was not the influence of R&B, which had already become an important component of the pop field, but the renewed prominence of country styles. As Presley's Sun recordings began to achieve national popularity, the *Billboard* journalist Paul Ackerman reported that "the pop field, which has dipped heavily into the rhythm and blues fount in the past year, is now making more frequent forays into the country and western field in order to come up with likely material." A few months after Presley's RCA contract had been signed, Bill Sachs led *Billboard's* annual country and western issue with an article that cited Elvis as the primary example of "how country music is being accepted by the general masses." An accompanying article on record sales noted that, while "the country market is not at the same exalted heights of yesteryear," nonetheless, "the tremendous popularity of such artists as Elvis Presley has stimulated country music activity to its highest point in recent years." The same theme dominated the next year's country spotlight, which remarked again upon country's "continuously widening impact on what has always been known as the pop market."[66]

For the first several years of rock and roll's popularity, the country music trade press echoed similar sentiments. Touting itself as "an economic Baedeker" for pop executives who were "reaping the new harvest" created by the mingling of formerly separate fields, Nashville's newest trade journal, the *Music Reporter*, seized every opportunity to remind the music industry that Tin Pan Alley no longer exercised unrivalled influence over the pop scene. "The great music centers of the big cities, which are no longer monopolies, might look thankfully to the hinterlands which have given the business its size and vigor today," wrote *Music Reporter's* editor Charlie Lamb. And among the outposts, Nashville now reigned supreme "on the national music throne by virtue of the undisputed dominance of rockabilly music, produced by one-time country singers to whom the style comes as naturally as breathing."[67]

The *Reporter's* analysis was largely correct. For all the later remembrances of the rock threat, it was the success of rockabilly that finally established Nashville as the undisputed center of country music recording. Not all sectors of the Nashville industry benefited equally. The Grand Ole Opry suffered as a result of its traditional reluctance to embrace new styles. The show could accept no credit for Elvis Presley's success, as he had appeared on the Opry only once, in 1954, and was thereafter a cast member of the *Louisiana Hayride*, the Opry's chief rival. The missed opportunity was a significant loss to WSM, which relied on the Opry for two-thirds of its advertising revenue as early as 1949. Nor did Acuff-Rose, the traditional engine of the city's musical economy, share in the profits. When Colonel Tom sought a publishing contract for his young star, he went to Los Angeles publishers Hill and Range, with whom he had worked on Eddy Arnold's publishing rights. The final calumny occurred when Hank Snow, nominally Parker's partner in the management of Presley through the offices of Hank Snow Enterprises–Jamboree Attractions, asked Parker when the money for the RCA contract might reach the agency's coffers. Parker "flew into a rage" and immediately insisted on dissolving the partnership, informing a chagrined Snow that "Elvis is signed exclusively with the Colonel."[68]

But while the traditional institutional leaders of Nashville's success were dangerously buffeted by the rock craze, the popularity of rock and roll provided the city's advocates in the pop industry—men like Steve Sholes and Paul Cohen—with the clout to invest significantly in a production center outside New York or Los Angeles. Paul Cohen had moved the bulk of Decca's country recording to Nashville in the late 1940s, when two WSM engineers opened Castle Studios, the first commercial recording studio in the city. Cohen and other major label A&R men relied on local studios throughout the mid-1950s—first Castle and then, when it closed as a result of WSM's pressure on the engineers to choose between the studio and their broadcasting jobs, Owen Bradley's Quonset hut. As late as 1955, Cohen considered moving Decca's country headquarters to Dallas but was persuaded to stay in Nashville when Bradley offered to build the new studio. No major label constructed its own studio in the city until 1957, when Steve Sholes used the influence he had gained from signing Elvis to convince RCA to commit to locating all of its country operations in Nashville. The all-important position of head of A&R for the division went to Chet Atkins, who had been supervising Nashville sessions for Sholes for several years and had produced "Heartbreak Hotel," Elvis's first hit for RCA. A year later, Decca turned over its country operations to Owen Bradley.[69]

The success of rock and roll thus symbolized not only country's increasing absorption into the pop mainstream but also the consolidation of production in Nashville. Indeed, only after the Nashville recording sector had been firmly established did the industry unite in its rejection of rock and roll. Several things about the timing of this repudiation, which occurred near the beginning of 1958, bear note. First, it took shape after rock's chart influence had peaked. By the spring of 1957, country artists had produced the first hits with what would soon be labeled the Nashville Sound. Ferlin Husky, Sonny James, and Marty Robbins all released significant crossover successes during that year. Sales of rock and roll records generally were down and broadcast advertisers were beginning to seek an alternative that would capture the attention of the adult audience. The realization that the adult market had been neglected coincided with a significant shift in marketing philosophy. Increasingly, class and race were being recognized as factors that conditioned all kinds of consumer choices, and advertisers sought to tailor messages and products for narrower segments of the population, based not only on demographic information but also on what would ultimately be called psychographics—lifestyle choices and values. Country's unique appeal to the white working class had been the source of its marginalization; now it was poised to become the genre's chief strength.[70]

Joli Jensen has argued that the story of generic warfare, in which rock nearly routed country, was a rhetorical strategy developed after the emergence of the Nashville Sound in order to justify the commercialization of country music to reach a broader audience. The country industry's efforts to patrol the border between the genres in the late 1950s, though, were aimed as much at isolating a delimited country audience and rejecting the very idea of mass appeal as they were at justifying a broader reach for country. This shifting consensus was evident in the pages of the *Music Reporter*. In mid-1957, the magazine, which had been published as the *Country Music Reporter* for its first few months, dropped the generic designation from its masthead and introduced the "one big chart," which listed records by popularity rather than category. Much of the paper's editorializing also revolved around discussion of the vanishing boundaries between categories. "Rock 'n' roll is considered Pop, yet it comes about as close as any type of music has ever come to being based upon the same principle upon which C&W music is based," editor Charlie Lamb pointed out. Yet, while the "snob barriers" of classification had come down in industry practice, the trades continued to perpetuate false distinctions, in spite of what the *Music Reporter* insisted was country's "multiple-market appeal."[71]

Within this wholehearted embrace of the pop market, though, was a contradictory message about the proper limitations of country's audience. "C&W music, on the whole, has more lastingly loyal fans than any other brand of music," the paper argued, "and these record buyers continue to shell out for the artists who plunk the guitars and sing from the heart." While the avenues of exposure within the industry must not reflect the "class segregation" that had traditionally relegated country to second-class coverage, the audiences would remain distinct. "The individual music buyer is predominantly still devoted to either one field or the other. However, the constantly expanding acceptance of C&W music . . . is accepted proof to the industry that there is big money to be made in both fields."[72]

By the middle of 1958 the *Music Reporter* reversed its earlier policy and extended the division between audiences back to the industry. The "one big chart" became three—for pop, R&B, and country—and then four, as a special chart was added just for rock and roll. The "multiple-market appeal" the paper had earlier boasted for country music gave way to loud protestations against the "two-headed evil" of "so-called 'all-market' tagging of a tune, by which it is supposed to be some hybrid monstrosity that pleases everybody but may not end up pleasing anybody." When the three most important men in country music publishing, Jim Denny, Jack Stapp, and Wesley Rose, went to New York and Los Angeles to hold "personal pow-wows hoping to convince [*Variety* and *Billboard*] to eliminate R&R from C&W charts," the *Music Reporter* professed the immanent good sense of the division. "Good luck boys," Lamb wrote, "THE MUSIC REPORTER sympathizes with your feelings when you see more than half of their C&W charts' top 10 grabbed by R&R disks." Ultimately, the magazine returned to the position expressed earlier by disc jockeys and by its predecessor, *Pickin' and Singin' News*, averring that exclusive focus on any charts was unhealthy. To "start the development of a truly popular music representative of the entire American public," Lamb opined, industry leaders should "stop reading the sales charts of hit records . . . and start playing songs which assume the listener is an adult and wants some expression of his adult experience."[73]

Thus, in some ways, the arrival of rock and roll represented the apex of the effect that mass culture as a marketing philosophy would have on country music. Having created a production and distribution structure with a truly mass reach, the industry's vision of its target audience over the next few years would become increasingly more specific and refined. Rock and roll's popularity had attracted investment from the major labels and, perhaps even more importantly, had convinced New York and Los Angeles to relinquish production control to local A&R men like Owen Bradley and Chet Atkins, whose pop sensibilities were tempered by their long experience with country music and the people who made up its audience.

But the impact of rock also shifted the terms in which the country industry argued for its own legitimacy in ways that made the principle of mass acceptance central to the genre. The folk-based synthesis presented in the late forties by men like Art Satherly and Fred Rose, which portrayed country as the musical expression of the nation's pioneers, was being replaced by one in which commercial success equated with respectability. This was true not only of the way the audience was characterized but also of the industry's presentation of its own professionalism and business savvy. Country music demanded respect because it commanded money, not because it tapped the spiritual wellspring of the American frontier. While the strategy had obvious appeal for those within the industry, it unreflectively conflated consumption and respectability. In the sixties, this emphasis on consumerism as respectability would combine with the increasing focus on psychographic market segmentations to reconfigure the image of the country audience in the eyes of the broadcasting industry, Madison Avenue, and ultimately the nation as a whole.

Throughout the course of the 1950s, concerns over the specific institutional forms that commercialism might take as a national market developed divided the country music industry and conditioned the field's response to rockabilly. At the beginning of the decade, deejays had momentarily emerged as the industry's critics and arbiters of taste. For those few years, they collectively determined exposure and, as a result, defined the boundaries of the genre. As the decade wore on, that function was appropriated by the record labels, aided by trade charts and station managers. In this regard, the battle over how to imagine rock and roll was also a controversy over how the country audience and the country market would be defined: by the daily ethnographies of deejays or by the mass marketing measurements of the popular music industry. By the end of the 1950s, a consensus had reemerged around the notion of a distinct audience and a rejection of the undifferentiated mass market. But the relationship between the audience and the industry was forever changed. No longer mediated by the deejay, communication between the audience and the industry would take place through marketing studies, surveys, and ad campaigns.

3

Country Audiences and

the Politics of Mass Culture, 1947–1960

The advent of rock and roll forced the newly formed country industry to reevaluate its relationship to the popular music business and to the very idea of mass culture. The unprecedented popularity of the new style also caused a "social repositioning of country music" among the latter's audiences and critics. For many observers, the notional unity between country music and the Southern white working class was finally and irreversibly cemented in the 1950s. As understandings of the genre and understandings of its audience became increasingly difficult to separate, the class politics of country music intensified. At the same time, issues of culture and consumption moved toward center stage in American intellectual and political life, perhaps because, as Jackson Lears has suggested, intellectuals could identify few other arenas in which they still wielded sufficient authority to influence society. The two developments converged to make country music a focal point for expressions of class suspicion. On the one hand, the traditional disdain with which many urbanites viewed rural migrants was augmented by the specter of hillbilly TV demagogues and volatile masses beguiled by meaningless commercial culture. On the other, country music fans, encouraged by the country industry, marched to the front lines of the "stylistic war between plebian and patrician" that represented one of the most legible remnants of explicitly working-class sentiment in the 1950s.[1]

This friction across class-cultural lines flourished in spite of the striking similarities between working-class country fans' responses to the increased dominance of mass culture and the responses of middle- and upper-class public intellectuals. Country music fans understood the power relations inherent in mass media, and resented them deeply. Yet, as Michael Denning has argued, the left's failure to take country music and the rise of working-class popular culture seriously resulted in a "missed connection" that greatly influenced the development of American culture and politics in the post–World War II era. By reducing industrially produced popular culture to little more than "an advertisers' plot," the left disengaged from the most obvious arena for pursuing the cultural politics that had helped to make it an important political voice in the 1930s and 1940s.[2]

In one sense, fan mail from the 1950s supports Denning's assertion, illustrating the expanse of common ground that might have been exploited in the struggle against corporate hegemony. But in other ways, the radical potential of country music was limited from the outset. This was not because, as many scholars have asserted, country music necessarily "marked out a politics . . . of patriotism and traditionalism," though it frequently did, but instead because the politics of class division became so central to the marketing of country music. The liberal reaction against mass media and commercial culture invoked the authority of the traditional cultural elite against the ominous masses, threatening the newfound cultural power of the entertainment business. The country music industry, by contrast, articulated a simple populist equation between commercialism and democracy. The popular will, this equation asserted, was expressed in the accumulation of record purchases, the accretion of crowds at the Opry's Ryman Auditorium, and the accrual of listener mail addressed to country musicians. In this formula, the commercial success of country music signified both the power of the white working class and the vigor of American democracy.[3]

The fan-oriented elements of the industry promoted and capitalized on class distinctions in order to develop a sense of loyalty in its audience. Country listeners were encouraged to recognize and reject the influence of middle-class taste in their music. This phenomenon was most visible

Country Audiences and Mass Culture

in responses to rock. While the dominant interpretation of country music in the 1950s and 1960s would argue that the country audience's antipathy to rock was based on racial prejudice, there is significant evidence to suggest that it originated equally in class hostility. The transformation of marginalized rhythm and blues and country into mainstream rock, as George Lipsitz has argued, "entailed a shift from working people's culture to anyone's culture." While many country fans objected to the infusion of "black" styles into their music, others resented more the appropriation of both white and black working-class music by the white middle class. But although the fan press capitalized on a sense of rebellion against the middle class to distinguish country from other genres, fans were nonetheless encouraged to subscribe to middle-class values by equating consumerism with respectability and democracy.[4]

HILLBILLY TOXIN: IMAGES OF THE RURAL
MIGRANT AND MASS CULTURE IN POSTWAR AMERICA

As World War II came to a close, many observers expected a reversal of wartime migration trends. Indeed, one of the central themes of wartime advertising revolved around the premise that Americans were fighting for a return to the farmsteads and small towns that had dominated the metaphorical geography of the United States through the 1920s. But the causes of the rural-to-urban migration transcended the ready availability of wartime jobs. The consolidation of agricultural production in the Midwest and Plains states and the continued decline of the Southern wage economies of sharecropping and coal mining ensured that the cities and suburbs of the North and West would continue to swell with wary new arrivals. As the nation struggled to come to grips with its modernist, urban present, images of the rural past, and of the rural dwellers imported into the urban industrial order, took on a particularly troublesome cast. After several decades of celebration and cultivation, the place of the "masses" and their cultures in the national scheme was reevaluated in the academy, in government policy, and in popular culture. Country music stood at the crossroads of the ensuing debates over mass media, cultural hierarchy, and the nature of the "folk."[5]

Throughout the 1930s and 1940s, intellectual understandings of folk and popular culture had become increasingly liberal and inclusive. Popular Front and New Deal cultural programs were supported by a growing cadre of academics and culture workers who viewed folk culture as an important contribution to the national character and a necessary component of contemporary social life. The symbol of the pioneer, representative of the patriotism and dignity of the common man, figured as the primary vehicle for celebrating the achievements of the nation. As World War II receded, however, the imagery surrounding the average American shifted. Government-sponsored arts programs curtailed by the war effort were never resumed, and commemorations of national grandeur focused increasingly on the material progress produced by the interaction of all groups rather than on the image of the ordinary man as the foundation of the nation. This shift was accompanied by a pervasive reconsideration among intellectuals of the role of the masses in past and present American life.[6]

In the field of history, this shift was typified by the work of Richard Hofstadter, who vigorously questioned the existence of the self-sustaining yeoman and his culture, and the relevance of either to the modern industrial order. In 1948, Hofstadter opened his treatise on the American political tradition with a rueful reflection on the "increasingly passive and spectatorial" state of mind of his contemporaries. Americans, he argued, looked to the past with a sense of "overwhelming nostalgia" that substituted "a ravenous appetite for Americana"—expressed in the popularity of historical fiction, comic books, picture books, and, one might add, square dancing and country music—for a critical appreciation of the lessons of history. As McCarthy's reactionary populism gained momentum, Hofstadter returned to his argument more pointedly. The "cranky pseudo-conservatism" of the time, he suggested, was a reflection of the spirit that had always animated the masses, in periods of both reform and retrenchment. The story of a noble, patriotic yeomanry was a myth, and the popular liberal reform movements of the nineteenth and early twentieth centuries represented little more than a fortuitous alignment of varied pecuniary interests. Intellectuals, Hofstadter wrote, succumbed too often "to a tendency to sentimentalize the folk," thereby ignoring the fundamental illiberalism of the majority, especially the rural majority. Conservatism in the 1950s was merely the "development of certain tendencies that had existed all along, particularly in the Middle West and South," including a suspicion of "intellectuals, the Eastern seaboard and its culture." The tone of the argument marked a significant shift from earlier discourse; even Hofstadter admitted that this opinion of the folk was one he would not have expressed fifteen years earlier.

Mountaineers and cowboys might have stood the country industry in good stead in the 1930s and 1940s, but their utility as claims to cultural legitimacy required buttressing in the 1950s.[7]

The same withdrawal from the general public and its cultural predilections characterized intellectual movements in other disciplines as well. In the 1940s, intellectuals such as B. A. Botkin and Charles Seeger had reinvigorated the study of folklore and folk music by working to popularize its fruits and, more importantly, by arguing that folk culture encompassed some aspects of contemporary commercial and mass culture. In contrast to the revivalists of the 1920s and early 1930s, such as Annabel Morris Buchanan, Botkin and Seeger viewed commercial hillbilly as an extension of, rather than a threat to, folk traditions, and thereby gave the music an imprimatur of intellectual worth. By the late 1950s, though, this inclusive vision of folklore and its value had notably fallen from favor. Seeger, who had been appointed to lead the Pan-American Union's music division, was so frustrated by the traditional conception of cultural hierarchy promoted by other members of the group, and so concerned about his position as a representative of the government during the Red Scare, that he resigned in 1953. That same year, Indiana University awarded its first doctorate in folklore. As folklorists struggled to carve out a niche in academe, they increasingly rejected popularized forms of folk culture. Richard Dorson, who became the head of the Indiana University program in 1957, lambasted Botkin and other folklorists from the governmental and popular sectors for their willingness to tailor folk forms to popular taste. Echoing Richard Hofstadter's complaint, Dorson wrote that in the 1940s, "Folklore started to become big business. . . . The cavernous maw of the mass media gobbled up endless chunks of folksiness, and a new rationale appeared for the folklorist: his mission is to polish up, overhaul, and distribute folklore to the American people." Dorson dismissed such efforts as "fakelore," and led his field toward an increasingly insular vision of folklore, its proper audience, and its place in popular and mass culture.[8]

Dorson's critique of popularized folklore revealed much in common with the writings of other intellectuals who sought to regain their traditional cultural authority as the arbitration of taste devolved to multiple points within the commercial culture industries themselves. Figures as diverse as Walt Disney, Fred Allen, and Irving Howe encouraged Americans to challenge traditional authorities. Russell Lynes's irreverent elaboration of cultural hierarchies in popular publications like *Harper's* and *Life,* along with Vance Packard's best-selling book *The Status Seekers,* served to demystify questions of taste and undermine the power that critics had once wielded. At the same time, though, many observers lamented the passing of clear cultural hierarchies. Irving Kristol bemoaned the loss of an older generation of critics who had been able to shape not only aesthetic values but also moral reason in society at large. "*Someone* has to be able to say, with assurance and a measure of authority, what is culture and what is not, what is decent and what is not," he wrote. "There must be some group or class that is admittedly competent to decide—not without error, but more wisely than anyone else—questions of moral and cultural value. Otherwise a necessary and vital element of order in the life of a society will be lacking." David Riesman observed that the political glad-handing required of those who actually held economic and social power put them at the mercy of popular opinion: "the desire of businessmen to be well thought of," he suggested, had vitiated individual leadership.[9]

The hillbilly in the 1950s became one symbol for expressing this widespread ambivalence about the vestiges of the nation's rural mythology, the nature of the masses, and the effects of corporate-controlled mass media on cultural hierarchy. To some degree, this discourse relied on traditional urban stereotypes of rural hicks. A 1958 article on Chicago's migrant population in *Harper's* ran through the familiar elements of the hillbilly caricature. The new migrants, like the old, were "proud, poor, primitive, and fast with a knife," "fecund," "anti-social," unable to maintain an orderly home or watch over their rampaging children—"on the streets of Chicago [Southern migrants] seem to be the American dream gone berserk." The article echoed an earlier exposé in the *Chicago Tribune* that spoke of the migrants in similarly degrading terms. "The Southern hillbilly migrants, who have descended like a plague of locusts in the last few years, have the lowest standard of living and moral code (if any), the biggest capacity for liquor, and the most savage tactics when drunk, which is most of the time." Opinion in other Northern cities was hardly more favorable. A 1956 poll in Detroit showed that citizens objected more to the presence of "poor southern whites and hillbillies" in their city than they did to "transients, drifters, dole types."[10]

The hillbilly's inability, or unwillingness, to adjust to modern life had long been a key element in the popular stereotype, but images of the rural migrant in the 1950s were updated in a way that made his relationship to mass culture and the organizational imperatives of industrialized society particularly important. Even when he was outwardly successful, the new media hillbilly was a savage underneath, lurking behind a mask of suburban respectability and technological sophistication. This, at least, was the story told by the best-selling novel *No Down Payment*, which was adapted for the screen in 1957. Part of a spate of suburban potboilers that reflected fascination with the nation's newest consumer lifestyle, *No Down Payment* was a melodramatic reflection on America's evolution from benighted ruralism to sleek suburbanization. The book's climactic scene warned of what could happen if the primitive hillbilly were not kept in check on the long march of progress. In it, Troy Noon (Boone in the film), a World War II veteran from the hills of Tennessee who has been relegated to a job as a gas station attendant in the California suburb of Sunrise Hills, self-immolates in a frenzy of violence aimed at the symbols of suburban gentility and class immobility. Consumed by envy at the ease with which his college-educated neighbors manage the modern order while his own Southern accent and lack of organization-man social skills brand him an outsider, he assaults his neighbor's wife and dies trying to escape the scene of the crime. Like most treatments of suburbia in the 1950s, the book is critical of suburban conformity and pretense. But while the novel encourages a degree of sympathy for Noon's plight as a symbol of obsolete frontier independence (and lawlessness), in the end it is clear that hillbillies like Troy Noon must go the way of all creatures that have been passed by in the course of evolution. In the nuclear age, Americans needed to reject the rural past and join the brave new world of consumerism and technology.[11]

Richard Hofstadter's concern with the "cranky pseudo-conservatism" that grew from the phobias and hatreds of the rural South and Midwest found its most articulate popular echo in Elia Kazan's 1957 film *A Face in the Crowd*. A dark satire that fused fears about the effects of the mass media with the urbanite's traditional disdain for country music, the screenplay by Budd Schulberg cast the hillbilly as a symbol of social and political decay in a classic denunciation of the totalitarian potential inherent in mass communications. In it, an uneducated but wily hillbilly singer named Lonesome Rhodes, played by Andy Griffith, is molded into a popular icon by the broadcasting and advertising industries. The film called attention not only to the demagogic potential of television but also to the artifice of the down-home country music image. When the television cameras focus on Rhodes for the first time, his handlers slap a cowboy hat on his head and a straw in his mouth and instruct him to "be perfectly natural, easy, and relaxed—and real country." Moving from

4 Hi-tech redneck: Andy Griffith, as the hillbilly singer Lonesome Rhodes, confronts the machinery of mass media in Elia Kazan's 1957 film *A Face in the Crowd*. The film fused the image of the hillbilly as a symbol of social and political decay with concerns about the deleterious effects of mass media.

Pickett, Arkansas, to Memphis to New York, Rhodes begins as a singer, becomes a musical spokesman for a do-nothing patent pill, and winds up as a mouthpiece for right-wing political interests. He is ultimately ruined when he inadvertently calls his loyal fans "a bunch of trained seals" and "stupid idiots" on the air. But the film confirms Rhodes's impression of his audience, alternating between close-ups of hysterical fans and distant shots of an amorphous audience to convey the gullibility and irrationality of the rural crowd from which the hillbilly singer has sprung. In *A Face in the Crowd,* the danger of the mass media lies in the ignorance of the audience that believes in the just-plain-folks hokum being peddled by advertisers and the country music industry.[12]

Ironically, the film reflected, in its production as well as its message, the humiliation born of many Americans' personal experience with the hillbilly stereotype. Kazan discovered early in production that Griffith still agonized over the insults he had suffered as a child growing up in North Carolina, where he had been taunted as white trash. Throughout filming, whenever Kazan wanted to transform Griffith into the deranged

Country Audiences and Mass Culture

hillbilly demagogue, he would whisper "white trash" to the actor before rolling the cameras. This meshing of Griffith's own experience with the biography of his character reached sadistic proportions as production progressed. Kazan encouraged the cast and crew to ostracize Griffith and, on one occasion, to ridicule him openly for the "dumb-hick ignorance" of art and literature he had displayed at a cast party the night before. Griffith barely survived the filming with his marriage and psyche intact.[13]

A Face in the Crowd typified the shift away from sympathetic portrayals of the white working class, especially migrants, in mass culture and toward the authoritarian and pathological interpretations that would dominate academic treatments, public policy, and popular culture in the 1960s. It also bespoke increasing unease among intellectuals about the nature of the folk and about their own inability to counterbalance any longer the power of mass media with traditional critical authority. Certainly, by the late 1950s, Hofstadter's charge that intellectuals tended to romanticize the folk could be leveled only if one had in mind the imagined virtuous folk of a bygone era. In the present day, the folk had been replaced by the crowd in the intellectual imagination, and it was viewed with suspicion at best, and hostility at worst.[14]

THE SMATHERS HEARINGS, COUNTRY MUSIC, AND THE POLITICS OF CULTURE

A Face in the Crowd captured and dramatized the assumptions about culture, class, and the mass media that animated intellectual discontent in the 1950s. These concerns were effectively brought to life during congressional hearings on the broadcasting industry held in 1956 and 1958. The hearings originated in the interminable struggle between ASCAP and BMI for control of the licensing rights to popular music in the United States. This conflict had always contained elements of highbrow versus lowbrow, with the former somewhat incongruously represented by the composers and publishers of Tin Pan Alley, while the impresarios of commercialized vernacular forms such as country music served as standard-bearers for the latter. The congressional hearings turned the highbrow/lowbrow divide into a debate over consumer democracy and suggested the ways that corporate dominance of American culture was legitimized in the late 1950s.

In November 1953, just as WSM was putting the finishing touches on the program for its first full-scale Disc Jockey Festival, and at least a year before rock and roll would become a popularly recognized movement, a group of ASCAP songwriters and composers, including Ira Gershwin and Alan Lerner, filed a civil antitrust suit against BMI. The complaint accused BMI of colluding with its broadcaster-owners and the major record labels, owned by the same broadcasters, in a conspiracy "to dominate and control the market for the use and exploitation of musical compositions." In truth, the suit was as much a reflection of songwriters' discontent with ASCAP as with BMI. But the claim that BMI was unfairly limiting access to the airwaves also expressed the frustration of the pop music business's old guard at their own loss of control in determining what the public would and should hear. As one Tin Pan Alley hand told *Variety*, "Don't tell me that in the final analysis the public really picks [hit songs]. We [Tin Pan Alley publishers] used to have a pretty good concept of quality and values in songs that we published." By the 1950s, though, publishers no longer wielded the power to shape the content of popular music. That role had been usurped by performers and record companies, whose tastes and motives the traditional Tin Pan Alley elite considered suspect at best. "Today, we don't dare publish a song until some artist perhaps likes it," the same publisher complained. "A record should be a by-product of publishing; not the sparkplug of songwriting and publishing."[15]

Though the lawsuit itself, *Schwartz v. BMI*, ultimately proved unspectacular, evidence gathered for the action provided New York congressman Emanuel Celler with the entertainment value he sought to draw attention to his investigation of unfair practices in the broadcasting industry. The inquiry began as a broad attack on the centralization of control of radio and television in the hands of the major networks. At the outset, the hearings provided the broadcasting industry with at least a modicum of amusement. Questions posed by committee members "represented the broadest type of humor" to professionals, betraying the committee's ignorance of the rudiments of network competition and their view of the media as monolithic and malevolent. Near the end of the hearings, encouraged by Arthur Schwartz and ASCAP, Celler turned his attention to the relationship between BMI and network radio broadcasters. Ironically, Celler's own law firm had successfully represented the plaintiffs in a similar suit against ASCAP that focused on the association's control of film music, the second most important avenue of exposure after radio. But the tone of the new investigation was decidedly in ASCAP's favor. And while most observers in the entertainment business saw the hearings as little more than a "headline hunting ball," they also recognized that the effort was a tremendous success on those grounds and that it would have to be handled with care.[16]

In truth, of course, BMI was itself battling ASCAP's more established monopoly over popular music rights, but there were indications to support the claim that broadcasters consciously worked to limit the use of ASCAP music and promote compositions controlled by BMI. As late as 1948, BMI president Carl Haverlin had suggested to the National Association of Broadcasters a numerical target for use of BMI compositions by member radio stations, citing the millions of dollars the licensing firm had saved the broadcasters over the contract ASCAP had proposed before BMI's formation. Whatever the legitimacy of suspicions that broadcasters were controlling access to the public's attention for their own profit, the hearings quickly devolved into an extended rumination on the decline of American taste, and the role of the mass media in hastening that degeneration. ASCAP supporters soon grabbed daily headlines with declarations warning the public about "the enormity of the conspiracy against good music" and charging that BMI songs were "obscene junk, pretty much on a level with dirty comic magazines." Congressman Celler made radio appearances with members of ASCAP lambasting the poor quality of BMI music and calling for the Commerce Committee to prepare legislation that would force the networks to divest their publishing interests. Bing Crosby wired Congress with his support for further investigation, blaming BMI for the "deplorable" songs dominating radio sets, and senators John F. Kennedy and Barry Goldwater found an uncommon point of agreement in their complaints that "the airways of this country have been flooded with bad music since BMI was formed."[17]

Though the uproar surrounding the Celler hearings was stimulated primarily by the popularity and perceived effects of rock and roll, country music also fell within the purview of the "bad music" for which BMI was being blamed. The industry was quick to recognize the potentially devastating material effects of the high-flown rhetoric surrounding the hearings. Few in the business had forgotten that the formation of BMI had paved the way for country to become a profitable field, and few doubted that what harmed the licensing firm would also hurt country music. Tennessee governor Frank Clement vowed to defend country music before Congress, telling those in attendance at the 1956 WSM celebration that "the fight against BMI is a plot by a small inside group in New York and California to gain complete control of the music business, to stifle competition and to stifle country music." Clement portrayed the fight for country music as a defense of the hinterland against the tyranny of urbanites, and of the common man against the cultural elite. "Prior to 1941 when BMI came into being almost all the economic rewards for the writing, publishing, and singing of songs went to a small handful of songwriters in New York and Hollywood," he said. The growth of the Nashville-based country music industry had been "a triumph for the great American concept of small business."[18]

In the summer of 1957, Celler released his report, which backed away from his original attack on the television networks but called for further investigation into the music field, with an eye toward determining whether broadcasters were violating antitrust laws through their control of BMI. Though the Justice Department declined to investigate, Senator George Smathers of Florida introduced a bill before the Communications Subcommittee of the Committee on Interstate and Foreign Commerce that would make it illegal for any company or individual engaged in music publishing, recording, or licensing to hold a broadcasting license. Hearings were scheduled to begin in the spring of 1958.

ASCAP's supporters opened the hearings with a broadside attack on the poor quality of BMI music and assertions that commercial drivel was crowding "good" music off the air. Oscar Hammerstein led the charge, and was followed by a Brown University professor who argued for the need to "upgrade our national musical taste." As radio and television had come to dominate the musical life of the nation, Professor Arlan Coolidge argued, Americans had "allowed commercialism to dominate ... to the detriment of our taste." Radio put forth "a perpetual blanket of banality" that prevented teenagers from appreciating concert and symphony music. The "almost complete absence of fine tunes by Berlin, Jerome Kern, Cole Porter, and many other gifted composers in the area of musical comedy" hindered the natural progression "from music of this kind to much concert music of high quality." In addition to identifying popular taste with poor quality, Coolidge connected cultural hierarchies with social order. "It may not be possible to force the acceptance of high moral standards or fine taste by means of laws," he complained to the committee, "but surely there must not be tacit approval of a condition which favors the cheap and restricts the worthy." Committee member A. S. Mike Monroney of Oklahoma agreed. Monroney particularly lamented the fact that research on audience preferences, or as he called it, "this new system of automatic mind reading which Madison Avenue—that controls the advertising agents—considers to be the Sermon on the Mount," was replacing arbitration by experts as the basis for determining good programming.[19]

Like a number of witnesses against BMI, Coolidge represented the educators and intellectuals who had traditionally shaped musical taste, at least among middle-class Americans. Their sense of dismay at having been superseded by the disc jockey, the audience survey, and ultimately by popular taste was palpable in their testimony. But their testimony was also shot through with contradictions. They championed diversity of musical offerings but hoped to curtail the broadcasting of "cheap" music. They suggested that musical comedy and opera would be as popular as rock or hillbilly if only they could be heard over radio but also suggested that quality and popularity were somehow mutually exclusive. Most difficult of all, they objected to commercial contamination of cultural life in a hearing designed to defend the economic prerogative of ASCAP. The conflict between popular opinion and educated exclusivity as measures of value was noted by one of the congressmen involved in the Celler hearings, who observed with some exasperation the efforts of each side to minimize its own commercial success in order to emphasize aesthetic worth. "I never encountered anything like it," he told a reporter. "Each side claims the other does more business." ASCAP composers bemoaned their inability to get their music played because of their licensing affiliation but simultaneously offered their popularity as evidence for the notion that the shut-out could only be based on discrimination against ASCAP, not on their own lack of appeal. Thus, while ASCAP supporters stingingly criticized "music which is commercially instead of artistically inspired," they also seemed to concede that music was, after all, entertainment, and as such was only as good as the response it drew from the audience.[20]

The tension between cultural hierarchy and popular taste was particularly evident when, on the second day of the hearings, Vance Packard appeared before the committee to testify on BMI's deliberate manipulation of the public taste for commercial gain. His argument ran parallel to that presented in *The Hidden Persuaders*, his exposé of the advertising industry, which had recently been released. Through constant repetition, Packard reasoned, broadcasters had successfully "manipulate[d] the public into accepting cheap music," especially rock, hillbilly, and

Latin American music. The committee's response was openly hostile, not because they disagreed with Packard's conclusion but because his argument separated concern over abuse of cultural power from matters of good and bad taste. Packard's primary concern was not the quality of broadcast music, though he clearly felt that hillbilly and rock and roll were tasteless, but rather the possibility that "fundamental freedoms [were] being nibbled away by all this overcommercialization and this slickness coming over American life." For Packard, the important issue was not what people chose to like but how much freedom they had in choosing. Thus, while the committee viewed the poor taste of the masses as the central issue, Packard insisted that the real threat was the power of capital to control cultural life.[21]

Though Packard's philosophy was actually kinder to the popular taste than that of many of the other witnesses, the committee perceived him simply as a snob, simultaneously dismissing him for intellectual hair-splitting and castigating him for his disinterest in uplifting the musical taste of the average American. Senator Pastore, steadfastly ignoring the connection between taste and economic power that Packard sought to explain, warned him that "if we are talking the esthetic qualities of this business, I am very much interested. If we are talking about the economics . . . I wouldn't want to waste the time of Congress with that." But Packard's attack on hillbilly music drew even more ire, in part because of the country industry's astute mobilization of political connections in its defense. Prior to Packard's testimony, the committee was made aware that at the close of his remarks, Senator Al Gore Sr. would present a rebuttal on behalf of Governor Frank Clement and the citizens of Tennessee. Michigan senator Charles Potter interrupted Packard's testimony with the objection that "we have liked hillbilly music out there" in the Midwest. Senator Gore more emphatically warned the committee that Packard's statement to the effect that "country music is cheap economically and intellectually" was "a gratuitous insult to thousands of . . . Tennesseeans, both in and out of the field of country music." He reiterated the industry's traditional claim to legitimacy, telling his fellow senators that country music was the folk music of the pioneers and reflected "the pathos, the sadness, the hopes and the aspirations of the people." ASCAP supporter Arthur Schwartz caustically speculated that apparently, "if you attack country music you attack southern womanhood," but New York and Chicago dailies seemed to side with Senator Gore.[22]

BMI's defense responded both to the charge of conspiracy and to the

Country Audiences and Mass Culture

charge that music licensed by the company was cheap and inferior. Country music became the cornerstone of the company's largely successful effort to convince the committee of the cultural worth of its catalogue and helped to legitimize commercial culture by linking it with the sacred national traditions of patriotism and pioneers. The list of country industry witnesses clearly reflected this strategy. The committee heard statements from two governors and a gubernatorial candidate; from popular country artists who were veterans and servicemen; from performers who had served their country by entertaining American troops overseas; and from Gene Autry, whose career as a singing cowboy made him one of the most popularly recognized icons of frontier mythology, and whose personal political connections were impressive in their own right. Indeed, the first day of testimony on behalf of BMI was dominated by Autry's long statement about his own struggle to join ASCAP, which was liberally peppered with digressive but calculated anecdotes about his appearances at the White House and his meetings with Will Rogers and Franklin Roosevelt. Autry also introduced the patriotic tone that would dominate the testimony of representatives of the country field. "American music, American performers have become, perhaps, the greatest ambassadors of good will throughout the world," he told the committee. "I believe there is a duty . . . to encourage the creation and dissemination of American music . . . in order to keep our great American heritage alive."[23]

As he had promised, Governor Frank Clement appeared to defend the country music industry as well. Clement's testimony provided a dramatic illustration of the bridge between the industry's older claims to respectability—based on patriotism and pioneer tradition—with the theme of economic power that would dominate the field's public relations stance thereafter. Clement emphasized that country music was "you and me and our friends and neighbors put to words and music," the music of the pioneers which, "in its present-day form," proved that "we still have pioneers today." He also connected commercial and folk idioms by asserting that "the country music of today [would] remain the folk music of tomorrow." At the same time, though, he dwelt at length on the commercial power that country music wielded as a $50 million-a-year industry and compared the sale of cultural goods to the more manifestly commercial enterprises of selling groceries or cosmetics. Yet he was careful to point out the difference between the historical spirit of American entrepreneurship that animated the country industry and more modern, and threatening, variations of commercialism, and to distance country music from its past position as an adjunct to radio advertising. "To the many writers and publishers who live in Tennessee and who are actively engaged in the creation of music sung around the world," he assured the committee, "Madison Avenue . . . is merely a street in New York and not a way of life." Finally, Clement and other witnesses dwelt on the democratization of cultural value through mass media. "Twenty years ago, the United States was the only country in the world where the body of folk music was separate from so-called popular music," he testified. "This is not true today, and that is as it should be. Music should basically be an expression of the people, for it is the people who make music popular." Roy Acuff wrote in his statement to the committee that the "choice of music is in the public's hands and that is where I think it belongs in a democracy."[24]

Although the majority of the testimony revolved around the success and wide acceptance of country music, witnesses also openly impugned the cultural and social hierarchies that ASCAP supporters promoted. "I think that when they refer to country and western music as trash, they are referring to the American people as trash," wrote the Grand Ole Opry star Little Jimmy Dickens. "My folks and their neighbors love country and western music. They are simple, everyday, hard-working God-fearing people and they certainly are not trash. . . . This isn't the kind of music that you have to force down the public's throat." Faron Young, another Opry star, and a proud U.S. Army private, first class, also tilted at snobbery when he told the senators, "Maybe country music doesn't sound like much to sophisticated people, but it sounds good to the American people because it talks their language." Governor Jimmie Davis of Louisiana concurred. "The notion that this kind of music is degrading, or cheap, or inferior, or has been foisted on an unwilling public is an insult to the millions of Americans who enjoyed folk music."[25]

The development of the argument against BMI and the corporation's defense of its catalogue revealed the extent to which consumer choice and public interest had come to be viewed as one and the same. As it became clear that the committee rejected ASCAP's supporters' "scattered, shotgun style attack on hillbilly, rock 'n' roll and Latino music as in poor taste and effect upon youth," testimony began to focus more tightly on the notion of broadcasters' responsibility to the public interest. "Those to whom the use of the broadcasting channels is now entrusted, should not only be innocent of any conflict of interest, but they should be free from the temptation to misuse their public trust," ASCAP supporters argued. At the same time, though, what had seemed a nearly universal assumption at the outset of the hearings, that the public simply accepted what was put before it, gave way to a growing consensus that audiences could and did influence the content of mass media. According to this argument, the public interest was being perfectly served, as audiences demanded and received what they liked from radio and television. Corporate gain and public interest were thus brought into perfect harmony by the law of supply and demand. Senator Pastore reported the results of his own test of "freedom of music on the air," telling the committee that several phone requests he made to different stations to hear "Louise," an ASCAP song bearing his daughter's name as its title, were all honored. Ironically, the chairman ultimately agreed with Vance Packard in his assessment of popular taste, if not in his concern over corporate cultural authority. "Do you believe that by breaking [the BMI–network broadcasting] combination you could stop rock 'n' roll and hillbilly? Can a person be made to like 'Rigoletto'?," he asked one of the bill's supporters. "I will always rely on the intelligence and cultural stamina of the American people to make the right choice."[26]

In the end, the Smathers Bill was allowed to languish, but the charges of disc jockey payola that emerged from the hearings would prompt another round of more sensational investigations in 1960. As it happened, the broadcasting industry was pleased to have the power of the disc jockey curtailed, as personal tastes were increasingly viewed as an obstacle to the power of broadcasters (and record companies) to determine programming. The technologies of audience research made it possible to assess public preference directly, and the disc jockey could only impede the process of corporate communication with the audience. The increasing centralization of cultural control in the hands of record labels and large broadcasters was in a certain sense anti-democratic, but the hearings nonetheless demonstrated how creators of commercial popular culture could be presented as defending the interests of consumer democracy against the power of the cultural elite. The country music industry, at least, would henceforth explain its value less in terms of the common man as citizen and more in terms of the common man as consumer. Such rhetoric helped to construct a legitimating continuity between the political traditions of the past and the consumer society of the present.

Vance Packard and other intellectuals called before Senator Pastore's congressional committee to testify as experts on cultural value were late-comers, not only to the fracas between ASCAP and BMI but also to the struggle for cultural authority in the age of mass media. In the postwar era, corporate power—expressed through the ascendancy of white-collar values as well as through the dominance of commercial leisure and enter-tainment—appeared to reach unprecedented preeminence. On the one hand, as Jackson Lears has suggested, the importance that intellectuals assigned to good taste in the 1940s and 1950s represented a somewhat desperate attempt to identify an arena in which they could still claim authority against the dictates of bureaucratic hegemony. Yet, as Lears also points out, this retreat to the role of "high-grade consumer advisor," with its insistence on the homogeneity and aridity of mass culture, also paradoxically served to support the corporate regime by obscuring the vitality of cultural alternatives. Equally paradoxical was the role of corpo-rate influence in stimulating expression of such alternatives. The interac-tion between the country music industry and its audiences is one example of how supple and multifaceted corporate influence on cultural life be-came in the 1950s. In the country music press, readers were encouraged to view commercialism as a form of liberation from the rigidity of cultural hierarchies, pointedly rejecting the values of the professional and man-agerial elite in favor of cultural populism harnessed to commercial gain.[27]

The role the emerging country industry played in promoting audience discontent with the power relations of mass media and with elite disdain for popular entertainment was clearly evident in the pages of Nashville's first trade paper, *Pickin' and Singin' News.* The paper's editors, reaching out to both professional and fan audiences, wrote frequently about the social positioning of country music and challenged the authority of tra-ditional arbiters of taste. The paper not only denounced "highbrows" who looked down on the musical expression of the common man but suggested specifically that, left unchecked, the snobs would determine the listening habits of all Americans. These were the people "who think folks should have the music others think they ought to like, rather than the music they DO like." Readers were encouraged to judge quality by popularity rather than by expert fiat, an argument closely linked to the genre's claims to emotional and artistic authenticity. "Country Music is the outlet of the emotions of the masses of people in this country. They like it because they choose what they like and pay no mind to what they don't like—regardless of what some 'expert' says about it."[28]

Coverage of specific events in the culture industries helped readers to locate the "experts" whose tastes unfairly determined what the public would see and hear in the media. In its inaugural issue, for instance, the paper carried a short article on Tex Ritter's performance of the theme song for *High Noon*. Though the song received an Oscar, Ritter had not appeared on screen during the film, a fact the editors put down to snobbery. Emphasizing the status difference between a B western and a picture calculated to win Academy Awards, and between the tastes of audiences and producers, the article began, "Most followers of Country Music think Tex Ritter is a right nice-looking gentleman, as do the cowboy 'shoot-em-up' movie fans. Evidently, the folks who make the best movies don't think so, or sumpin.'" But, like the pop music businessmen who sought to capitalize on the popularity of country music, the article implied, highbrow filmmakers had been willing to exploit Ritter's talents, so long as he didn't play a large enough role to contaminate the proceedings. In truth, Ritter had earned more respect in Hollywood as both an artist and a businessman than the article suggested, but the story was pitched to support the paper's position that those who wielded cultural power were having their cake and eating it too. They sneered at commercially successful popular entertainment while appropriating whatever they could for their own profit.[29]

A similar message was conveyed in coverage of the Helen Traubel story. Traubel, a soprano with the Metropolitan Opera, had run afoul of Met director Rudolph Bing when he discovered that she was singing nightclub engagements during the opera season. Bing put Traubel on leave until she was prepared to return to "the more serious aspects of [her] art," noting that high culture and nightclub singing "do not really seem to mix very well." Though his concern probably stemmed as much from a desire to keep the shows from competing with the Met for ticket proceeds as from any aesthetic agenda, Bing was lambasted in the music press as the worst kind of highbrow snob. Echoing Fred Rose's letter to his colleagues in *Billboard* some years earlier, Traubel defended Tin Pan Alley's popular tunes as the folklore of America. "In other countries in the past, this would have been called folk music and would have been highly regarded," Traubel told a reporter for *Down Beat*. "To assert that art can be found in the Metropolitan Opera House, but not in a night club is rank snobbery that underrates both the taste of the American public and the talents of its composers."[30]

Ironically, the incident placed Nashville and Tin Pan Alley on the same side of the battle between highbrow and lowbrow when Minnie Pearl, upon reading of the controversy, invited Traubel to appear on the Opry. Traubel agreed, and *Pickin' and Singin' News* ran a front-page story on the singer, quoting Pearl's invitation at length. "In view of your recent expression of your love for American Music," Pearl wrote, "I would be greatly honored to have you as my personal guest on the Grand Ole Opry. . . . You will find our listeners are closer to the rank and file of American music lovers than any other single group, and your magnificent voice would be greatly appreciated." The paper encouraged Traubel to stick by her decision to "sing what the people wanted to hear" and pointed out that her appearance on the Opry would put Traubel before her largest audience ever. The editors were also careful to compare the artistry of country music favorably with the artistry of high opera. The announcement of Traubel's appearance included a photo of the soprano over the caption "Can She Do It?" and the review of her performance emphasized her nervousness and the technical difficulty of the song she chose, "It May Be Silly (But Ain't It Fun?)."[31]

Not surprisingly, issues of respectability, for both the audience and the industry, were most clearly elaborated in discussions of the term "hillbilly." In 1953, when Congress moved to recognize National Hillbilly Music Day in honor of country music, *Pickin' and Singin' News* leapt at the implied snub to "all who appreciate the great part Country Music plays in the American way of life." In an open letter to the U.S. Congress, the paper quoted the *New York Journal's* 1900 definition of a hillbilly as "a free and untrammelled white citizen of Alabama who lives in the hills . . . dresses as he can, talks as he pleases, drinks whiskey when he gets it and fires off his revolver as the fancy takes him." Congress would have to change the proposed name or suffer the consequences of offending their constituents. "There may have been a time when high-brows and city slickers could poke fun at the music the masses of rural Americans indulge in and appreciate," the editors noted, "But, today, the self-styled snobs are in the MINORITY, and country music lovers are in the MA-JORITY." The notion that the best music would be appreciated by the greatest number of people upended traditional, elite assumptions about good taste, which dictated that the finest cultural expression would speak only to the most refined of audiences.[32]

The challenge to traditional cultural authority was accompanied by a conservative message that proposed commercialism itself as somehow revolutionary. In addition to becoming a symbol of quality, the commercial success of country music was becoming a symbol of the audience's success, of listeners' own progression into the middle and upper classes. And, as in so many other arenas in the 1950s, consumerism defined respectability and the American Way. *Pickin' and Singin' News* reminded members of Congress that the people who played and listened to country music were "home-owning, tax-paying, Cadillac-driving, sartorially splendid citizens with the highest ideals and morals." The letter concluded by entreating congressmen to "take a few minutes to consider whether or not you would be joining the 'Upper-Crust' in passing a Resolution lending Congressional sanction to an insulting description of a beloved endeavor." Given the conflicting messages about the cultural meanings of consumption, it was anyone's guess as to whether joining the upper crust was a good idea or a bad one.[33]

Yet, for all its efforts to improve the image of country music and to legitimate the taste of country fans, *Pickin' and Singin' News* perpetuated a comic hillbilly image for the consumption of country fans and professionals and even mocked the field's pretensions to cultural respectability. While editors worked to create an uproar over the proposal for a National Hillbilly Music Day, the paper's coverage of "Hillbilly Homecoming" in Maryville, Tennessee, made no comment on the name, nor did it protest Governor Frank Clement's declaration of "Hillbilly Homecoming Week" in conjunction with the festival. When Madison, Tennessee, home of a number of Grand Ole Opry stars, announced its own "Madison Hillbilly Day," the paper reported without editorial remark that Madison residents planned to dress "country" for the festival and that "the men of the town have been growing beards for the past two months. A shave during that period costs a $2 fine." Indeed, the editorial letter to the U.S. Congress protesting use of the word "hillbilly" appeared next to a cartoon that depicted a scrawny guitarist with a single tooth bellowing, "Oh you broke my heart when you left me, little darlin', but I'll break your dern fool neck when you git back," in front of a sign that read "Hillbilly Audition Today." The same willingness to accept the hillbilly stereotype as good humor was evident in another article in the same issue that announced the opening of the "Hill-William Jamboree" show in Texarkana, a name that recalled the Hoosier Hot Shots' 1936 novelty recording, "Them Hill-Billies Are Mountain Williams Now."[34]

The editorial policy of *Pickin' and Singin' News* concerning use of the term "hillbilly" clearly depended on the context in which the term was invoked, and by whom. By making explicit reference to the migration of rural Tennesseans in pursuit of jobs, Maryville's Hillbilly Homecoming used the term to foreground nostalgia for the simplicity and camaraderie that many migrants associated with their one-time communities. Madison's Hillbilly Day, as the plan to wear costumes and grow beards suggests, emphasized the difference between the isolated mountaineer of the past and the modern rural denizen of the New South. Each in its own way, these events used the term "hillbilly" to celebrate rural roots and to measure and ratify the transition to modern life. These uses of the term "hillbilly" persisted in popular dialogue long after the industry's efforts to eliminate more official uses of the word had removed it from chart listings, record catalogues, and honorific proclamations. Indeed, one fan magazine in the late fifties found it necessary to provide its readers with a brief lesson in the meaning and etiquette of the term. Though it conceded that "hillbilly" had "perhaps even gained a little respectability through long usage," it urged country fans to avoid the label as much as possible. "Although some, primarily disc jockeys, use hillbilly today to cover the whole field of country music, this was never intended and should be discouraged. If used, it should be restricted to the style native to the southern Appalachian and Ozark areas of the south, and typified today by Bill Monroe, Flatt and Scruggs . . . and many others. But it should probably be discarded completely in favor of more descriptive terms."[35]

The approach to cultural hierarchy taken by *Pickin' and Singin' News* served to elevate "the masses" of Americans who loved simple country music above "the experts" who dictated proper taste. But beyond the vague indication that they lurked in the executive offices of institutions of both high and mass culture, the experts remained mostly anonymous, and the mechanisms that determined the cultural content delivered by mass media seemed equally obscure, and beyond the reach of the average fan. Only a few years later, however, *Country & Western Jamboree*, a fan magazine based in Nashville and edited by a reporter for the *Nashville Banner*, brought the economics of mass culture, or at least radio broadcasting, into sharp relief for its readers when it announced its "Crusade for Country Music."

The Crusade for Country Music was clearly a product of its times. Where *Pickin' and Singin' News* had lampooned the highbrow minority at the height of country's post–World War II popularity, *Country & Western Jamboree* worked from a less enviable position. When Ben Green accepted editorship in 1957, country music was at the nadir of its market share in radio broadcasting and its strength in the record charts. Though Nashville continued to blossom as a recording and business center, the amount of country music played on the radio had diminished by at least half over the preceding four years, as programmers rushed to join the Top 40 formatting revolution. The effort to mobilize country fans was, therefore, not only an attempt to keep listeners involved and dedicated but also an earnest, if somewhat unorthodox, bid to influence radio programming in favor of country music.

Green announced his Crusade for Country Music in the editorial section of his second issue. The inspiration, he told readers, came from "letters from hundreds of disc jockeys, fan club presidents, and others [which] convinced me we are united in a great cause" to promote country music. The goal would be to "strengthen our fan clubs, help our artists and in truth—help spread happiness and peace to all the world." Fan club presidents would "lead squadrons in the crusade" but everyone could contribute if they would "learn to know [country music] and to love it like we do." Though editorial statements often slipped into grandiose rhetoric, the heart of the campaign was much more pragmatic and, in addition to spurring fans to action, served as a tutorial in the power relations of mass media. Such was certainly the case in an article based on an interview with Starday Records president Don Pierce. Bemoaning the lack of radio outlets for new country records, Pierce identified both economics and control of the media by a cultural elite as barriers against fans hearing the music they liked, and he suggested that organized action by the Country Music Disc Jockey Association was needed. "Until this is done, we are at the mercy of the people who own stations and like long-haired music, and those who might be prejudiced against country music," he told readers. "Or we are at the mercy of the sales manager who might not like Country Music or be totally indifferent to the potential if he did like it. Also he would have a hard time selling it to sponsors who do not realize the potential." A handful of individual tastes determined what the public would hear, the article implied, but everyone listened to the language of money.[36]

While Pierce envisioned an industry organization to carry forth the sales effort for country music, the editors of *Country & Western Jamboree* had in mind a broad audience offensive. The magazine ran testimonial stories on the sponsors of country radio shows to expound on the advantages of advertising with country music. An article on longtime Opry sponsor Martha White Mills ran under a note from the editor encouraging readers to show the story to local advertisers. In case the message hadn't gotten across the first time, the following issue included a reminder of the story. "We encourage all our readers to show this story to business people so they can understand the potential of Country Music. This is just a small part of our Crusade for Country Music Appreciation. But it's an essential part." Every country music fan, Green told his audience, should be willing to "reach for a telephone and urge some station manager to give Country Music a chance." If the station manager was reluctant, readers could share the information that in many radio markets, a country station could garner 25 percent of the listening audience uncontested, while ten or twenty stations competed for the 50 percent who wanted to hear rock.[37]

And if this explanation was not quite clear enough, Green offered a more detailed account of how listeners could exert pressure on local radio broadcasters, outlining the relationship between programming and commercial sponsorship.

> In a real way, the key to more Country Music on the air over radio is an "economic situation." Radio stations and their managers are usually alert to give listeners what they ask for—provided sponsors are available. It occurs to us that the best way to get more Country Music on radio in a given situation is to approach the radio station and offer the suggestion; and then see the potential sponsors with the proposal that they try Country Music on some of their radio time. The combination selling approach—first to the radio station, then to a potential sponsor—should do the job.

Another article, three pages long, explained how to put on a concert, including sections on "Selecting a hall or auditorium" ("Lease the concessions, if possible, or request a per cent of the net profits"); "Selecting artists" ("Record artists with hits in the Billboard or Cash Box charts . . . draw best); "Advertising suggestions"; and "Disc jockey promotion."[38]

While such information was partly a testament to the still blurry boundary that separated fans from professionals, it appeared in a publication that was clearly aimed at fans, not the industry. For, although it regularly presented relatively sophisticated and detailed information about how the music business worked, the magazine also engaged in overblown pronouncements and self-promotion so transparent that even the most impervious sycophant could not have failed to recognize it. The announcement of phase two of the crusade outlined seven steps designed to make the crusade "intensely interesting to you," the reader, three of which involved subscribing to *Country & Western Jamboree* or soliciting subscriptions from friends. "There can be no substitute for crusaders who will carry the message," the article read. "They cannot know the message or what to do with it unless they read *Jamboree*." And, not surprisingly, the magazine contrasted the order of business in the general entertainment industry with that which ruled the country music subfield. Here, fans reigned supreme, defeating the experts and contributing valuable ideas to the entertainment world. The story of the Everly Brothers was used to demonstrate "that the fans recognize the stars and actually 'make' them—before they are discovered by the recording companies, talent scouts, etc." An article on the Jimmie Dean show told readers "how every piece of mail is read by somebody connected with the show; how ideas are screened and analyzed; how the best ideas are made part of this big, coast-to-coast television show." Such stories, the magazine pointed out, were just a few among the "thousands" of cases "in music, movies, politics and all fields, where the fans knew, but the experts didn't."[39]

Contrary to the widely accepted notion that the country industry sought to conceal its artifice behind a mask of authenticity, the interpretation of the business presented to fans by magazines like *Country & Western Jamboree* was considerably more complicated. Readers of publications like *Pickin' and Singin' News* and *Country & Western Jamboree* received conflicting messages about class, culture, and the meaning of mass media. They were encouraged to reject traditional notions of cultural hierarchy but were also encouraged to accept class standing, defined by consumption, as a measure of respectability. They were simultaneously made aware of the mechanics and economics of mass media and encouraged to believe that they had the power to intervene as individuals to affect the content of the media in specific ways. Perhaps most importantly, they were encouraged to get in touch with each other, to construct a network of knowledge outside of the channels of mass media. Their responses to these exhortations, however, were even more varied, and more revealing of the ambiguous effects of mass entertainment.

As early as the 1930s, country music fans had relied on their understandings of the relationship between audience and performer to help smooth the transition to modernity and mass culture. By assimilating the new relationship between ethereal performer and unseen audience to familial and neighborly bonds, radio listeners made sense of the new medium and of the mobility and urbanism that attenuated community ties (and controls) which had circumscribed for many their sense of place in the world. The readily ascertained fact that the rustic image of friends and neighbors was a profitable theatrical illusion did not undermine its emotional utility. By the 1950s, however, the meaning of commercialism had taken on a more disquieting note. Country music fans did not need to subscribe to music magazines to learn about the impact that advertising sponsorship and financial power played in shaping their entertainment. Long before *A Face in the Crowd* incited fear of the hillbilly demagogue, the corrosive influence corporate power exerted on American culture was becoming a public preoccupation, especially where that power related to the persuasion of advertising. Frederic Wakeman's popular 1946 novel *The Hucksters,* and a year later the film of the same name starring Clark Gable and Deborah Kerr, lampooned Madison Avenue admen and the philistines whose commands they obeyed. The novel was followed by at least half a dozen similar efforts, many of them written by former advertising executives or scriptwriters for network radio shows. Concern over the relationship between culture and commerce grew to a fevered pitch in the late 1950s, and, as Vance Packard himself had so ably demonstrated, it was a short hop from arguing that the public's taste in toothpaste was manipulated to concluding that its taste in entertainment was also being controlled.[40]

Whatever they may have thought of the "experts" who denounced mass media and much of the entertainment they distributed, country music fans absorbed the message of elite dominance and media manipulation. While Michael Kammen has suggested that "ordinary people simply 'tuned out'" the debate over mass media, evidence from fan mail to country music magazines suggests that, quite to the contrary, they retooled intellectual debates for their own purposes. Fans frequently expressed their frustration with commercial mass culture in their letters to *Country & Western Jamboree.* One reader in Baton Rouge explained her predicament in a long letter to the editor. Remembering the days of block programming, she explained that at one time, by "tuning in the different towns all during the day, it was possible to get almost eight hours of Country Music from morning until late evening." Since the advent of format radio, though, the stations all played the same rock and roll songs. The few country shows that were still available remained at the mercy of station managers who discriminated against the genre. She wrote:

> These shows, you understand, will last only as long as the management can take it—then "poof" off again! . . . If there were only some way to get your Country Music Crusade going down here it would be wonderful. Showing various program directors or prospective sponsors some articles on the success of Country Music would not be of any help. They are so stubborn they would not listen to reason. . . . We could probably get more co-operation from a corpse than the supposedly alive people who are responsible for providing entertainment in this city.[41]

Another fan wrote to complain of the lack of country programming in Columbus, Ohio, invoking her personal experience to challenge the assumptions of biased station managers. "I think every Columbus station is against this music. It don't make sense to me. I know so many people that like Country Music. . . . We have tried about every way there is to get Country Music in here but we don't seem to get anywhere." Another correspondent echoed Vance Packard's testimony before Congress when he wrote, "I feel the reason this type of music is not as popular as the other kind is because it is not played as much. . . . I feel that if the old type of music is played more it will soon become as popular as the so-called country music that is played today." One young woman wrote in on two separate occasions to complain about the situation where she lived. "I would like to join you in your 'Crusade for Country Music.' It is a wonderful plan and I would like to help in any way I might. It is a cause very close to my heart," she began, before opining that country music's real problem was lack of exposure. "I feel certain . . . that if people would just listen to hillbilly music they would instantly like it. But no, they wouldn't dare listen to that 'corny, square stuff.' . . . Let's expose those folks to it so much that they can't help but like Country & Western Music." A year later, she wrote to inform the editors that, although she had shown the *Country & Western Jamboree* article on advertising with country music to her local station manager, it had done no good, for he "wanted no part of country music."[42]

Occasionally, frustration with the sponsors who effectively controlled the listening privileges of country music fans gave way to a more poignant sense of powerlessness in a world dominated by money. Listeners understood that the availability of the music they wanted to hear depended ultimately upon their ability to pay for it at sponsors' retail counters. Those who could not afford the products they heard advertised were conscious that their taste counted for less than that of more affluent radio listeners. Country's lack of popularity, one fan surmised, was due to a lack of purchasing power, "and since 90 per cent of us are just plain, down to earth folks, our bread and butter must come first." Writing to Washington, D.C., station WGAY, one country fan hoped that future goodwill might stand in for immediate buying power.

> We all realize that unless you all keep the sponsors happy, the pickin' will end. This is real bad because if most of the listeners are like us, the pickin' is sure to end. Why? Because we are just not in the market for a Muntz TV etc. I'll grant you one thing, though. If I am ever in the market for any of your sponsors products, you'd better believe that I'll let them know that I heard about it on WGAY and that is the reason that I came to them. I am like many others. We feel as if we owe you something for bringing OUR music back to the Washington Area.

A pair of listeners who owned a Tastee-Freez in La Plata, Maryland, suggested another possible bargain in the postscript to their letter of appreciation: "P.S. As soon as we can afford it, we will buy one of your T.V. sets for this place."[43]

As these letters suggest, the temporary homogenization of mass culture may have contributed to reactions against rock and roll as much as racism. Indeed, to the extent that we can identify particular stylistic codes for black and white influences on country music—the beat, for example, versus the angelic chorus—writers to *Country & Western Jamboree* were much less worried about the incorporation of "black" sounds in rockabilly than they were about the co-optation of country music by the upper-class whites who controlled the culture industries. Occasionally a reader singled out the absence of a repetitive beat as the quality that made country music enjoyable, or called for separation of different genres in words that strikingly resembled arguments for segregation, as when one correspondent complained, "The way it is, one cannot tell just where the 'line' is supposed to be between rock & roll, popular, and hillbilly! . . . This is a free country, lots of room for all kinds of music fields; why not do some dividing and prevent this constant 'mixture' and have clean fields once and for all!" But for the most part, the thinly veiled racism that underlay the comments aired in Congress about savage rhythms and jungle beats was remarkably absent from country fans' responses to the dominance of rock and roll.[44]

In their place were myriad complaints about the appropriation of country music by people who, fans felt, did not appreciate it or understand it. "These teenagers down here are all pop music lovers," wrote a young woman from Arkansas. "They don't appreciate my kind of music until a really good song comes out in the country music field, and then they say it's popular music." This resentment often bore obvious class connotations, as when one man remarked that it was a "shame" to see country music stars "decked out with a business suit, sport shirt, and, worst of all, black and white shoes. . . . Nobody wants to hear country artists and country bands playing and singing pop tunes backed up by some pop group of vocalists covering up the artist's singing." Another country radio listener wrote to his local station with words of praise and a similar caution. "WSHO is exactly the kind of program we dig. Please don't put on any of that longhair stuff, as there's too much of this already."[45]

George Lipsitz has written that those who wished to censor music in the 1950s deployed the threat of sexuality to cover for more pervasive concerns about "the 'transgressions' perpetrated by middle-class white youths when they embraced 'prestige from below' and undercut the ideological hegemony of their own race, class, and family." Country music fans appear to have understood the controversy over rock and roll in just these terms—as a confrontation between different elements of the middle class in which the working class, black and white, was merely a conversational object. Here, as in other cultural discourses, the hillbilly and the white working class were cast as threatening social order through the media. The debate over culture and juvenile delinquency reduced the lives of poor whites to symbols of youthful middle-class rebellion, a tendency many country music listeners obviously found insulting. "I think that music belongs to the older folks as well as the teenagers," wrote one fan in the pages of *Country & Western Jamboree*, "I wish you would feature Hank Williams more often because he's the one that made country music great. . . . Why take it from [him] and give it to Elvis?"[46]

Country music fans in the mid- and late 1950s thus simultaneously echoed the anti–mass culture statements of "highbrow" intellectuals and rejected the aesthetics and authority of the professional elite. This was particularly evident in the continued embrace of the "hillbilly" label, in spite of efforts by the country industry and press to curtail its use. Many fans agreed that "there should be more dignity involved when it comes to country music" and fretted "that it is regarded as 'low-life' and something to be scorned by quite a majority of Americans." Most, however, persisted in using the term "hillbilly" not only to express their rejection of cultural hierarchies but also to emphasize a sense of belonging and of progress, in much the same way that Maryville and Madison, Tennessee, had invoked the word. Many of these people also seemed to view the growing acceptance of country music as an indicator of their own respectability. "I never wrote a letter to a station before so please excuse the poor writing and expressions," wrote thirty-two-year-old W. B. Williams to a Washington, D.C., radio station. "I came here in the mid 40's when hillbilly music was classed poor in the D.C. area but *you* promoted & led the hillbilly music to the top. The Air Force broke the sound barrier but you had already broken the listening barrier." Harland Anderson from Ranson, West Virginia, expressed a similar sentiment in his letter to the same station. "I will take time to let you know how much your radio program means. It's the best station that's on the air. I am an old hillbilly," he began. "You have really done more than anyone I know of for us hillbillies. That's my music." Another fan put it more simply. To the "people who ridicule us," she replied, "all I say is, 'I'm a hillbilly and I'm durn proud of it!' "[47]

FAN CLUBS AND PARTICIPATORY COMMERCIALISM

The commercial success of country music helped listeners to imagine their position in the world, to articulate a sense of belonging and exclusion, and to measure their progress in terms they defined. For many, this sense of belonging was both real and imagined, for the networks that fans developed through club work and pen pal contacts made mass culture an active social endeavor. "Your 'Crusade for Country Music' is the greatest idea to take shape in a very long time," a *Country & Western Jamboree* reader wrote. "Personally, I think it will not only bring a helping hand to c&w music, its stars, promoters, and those connected with this field, it will (and does) bring new friends together." This prediction was frequently confirmed by other readers. "Country music means more to me than anything and I'm in 66 fan clubs to prove it," wrote Dorothy Paul of Morrison, Illinois. "I've made many friends through this fine magazine and love to hear from anyone who loves Country Music as I do." Another fan wrote, "Ever since I fell in love with Country-Western music I've tried my best . . . to promote [it] as much as I can. I've worked with quite a few fan clubs, write to many deejays, magazines, etc., and just do what I can. I've corresponded with many (and I do mean many) fans and find it's the greatest hobby I've ever run across."[48]

In addition to pressing fans to contact radio stations, television shows, and particular artists, fan magazines encouraged the development of personal networks among country listeners through fan clubs and pen pal pages. The extensive reader mail section of *Country & Western Jamboree* was often the most lively part of the magazine and certainly drew the greatest response from readers, who engaged in lengthy debates over the merits of various styles and artists. In addition to this section, the magazine also featured "Fan Club Corner," a collection of letters from club presidents that offered fans a chance to correspond with each other. As one fan club member put it, the magazine not only reported on the stars of country music but "report[ed] also the many loyal fans and followers of this type of music which we one and all love so much." Another fan magazine, *Country Song Roundup,* included both a section for fan club presidents and a pen pal section that served as a clearing house for country music listeners with interests as diverse as record collecting, penmanship, career advancement, and romantic aspirations. For the most part, however, these fans sought companionship and personal reinforcement of their engagement with the music they liked. "I am one of very few Country and Western music fans in the high school which I attend," wrote one young man. "I would certainly enjoy exchanging letters with guys and gals who share my musical tastes. . . . So please write soon and I'll answer soon."[49]

The industrial fan press was thus partly responsible for the dramatic expansion of country music fan club participation during the early 1950s, but its invitations were directed at a club culture that had been developing since the 1930s. By the mid-1940s, the country artists most likely to have fan clubs were those, like Gene Autry and Roy Rogers, whose careers as singing cowboys straddled the country and movie businesses.[50] As the wartime migration ushered in the national hillbilly boom, however, country music began to develop a fan club culture of its own. Ernest Tubb, whose sales figures during the mid-1940s rivaled those of pop stars like Bing Crosby and whose stage performances set female audience members swooning in the aisles, was among the earliest country stars to have a substantial club. Tubb's first club was established in 1942, but after running into difficulty with his club president, Tubb shifted responsibility for the organization to a young fan in rural Oklahoma named Norma Winton (later Norma Barthel) who had launched her own, unofficial club in 1944. The first issue of Winton's journal, *Melody Trails*, listed thirty members, twenty-seven of whom were women; within a year and a half, membership had risen to 1,500. By the early 1950s, other prominent stars, including Eddy Arnold and Hank Snow, had formed clubs to keep fans abreast of their personal appearances and record releases.[51]

The networks fans created to distribute information and forge social ties became an important component of the fledgling industry's promotional apparatus. When a new fan magazine such as *Pickin' and Singin' News* appeared, editors appealed to fan club presidents to mention the new publication in the next issue of their journals. The same was true of new fan clubs. Willis Glenn tried a number of different approaches to announce the Roy Acuff Fan Club, including contacting deejays and getting announcements on several major national deejay shows. Finally, he wrote to Norma Barthel for help. Norma responded that "the best and about the only way to really get members is to write to as many fan club presidents as you can find addresses for, and ask if they would kindly list the [Roy Acuff Fan Club] in their next journal." While club presidents and members wrote in to commercial magazines often to request stories on their stars, a more fruitful approach was to correspond with other presidents to get a feature in their journals. Like Tubb's *Melody Trails*, most fan club journals offered more than just news of their honorees. General news items, editorials on the state of the country field, and reciprocal spotlight articles on different artists exchanged between club presidents made many journals resemble a fan-produced alternative to the industrial fan press as much as a running paean to a single artist. The trading of features and expertise became an important way of constituting a network of leaders, establishing standard practices, and circulating information.[52]

Indeed, fan club presidents organized informally as a group almost as early as the country industry's professionals. In 1953, just as the Country Music Disc Jockey Association was being formed, Hank Snow's fan newsletter called fan clubs the field's "unheralded publicity agents" and suggested that club presidents join forces to organize a national convention. "The resulting publicity of such a convention is bound to be a great step forward for our stars," the article argued, "and would tickle the cockles of any Chamber of Commerce's heart for the publicity brought to the city where it would be held." By 1955, a report on the Disc Jockey Convention described also the first "Fan Club Convention," held in conjunction with the deejay meeting. Norma Barthel described the meeting as an impromptu affair organized when Teddy Wilburn hastily gathered all the presidents he could find so they could talk to one another. Presidents of fan clubs for George Morgan, Faron Young, the Wilburn Brothers, and Justin Tubb, among others, along with the head of the International Fan Club League, gathered to talk about their activities and compare notes. Though many club presidents corresponded with one another, as did Barthel and Jim Evans, she emphasized the lack of cohesion in the group when she noted that she had met very few of her peers prior to this gathering. Fan attendance and events continued as part of the convention over the next several years, but the clubs did not sustain an organization or a systematic program.[53]

Fan clubs of the 1950s took on new qualities that distinguished them in several respects from the clubs of the prewar era. Like movie fan clubs, country fan clubs of the 1950s engaged in "boosting," concerted efforts to promote an artist by writing to industry decision makers on the artist's behalf. In the case of movie fans, boosting involved letter-writing campaigns to producers and studio heads like Louis B. Mayer, frequently requesting a specific role for an artist in a film fans knew to be in preparation. For country music fans, it meant request campaigns aimed at disc jockeys, distribution of independent recordings, and attempts to convince station management to offer more country airtime. In both cases, fans sought to intervene in the workings of the mass media, claiming their own authority to shape the content of those media. However, the diffuse nature of the recording and radio broadcasting industries, compared to the centralized studio system of Hollywood, made meaningful audience participation in the business much more accessible for country fans than for movie aficionados, and country fan clubbers thus engaged in a wider range of activities aimed at influencing the operations of the country business.[54]

Treva Miller, a seventeen-year-old from east Tennessee who served as president of Patsy Cline's fan club, carried out important business functions for her star, as did many presidents. She performed a host of public relations duties, from answering fan mail to finding a place to print picture Christmas cards featuring Cline for deejays. In addition to producing a newsletter and a more ambitious periodical journal, Treva corresponded with other fan club presidents to place articles on Cline in their journals. Although organizers were almost always volunteers who subsidized the clubs out of their own pockets, stars like Cline relied on their club presidents to be businesslike and professional in their demeanor. For instance, Cline did not hesitate to complain to Treva about fans who did not understand the appropriate boundaries of the club relationship. "This Joan Dove is worrying me to death," she wrote about another young woman who wanted to run a club for her. "She thinks I should tell her what to do and how.... See if you can't get her straightened out.... I know she wants to help and I appreciate it but I wish she wouldn't call every day and write me letters two and three times a week."[55]

In addition to boosting and fulfilling public relations functions, country fans could easily serve as amateur disc jockeys, as promoters for local concerts, and even as record distributors, roles not generally available to fan club members in more centralized media such as film. Fans eagerly played such roles through the 1960s, demonstrating the gradual nature of the transition from a participatory vernacular culture to a more spectatorial relationship between audience and industry. Jim Evans, who revived a fan club for Jimmie Rodgers in 1947 as an outgrowth of his activity as a record collector, advanced Rodgers's historical legacy in a number of ways; indeed, the variety and nature of his efforts ultimately led him to change the organization's name to the Jimmie Rodgers Society in order to reflect the historical and preservationist bent of the group. In addition to producing *America's Blue Yodeler*, a quarterly newsletter that reached a circulation of nearly 4,000 in 1952 and 1953, Evans maintained a steady correspondence with executives at RCA Victor and Peer-Southern Music in order to promote Rodgers's work. Evans suggested song line-ups for memorial albums to RCA A&R director Brad McCuen, provided reports on how reissues of Rodgers recordings were selling in the Lubbock area, and furnished discographical and historical information that the label itself apparently did not have. Indeed, in one exchange he chastised the label for errors in the liner notes issued by the company, which had resulted in extra work for Evans as he tried to straighten out inquiries from confused fans. The note on the *Jimmie the Kid* album, he wrote, "was very nice [but] it was full of errors. I do hope you will let Prynce [Wheeler, another fan] or myself check over the next one before going to press with it. The errors in it have added greatly to my correspondence." Evans also served informally as a record distributor, ordering reissues in quantities of twenty to fifty copies to sell by mail to fans who couldn't find the records in local stores. Roy Horton at Peer-Southern Music relied on Evans both for information and for distribution services. When fans contacted Horton with inquiries about where to obtain Rodgers's records, he sent their names not to RCA Victor but to Jim Evans, and on at least one occasion he asked Evans to "send me a list of the acts that play folk music down your way," presumably in an effort to scout talent.[56]

Fans' active participation in promoting and distributing country music was particularly important to a field that was still struggling to gain access to the publicity, broadcasting, and retail distribution channels that provided exposure for the rest of the popular music business. With varying degrees of effectiveness, fan club activists attempted to constitute an alternative gate-keeping structure that would allow them to combat the power of radio and record executives to determine what they heard. Just as the country music barnstormers of the early radio era had relied primarily on local social organizations to book the shows that provided their livelihood, so artists and record labels during the transition to full articulation with the pop industry depended on fan journals, deejay requests, and person-to-person record distribution to provide a functional alternative to a truly mass distribution system. As such, fans formed an important, if unofficial, part of the burgeoning country industry.

Nonetheless, throughout the 1950s, many in the industry remained ambivalent about or unaware of the promotional possibilities that fan clubs represented. Even as late as 1955, a new artist like Patsy Cline—with one single on an independent label and a few appearances on a regional TV show to her credit—could be generally unaware of the purposes a fan club would serve or how one was organized. "Please send me the information on just what [a club] does and what all there is to do to get one started," she asked Treva Miller in one of their earliest exchanges. After receiving Miller's explanation, Cline modestly decided that a fan club was beyond her needs. "I'm waiting a little while until people know who Patsy Cline is a little better and then I'll start a club," she wrote. Within months, fan requests for a club prompted Cline to ask Miller to start one up. "I've got to get a fan club president right away," she wrote, "because everyone keeps asking me can they join my fan club, and I don't have any . . . except what you've been doing. A girl up here promised to be the club president for me but she knew about as much as I do about it, and that's nothing. So I want you to take the job." Miller accepted, establishing a relationship that lasted until she was killed in a car accident in September 1960, at about the time Cline signed with Decca records and "I Fall to Pieces" became a crossover hit.[57]

The majority of club organizers were working-class women, married and single. Single presidents reported occupations such as nurse, beautician, secretary, and factory worker (at Haggar Slacks), while housewives frequently identified their class by mentioning husbands' blue-collar jobs with companies such as Colorado Fuel and Iron and Kaiser Aluminum. As one club organizer, Blanche Trinajstick, put it, "If you've known many fan club presidents you must be aware that they are not usually 'ladies of leisure' . . . they are more likely to be middle class working people . . . seldom from the 'Country Club' set." While men like Chaw Mank, Jim Evans, and Willis Glenn were an important part of the fan club community, the predominance of women was such that writers referring to fan club presidents in the abstract invariably used feminine pronouns. One offended male president finally felt compelled to complain about the practice to the editor of a fan club journal. "Why do you almost always refer to a fan club president as 'she' or 'her'? . . . [M]aybe [men] are a minority, but presidents just the same!" In response, the editor explained that for many years she was unaware of any male fan club presidents at all but said she was pleased to see men taking a more active part in clubbing and offered her "apologies to all you male fan club presidents" for the implied exclusion.[58]

Whatever pronoun editors used in referring to presidents, they presented the experience of fan clubbing in heavily gendered terms, both because these were the terms in which they felt they were perceived by outsiders and because their experiences as wives and mothers provided a point of social commonality beyond their interest in country music. Fan clubbers were especially anxious to combat the popular image of fans as erotically fixated teenage girls, and they labored to communicate a more mature, less sexually charged image. The average observer of a gathering of fan club presidents, one clubber wrote, would "be surprised to find a group in which most are happily married women—most of them mothers and some even grandmothers! Some younger, unmarried girls, too, who are sincerely devoted to the promotion of their star—ALL of them dedicated country music fans who work—without pay!—to help country music and the artists."[59]

Club presidents also couched their clubbing in gendered terms by writing about the ways they balanced volunteer club work with family commitments. In response to a fellow club president's inquiry on how to maintain a journal production schedule, organizer Blanche Trinajstick teased, "You, who ask this question, are a mother of three, I believe, and you ask me about a schedule? . . . I have never tried to stick to any kind of schedule. How could I, when there are always skinned knees to be treated, thorns to be extracted from little hands, or peanut butter sandwiches to fix???" Nonetheless, she estimated that she spent an average of forty-five to sixty hours a week working on her fan club–monitoring organization, an estimate many club presidents echoed in the oft-repeated assertion that clubbing was practically a full-time job.[60]

Most women had to negotiate the time and resources they devoted to club work with their spouses. Trinajstick told fellow clubbers that she would not be able to carry out her duties without the support of her husband and children, whose assistance ranged from providing the financial support necessary to produce and mail her journal to helping out with mimeographing and collating. "I couldn't even keep up with it if [my husband] wasn't agreeable to it," she confessed. "I'll admit there have been times when an issue of K-T was under way, that the family had to eat a lot of sandwiches, and Frank pitched in and helped with the housework so [I] could maintain a mailing schedule!" In fact, one reason why fan clubbing may have been particularly attractive to married women in the 1950s and 1960s was that it offered some of the intellectual and social fulfillment associated with work outside the home, but as unpaid work it seemed not to threaten traditionalist expectations about female domesticity. Fan club organizer Ruth Slack told her life story primarily in terms of her family and noted that while her husband "never was in favor of me [working] in the first place" and ultimately asked her to stop working outside the home, he fully supported her fan club activities. Occasionally, though, fan clubbing could be an expression of independence as well. Norma Barthel, highlighting the extent to which clubbers had to find ways of subsidizing their own activities, with or without spousal assistance, confided to Jim Evans that she had undertaken her latest publishing project without the consent of her husband. "I had to borrow every cent to print and mail this first edition as my hubby would have nothing to do with it," she wrote, "and [he] doesn't know I've done this!"[61]

The most dedicated of country listeners, those who organized fan clubs, thus found their activities embedded within two potentially competing social contexts: the increasing professionalization of the country industry and the gendered sociability within which they created their relationships to family, friends, and one another. This tension would continue to intensify through the 1960s, and by the early 1970s their status as volunteers and as women would ultimately become the basis for their exclusion from the industry's business community.

Encouraged by their favorite artists and by the fan-oriented press, country music listeners wrote often in fan magazines about their perceptions of excessively centralized, elite control of mass media. Their defenses of country music revealed that their antipathy toward rock was based as much on class antagonism as on racial hostility. While the middle-class trade press fretted about the influence of rhythm and blues, country listeners railed against the infusion of tepid white pop into their music. The social practices that surrounded country listening also reveal the extent to which the homogenization and passivity that the left so feared had, even by the late 1950s, failed to penetrate audience understandings of the music or the media. Audience engagement in the Crusade for Country Music and in the growing number of country music fan clubs demonstrated the continued appeal of alternatives to the mainstream, and the hope that mass culture could be made to reflect diverse tastes.

And, in light of the return to formalistic approaches to cultural worth in the sectors of government and academe, mass culture indeed seemed to become the best hope for assigning value and dignity to country music and the elements of working-class culture it represented. Though positive images of the working class were progressively erased from television and movie screens across the nation, country radio embraced and enhanced its working-class identity and reached out to affluent blue-collar America. Even Bing Crosby, who had deplored the condition of popular music in 1956, acquiesced to the rule of consumer democracy over cultural guardianship. In 1959, KFOX, Bing Crosby Enterprises' major outlet in the Los Angeles market, switched to a full-time country format and became a pioneer in developing the form. The station's success, carefully publicized and frequently replicated under the stewardship of the Country Music Association and its members, became the model and marker of the genre's economic recovery and cultural rehabilitation.[62]

4

Masses to Classes

THE COUNTRY MUSIC ASSOCIATION AND THE

DEVELOPMENT OF COUNTRY FORMAT RADIO, 1958–1972

In 1957, Goddard Lieberson, the president of Columbia Records, wrote an article for the *New York Times Magazine* that described, for the presumably shocked residents of Manhattan, country music's development into a $50-million-a-year business. The article dwelt at length on the simultaneous increase in country's profitability and respectability and concluded its exploration of the subject with a quote from Minnie Pearl. Asked when hillbilly music became country music, the comedienne reportedly pulled her blue mink stole around her shoulders and laughed, "Hillbilly gets to be country when you can buy one of these!" By the time Pearl made her comparison, the transformation from hillbilly to country was complete. But, as her joke suggested, the change involved much more than nomenclature. In clutching her mink stole, Minnie Pearl was making a comment not only about her own success as an entertainer but also about how country music and its audience were perceived and labeled by outsiders, and how economic success affected that labeling process. Over the next decade, the country music industry redefined itself by reference to its commercial power and, in the process, helped to remake the popular image of the Southern white migrant.[1]

The outburst of optimism expressed in Lieberson's article was both late and short-lived. The commercial success first of honky-tonk styles and then of rockabilly had paved the way for the development of a fully formed and relatively autonomous music production center in Nashville. And while the spectacular growth in mainstream popularity that had characterized the decade's first years could not be replicated, the genre continued to make steady gains in radio airplay through 1957. The industry remained divided, however, and the turmoil created by the advent of television and development of Top 40 radio programming created new challenges. The period has traditionally been identified in the collective memory of the country business as one in which the nascent Nashville establishment was seriously threatened. That threat has generally been attributed to the popularity of rock and roll but, as we have seen, the causes of the industry's instability stemmed from more endemic changes in the entertainment business, the reconfiguration of mass media, the centralization of the country business itself, and the social changes associated with the migration of rural Southerners and Midwesterners to urban industrial centers.[2]

Perhaps because stylistic changes in popular music have been widely accepted as the root of the problem, interpretations of the country industry's response have focused on the changes in the sound of country that took place during the late 1950s. The new cadre of producers and studio heads who dominated the Nashville recording industry—Chet Atkins, Don Law, and Owen Bradley chief among them—generated a remarkably uniform shift toward a smoother sound characterized by backing vocals, lush string arrangements, and more polished singing styles. Dubbed the Nashville Sound, these stylistic changes brought country closer to traditional pop music and have been interpreted as an attempt to appeal to a new, more middle-class audience.

If we look beyond the recordings themselves, to the country music industry's marketing campaign during these years, however, we find a different story. Discussions of the country field within the music trade in the mid-1950s focused on its mainstream appeal, but by the late 1950s, spokespeople for the industry became increasingly aware that their audience was quite different from the middle-class mainstream to which pop music and rock and roll were targeted. Rather than explaining country's commercial value in terms of the mass market, country broadcasters and businesspeople began to emphasize the unique characteristics of the country audience. This audience was not imagined as comprising new listeners won over from the ranks of pop aficionados. Instead, the country industry worked to revise understandings of its traditional audience: the rural-to-urban white migrants from the South and Midwest who made up a significant portion of the newly affluent blue-collar middle class. In the same way that residents of Maryville and Madison had used the image of the hillbilly to measure their progress into modernity, the country music industry used its commercial power to combat the popular stereotypes surrounding its migrant audience. According to the philosophy the industry developed, country music appealed to a more sophisticated audience not because it had attracted new listeners but because its traditional listeners had achieved the economic success they sought in their new communities.

A CHAMBER OF COMMERCE FOR COUNTRY MUSIC

In November 1958, as Congress began to turn its attention away from broadcasters and toward disc jockeys in its search for a conspiracy against the public taste, the country music business converged on Nashville for the seventh annual WSM Disc Jockey Convention. On Thursday evening, just as the convention got underway, Jack Stapp, who had recently left his position as program manager for WSM to open his own publishing firm, delivered a keynote address and organizing speech for the newly chartered Country Music Association (CMA). The country music industry, Stapp warned, was in a dangerous position "created by bad publicity we cannot fight as a group" and "by inroads on the taste of people." Executives in New York and Los Angeles and radio programmers around the country were woefully ignorant of the country field, he said, and viewed the country artist as "an uncouth, unintelligent, no talent, no appeal individual." The chief goal of the CMA would be to "educate the people behind the closed doors" of the television networks and radio stations, to help them understand what country music could do for their ratings and for their sponsors. This educational campaign would need to be extended to the public as well, Stapp pointed out, for without attention to exposure, the country business would be "relying to a dangerous extent on the tastes of [its] loyal followers." And while Stapp spoke of the need to get country music into markets that were still "virgin territory," he explained that this effort was aimed particularly at keeping country music before its existing audience. Without "constant reminders" the loyal country audience would simply vanish. "If country music does not become more accepted nationally . . . if we do not saturate the country with good publicity, if we do not educate the public," he told the crowd, "we must be prepared to suffer the consequences."[3]

The evident alarm in Stapp's speech attested to the difficulties the country music business faced in the late 1950s. He almost certainly had in mind the recent congressional hearings when he spoke of "bad publicity and other mud that has been thrown at our business." Combating allegations of corruption and underhanded tactics in the music business would continue to be a part of the CMA's role over the next several years. The more important educational campaign, though, was aimed at the radio industry itself. As the 1950s progressed, Top 40 formatting had progressively overtaken the more eclectic block programming principle that had dominated broadcasting from radio's inception as an entertainment medium. The results for styles, like country music, that aimed for a relatively targeted audience appeal were ruinous. In 1953, 65 percent of the nation's radio stations played country music on at least one show, and 236 offered their listeners twenty or more hours of country. A 1957 survey of radio programming conducted by *Sponsor* magazine revealed fifteen stations that played exclusively country music, and another 2,024 that included country in a mixed lineup of offerings. But this number represented a diminishing percentage of radio airplay and began to decline in the final years of the decade. By 1961, when the CMA conducted its first survey of AM radio stations, it estimated that only 36 percent programmed country music, and only 112 played even eight or more hours of the genre.[4]

Moreover, the declining power of the deejays and their promotional organization, the Country Music Disc Jockey Association (CMDJA), had divided the industry and hampered collective action. The structure of the new organization was designed to balance the conflicting interests of the varied pursuits that made up the industry. Stapp told his listeners that the country music business was "an industry just like the automobile industry, the furniture industry, the radio industry," and, like these industries, needed an organization that would allow it to "work with a solid front . . . as a bold group." Hinting at the problems that had plagued the CMDJA, Stapp explicitly distanced the new organization from the old, assuring the crowd that the CMA would not be "an organization that will employ 'politics' for a select few." Instead, it would be industry-wide and would be led by a board of directors, elected by the membership and representing every facet of the business. The board would devote attention to only those projects that would benefit every aspect of the business. It had taken three years, but the organization envisioned at the grievance meeting after the 1955 Jimmie Rodgers Memorial Day celebration had finally taken shape. Nine categories—publishers, artists, management, deejays, radio, records, trade publications, composers, non-affiliated—were represented by two board members each who served overlapping two-year terms. Fittingly enough, Ernest Tubb, who had proposed such an inclusive organization at the Rodgers celebration, was the first representative to the board on behalf of artists.[5]

In addition to addressing the condition of the industry, Stapp also spoke to the personal histories of the individuals gathered before him. Like many people in the country audience, most of those who convened for the DJ convention had direct personal experience with the hillbilly stereotype. The cultural condescension in evidence at the 1958 congressional hearings had its roots not in the committee itself but in the popular music industry, and nearly everyone in the country field had endured ridicule at one time or another. By addressing his audience first as individuals deserving of the same dignity that so many other rural-to-urban migrants sought in the 1950s, Stapp put the assembled group in the shoes of country music listeners. "Country music," he said, "has helped to house you and your family, it has medicated your children, it has furnished you with the automobile you are driving. It's helping you to utilize your American heritage to progress and gather for yourself not only the necessities of life, but some of its luxuries." Underlying the educational mission of the CMA was the belief that country music could become a symbol of success rather than inferiority, for its practitioners as well as its audience.[6]

The CMA had actually been in existence for several months by the time Jack Stapp made his plea to the industry to ensure its future by pooling resources. As Connie B. Gay, one of the organization's founders and its first president, later remembered, the poor turnout at the 1958 CMDJA meeting in Miami prompted a small group to meet in his hotel room after the capstone show at the Dinner Key Auditorium. The group represented a cross-section of the industry and a number of the most important organizations in Nashville: Acuff-Rose president Wesley

Rose, Grand Ole Opry manager D Kilpatrick, talent manager Hubert Long, and artists Teddy and Doyle Wilburn. After some discussion of the problems that had beset the CMDJA, the men agreed that the structure of the new organization would need to reflect the complexity of the industry, balancing the sometimes conflicting interests of different groups. D Kilpatrick began drafting bylaws and, along with Rose and Long, planning for a series of meetings and events to get the association under way at the fall WSM convention in Nashville. In September, the association applied for a nonprofit charter from the state of Tennessee. The charter made the organization's central purpose clear. The new association would be dedicated to the "fostering, publicizing and promoting of country music, by bringing the commercial possibilities of country music to the attention of advertisers, advertising agencies, station managers, and radio and TV networks." The specific means by which this goal would be accomplished were less clear, however, and the CMA struggled to define its mission and strategy for several years.[7]

In January 1959, the CMA board, which had been elected at the WSM convention in November, appointed Harry Stone, former station manager of WSM, to be the association's executive director. Stone's past experience suggested something of what the CMA hoped to accomplish. Working with the Grand Ole Opry from 1928 to 1950, Stone had been instrumental in transforming the show from a regional phenomenon into a national institution. His strategy had involved not only the selection of artists with a more modern sound than that which had previously characterized the roster but also the restructuring of the show to make time slots more appealing to advertising sponsors. When R. J. Reynolds picked up the Prince Albert Show for national network sponsorship, it was Stone who helped develop a program that would retain its dedicated listeners throughout the South and appeal to a new audience unfamiliar with the Opry tradition. Few men in the industry in the late 1950s could point to a more impressive record of shepherding country music to success before a national audience, or of convincing advertisers of the genre's commercial potential. Wesley Rose announced on behalf of the board of directors that the CMA's new executive director would "expound [country music's] commercial advantages . . . through personal contacts with advertising agencies and supplying a steady flow of information to station managers and program directors."[8]

Unfortunately, the fledgling association was in no position to take advantage of either Stone's expertise in broadcasting or his personal contacts in the advertising industry. Instead, he quickly found himself occupied almost exclusively with fundraising. At the outset, the CMA's organizers imagined that only about a third of the money to support the group would come from the annual ten-dollar membership dues, with the remainder to be raised through benefit spectaculars and other fundraisers. Stone accepted the directorship under the mistaken impression that the major record labels had already committed to financial support of the association. He must have been considerably dismayed to discover, when he took up his post on February 1, that his treasury consisted of a few thousand dollars in individual membership dues, plus $1,200 that had been carried over from the treasury of the defunct Country Music Disc Jockey Association. The sum would not even cover the organization's most basic expenses—his own salary and that of his assistant and office manager, Jo Walker. Faced with the desperate need for funds, Stone set about arranging a series of benefit concerts. The first spectacular was planned for March 8 at the Kentucky State Fair Coliseum in Louisville. Showering city and county newspapers throughout Kentucky and Indiana with promotional material, Stone hoped to attract small-towners from miles around for "the biggest influx of visitors since the running of the Derby." But in spite of a scheduled lineup that included Johnny Cash, Ray Price, and Ernest Tubb, the show attracted only about ten thousand people, filling just over half of the coliseum. A second benefit in June at the Jimmie Rodgers Day festival drew about seven thousand fans, less than a third the number who had attended the first festival concert in 1953. Between the two benefits, the association raised less than $15,000.[9]

In addition to raising money, the shows had been meant to generate media exposure for country music by demonstrating the size and devotion of its audience. As recently as 1957, Jim Denny's Philip Morris package shows had brought in crowds of thirty to forty thousand weekly throughout the South, frequently with the same talent that donated services for the CMA benefits. The Philip Morris shows had been free, but they had set the attendance standard for package extravaganzas, and the comparative size of the crowds at the benefits was discouraging and could not have been considered newsworthy except at the local level. The CMA also found itself at cross-purposes in relying on performances for income. First, the arrangement demanded a disproportionate contribution from artists, who donated their time and paid their own expenses to get to the shows. The organization could not long rely on a single category of the membership for support before resentment began to surface. Moreover, in arranging the benefits, the CMA had to avoid competing with the regular engagements upon which artists and booking agents relied for income. As a result, locations for benefits were selected in part precisely because they were less likely to produce large crowds and were therefore less desirable for commercial shows. Ironically, rural areas had always been a challenge for promoters of large-scale events, and as the countryside was progressively depopulated between 1945 and 1960, the challenge intensified. It soon became apparent that benefit shows were not particularly well suited to any of the purposes for which they had been intended: publicity, fundraising, or audience development.[10]

The addition of institutional members in July 1959, the largest of which paid $1,000 annually, afforded the CMA a temporary reprieve, but not a permanent solution to its financial woes. By the time the general membership met at the WSM Disc Jockey Convention in November 1959, the fledgling organization could point to only a few specific steps toward its central goal of promoting the commercial potential of country music among the public, advertisers, and broadcasters. Stone had presented the board with a number of proposals for projects, including the idea of a promotional album like the one that would eventually fund construction of the Hall of Fame, but they were deemed unworkable with the existing staff and funds. The most notable achievements for the year had been the institution of a regular newsletter, *Close-Up;* the creation and distribution of a logo for the association; the mailing of five thousand copies of a promotional brochure titled "Country Music—Approved Everywhere"; and Mississippi senator James Eastland's motion to declare National Country Music Day in conjunction with the Jimmie Rodgers Day celebration. As participants arrived for the WSM event, a meeting of the officers and directors of the CMA focused on financial issues and on how to salvage ticket sales for the first annual CMA banquet to be held on Friday evening at the Brentwood Country Club. The same tone dominated the full membership meeting the following day. "Money is what we need and what we have very little of," Hubert Long, the CMA treasurer, told the members after outlining the costs involved in running the organization. Harry Stone made an urgent plea for support, telling those assembled, "Country music has its best chance in a long time to sell itself to the American people." In spite of these appeals, though, the financial situation had already reached a critical pass. When the newly elected board met at the end of the WSM festival a few days later, the directors voted to remove the executive director and cut the association's staff back to its secretary, Jo Walker. Stone, frustrated by the lack of support and unhappy with the way his position had evolved, readily agreed to resign. As Walker later explained, "We just didn't have the money to pay both of our salaries. Mine was a lot less and, besides, I could type."[11]

In February 1960, the officers and board of the CMA convened in Shreveport for the first quarterly meeting since Stone's departure. The night before the business meeting, Jo Walker met with President Connie B. Gay to discuss the state of the organization. The CMA's two bank accounts, she told him, contained only about $735. If the gathering the following day was not opened on a positive note, Walker feared the directors would vote to disband. Gay was both a successful broadcaster and a consummate promoter whose career had encompassed stints as a streetcorner pitchman, an agricultural extension agent, a speechwriter for the Farm Security Administration, a deejay, and a television and radio producer. When the directors arrived for the meeting, his public relations acumen was put to good use. He told his fellow directors that he had just finished a cross-country drive from Washington, D.C., to Texas and was pleased to report that their efforts were having an effect. More stations were playing country music, a few had even started a full-time country schedule, and they were meeting with success. RCA Victor vice-president Steve Sholes remarked that his company's country record sales had improved. As the discussion continued, optimism grew, and by the time the finances were discussed, all agreed that they had made enough headway to justify continued effort. D Kilpatrick, who had moved from the Grand Ole Opry to the Acuff-Rose Artists booking agency, suggested that, in order to keep the association afloat, the institutional members might be persuaded to pay their annual dues right away, rather than waiting until they came due in July. The representatives of the institutional members who were present agreed. Jo Walker later remembered this as the turning point for the organization. "People just began to get a little enthusiastic and from that day on I never had any doubts that it would be successful, that it was here to stay . . . of course, they had a little hype in there too." In June, the board reported that the treasury was on firm footing.[12]

Changes in broadcasting had been at the root of the country industry's problems in the late 1950s, and the rebirth of country radio provided the foundation for the CMA's promotional efforts, and for the organization's success. Measuring and publicizing the growth of country radio, both as an argument for the music's essential appeal and as an index of the association's impact, became one of the CMA's central concerns. *Close-Up* provided the most obvious vehicle for drawing attention to the nascent trend. The same issue that reported the results of the pivotal Shreveport meeting listed four stations that had switched to an all-country format, and announcements of stations that had recently increased country programming became a regular feature in the newsletter. The announcements not only created an impression of country music's popularity but also helped record companies, booking agents, and concert promoters to identify deejays for their promotional lists. But it was not until August 1960 that the association formalized its radio campaign. At the quarterly meeting, the board appointed Capitol executive Ken Nelson to head a committee that would conduct "an educational campaign at the ad agency level . . . to acquaint time-buyers and other agency executives with the full facts relative to the mass popularity" of country music. Within a month, the committee had sent its first mailing to three hundred agents and buyers, a reprint of an article in *Sponsor* that had run under the title "Country Music: A Gold Mine for City Broadcasters."[13]

Like the larger radio campaign it initiated, the mailing was aimed at helping advertisers understand the audience for country music in new terms: as average, middle-class, urban and suburban adults, not listeners who had been lured away from the pop audience but country music fans who otherwise would not be reached by radio. The country music audience, the article from *Sponsor* said, was composed of "the every-day working people of any city, large or small—the housewife, mill worker, fisherman, truck driver—in short, the people the advertiser wants to reach." And while it suggested that this was where the advertiser would "find the immensity of the middle class," the audience the article described was clearly affluent blue-collar workers rather than the stereotypical suburban middle class. A properly run country music station in any of the large metropolitan areas of the Northeast or Midwest could reach "a listening audience never dreamed of in a general market format," "a vast untouched audience" commanding "many, many thousands of consumer dollars." In September, Charles Bernard, a New York advertising representative who had long specialized in country music, announced the results of a national survey of the country radio audience he had commissioned from a leading ratings firm. The survey reaffirmed the growing consensus on the nature of the country audience. Country listeners were loyal to country stations; they could not be reached by contemporary format radio. They were adults, "the man who works for the dollar and the woman who spends it." And perhaps most surprising to sponsors, their median income was actually higher than the national average. The idea that the country radio audience was somehow both average and unique, and that it encompassed an important segment of the buying public, would be the central themes of the CMA's marketing strategy throughout the 1960s. It was an image in sharp contrast to the white trash stereotype that dominated popular culture.[14]

THE DEVELOPMENT OF COUNTRY FORMAT RADIO

Although the CMA's campaign marked the first concerted effort by the industry to convince national sponsors that country music could sell products, it publicized changes in country broadcasting that had been under way throughout the 1950s, most of which originated outside of Nashville. In part these changes were a response to the growing popularity of television as a mass appeal medium. With television firmly in place as the primary family entertainment, radio stations no longer sought to provide universal appeal. The national network broadcasting that had characterized the 1940s gave way to a more personalized style that identified stations with a narrow audience by playing a single style throughout the broadcasting day. Rock and roll was the first genre to be programmed in this way, but by the late 1950s segmented markets had become the dominant philosophy in radio programming.[15]

Not surprisingly, one of the first full-time country stations appeared in Southern California, where the Dust Bowl migration had produced a community of Southern migrants whose similar backgrounds and social positions made them an ideal target for the new style of programming. The potential of the audience was not immediately obvious to broadcasters, though, and the first full-time country station broadcasting to the Los Angeles market, Pasadena's KXLA, became aware of the possibilities almost by accident. KXLA's sales manager, Dick Schofield, later recalled that the station's country shows were initially "somewhat of an embarrassment to the management of the station," and that local sponsors were the first to become aware of the genre's potential.

When a sponsor would give us a termination notice, I would go out to see him and try to talk him into staying on the station. He would usually say, "No! Not unless you can get me on one of those hillbilly shows that you people have on." . . . In deference to economic pressure we would add one of those hillbilly programs for this guy . . . we added more and more country music programs, just one at a time. All of a sudden our schedule was about 65 to 75 percent country music programming.[16]

By the mid-1950s, KXLA had assembled a remarkable lineup of announcing talent under the direction of Cliffie Stone, including Joe Allison, Biff Collie, "Squeakin'" Deacon Moore, Charlie Williams, and Tennessee Ernie Ford. The station's owner, Lowell King, relied almost exclusively on Stone's judgment in programming, with the result that the deejays retained absolute control over record selection. The deejays also had wide latitude in creating their on-air personalities. Joe Allison remembered that when he arrived at the station in 1952 the dominant announcing style was still a holdover from the barn dance comedy tradition: "I still had pet phrases and we'd even accuse each other of stealing our jokes. I'd say, 'I'll bet you a half a gallon of red ants you can't do that again,' you know. And then somebody else would do it and I'd say, 'Hey you're stealing my stuff.' But it was a holdover . . . I was Uncle Joe and there was Smiling Eddy Hill and Jolly Joe Nixon, and still doing a lot of that stuff."[17] But announcers like Allison and Charlie Williams were also working toward a more dignified style. This shift was driven as much by the deejays' personal feelings as by the response they expected from their audience. "I didn't like people putting our business down the way they did," Allison recalls, "and most of us didn't."

> You could call me a hillbilly if you were in the same business I was in. But some outsider who wasn't in it couldn't call me a hillbilly. . . . I could say to Charlie Williams, "Hey, you hillbilly, hand me that record," and he wouldn't get mad. But if it was somebody who didn't know what he was talking about, it would really make him angry. So that little phrase there might make you know why we were trying to get out of that old haybales and horse collar image. Because we didn't like it. We didn't feel we were that way and we didn't like for people to think of us as that way.

Dick Schofield drew on his own personal experience to imagine the station's audience. "All of my radio background was major market. I just happened to grow up in Texas and Oklahoma. And my own concept was that you couldn't communicate with this audience by talking hillbilly. We began to refine that concept the last couple of years I was at KXLA."[18]

Although KXLA became tremendously successful, its programming strategy was still bold enough to require a personal dedication on the part of its owner and staff. In 1959, Lowell King found himself in failing health and sold the station to new owners whose interest in country music was limited. The full-time format quickly dissolved, and the staff left, almost en masse, to try again at Long Beach station KFOX. Although it had received scant attention from the industry while it was on the air, KXLA was ultimately the foundation for the development of the country format. It and its successor station KFOX functioned as a training ground for disc jockeys to develop a more sophisticated sound and a sales approach that could appeal to national sponsors.

> At KFOX we had a bunch of guys who I would call . . . gold stars, you know, they were really good deejays. And we didn't do a format, but in a way we did because we knew how to keep a show going and how to keep it smooth and how to tighten up your cues and not let all the dead airspace come in and try to balance your fast ones with your slow ones. And even your keys; you put somebody to sleep if you play four songs all in the same key, you know.

Many of the deejays went on to apply the lessons learned at KXLA and KFOX to other stations. Both Dick Schofield and Joe Allison later did consulting work on behalf of the CMA, helping to refine and codify the programming philosophy that dominated the country broadcasting field through the 1960s.[19]

In the meantime, other stations were also moving toward a more refined format. While still at KXLA, Allison had begun working at Los Angeles station KRKD, the only full-time country station in the city itself. In 1957, that station tried a new programming technique that brought it closer to a defined format. KRKD's *Giant Jukebox* applied some of the lessons of Top 40 to the country field. Its deejays, Jolly Joe Nixon, Joe Allison, and Tom Brennen, selected the top fifty country tunes based on audience opinion, sales charts, and national play surveys. The top five hits were put into heavy rotation, and a "country classic" was included in the mix. Though the KRKD format was rudimentary, the basic concept of mixing current hits with more established songs, and keeping the mix the same across different deejay shows, was the essence of the country format as it developed over the next few years. A similar approach was developed at Lubbock, Texas, station KDAV. The station's program manager, David Pinkston, initially relied on the expertise of his disc jockeys for programming, but by the early 1960s his desire to even out differences in shows led him to create a system for identifying and placing different elements of the genre. By means of music wheels, he categorized songs into groups such as hit parade and classics and specified the times at which a selection from each category should be played.[20]

While the components of formula country radio were converging, the CMA was also beginning to codify a preferred approach to announcing based on assumptions about the changing social position of the country audience. The *Music Reporter* told those attending the 1960 WSM convention that the CMA's advice in its correspondence with radio stations focused on retaining the personality and warmth of older announcers without the hokum of cornpone characters. "Foremost is the jockey's sincerity. . . . Any announcer who does not or cannot project to his listeners a feeling of sincerity and friendliness has no business doing a show," the CMA's standard counsel ran. But equally important was the title and presentation of a country show. "There may be some frankly ashamed to admit that they listen to 'Corncob Hoedown,'" the CMA told stations. "The industry has come a long way in recent years and no one can deny that C&W has grown up. We are not a group of raggedy, country boys and girls with missing front teeth. We have acquired status. In choosing a title for your show, make it one that a listener would not hesitate to tell a friend about." Detroit-area station manager Bob Staton struck a similar note in his remarks at a 1962 programming seminar at the convention. "Let's face it. There is very little difference in the city slicker and his country cousin. Their way of life today is almost identical: each has electricity, refrigerators, freezers, telephones and indoor plumbing. So why try to create an image for something that does not exist?"[21]

The central challenge before the CMA was to bring its vision of modernized country broadcasting to life. The organization targeted individual stations in medium and major markets that might be persuaded to change their programming once they understood the country format better. "Part of it was knowing kind of how to program it. Because they'd been doing pop and with so many rock stations in a market, somebody had to be suffering. So that's kind of who we went for to try to get them to change to country. . . . Some of them needed help as far as how do you sell? Who do you sell it to? How do you sell it?" The association subscribed to PULSE and used its ratings data to identify struggling stations.

Once a potential station had been identified, Jo Walker would write a personal letter outlining the benefits of switching formats and offering to have a broadcasting member of the association visit and discuss his own experience. Joe Allison and Dick Schofield were among the consultants most often called upon, and their involvement with dozens of stations helped to create a uniform approach to programming country and to the sales message the CMA sought to communicate. Several of the association's other efforts also contributed to the codification of programming styles. Though the CMA and the consultants it recommended always emphasized that "every market, every situation, is, of course, different," they did underscore a few basic points to every station considering a switch to country format, almost all of which were aimed at eliminating the older friends-and-neighbors style of country broadcasting. The printed programming guidelines the CMA eventually produced stressed over and over that the country audience was respectable and intelligent and should be addressed accordingly.

> Don't approach the Country Music listener as a "different" type animal. . . . Don't instruct your announcer to "sound country." There is no reason for deejays to take on a phony accent, or drawl, because they're programming Country Music. Don't assume the Country Music listener is less intelligent than any other. . . . Be careful that your programming is not slanted down to your audience. Country Music fans are intelligent people.[22]

By the early 1960s, Joe Allison was in a unique position to help the association capitalize on the experience and success of broadcasters in Southern California. Allison had spent several years in Nashville before moving to the West Coast and traveled between the two for several more years, working as an announcer for the Grand Ole Opry and as a deejay on WMAK. In 1959, while on the staff at KFOX, he joined the board of the CMA as a representative of the radio category and quickly became instrumental in helping the CMA expand the full-time country format by serving as a consultant to stations changing their programming to country music. In 1960, Allison undertook his first project for the association: changing ten-thousand-watt KSAY in San Francisco to country music programming. "Jo Walker called me from the CMA and asked me," Allison remembers. "She said, 'A station in San Francisco wants to go country.' . . . They were in the basement of the Fairmont Hotel on Nob Hill. Well, you think that didn't cause some consternation up there!"[23]

Allison's approach at KSAY differed from later efforts in that he focused on developing the deejay staff rather than the format. Rather than training existing staff, he hired veterans Joe Nixon and Charlie Williams, who could be relied upon to select appropriate records and deliver the sophisticated announcing style they had perfected in Los Angeles. Though the station was ridiculed in the local press, it quickly increased its market share. By 1961, a survey conducted by the station showed that 62 percent of listeners in the Bay Area listened to country music at least some of the time, and that country accounted for 31 percent of the records sold there. In spite of the station's success, though, Allison was ultimately unsatisfied with the results. The station's management refused to stick to the full-time format he felt was critical to maintaining audience loyalty. He had begun to realize that the key to a successful urban country station was to guarantee that listeners tuning in at any hour would be assured of hearing the same country sound, but KSAY's management was not convinced. "If they didn't change their block programming over and commit themselves to country, they weren't going to make it," Allison told them. "And they wouldn't do it. If they had a program, *Harry's Garden Club*, right in the middle of the afternoon, but it was sold and they were making money, they weren't willing to change it." Williams and Nixon were also dissatisfied and returned to Los Angeles after a few years. KSAY continued as a country station, however, billing itself to advertisers as "the Bay Area's Blue Collar Giant."[24]

In the summer of 1962, the CMA called on Allison again, this time to help KRAK in Sacramento switch from an "upbeat, middle-of-the-road good music station" to country music. At KRAK Allison was forced to work with the existing staff, and it was this constraint that finally led him to develop an explicit format that would guide the selection of records and the specific mix of old and new tunes. "The station had a union problem, and they couldn't fire the staff that they had. So what we had to do was take that staff and convert them to operating a country station. I had to come up with a format and a formula for people who knew absolutely nothing about country music," Allison later recalled. He developed an hour-long rotation that drew together the diverse sounds contained within the country rubric. The idea of playing a little bit of everything was determined in part simply by necessity. "The truth of it was we had to play it all because there wasn't enough music without playing all of it to program a whole radio station," Allison says. But the audience was also becoming fragmented as the folk revival gained momentum. Broadcasters hoped that a format that mixed fiddle and blue-

5 San Francisco station KSAY was Joe Allison's first effort to implement a country radio format. Though Allison was unsatisfied with the results, the station successfully advertised itself to potential sponsors as a way of reaching affluent blue-collar workers, as evidenced in this ad from the broadcast advertising trade magazine *Sponsor*.

grass with contemporary Nashville Sound hits would appeal to college-age listeners as well as more traditional country fans. Allison made piles of records according to categories—up-tempo, old-time, classic, number one, album selection, inspirational, and so on—so that inexperienced deejays could work the format. Songs were interspersed with news, weather, and local bulletin board announcements that also reflected the segmented audience. "On Campus" covered activities at Sacramento State College, while "Covering the Bases" offered announcements of interest to the ninety thousand people dependent upon the five military installations in the station's listening area. Within a few months of the station's switch to country in October, it had become the number one station in Sacramento.[25]

In addition to providing the impetus for defining the elements of the country format, Allison's experience in Sacramento demonstrated why the CMA's effort to project a more professional image for the industry was so important. When he arrived at the station to meet with the sales staff, he discovered that station manager Manning Slater had bought each of his salesmen a bright red cowboy hat and a walking stick. "They came to the meeting with those things on! After the meeting was over he said, 'What do you think?' I said let's lose the hats and let's lose the canes. And you could see these salesmen going, 'Oh God, I hope he means it!'" Allison realized that this kind of misconception about country music within the broadcasting industry was one of the central barriers to expanding country's market, an observation he would later bring to bear in his work on CMA sales presentations. "If you're not careful you can take these regular businessmen and make caricatures out them," he said. In order for country music to gain more airplay, the professionals who would have to work in the field needed to be able to maintain their personal sense of dignity.[26]

The same was true of advertisers. In spite of KRAK's success, Slater later told reporters for *Broadcasting*, "there was a terrible reaction when we first made the switch. Advertisers were obviously prejudiced against our music, relying strongly on the erroneous cliché that people who listen to country music were poor credit risks." This prejudice was not rooted in pecuniary interest alone. The white-collar professionals who worked in sales and advertising were loath to be personally associated with the popular image of the uneducated and uncouth country audience. As a result, according to Allison, salesmen and advertisers often tried to influence the programming in favor of more pop-oriented sounds. Allison responded by refocusing their attention on the advertising power of country music, using the genre's commercial success to validate its traditional sound and its audience.

> They'd get into saying, "What about playing the new country music as well as the old?" I said, "Don't get involved in what's played, let the program director and the deejays be involved in what's played on the air . . . because your main job here is how many cars can it move off a lot, how many cans of pork and beans will it move off the shelf." . . . And I would always add, "If your wives don't think it's dignified for you to be involved in, tell her how much money you're making . . . that'll take care of everything."

One consultant, Bill Hudson, took a different approach to dealing with these concerns. When he changed Dallas station KBOX to a country format, Loretta Lynn's "Don't Come Home A-Drinkin' (With Lovin' on Your Mind)" was a major hit, but he did not allow the station to play it for several weeks. "I knew the agencies and everybody else listening would be looking for that hard country sound. So we went with Glenn Campbell and the softer country for the first three weeks or so and we got people to say, 'I didn't realize it but I kind of like country music.' . . . Right after that we'd begin to play any country record, no matter how hard it was."[27]

The impetus for the country format thus developed from a variety of sources, many of them related to the personal experiences and desires of professionals in the broadcasting and advertising industries. Whether through projection or through direct contact with the audience, however, most in the industry assumed that their experiences paralleled those of their listeners. And, as the expansion of country radio exhausted the pool of announcers steeped in the field, the need to be able to explain the country sound to those unfamiliar with it became increasingly acute. The triple mission of gaining personal respect, recasting the audience, and interpreting the essence of country music to those outside the industry was evident in the CMA's every pronouncement. Once the country format sound had been established through a diffuse process of experimentation, it was quickly and relatively uniformly replicated by the CMA and a handful of consultants. By 1965, the success of the formula in medium metropolitan markets such as San Diego, Sacramento, and Seattle had paved the way for the next wave of urban country broadcasting.

The sound of the new country stations was calculated to convey an image of professionalism and intelligence, but the CMA and country broadcasters also worked to present more direct portrayals of a modern, sophisticated country audience. A station manager in Arizona succinctly summed up the task. The country industry needed to "educate the time-buyers so that they understand that the people who listen to country-western radio stations are as normal as everyone else, and aren't a bunch of freaks." The lengths to which stations went to convince sponsors of this fact sometimes reached comical proportions. When a man arrived at a country show sponsored by KSON in San Diego wearing a dinner jacket, he was besieged by the station's public relations staff. "We took so many pictures of him he thought he was a celebrity," owner Dan McKinnon told a CMA broadcasters seminar. Don Nelson at WIRE in Indianapolis used a similar tactic. "We'd put on a show and photograph the cars in the parking lot to show that they weren't all pickup trucks." A Knoxville station owner who wanted the city's Mercedes dealer to advertise on his station conceived an even more inventive solution. He asked the recalcitrant dealer to have his service man keep track of which station was tuned in on cars that came in for service. The dealer finally agreed to buy time when the straw poll came out in the station's favor.[28]

But if the audience the country industry tried to sell to advertisers was prosperous, it was also decidedly working class. KSIR in Wichita advertised that it delivered "blue-collar radio—the sound with the majority in mind. Blue collar radio is programmed to appeal to . . . the man in the factory, the bricklayer, the family next door . . . the everyday people who constitute the majority of the buying audience." KSAY featured a socialist-realist silhouette of a construction worker, sleeves rolled up and lunchbox in hand, over its appeal to "Cash In on the Bay Area's Blue Collar Giant." WKMF in Flint, Michigan, "Home of the Award Winning Factory Whistle Show," announced to potential sponsors that it "corner[ed] the Adult Blue Collar Market." Such claims were supported by PULSE research, as *Sponsor* told its readers in 1966.

> He lives in San Francisco or New Haven or Cleveland; he's 45 and most likely owns a brand new Chevrolet; he also owns his own home and has a wife and two children to make some noise in it; he spends his days operating a machine that requires an experienced hand at the controls; his annual salary is about $6,000 a year, most of which he spends on consumer goods for his family and the rest of which he saves. Who is he? According to a special Pulse survey, he's the typical Country music listener.[29]

THE SELLING SOUND OF COUNTRY MUSIC

The CMA tried to communicate its message about the country music audience at every opportunity: in press releases about concerts (such as the one that referred to the first Grand Ole Opry appearance at Carnegie Hall as "a great meeting of the white collars and the blue denims"); in sales materials for radio time-sellers; in the comments of CMA directors and officers in the trade press; in programming guidelines distributed by mail and in the press; and in personal correspondence between the CMA and station managers around the country. One of the most notable vehicles for promulgating the image of the prosperous, working-class country listener was the CMA sales presentation, "The Selling Sound of Country Music." In the four-year span between 1963 and 1967, the show was presented to several thousand potential sponsors and advertising executives in New York, Chicago, and Detroit. The basic text was also modified for smaller presentations to groups in Norfolk, Virginia; Nashville; and San Diego, among other cities. The scripts for these sales shows offer a unique perspective on the message of the CMA, a rare record of the face-to-face interaction between the country industry and the people the industry perceived as being "behind the closed doors" of the broadcasting and advertising industries. Perhaps because the relatively informal atmosphere of the live performance allowed for directness without offense, the scripts dealt head-on with the stereotyping and class divisions that characterized images of the country audience and the country industry. In addition to being an effort to sell country airtime, the shows were clearly meant to disprove what the CMA felt to be "the widespread feeling in New York that country is a medium run by hillbillies for hillbillies." Though the content of the scripts varied slightly from performance to performance, the basic message was always the same: country listeners were consumers and therefore deserved to be treated as respectable, intelligent citizens, not ignorant hayseeds; and country artists, like their audience, had become reputable, successful craftsmen.[30]

The concept for the sales shows developed over the course of several years between 1960 and 1963. In the fall of 1960, Connie B. Gay told the CMA membership that potential sponsors should be the association's main focus. "Country music's most urgent, immediate need is a 'crash program' on Madison Avenue and elsewhere," he urged, "to place the sales story of country music in the hands of large commercial sponsors and advertising agency decision makers." The first step was taken in January 1961, when the board and officers of the CMA met in New York and sponsored a luncheon for advertising agency representatives. After lunch, Gay delivered a brief speech on the commercial potential of country music and the mission of the CMA. Though the agency guests expressed interest, the lunch seemed to produce little in the way of concrete results. But at the quarterly meeting a year later, Charles Bernard reported that the Radio and Television Executives Society of New York had contacted him about the possibility of presenting a show for the society's annual newsmaker luncheon.[31]

The luncheon took place in February 1962, with Ferlin Husky appearing before five hundred of the society's members as the emcee and star of a show titled "A Salute to Country Music." The choice of Husky as presenter suggests that, from the beginning, class was a central theme of the presentations. Husky was a well-known star, and his 1957 hit, "Gone," had ushered in the big, smooth sound that characterized Nashville production for the next decade. But Husky's stage act had always relied on the presence of his comic alter-ego, Simon Crum. Crum started out as a standard hick rube, but in the mid-1950s Husky inverted the joke and became the country fool who fools the city slickers. Rather than aiming at the uneducated mountaineer, the traditional target of rube comedy, the new Crum—a well-dressed, pretentious fop whose ignorance betrays him as a hick on the inside—satirized the class snobbery of upwardly mobile middle-income America. In 1958, Husky took his character to the big screen in *Country Music Holiday*. An unexpected box-office success, the film featured Husky/Crum as a gullible Tennessee boy transplanted to Manhattan, where he absurdly manages to charm a beautiful, high-society knockout (Zsa-Zsa Gabor) and is whisked away to a world of fox hunts and country mansions. Husky spent much of the New York luncheon in his Crum persona, dressed in white slacks and loafers, a dinner jacket, and a cummerbund. The inversion of clever hick and ignorant snob was completed when Crum crowned the society's staid president with a white Stetson, as if to suggest that broaching the class distinctions surrounding country music was as easy as a quick costume change. Bernard announced that the event had been a success and that the society was considering making it an annual affair.[32]

Whatever the use of humorous stereotypes in "A Salute to Country Music," familiarizing New York advertising executives with the sales potential of country music was a particularly serious issue for the CMA. The association estimated that 75 percent of the advertising campaigns that bought time on country stations had to be cleared through New York offices. The lack of country music programming in the city meant that the executives who made decisions about time purchases had little opportunity to familiarize themselves with the sound or style of a country station. The problem was eased somewhat when WJRZ in Newark, New Jersey, added an hour of country programming to its weeknight schedule, but a single show could not approximate the results a full-time country station would produce. The connection between the show for the Radio and Television Executives Society and the addition of country to the WJRZ schedule was probably tenuous at best, but letting the music speak for itself seemed to be an effective strategy. In December, the directors of the CMA announced that they had formed a committee to plan for a country show to be presented to the Sales Executives Club of New York the following May.[33]

Unlike the earlier presentation to the Radio and Television Executives Society, the New York show in its very execution would demonstrate that country music was serious business. The show was to be a scripted stage production featuring half a dozen artists, and in addition to the presentation itself, the committee planned to produce a souvenir program and to record the show and press a promotional album to distribute to those not in attendance. The talents and resources of the entire industry would be on display. Early in the planning, the CMA contacted Joe Allison and asked him to prepare the script for the show. His experience as a disc jockey, radio consultant, master of ceremonies, television producer, and songwriter influenced his approach to the script, though he had never worked on a trade show. In this first show, Allison sought not so much to demonstrate the demographics of the audience as to familiarize the admen with country music itself. "You couldn't tell them anything about demographics," he later recalled. "They had the numbers. They could tell you [who] would listen to country music [and when]. . . . But what they didn't know was anything about country music." Allison designed the show to include a broad range of styles and to demonstrate for the executives the country influences in music they heard every day, from Ray Charles to Flatt and Scruggs.[34]

Allison also applied to his scriptwriting the lessons he had learned about advertisers and broadcasters in his work as a radio consultant. One of his chief goals in the New York presentation was to allay the audience's fears that they would be somehow degraded by working the country field. It was critical, Allison felt, to convince the advertisers that they would be dealing with professionals, and indeed "not just [with] professionals, but top professionals." This goal was achieved in part by the choice of Tex Ritter as master of ceremonies. In addition to being a well-known star, Ritter was himself a successful businessman and an outstanding speaker. "When Tex spoke you thought God was talking to you. He was like Franklin Roosevelt . . . when he was in a room and he talked, everybody listened." Between songs by Leon McAuliff, Don Gibson, and the Anita Kerr Singers, Ritter emphasized again and again that the modern country artist was an everyday businessperson. Country artists in the 1960s had to be sure to leave time to "confer with their brokers, tally their oil stock dividends, buy and sell real estate, send out the laundry, and regulate their highly successful lives in general." In other words, they behaved like any successful entrepreneur. The status-conscious executives of the broadcasting business, Allison felt, "were trying to find something that their wives could talk about at the country club and not be ashamed of it." The sales show supplied that something by emphasizing the professionalism and profitability of the country field.[35]

By the time the show was presented to the Adcraft Club of Detroit the following year, Allison had widened his focus to include the audience as well as the professionals of the country industry. The sophistication of the country entertainer was still an important point, but it was treated with a more delicate touch. "The songwriter who once tended stock on his daddy's farm is now consulting his broker regarding another kind of stock," Ritter told the audience, and like other affluent Americans, wise to the ways of the consumer world, he "[did] not consider his Cadillac a luxury but a commodity." In this second presentation, the country audience took center stage, with a narrative that explicitly contradicted the popular image of the destitute, ignorant hillbilly migrant. Using survey and sales account data collected by KFOX in Los Angeles, Ritter demonstrated that the all-country station was the most successful sales vehicle for new cars in the Los Angeles area. "Who are the people who enable the country music station to sell more cars than any other radio station?" Ritter asked. "Metropolitan population influx figures show that the largest percentages have their roots in the middle-west and south. Craftsmen, technicians, laborers, and home folks who are the working force." The audience the CMA was selling was not a new, more middle-class audience attracted by the modern sound of Nashville production. On the contrary, the country listener potential advertisers were encouraged to envision was the same rural-to-urban migrant who had made up the bulk of country's fans since the late 1940s. The goal of the marketing campaign was to cast this traditional audience in a new light: as citizens, workers, and consumers. "The fans of our music elect the presidents, run the factories, grow the food, transport our goods and in general manipulate the gears of this country every day," Ritter told the Detroit advertisers. The "pseudo-intellectual" sponsor who overlooked the country audience "while searching for more so-called intellectual advertising pursuits might very well be cutting off his nose to spite his own face."[36]

In the fall of 1964, the CMA decided to take its presentation to the Sales-Marketing Executives Club of Chicago. Though the city had no full-time country station at the time, management at fifty-thousand-watt WJJD had already contacted the CMA about changing to a country format. The switch was viewed dimly by many of the local agency offices, and the show was no doubt intended to bolster the station's chances for success in the country's second largest northern urban center. In addition to inviting representatives from key ad agencies throughout the Midwest, the association invited country station managers from around the United States to discuss their success with the country format and offer advice to potential sponsors. The purpose of the show would be "to sell country music to advertisers and their agencies with emphasis on the responsiveness of audiences to radio programming of country music."[37]

In the Chicago script, the themes of cultural snobbery and audience respectability were fully developed, particularly in a segment that dramatized the interaction between the country station salesman and the advertising time-buyer. "If all the sales managers of the Country Music radio stations could collect and print their experiences connected with the objections of retail advertisers, media directors, and time buyers, the resulting work would have to be classified as a study in snobbery," Tex Ritter told the admen. He pointed out that country music offered an acceptable outlet for class derision that was otherwise inappropriate in a pluralistic society.

> What a capital opportunity existed when the buyer of advertising used to open the door to a country music salesman! If the buyer happened to be in need of therapy, how good it was to say, "You don't expect me to advertise with that (cuckoo) hillbilly music, do you? . . . We simply do not feel that your (cuckoo) music is right for our product. Our marketing objective is the middle income consumer, and your gravy-sopping, hog-calling, barefoot itinerant hardly fits the image!"

Again using survey data from stations in major metropolitan areas, the script went on to sketch a very different profile of the country audience. The country listener was an educated adult homeowner but was also clearly part of the working class, not the white-collar world. Country listeners were "bricklayers and plumbers, carpenters, truck drivers and stevedores . . . electricians, machinists, electronic specialists, technicians, and craftsmen." Though migrants from country to city, they were "*not* from some other planet" but were ordinary, respectable folk. The advertising executive who looked down on the country music audience could only be described as a class snob, "an otherwise bright person . . . so eager to display his 'status quotient' that he becomes a victim of his own propaganda."[38]

Such open attacks across class lines hinted that the suppressed cultural tensions of the 1950s were finding new voice in the 1960s, and they

THE SELLING SOUND OF COUNTRY MUSIC

6 Tex Ritter sings for the Sales-Marketing Executives Club of Chicago during a 1965 CMA sales presentation. The CMA used the sales presentations to revise advertisers' perceptions of the country music audience, replacing the hillbilly image with one of ordinary consumers. *Photo courtesy of Country Music Hall of Fame and Museum.*

indicated the role that the popular culture industries had begun to play in constructing definitions of class identity based on consumption and taste. Yet if the tone of the sales presentations echoed the emerging reaction against liberal politics, it was inspired by the same pluralistic values that animated other social movements of the 1960s. Joe Allison remembered that "almost everything we did back in those days was very defensive . . . because we still had people hacking at us and calling us hillbillies and all that kind of thing," and he specifically compared the effort to recast the country audience with other, contemporaneous struggles for equality. "Being country was like being a Jew or being black or being any other ethnic derivation that had to fight its way out of the criticism into the light," he maintained. "It was the same thing. I don't know if it socially was as important, but we felt that way." The CMA was not alone in this perception, as a *Sponsor* feature on country programming acknowledged in 1966. The days of programming country music as "almost 'ethnic' stations" were passing, the magazine declared. "Now these same 'limited appeal' outlets are pulling in healthy shares of markets and turning up an audience that is a far cry from the Yokum-family image so long associated with the country idiom."[39]

THE BIG COUNTRY SOUND FOR BIG CITY FOLK

By 1965 the tide had clearly turned for country radio programming, in part because of the CMA's success in advertising the format's achievements. A handful of stations along the West Coast—KFOX in Los Angeles, KSON in San Diego, KAYO in Seattle, and KRAK in Sacramento—had proven that a full-time country music format could capture a significant share of the audience in metropolitan areas. While this success augured well, many broadcasters and advertisers harbored doubts about the format's appeal in the urban industrial Northeast; and the nation's first and third largest markets, New York and Chicago, had yet to be conquered. The potential for a country station in these markets was evident. In 1963, *Sponsor* magazine reiterated its earlier observation that industrial centers were ripe for country music. Station survey results showed that "the blue collar worker or the industrial worker . . . is the chief country & western radio fan." Department of Commerce statistics indicating a 500 percent increase in the average industrial wage over the previous twenty years completed the story. *Sponsor* told its readers: "58% of the nation's spendable income is in the hands of the blue collar industrial worker. He's the 'middle income majority.'"[40]

Chicago, of course, had never been without country broadcasting. WLS continued to broadcast the *National Barn Dance* until *Prairie Farmer* sold the station in 1960, and a similar show, featuring most of the old *Barn Dance* cast, was broadcast over WGN throughout the sixties. But by that time a live variety show broadcast as part of a block-programming scheme was little more than a nostalgia piece, and the popularity of the *National Barn Dance* had been declining since the late 1940s. As the *Barn Dance* waned in popularity, rival station WJJD began to adjust to the newer style of country broadcasting with its popular deejay show *Suppertime Frolic*, featuring Randy Blake. (In fact, the show was managed for a time by Ken Nelson, the Capitol Records executive who initially engineered the CMA's radio campaign and succeeded Connie B. Gay as president of the organization in 1960.) During the late fifties, though, WJJD abandoned its mix of pop, country, and rhythm-and-blues in favor of a full-time rock Top 40 format. Country stations in Gary, Indiana, and rural La Grange, Illinois, captured fractions of the Chicago market, but their relatively weak signals and remote locations distanced them from the metropolitan audience, and neither station followed the new full-time format formula.

Ironically, it was WLS's switch to a rock format that induced WJJD to change over to country programming. With the Top 40 market split, WJJD's share dropped dramatically. The station first tried a more adult, middle-of-the-road pop appeal but was still unable to capture a large enough audience even to register in PULSE ratings for the city. The station's general manager, George Dubinetz, began to study record sales figures in the Midwest in an effort to discover an unmet demand for his station. He found that country music, even without a major outlet in Chicago, accounted for up to 35 percent of total sales for several major labels. In the fall of 1964, he contacted the CMA for advice on changing the station's format. Dubinetz originally tried to hire Joe Allison as program director, but Allison turned down the offer because he didn't want to live in Chicago. Instead, he suggested that the station contact Chris Lane, whom Allison had trained at Seattle's KAYO.[41]

Lane brought with him the programming philosophy he had learned from Allison. As he later reported to *Close-Up*, he "used a completely modern approach in presenting [the] C&W sound to Chicago." The station dubbed its deejay staff "the Western Gentlemen" and commissioned a slick station identification jingle package from Pepper Studios. But while the format was even more closely modeled on a Top 40 formula than Allison's earlier stations had been, the song selection favored traditional sounds over pop-oriented production. Lane opened his very first show with Buck Owens's "Tiger by the Tail," and one was as likely to hear a George Jones or Hank Thompson honky-tonk tune as a Chet Atkins instrumental. Just before the bottom-of-the-hour news break, listeners could expect their hourly "song of faith," and the station reached out to the college set by including a fiddle or bluegrass song once an hour. The play formula replicated almost identically the one in use at KRAK.[42]

Whatever the station's efforts to reach passing pop fans or college-age folk aficionados, its primary audience was clearly the white working class and the Southern white migrants who, as *Variety* remarked, "comprise[d] quite a little city of their own in the Uptown sector of Chicago." Songs like Jim Nesbit's "Still Alive in '65" ("some's got a little, some's got a lot, me I ain't never done too hot") certainly stretched the bounds of the new audience image the country industry was trying to promote. But in Chicago as elsewhere, consumerism created the cultural space necessary to make hard country acceptable, if not respectable. Reflecting on the station's choice of target audience, *Variety* tempered its pathologizing of Southern migrants with a grudging acceptance that they did, after all, purchase goods. "As for the southern migrant in Chicago, while he's somewhat of a sociological problem, he's nevertheless without representation in the communications media. Since he has little to identify with in urban culture, wjjd could fill an important void for him. Also, as a consumer, he's anything but negligible, especially when it comes to the living essentials."[43]

Within weeks of its February 15 debut, wjjd moved from undetected in the PULSE ratings to the number four position overall. A special survey identified Chicago as the market containing the greatest number of "country-western music households." The station was estimated to be broadcasting to nearly half a million households, pulling in a full 25 percent of the city's radio audience during parts of the broadcasting day. When the *Chicago American* asked its readers to write in with their station preferences the following month, the response came as a surprise. "The vast majority of the overwhelming number who have written to tell us their preferences say they like country-western music," the paper reported. One listener submitted her choice of wjjd along with an effort to distance herself from the obvious stereotype of the country listener. "I'm not a transplanted hillbilly. I was born and raised within 65 miles of Chicago," she told the editors.[44]

In spite of the station's popularity, many advertisers were slow to respond, particularly those, like airlines, who imagined middle-class consumers for their products. "The so-called sophisticated accounts wouldn't even touch us," recalled the station's general manager. The difficulty involved in overcoming the hillbilly stereotype in Chicago was evident in responses to the CMA sales presentation. While the *Chicago Tribune* reported that "there was nothing naïve or unsophisticated" about the presentation or the music, the *Chicago American* ran its description of the show under the headline "Yahoo! They Brought the Mountains to Chicago" and told the improbable tale that Tex Ritter had opened the show by declaring, "Dang it all. We've ahrahved!" wjjd approached the problem not by changing its programming to a smoother sound but by continuing to collect facts about its audience to disprove prevailing wisdom. Like outlets on the West Coast, the station relied heavily on the visual impression audiences at live shows could make. A series of concerts at the Arie Crown Theater provided an opportunity to physically substantiate claims to respectability. Photos showed well-dressed, average-looking men and women quietly studying their programs as though at a classical concert, though the fans waiting to take pictures in orderly rows at the foot of the stage slightly betrayed the image. The shows also provided an opportunity to survey audiences about their income and lifestyle, and this information was assiduously relayed to advertisers in the area. "We would ask a lot of questions about income, home ownership and all the rest," George Dubinetz recalled. "We took this material to the advertising agencies and said, 'Look, there's nothing wrong with these people. They work for IBM, Illinois Bell and there's nothing strange about them.' "[45]

By the end of 1965, WJJD was universally embraced by the broadcasting industry as a tremendous success. Plough, Inc., the Memphis broadcasting company that owned WJJD, was so impressed with the progress of the station, their first country effort, that they decided to use the same strategy for their Atlanta and Boston stations. In part, this success reflected the CMA's achievements in recasting the country audience. "The 'status' of country formats and country broadcasting has been improved," *Sponsor* reported, and advertisers were no longer "afraid of the country image." But it also reflected a new attitude toward the radio audience as a whole. Commenting on the changes in the Chicago market that had resulted in WJJD's switch, the *Chicago American* noted that the only universal characteristic of the city's radio stations was that they were all seeking a greater share of the market's audience and all adopting narrow formats in the process. "This is the era of specialization," the article informed listeners. As consumers, listeners were interchangeable, and sponsors cared less and less about the cultural predilections and tastes of specific groups, so long as they could patch together the largest audience possible by using a variety of outlets. "Country is just a word for another kind of specialized radio," said one sponsor. The segmentation of the radio market was a major selling point for the CMA. The organization boasted that country format stations reached "the largest unduplicated audience in the world," stressing the fact that most country listeners tuned in a single station all day. Half of WJJD's audience listened to the station almost exclusively.[46]

But if advertisers were increasingly indifferent to cultural hierarchies and more attentive to the mathematics of audience accumulation, the symbolic importance of the Northern cities, especially New York, remained paramount within the country industry. For all of the declarations of independence from the traditional centers of cultural prestige, most in the country business viewed New York as the last bastion of highbrow sophistication, the pinnacle of the cultural pyramid the business had been scaling for twenty years. The CMA carefully publicized indications that country was becoming acceptable in the nation's largest city. When a Grand Ole Opry troupe performed in front of a standing-room-only crowd under the chandeliers at Carnegie Hall in 1961, the show was viewed by many as an indication that country music had finally arrived, in spite of Dorothy Kilgallen's complaint that the city was being overrun by "hicks from the sticks." And the addition of an hour of country music each day on New Jersey's WJRZ prompted the *Music Reporter* to celebrate: "At last in this dapper, debonair city of sophistication, air time has been obtained for C&W music." In addition to being a potent cultural symbol, New York was also a source of commercial power, and the CMA was anxious to give media departments and advertising agencies the opportunity to hear the new image of country broadcasting firsthand.[47]

In the summer of 1965, the CMA fulfilled its fondest wish when WJRZ decided to change to a full-time country format and hired Joe Allison to consult. The implementation of the format at WJRZ recapitulated years of development. In spite of the ballyhoo surrounding the New York market, Allison approached the new project just as he had previous stations. The hourly rotation that he had developed at KRAK and KAYO was again pressed into use, this time in physical form as a painted collar around the control-room clock. Allison also sought the same warm but professional announcing style that had become the standard in country broadcasting. As he had been at KRAK, Allison was forced to work with the existing staff and advised station owner Lazar Emanuel on which of his deejays could make the switch successfully. The format would demand professionalism, but Allison was also wary of announcers who might alienate the audience. One deejay was relegated to the news department because Allison feared that "a country and western audience would find him condescending," and another had to be warned to eliminate his "hippy talk," which Allison thought projected an image that was too pretentious and too modern.[48]

Even if their personal announcing styles could be adapted to the new format, though, the deejay staff had to be carefully controlled in order to produce the right sound and image. "All albums and singles, except those that are to be used on the air, should be removed from the control room," Allison advised Emanuel. And when the deejays began injecting their own tastes into the song selection, program manager Ed Nielsen made very clear the limits on their programming power. "For the last two weeks, I have noticed personal preferences popping up in the programming," he told the deejays in an internal memo. "Rather than attempting to 'reason with you,' I am taking the matter entirely out of your hands. You will receive a rotation system regarding music which WILL NOT be violated." Tight managerial control of playlists at Top 40 stations was generally intended to limit deejays to a narrow selection. But the rotation system at WJRZ, predicated upon "complete exposure of the list," was clearly meant to force the announcers to play the full range of styles dictated by the format, even if they found some objectionable.[49]

The station's technique with its sales staff also reflected lessons learned at other stations. In a memo announcing the format change to the station's salesmen, management was at pains to point out that the new format would not humiliate them. "It will be sophisticated, it will not be 'hokeyed' up, it will be a tight Top 40 format, but with country music." And, appealing as always to the mollifying commercialism of the genre, the memo added, "Believe me, fellas, I have never been more excited about anything than I am now. We are all going to get rich with this." Salesmen were given statistics regarding the success of other stations that had switched to the country format, along with account lists of national sponsors who had advertised with country music. They were also given a list of random sales points that consisted, almost verbatim, of the central themes of commercial power and misplaced snobbery from the CMA's sales presentations: the country artist was not "an illiterate rube," "the day of the haybales and horse collars [was] passé." Finally, Allison encouraged the salesmen to use the strategy he had been using with sponsors and stations for years, "sell the '*effects*' . . . not the music."[50]

But while the station's sales materials and press releases urged New Yorkers to view the country audience in the sophisticated light the CMA tried to cast, its programming philosophy also revealed that the listening audience had become somewhat secondary to the format's appeals. The press statement announcing the format change confronted rural stereotypes by remarking that the mention of country music unfairly evoked an image of "an illiterate, overall-clad hill billy" and insisted that some

Masses to Classes

part of country music would appeal to everyone, "whether you are an urbanite or a suburbanite." In fact, Allison used the word "suburbanite" as an oblique reference to the music's rural image and past and to the thousands of migrants who had moved to the urban fringe, he felt, in an effort to regain some connection to rural life. "That, to me, was the out of town audience," he later said, and he used the image of suburbia "instead of saying backwoods." But the days of schoolhouse tours were gone, and with them the controlling influence of listener preference. Allison largely ignored the specific demographics of the markets in which he consulted, instituting instead a formula based on his own intuition and vision of what country music should sound like. That vision was, on the whole, fairly inclusive, encompassing gospel and honky-tonk, modern and traditional sounds, but Allison was aware that many country listeners would be disappointed by the format. "Please do not tumble to crank phone calls and letters criticizing the format," he wrote to WJRZ's owner, "These are hard-core country listeners, who will certainly affect your thinking if you allow it. Besides the fact, we know they are going to listen to WJRZ in any case."[51]

Whatever the feelings of "hard-core country fans," the response to WJRZ was immediate and impressive. Within weeks, the station was pulling a large enough audience to appear in market share ratings for the first time. When management formed a promotional "country club," requests to join arrived in such numbers that a special service had to be retained to process the mail. Letters addressed simply to "the country-politans," the station's label for its deejay staff, were successfully delivered. But the station's greatest impact was felt beyond the reach of its broadcasting signal. As the CMA had always suspected, New York was in some sense the key to swinging the public relations pendulum in favor of country music. With the success of WJRZ, the popular press finally embraced the new image the CMA had been promoting for years. The *Saturday Evening Post* proclaimed,

Even New York City—where there are restaurants for Polynesians, north-ern *and* southern Italians, northern and southern Chinese, Moors, Scan-dinavians, Lithuanians and Romanians, but where you can't buy a decent plate of turnip greens, purple-hull peas and fried okra—even that market has been opened up. [WJRZ] has been beaming Lefty Frizzell and Ferlin Husky across the Hudson all day and all night, and it has increased its audience 1,000 per cent.

Almost by virtue of its arrival in New York, country music had achieved "a new acceptance and a new dignity." *Sponsor* and *Broadcasting* initiated regular feature sections on country music, and stories about the Nashville Sound appeared in newspapers and magazines across the country.[52]

By the end of 1960s, the cultural redemption of the country audience was nearly complete. In October 1965, *Broadcasting* published a special report on programming the country format. While the sound of country music had become more sophisticated, the key change the magazine cited for country's resurgence as a programming choice was "the awareness by broadcasters that their country music audience isn't limited to hayseeds, Okies, rubes, or Jed Clampetts." The magazine enumerated the healthy economic characteristics of the country listener along with a list of sponsors that included airlines and Cadillac dealers. Some station managers reported that they still had to deploy "great sales effort and unlimited patience" to overcome the "'Grapes of Wrath' stigma," but advertisers seemed to relinquish the stereotype with naïve good humor. When WJJD encouraged one of its sponsors to attend a country music concert and actually see the audience firsthand, she told *Sponsor,* "I never believed I would see so many sophisticated and affluent people at a Country show." "They may not all show up in Cadillacs and minks but neither do they qualify for aid from the poverty program," *Broadcasting* told its readers. An executive quoted in *Sponsor* echoed the sentiment, pointing out that, perhaps to some sponsors' surprise, "Country listeners eat and sleep and go on vacations and buy cars just like everyone else."[53]

There are many reasons to wish that the country music industry had clung more tightly to an alternative vision of respectability—one that did not rely so heavily on consumerism and commercialism—but the terms of value were set in cultural dialogues that transcended the world of country music. In Cold War America, prosperity was a resonant political and cultural language. It was invoked to illustrate the ideological superiority of democracy over communism and the cultural superiority of the urban North over the rural South. To a greater extent than in any previous era, consumer culture became one with the American Way in the 1950s and 1960s. As Lizabeth Cohen has written of what she calls the consumers' republic, the postwar period witnessed the construction of a political and economic regime "that expected a dynamic mass consumption economy not only to deliver prosperity, but also to fulfill American society's loftier aspirations: more social egalitarianism, more democratic participation, and more political freedom." Country music was the perfect cultural mirror for the new consumer citizenship, not only in the way its fan press encouraged "voting" through record choice but also in the way the CMA abandoned Nashville's earlier mass market dreams in favor of targeting and publicizing an audience narrowly defined by class and race.[54]

But the cultural importance of commercial success reflected more than the interests of the business, government, and labor leaders Cohen identifies; it represented the aspirations and achievements of many Americans. The thousands of rural-to-urban migrants—country music professionals among them—who left small towns and family farms for work in the city were motivated by the pursuit of more affluent lives. Their identity as consumers, symbolized partly by the commercial success of country music, was the measure of their success in attaining that goal. The CMA's efforts to revise popular understandings of the Southern migrant and the white working class, to counteract the pathological images that prevailed in other forms of commercial culture and intellectual discourse, had other consequences as well, though. Complaints that the country industry was changing its sound to appeal to a more middle-class audience were somewhat misdirected. The middle-class audience the CMA worked to capture was composed of the white-collar representatives of ad agencies and station sales staff, and what it sold was not a more polished sound but a refurbished veneer on its old audience: the effects, not the music. Country music listeners had themselves become a commodity, and their identity as consumers threatened to overwhelm their identity as an audience.

5

Commercialism

and Tradition, 1958–1970

Many country music fans in the 1960s worried that they were being sold out and, in the most literal sense, they were. The Country Music Association's promotional efforts were not aimed at making white-collar advertisers and sponsors like country music but at selling the country audience as a prosperous and powerful segment of the buying public. The CMA sold listeners: "the largest unduplicated audience in the world"; the millions of Southern uplanders and rural Midwesterners who had made good in the Northern urban economy and moved to the suburbs; and the additional millions who remained in the rural South and Midwest. Fans' suspicions that they were being snubbed by the country music business in favor of a more upscale urbane audience missed the mark. The Nashville Sound and the marketing campaign of the Country Music Association did not abandon the traditional battle for the country audience's respectability; they simply transposed it from the realm of pioneers and citizens to the aisles of the consumer marketplace. The country music listener was no longer a simple hayseed, a poor but proud exile, or a dignified citizen; he was a Chevy owner, a Delta passenger, a Pepsi drinker.

The country audience responded to this new discourse of commercialism in conflicting ways. By the late 1950s, thanks in part to country's industrial fan press, many country listeners were thoroughly familiar with the economic imperatives of the music business. Their responses to the increasing popularity and mainstream respectability of their music in the 1960s revolved largely around acceptance or rejection of the financial economy that underpinned the dissemination of country. Some fans argued for a form of consumer activism to influence the kinds of country music being produced by Nashville; others proposed withdrawing from the cultural marketplace to protest their lack of power. For some, commercial success meant validation of their own tastes; for others it signified a cynical desertion of the music's tradition. Class tensions simmered below the surface of much of this debate and occasionally erupted to the surface with striking clarity. Thus, commercialism was a rich language of emotions and aspirations for fans as well as professionals. But the audience concerns revealed in letters to fan magazines were particularly notable for their insistence on the continued importance of older definitions and social meanings for country music.

Even when they did not reject its commercialism, fans sought also to express the less tangible values they found in country music. More often than industry voices now did, country listeners returned with conviction to the notion that this was the people's music, a reflection of America's simple folk traditions. Ironically, this same notion underlay the Country Music Association's most conscious effort to appeal to a more upscale audience. In the Country Music Foundation and Hall of Fame, the CMA celebrated commercialism, but it sought also to preserve a historical identity for country music, in part because the pre-commercial tradition from which country sprang had always attracted the interest of middle- and upper-class cultural reformers. The history-making institutions of the CMA produced a synthesis of commercialism and tradition that became a powerful means of popularizing the genre's past and of making it more palatable to the intellectuals and academics who had persistently denigrated country music.

A THING THAT MONEY CANNOT BUY:
THE COUNTRY AUDIENCE IN THE CMA ERA

More than a decade after the country field's first efforts to organize on a national basis, the institutional development of the industry had profoundly affected the ways fans interacted with the music they enjoyed. Country fans in the 1960s found themselves in a new position with respect to the mass media. The genre's growing popularity meant that some form of country music was available in almost every radio market. Syndicated and national shows made country artists regular fixtures even on television, citadel of the mainstream. Nashville, now the nation's third most important recording center, had clearly become a major media hub in its own right. Cultural condescension about the music had by no means disappeared, but it was difficult to argue any longer that a small group of elitists in the larger entertainment industry were keeping fans from listening to the music they wanted to hear.

Nonetheless, the lessons promulgated by the country industry during the 1950s were evident in audience responses to the countrypolitan sounds produced by Nashville in the 1960s. For years, the commercial fan press had carefully promoted the cultural and social divisions between country and pop. Magazines like *Pickin' and Singin' News* and *Country & Western Jamboree* made clear to their readers that country music was despised by snobs who looked down on simple people and their pleasures. Articles encouraged fans to defend country music and remain loyal to "their" music in spite of sneers from "longhairs" and pop fans. Country fans during these years were constantly reminded that individual taste was just as important as the pronouncements of highbrow critics. The same magazines that carried this message of cultural rebellion carefully outlined the economics of the culture industries and spurred readers to consumer action. They offered guidance on how to participate in phases of the country business from concert promotion to public relations. Fans were thus encouraged to assume personal responsibility for advancing country music, not only by buying and requesting records but also by becoming familiar with the workings of the business.

During the 1960s, fans applied these lessons to their experiences of the burgeoning country industry in Nashville. Whatever they thought of the music's commercial success, they took into account the business of country music in their assessments of changing sounds. This was most evident in the frequent complaints, made by fans who preferred honky-tonk and hillbilly styles, that the Nashville Sound was nothing more than a marketing strategy. Similar complaints about rockabilly in the 1950s had been aimed at centers of cultural power beyond the country field and reflected concern that country music was being co-opted by "outside" forces, especially middle-class youth and the larger music industry.

Complaints during the 1960s contained many of the same surface features: that the instrumentation was too modern, that the music sounded too much like its mainstream pop counterpart. But fans in the 1960s were less worried about co-optation from without than about corruption from within. The country music business itself, once the victim of external cultural power, had become the problem. One fan noted with disgust that fans could do little to affect the kinds of music available to them. "But the ignorant people of Nashville, where country music originates, can do something about it," he wrote. "They're just too damn gullible. . . . These so-called creators of fine music don't even know themselves what Country music is." Audience tastes had been superseded by the preferences of misguided producers and artists in search of hits. "What about us country fans?" the same correspondent asked. "Why doesn't anyone care? I guess everybody's too busy making money to care." Another reader wrote in with her support of this assessment. "Perhaps the Nashville Sound does satisfy a lot of people's musical desires," she speculated, "but all of us true country fans can just look because you all are too busy to care about us."[1]

While many fans clearly thought they had been disenfranchised by the growth of the industry, they retained the notion of consumer democracy that had been fundamental in earlier calls to become boosters for country music. An Illinois man wrote to the fanzine *Music City News* about his interest in starting a nationwide protest. Country music lovers, he wrote, must "defend what we love and not accept what is being shoved down our throats." He reminded other disgruntled fans that the role of the audience in the commercial system offered them influence. "We must ask the D.J.s across the nation to not play any record if it hasn't got that good old Country flavor," he argued. "We must let our favorite artists know that they are going to have to keep the Country sound or else we will not buy or request their records." Another reader proposed the option of disengaging from the current commercial marketplace entirely. "I can't believe there won't always be someone that will sing my kind of music," she wrote. "But if there isn't, I've been fortunate to be able to collect a number of records that are my kind of music. I can always play them." "I am going to buy the records of those who are Country and not the ones who doesn't care if he sings [*sic*] Country or not," another reader declared.[2]

An understanding of the role that economic concerns played in shaping country music did not necessarily imply a rejection of or rebellion against industrial control of the music. Some fans accepted the influence of economic imperatives on the production of country music and assigned the blame for pop trends neither to the industry nor to a class of country listeners who were not "real fans." Instead, they invoked the principle of consumer democracy and looked to their own community for explanations. One club president, writing about the "modern country sound" that "the average country fan despises," explicitly discouraged theories about the conspiratorial use of cultural power and pointed fans instead to their own responsibility for determining trends through consumerism. "Most fans, positive in their opposition to the pop sound, are convinced it is being forced on them by some conspiracy," she wrote. "Sadly, I must argue that the bulk of the blame goes to the fan. When the performer sees that the top records on the chart belong to the country-pop idiom, he assumes this is what the fans want." Instead of railing against unresponsive Nashville executives, she opined, fans should institute "a nation-wide boycott of records utilizing a too-pop approach."[3]

When the honky-tonk artist Ray Price abandoned his traditional fiddle sound for orchestral arrangements in the early 1960s, he became a target for audience distress about the fate of the genre. One fan responded to the uproar with absolute pragmatism. "Although I prefer the steel and fiddle background I see nothing wrong with Ray Price using violins and a choral background on some of his recordings if it will help him financially," she wrote. Barbara Huss, a fan club president and frequent contributor to the letter column of *Music City News*, suggested that fans had no one to blame but themselves. Price's new singles were outselling contemporaneous releases in the older style, she argued, and "Columbia [Records] will naturally require Ray to record the songs in the manner in which the most sales are obtained." If fans wanted to hear a particular style, they would have to vote for it with their pocketbooks. "Where were all those DJs and fans who wanted Ray to record in his old style [when he released a traditional single]? It looks as though they just complained and did nothing in the way of playing and purchasing the record," Huss argued, before emphasizing again the importance of consumerism as a means of canvassing audience sentiment. "We can't expect Ray or the other artists to stay country just for our sakes when we don't do our part. . . . If we want more country sounds out on records, then we will have to do more than complain—buy, request, and play COUNTRY records."[4] Such responses revealed the extent to which country fans had accepted the logic of commercialism as both effective and just. Country listeners in the 1950s had referred regularly to the class discrimination at the heart of a system that relied on sponsors' sales results to determine what kinds of music would be available. By the mid-1960s, such laments had all but vanished.

The cultural contest over the meaning of country music's commercialism in the 1960s and early 1970s undoubtedly shaped the way audiences listened to country music and what they heard in it, but it did not overwhelm the intensely personal alternative visions of the genre that listeners created for themselves. A frequent contributor to one fan-produced magazine dismissed the controversy over the countrypolitan trend and privileged instead the emotional attachments country invoked. "I must admit I have been among those who have criticized the current trend toward 'modern' sounds, but putting all that aside, there is so much good in country music. . . . Country music is sitting alone and listening to all your favorite records, old and new, and not feeling lonely. Your friends are with you." Country, regardless of its particular style or its commercialism, provided her with a sense of friendship, home, and compassion. "No one is a stranger in country music. It is synonymous with America, although it is now popular in countries throughout the world. Country Music—Home—Friends . . . they're all one word."[5]

A New York woman expressed similar sentiments when she explained to *Country Song Roundup* that local station WJRZ had helped her through mourning for her husband, with whom she had played in a local country band for many years. "After he passed on," she wrote, "WJRZ came on with this beautiful music and you can't imagine what a wonderful pick up it was to me—it helped keep me going. I hope I haven't been a bore to you, but just wanted to let you know how this music rates with us and always will." Another woman interrupted a heated exchange over whether country artists were selling out with a reflection on some of the spiritual aspects that gave the music meaning for her. "This is what country music means to me," she wrote. "[God] gave us this music that we love. God is love, therefore He is in the beauty of music. . . . Music means more to a child of God than anyone else, because music is a thing that money cannot buy, a gift from God above." When *Music City News* published an editorial arguing that there could be no single definition for the many styles represented within country music, a Kansas man responded with a long prose poem that emphasized the role country music, whatever its stylistic bent, played in his daily life. "[Country music] is the sobbing at gravesides when a loved one has passed away. It is the clatter of rice and old tin cans at a wedding. It is the chiming of church bells calling us to worship and lifting our spirits on the Sabbath. . . . It is the sounds that we identify and live with."[6]

The personal and emotional meanings listeners attached to country music shaded easily into more categorical social identities such as class. This was particularly evident in responses to the *Music City News* editorial that elicited the poem above. The article was written as a response to fan complaints about the dominance of the Nashville Sound and the declining popularity of honky-tonk styles. The editors condemned "hot shot deejays and overheated fans" who predicted the genre's demise by dilution, arguing that it would be impossible to "take the country out of country music." The piece concluded, "No one really knows what country music is," noting that even the Country Music Association's search of two continents had failed to turn up an adequate definition. Fans leapt to the challenge, and their attempts to explain what they found upsetting about the changes in country music and how they defined the genre revealed the extent to which many of them hoped to preserve the eroding social boundaries once associated with country music.[7]

One of the very first responses rejected the editor's assertion that country listeners were "all lathered up over the use of horns, drums and strings on records by C&W stars" and suggested that the protest had more to do with the new, more genteel image countrypolitan artists projected.

> If, and I find this hard to believe, the CMA has searched two continents for a definition of country music they have wasted a lot of time and traveled to far off places for nothing. Connie Gay once said during the era of rock and roll that country music would never die because "It is the music of the land and its people." . . . That's it, the songs of life. . . . So you see, Editor Scutt, it's not the use of horns and drums the "clan and fans" are lathered up about.

Another reader wrote that he found the "hassle among MCN readers" over instrumentation and vocal backings ridiculous. Battles over stylistic differences missed the point, he argued. "People are losing sight of what country music basically is: simple music about life . . . that can be understood and appreciated by ordinary people." A number of correspondents echoed the sentiment that country music was best defined by the kinds of people who listened to it and whose lives it had most often portrayed during the preceding twenty years. A reader from Prestonsburg, Kentucky, suggested that if the CMA needed to define the genre it should "look where Country Music originates, in the country—visit the backwoods, small hamlets and towns. Ask the country people—What is Country Music? . . . Country music is country people. It's their life, their ups and downs." But the case for preserving a social definition of country music was stated most succinctly by James Kennison of Valley Station, Kentucky.

> Country music belongs first to the laboring and rural people of this country. They have no musical training and often can't even read music, but when the day's work is done they can take down the old guitar, banjo, or fiddle and play the simple songs that tell about their way of life. . . . They don't want your horns or drums—they don't want your chorus singing in the background or even the Jordanaires making little noises behind them. All that stuff is for the city people who jumped on the country music bandwagon when there turned out to be so much money in it.[8]

The Country Music Association demonstrated in market after market that its audience fell squarely into the blue-collar middle class. But income figures, home ownership statistics, and demographic studies notwithstanding, many country listeners clearly wished to preserve a rural and working-class identity for the music. In case the editors of *Music City News* had misunderstood his first letter, James Kennison followed up with another the next month. Complaining about the television coverage of the CMA's Country Music Week, he grumbled that the *Lawrence Welk Show*'s guest for its country salute was Eddy Arnold, "a man who gave up country music just as soon as he got rich enough to buy his first tuxedo."[9]

These class tensions were particularly apparent in an exchange that took place in the U.S. Army newspaper *Stars and Stripes* in 1961. The fracas began when the paper reprinted a UPI review of a country music television special that began, "The big question about country music is which country should take the blame for it. . . . If it was United States country music, it's no wonder we've become a nation of city dwellers." The paper was inundated with protests, many of which noted that while the paper covered pop and jazz weekly in its entertainment section, country music was rarely mentioned. Technical Sergeant Paul Graupp went so far as to equate the three genres with strict social divisions between their audiences and suggested the cultural skirmishes that took place around musical allegiances. "I know a lot of people within this small area who were angered by the article and a lot of hard feelings that were created by the three different categories of music listeners," he wrote. "Anyone who has the slightest idea of music and the entertainment field as it pertains to soldiers should know the basic lesson of how much these individual music traits mean to each of us. To blast one is to add to the dismay of those blasted and the glee of those on the other side." Whatever other identities might have been at play in the social contest over aesthetic worth, though, Graupp ultimately viewed it as a class conflict. "A retraction would be in order, but then this isn't an ordinary newspaper, is it? The viewpoint one gets from reading the various columns is that only the white-collar, blue-nose, and socially listed parties have any business reading the newspaper."[10]

Another letter writer, obviously working from the assumption that the reviewer's distaste reflected class condescension, argued that this critic should be careful about looking down on country artists who had surpassed him in class status. "Apparently Mr. Scott hasn't realized that [the artists on the show] are in a much higher income bracket than he is," he cautioned. Several felt that the review was out of keeping with the Army's policy of meritocracy and pluralism. One division stationed in Spain wrote a group letter reaffirming the need for tolerance. "We (the men of our division) are from different parts of the United States, including Pennsylvania, Wisconsin, Nebraska, California, Texas, Florida, and New York. We ourselves do not enjoy all kinds of music but we believe in 'live and let live.'" The Army rushed to agree, declaring country music a symbol of American heritage with the potential to affect troop morale. Senior commanders received orders banning the use of "hillbilly" and other derogatory terms to refer to country music in Army publications and official speech.[11]

In the 1960s, to an even greater degree than in earlier eras, fans were aware of and concerned about the commercialism of country music. The industry reaped what it had sown in the 1950s, as many listeners insisted that the genre maintain the class position it had so carefully staked out during its lean years. Others applied the notion of consumer democracy to argue that the stylistic direction of the industry justly reflected the preferences of the fans. But for the most part, fans adopted a philosophy that many of them called "live and let live." While they were aware of the influence of commercial considerations on the kinds of country music they heard on radio and record, they simply chose those songs and artists they liked and ignored the others. As it had for decades, country

Commercialism and Tradition

music, and the business surrounding it, continued to fulfill intensely personal needs.

"TO ENSURE THAT COUNTRY MUSIC RETAINS ITS INDIVIDUALITY"

While some fans continued to fume over the cultural condescension they perceived among audiences for more "highbrow" musical pursuits, the CMA embarked on a less combative strategy. The organization and the industry executives it represented were not particularly concerned about whether advertisers or other white-collar professionals enjoyed country music as listeners, only whether they saw it as an effective sales vehicle. But in the 1960s the association undertook a number of projects that would appeal to one unconquered audience it did care about: the critics and intellectuals who wielded traditional cultural authority and who had ridiculed the genre since its inception. Ironically, the industry, fans, and former critics alike all embraced the only part of the CMA's platform that actually *was* consciously aimed in part at making country music more palatable to those who might previously have scorned it. Through the development of the Country Music Hall of Fame and Museum and the Foundation Library and Media Center, the Country Music Foundation created a forum for the academic and popular study of country music history that finally unified vernacular and commercial forms of the music into a single canon.

In the early 1960s, the CMA's membership application form outlined a three-part mission for the organization. Two elements, making the advertising industry more aware of the selling power of country music and securing more broadcasting time on radio and television, were accomplished through the kinds of programming and promotion efforts already discussed. The third section of the statement of purpose seemed odd in its context, sandwiched as it was between the concrete pledge to increase country airtime and the concluding assertion that the CMA proposed to "make advertisers and broadcasters aware of [the] fact" that country music was a "tried and proven means of reaching the masses." This third section declared that the CMA intended "to promote Country Music in its entirety, with no selfish motives; to encourage the highest ethics throughout the industry; and to ensure that Country Music retains its individuality."[12]

This element of the mission statement clearly reflected the pride the organization's founders and members took in the heritage of country music, but it also spoke to the same legacy of cultural inferiority that was so sharply expressed in the advertising and broadcast marketing scripts. As soon as hillbilly became a recognizable genre of commercial popular music, preservationists, intellectuals, and cultural critics had dismissed it, not only on aesthetic grounds but because they perceived it as a vulgar commercialization of valuable folk art. In its broadcast marketing campaign, the CMA had found ways of using commercialism to gain the respect of executives in the entertainment field. But in this section of the mission statement, the organization betrayed the industry's own continuing unease with the effects of producing country music through the structures of commercial mass media. As it was executed, then, the full mission statement could be expected to present something of a contradiction. On the one hand, the CMA sought to improve the genre's cultural standing by reference to its economic power; on the other it sought to downplay the music's commercialism by emphasizing its preservation of cultural tradition and folk roots.

The ambivalence the CMA mission statement revealed about the effects of participating fully in the mass media marketplace was not new to the industry. It had been the source of much of the fractiousness that had prompted the formation of the organization. And while the CMA represented an effort to control that participation rather than retreat from it, the association continued to search for ways to mitigate the worst potential effects of the marketplace. The mission statement was abstract, but its concrete origins could be read through nonetheless. The specter of payola and underhanded business tactics had already been the source of attacks against the field's business interests and its cultural value during the 1958 congressional hearings. Centralization of production and loss of the disc jockey-promoter-entrepreneur created opportunities for abuses of power and excessive faddishness within the field. And while few in the business envisioned the kinds of apocalyptic scenarios of extinction or total absorption that fan writers to *Country Song Roundup* and *Music City News* forecasted in their letters, uncertainty lingered about how to manage articulation with the larger pop industry while still remaining distinct.[13]

These concerns, which would ultimately result in the formation of the Country Music Hall of Fame and then Foundation, attracted the board's attention as early as 1959, even while the future of the organization remained in some jeopardy. They emerged first in an extended discussion about devising a "definition" for country music. In part this was simply the old issue of nomenclature rearing its head once again. Some worried that the term "country" didn't go far enough in erasing the hayseed image that the label "hillbilly" had once evoked, or that the label imposed a false geographic limitation on the music and its audience. But the debate inevitably invoked the thornier issues of establishing generic boundaries and maintaining institutional and stylistic independence. Patrolling generic borders against interlopers and opportunists had been a central preoccupation of the CMA's progenitor, the CMDJA, so it was not surprising that one deejay representative, Cracker Jim Brooker, was particularly adamant that the board should make the formulation of a definition for country music its top priority. The first board struggled with the issue throughout 1959 and finally, just before the annual membership meeting, deferred further discussion to the incoming board, citing "differences of opinion" over one suggested definition.[14]

The issue of defining and renaming the field continued to occupy the organization over the next several years. A number of ideas were proposed: American music, countrypolitan, metropolitan, town and country. (Connie B. Gay, who owned the licensing rights to the phrase "Town and Country," ceded them to the CMA for use in its marketing in 1966.) The industry was no more able than fans, however, to reach consensus about an appropriate definition. In 1960, *Music Reporter* editor Charlie Lamb, who, as a member of the CMA's first board of directors, had suffered through much of the discussion himself, issued a tongue-in-cheek invitation to anyone with an idea for "a bigger, better, more descriptive name than 'country'" to step forward. The paper warned readers, however, that "the proponent of a new name for country music [would] probably encounter a shower of brickbats" for his or her trouble. The controversy was so heated in part because of fundamental disagreements over what, exactly, was being named. "Nobody could really give a concise definition," Jo Walker said later. "It's pretty difficult. How would you define rock or jazz or other types of music? And define it broadly to tell the story."[15]

As time went on, the CMA focused more and more of its energies on simply telling the story rather than on trying to define an essence for country music. This historically driven approach allowed for the inclusion of a broad array of styles and for a contextual understanding of what counted as country rather than one based on sound, instrumentation, or style. Joe Allison later remarked on the importance of these relative meanings and historical outcomes in understanding the boundaries of the genre. "The first time I ever heard Elvis Presley, I laughed my head off," he said, emphasizing the difference between initial perception based on sound and the complex constructions of meaning that audiences and the industry created over time. "After a while it's an image, not a sound." The Hall of Fame and Museum allowed the CMA and the industry to create a flexible image of country music that was still distinct from other genres.[16]

The importance of history as a method of controlling the contemporary meaning of the genre was evident in the origins of the idea for a hall of fame. The concept had been suggested as early as 1955, when, at the height of industry disunity, the CMDJA and WSM had simultaneously announced their separate plans to establish halls of fame. In that context, the hall of fame had been part of a struggle within the field for control over the centralization of the industry in Nashville; now it became a unified attempt to retain a measure of independence from the larger music industry. In August 1960, a good portion of the quarterly board meeting was again consumed by discussion of centralization and loss of identity. While Paul Ackerman, a trade publications representative, argued that "the centralization of the music business was the best tonic for American music as a whole," and that music production would never again be controlled by New York and Los Angeles, Cracker Jim Brooker countered with the fear that "with integration we lose identity." At some time during this meeting or the next, the notion of a hall of fame was resurrected. *Close-Up* reported after the first quarterly meeting of 1961 the cryptic information that items that had been discussed by the board "show some very promising news for the Country Music industry." The newsletter could reveal no more because plans had "not been finalized."[17]

In fact, the directors had apparently decided to follow Ackerman's advice that the industry should "honor the past—the roots—let the past serve as a fount of inspiration" but "gladly accept development and change which comes naturally." Rather than limiting the genre in the present by constructing a rigid definition, the CMA moved to create a historical definition through a hall of fame. Once the idea was conceived, plans were formulated with surprising rapidity. Steve Sholes of RCA and Roy Horton of Peer-Southern Music were dispatched to Cooperstown to visit the Baseball Hall of Fame and learn more about its electoral procedures. By the time preparations were being finalized for the next meeting of the board in May, news of the new Hall of Fame was out. *Close-Up* reported with obvious excitement that the issue would be on the agenda and that "near 100% attendance is expected at this important meeting." The board agreed to model the Country Music Hall of Fame on the principles of the Cooperstown hall (though it later amended these rules) and empanelled a committee of "100 well-qualified men and women in the Country Music business" to serve as electors. In July the organization reported that the idea had "met with widespread approval" and that ballots for the first election of inductees would soon be mailed.[18]

In November 1961, less than a year from the start of planning, the first members of the Hall of Fame were announced at the Third Annual CMA Banquet at the Hillwood Country Club. CMA president Ken Nelson unveiled three bronze plaques honoring Jimmie Rodgers, Hank Williams, and Fred Rose as the Hall's first inductees and presented the honorees' widows with certificates bearing the words of each plaque's inscription. In spite of the pomp and reverence, though, the Hall of Fame consisted of little more than the plaques themselves. Since the CMA owned no public space of its own in which to display the plaques, they were relegated to the lower level of the War Memorial Building in Nashville as a special exhibit in the Tennessee State Museum. The trades appropriately highlighted the Hall of Fame's founding and eulogized the inductees, but the Hall remained an institution aimed largely at the industry itself. The field's largest fan publication, *Country Song Roundup*, merely noted the formation of the new Hall of Fame in an article devoted to the WSM Festival and National Country Music Week. In its own homage to the Hall of Fame, the CMA dwelt on its importance to the industry more than to fans and contrasted the spiritual and commercial riches the field had produced. The purpose of the Hall, the CMA told its members, was not only to preserve an important part of Americana but also "to remind you that our industry has made contributions to this land of ours. To remind you that Country Music and the people who create it, love it and promote it, are people rich in the greatest assets of all—compassion, love and dignity." As soon as the Hall of Fame was announced, the CMA began to talk in general terms about the possibility of erecting a building that could house the Hall of Fame, a museum, and the organization's office space. But in the fall of 1961, the association had only just pulled itself out of the dire financial straits of its early years. A construction project of the magnitude a building would require was still far beyond the association's means, as *Close-Up* wistfully acknowledged. "Some day," the newsletter remarked, "CMA hopes to see a Country Music Building spring up where the Hall of Fame can find a permanent home."[19]

In the meantime, the association focused its efforts on other, less expensive symbols of tradition, respect, and individuality. The most notable of these was the institution of National Country Music Week in conjunction with the annual WSM Disc Jockey Festival. The CMA had declared and celebrated the first National Country Music Week in 1961, but in 1962 the organization launched a concerted effort to obtain official status for the observance. In June, Representative Otis Pike of New York introduced a resolution in the House calling for observance of the week as a "tribute to the native country music of America and to the men and women who devote their lives to its creation and preservation." While the rhetoric of citizens and pioneers had ceased to hold much meaning in the context of the industry's image of itself, it remained a central trope in efforts to establish respect among traditional cultural authorities. By October, as the CMA announced a series of special episodes on network variety shows and the mailing of celebrity radio spot announcements in honor of Country Music Week, the resolution had passed in the Senate. Ironically, one of the motion's key proponents in the Senate was none other than John Pastore, the senator from Rhode Island who had directed questioning during congressional hearings on the Smathers Bill.[20]

The success of Country Music Week in 1962 also marked the beginning of an accommodation between the country industry and its sometimes reluctant home. The country business and its participants had suffered the same slights and condescension from Nashville's social elite as from the cultured classes anywhere. This was not only because the city's upper crust thought country music was cheap and trashy but also because the growing popularity of the genre, and its association with Nashville, threatened to undo decades of cultural work that had earned the city a reputation as the "Athens of the South." As publishers and recording studios settled in along Sixteenth Avenue South—a working-class, racially mixed neighborhood that the city's wealthy had abandoned years before—the music industry and downtown business interests agreed to have as little to do with each other as possible. The journalist Patrick Carr later mused that a good deal of the industry's image polishing in the sixties and seventies was probably "motivated not by economics, but by the simple craving for full acceptance in Nashville's better country clubs." Carr may have overstated the case, but the CMA was

Commercialism and Tradition

founded in part on the promise that it could make the country industry a respectable business for its practitioners, and in its most practical form that required gaining acceptance in the community where they lived.[21]

Industry leaders and the CMA had had mixed success in gaining local and state support. Governor Frank Clement had appeared before Congress on behalf of country music, but his successor, Buford Ellington, consistently ignored the country industry, hampering efforts to promote the genre and develop industry-related tourism. Thus, when the CMA approached Nashville civic leaders about the possibility of collaborating on tourism connected with Country Music Week, the organization was prepared for the controversy that ensued. The CMA hoped that the city would welcome visitors to the fall WSM Festival and officially recognize a new nickname that had originated in the music trade press and begun to spread to popular usage: Music City USA. The image of the city was at stake, and Nashville's cultural elite was more than a bit dismayed. Even Jo Walker, executive director for the CMA, understood the ambivalence that many residents felt at the suggestion of the rechristening. She found herself caught between her pride in the work of the CMA and the image she knew outsiders would attach to her adoptive hometown as a result of its association with country music. Though she hoped that the city would officially recognize the music's contribution to Nashville, she "also wanted people to think that Nashville was a center of culture and learning," she later told an interviewer. "I guess I was thinking more at that time about the Yankees, or the Northerners, thinking that we Southerners didn't wear shoes, et cetera. But I thought it was kind of a reaction that we expected."[22]

The city fathers may have, as Walker recalled, "thought of us as more or less unwashed hillbillies out here on Music Row," but by the early 1960s, for the first time, the country industry in Nashville commanded enough economic power to demand at least the appearance of respect. The growth of the industry had fueled a substantial real estate and development boom in the run-down Sixteenth Avenue neighborhood. One real estate agent marveled, "What the music people did for this neighborhood is as sensational as some of the tunes they have produced. They . . . took a tired blood, worn-out area and gave it a transfusion of vigor." It was unclear whether the agent was more impressed by the role of "New York capital" investment in Nashville, or the fact that much of the development had been accomplished "with money the participants earned right here in Nashville in their chosen professions." In any case, the tangible benefits of being home to a major entertainment industry were beginning to be noticed.[23]

In light of this economic clout, the city negotiated a compromise position. Mayor Ben West announced that the city would post new signs on all of the highways into town reading, "Welcome to Nashville, Home of the Grand Ole Opry, Music City USA." The existing signs welcoming visitors to the Athens of the South would stay. But Mayor West's public remarks on the subject made clear that the arrangement was based on a common interest in economic development rather than on a reevaluation of country's place in the cultural scheme. "The city has procrastinated too long in recognizing its No. 1 tourist attraction, the 'Grand Ole Opry,'" he told those assembled at a small ceremony in October. "We are indeed proud of it and the $35 million music industry it has fathered in Nashville."[24]

The next month, when the new board met at the end of the WSM celebration to discuss its agenda for the coming year, the subject of a building to house the Hall of Fame was broached in earnest. In addition to housing the CMA's offices, a new building would allow for a significant expansion of the historical mission of the Hall of Fame. The proposal included plans for "an extensive museum of memorabilia" that would help make those in the industry, fans, and the general public more aware of the history of the genre. After the second quarterly meeting in May 1963, the *Music Reporter* boasted of the "CMA's plans for a 2-million dollar combination CMA headquarters and C&W museum." Such an expensive building would be "quite an investment," the paper conceded, but reminded tradesters and Nashvillians alike that, thanks to the millions generated by the country industry, "Music City [had] proved to be a very profitable place to invest." Too profitable, in fact, for the CMA to be able to afford land in the neighborhood that was now called Music Row, where real estate speculation was rampant. Instead, the organization approached the mayor of the newly consolidated city-county metro government for support, assuring him that the museum would stimulate tourism in the city.[25]

Mayor Ben West had cooperated cordially with the CMA, but Nashville-Davidson County metropolitan mayor Beverly Briley enthusiastically embraced the organization and the industry. In November 1963, Briley attended the Fifth Annual CMA Banquet to announce that he would grant the CMA a prime piece of land, Tony Rose Park, at the very head of Music Row. As gratifying to members of the CMA as the grant itself was Briley's

Commercialism and Tradition

rhetoric and symbolism. The music industry's contribution to Nashville was not only economic, he told his audience, but cultural as well. He even averred that country music had made "a major contribution to Metro Nashville and Davidson County" in popularizing its image as "Music City USA." Perhaps most important of all, he affirmed the role that many local residents in the business hoped they played; he appointed a dozen country music artists and businessmen Metropolitan Ambassadors, complete with sash and seal. Briley's willingness to recognize the country industry and its representatives as valuable cultural agents marked a seismic shift in the city's attitude toward its biggest business.[26]

Still, however much the mayor's enthusiasm set a new tone in the city, the CMA realized that his support alone would not be sufficient to overcome the series of financial, building, and zoning hurdles the organization would face as it moved forward with the building project. Indeed, no sooner had the grant been made than it was opposed in the city council, which eventually insisted that the land be leased rather than granted outright. The CMA also hoped that local businessmen with an interest in increased tourism would provide financial support for the Hall of Fame building. The scripted stage show had proven to be an effective way of communicating the CMA's new image to indifferent executives in other urban areas, so it was not surprising that the association's first attempt to "establish ourselves as a real industry and part of the community," as Jo Walker later described it, came in the form of a sales show for the Nashville Chamber of Commerce.[27]

The lineup of the show was nearly identical to the one presented for the Sales Executives Club of New York the previous May. Leon McAuliff, Sue Thompson, Flatt and Scruggs, the Anita Kerr Singers, and Jim Reeves (replacing Don Gibson) represented a range of country styles including western swing, rockabilly, bluegrass, and the Nashville Sound. The script differed significantly in its content and intent, though. Just as the other sales scripts had attempted to demonstrate the economic impact country music could have for sponsors, the Nashville show, retitled "The Nashville Sound," demonstrated the economic impact the industry had on the city. More importantly, it consistently positioned Nashville as a cultural center whose influence, at least in the music field, now matched that of New York or Los Angeles. The city might be forced to abandon its reputation as the pinnacle of Southern academic achievement, but in return it would become a global cultural power on par with any in America. "This music and its by-products do, in essence, *begin* in Nashville and *spread* to the far reaches of the globe and, in turn, re-direct the attention of the world to its source," emcee Tex Ritter told his audience. Within a few months, the city would even host its second world movie premier for Jim Reeves's new feature, *Kimberley Jim*, filmed on location in South Africa. Forward-looking civic leaders, the show suggested, would embrace and advance the city's new role as a world cultural center. "With the help of experts in sympathetic areas, who know a good thing when they see it," the text concluded, "the Country music industry can be a proud ambassador that can very well attract the eyes of the world, to be directed toward the center of its creation: the Country Music Capitol of the World, Nashville, Tennessee."[28]

In addition to proposing an image of Nashville as a new center of cultural production and influence, the show addressed more personal fears about the industry's impact on life in the city. Like the other scripts, this show emphasized the professionalism of the musicians and technicians who produced country music. But where the New York show had been aimed at making advertising executives feel comfortable doing business in the country field, the Nashville script undertook the more sensitive task of making its audience feel comfortable living next door to the industry and its agents. Whenever possible, it referred not only to the professional status of the participating artists but to their conventional, respectable personal lives as well. The songwriters Boudleaux and Felice Bryant were described as "that highly intelligent, extremely talented and not-to-be-disputed paragon of community integrity and his altogether charming wife," though the script's writer, Joe Allison, appears finally to have thought the portrait too hyperbolic and asked Tex Ritter to ad-lib something a little less exaggerated. The narrative harmonized the Boudleaux's private home recording studio with images of their luxurious suburban house, complete with the chaos of children who had to be watched lest they "drop a sandwich, track in mud with their sneakers," or wreak havoc with "the mysteries of their new chemistry set." Wesley Rose was portrayed not primarily as a successful publisher but as a responsible employer on his way to a company bowling team meet. Chet Atkins's wife became one of the "girls," playing "first up, closest, first in . . . during their golf match at the country club." The overt message of the text was the industry's impact on Nashville's economy, but the CMA obviously hoped that the audience would also take away an image of industry figures leading ordinary lives in traditionally respectable communities.[29]

In spite of its efforts to present the country industry as a good corporate neighbor, the CMA found little local support in its fundraising for the Hall of Fame building and soon turned to more promising avenues of assistance. In February 1964, the board named Judge Robert Jay Burton, a president of BMI, to chair the building's fundraising committee. The committee mobilized every possible constituency in its fund drive, but ultimately the museum was underwritten by music corporations and direct marketing record sales. In March, CMA members were informed that any individual or organization donating $10,000 would have its name placed on a bronze plaque in the new museum. The first donation was received from the association's founding president, Connie B. Gay, and other donors soon followed, including BMI, RCA, Columbia, Decca, Mercury, Peer International, and Hill & Range. After a fundraising luncheon for industry representatives in New York, the CMA announced that it had collected more than half of the $300,000 it hoped to raise by January 1, 1965. By May, the design of the new museum had been determined, and *Close-Up* sported a new masthead featuring an architect's sketch of the proposed museum, a barn-shaped building with a glass façade.[30]

Throughout the summer, the CMA continued to raise funds, but additional donations were coming into the coffers more slowly. Between January and May, the association had raised $170,000. In November, *Billboard* reported that the organization had about $200,000 in its fund. At the WSM convention that fall, Jo Walker was so busy that she couldn't make time to sit down with a visitor from California who wanted to make a business proposition. A volunteer assistant finally took a few minutes to talk with the man, who told her about the success he was having using television advertising and direct mailing to sell compilation albums of old rock hits. He wondered whether the CMA would be interested in working with him on a country equivalent. Harry Stone had suggested the same idea as a fundraiser in the very first days of the CMA, but at the time there had been no effective way for the organization to administer the advertising and sales effort the project would have required. Now that such a marketing mechanism was available, Jo Walker realized, a greatest hits album could provide the association with the remaining funds it needed to build the Hall of Fame.[31]

In January, Walker took the premium album idea to the board and received approval to pursue a contract with Martin Gilbert Advertising to produce and market *Famous Original Hits by 25 Great Country Music*

Artists. Gilbert agreed to make an initial "donation" of $25,000 to the Country Music Foundation and to pay not less than $85,000 in royalties, or 11.5 cents an album for the first half million copies sold, and 6.75 cents for each copy sold after that. (Dick Schofield later negotiated an increase in the per-copy royalty after 500,000.) Roy Horton negotiated with the artists, publishers, and record companies for rights to the album's songs for a period of eighteen months. Columbia pressed the albums, as it had Gilbert's previous projects, beginning with an order of 500,000 copies. Ironically, in spite of the album's historical mission, it was itself almost devoid of historical sensibility. The twenty-five selections chosen by the CMA board for inclusion represented a range of sounds, from the smooth crooning of Jim Reeves to the honky-tonk style of Ernest Tubb and Hank Williams. But the list of artists was conspicuously dominated by contemporaneous favorites such as Bill Anderson, Bobby Bare, Roger Miller, Don Gibson, and Marty Robbins. The artists who would become the mainstays of the country music canon before 1940 were absent, and even those whose careers touched on the pre–World War II era, such as Red Foley and Roy Acuff, were still active and well-known performers in the mid-1960s. The museum was not built, then, on the history that it would ultimately preserve, but on the commercially successful country music of its own day.[32]

The power of country format radio was also critical to generating the funds necessary to build the museum. Martin Gilbert Advertising had been founded on sales of television advertising time, not records, and Gilbert originally planned to market *Famous Original Hits* exclusively on television. The CMA insisted, however, that he exploit country's strongest medium, its new format radio stations. As the association had predicted, these outlets became the album's strongest sellers. WJRZ in New York sold over 15,000 copies of the record in three months, more than triple the sales of the local CBS-TV affiliate. KFOX in Los Angeles sold more than 8,000 copies, and Sacramento's KRAK sold an additional 6,000. Format stations far outpaced their block-programming rivals in the country field, demonstrating the power of format radio to command its audience's loyalty and sell product. Moreover, sales were strong throughout the country, in urban and rural areas alike. The album was released in June 1965, and by January of the following year it had already sold 600,000 copies, well on its way to the million and a half that it would ultimately sell. In December 1965, with the requisite $300,000 in its fund, the CMA signed a building contract for the new museum and broke ground at the site in March of the following year.[33]

When the museum finally opened in the spring of 1967, it proved to be an even bigger tourist attraction than the CMA had hoped. The first visitors through the door were the Marvin Posts of St. Paul, Minnesota, and they were followed by tens of thousands of others each year. The CMA estimated that during the peak summer months, the museum hosted about 4,000 visitors each week. By year's end, some 70,000 visitors had been through the museum, "not counting tours of school children." Ultimately, even city and state leaders realized that the tourism associated with country music was big business in its own right. By the end of the decade, the city's landscape was permanently inscribed with the symbolic geography of country music. The street in front of the Ryman Auditorium became Opry Place, and the CMA's home at the corner of Division and Sixteenth was renamed Music Square East. The airport was redecorated with a country music theme and "Tennessee Waltz" adopted as the state song. Even those who disliked the camp image the industry sometimes imparted to the city acknowledged its importance nonetheless. In 1969, the manager of the Nashville Area Chamber of Commerce Conventions and Visitors Division explained to a reporter that while some discomfort lingered, the city's "first-family people" were finally becoming accustomed to the idea that country music was just another business. Besides, he observed, "The top people are becoming more acutely aware of what country music means to Nashville. If the music industry left town today, can you imagine what it'd do to this place?"[34]

THE STORY OF COUNTRY MUSIC

Country music's economic contribution to the city was no doubt the most important factor in Nashville society's acceptance, however begrudging, of the industry. The attention the mainstream press had given what had become the nation's second-most important recording center also helped to legitimate the activities taking place on Music Row. But the change of heart also reflected important shifts in high culture, particularly the impact of the urban folk revival and another swing of the pendulum of intellectual attitudes toward popular and mass culture. By the mid-1960s, the CMA was well placed to take advantage of these developments. The organization had already recognized the importance of tradition and historical context in defining its unique appeal, and the historicizing project was just the kind of activity, benefiting the entire industry equally, that the association looked for. In 1964, the CMA formalized its educational and cultural initiatives in the Country Music Foundation, which soon oversaw the Hall of Fame and Museum and the Country Music Foundation Library and Media Center. Though the new entity was created primarily to allow for tax-deductible charitable donations to the Hall of Fame building from fans and other non-industry supporters, it gave a distinct institutional life and focus to the CMA's cultural mission. Together, the institutions of the Country Music Foundation helped to produce a historical tradition that unified a diverse array of styles—from string bands and western swing to bluegrass and rockabilly—into a single narrative. The elements of the narrative had always existed, but the tradition was neither clearly codified nor widely known until the economic and cultural powers of the commercial industry were harnessed to the task of promoting it. Through the efforts of the CMA and the Country Music Foundation, cultural power and cultural authority were fused in a single voice.[35]

In the late 1950s, the twentieth-century folk revival emerged from its McCarthy-era hibernation to sweep from Swarthmore, Newport, and Washington Square to collegiate coffeehouses across the country. The urban folk revival of the late 1950s and early 1960s pointed to possibilities for new relationships between commercialism and high culture. Commercial recordings by country artists like the Carter Family, Uncle Dave Macon, and even more recent stars like Flatt and Scruggs were suddenly transformed from "cheap tunes based on ancient Broadway hits," as the preservationist Annabel Morris Buchanan had scornfully labeled hillbilly music in her day, into iconoclastic statements of folk culture. This alchemy was accomplished, not as it had been in the past, through concealment or ignorance of the music's commercial origins, but simply, as Robert Cantwell has written, as "a matter of imaginative and material making." The folkniks demonstrated that they could make commercial products the basis of a rejection of mass and consumer culture simply by appropriating those products for their own purposes and creating through their own performances a new authenticity for the music.[36]

The same movement taking intuitive, emotional form on campus squares and dormitory floors was finding critical and theoretical expression in classrooms and academic journals. In 1960, a small group of folklorists and aficionados—Archie Green, Ed Kahn, D. K. Wilgus, Gene Earle, and Fred Hoeptner—chartered the John Edwards Memorial Foundation (JEMF) to curate the collection of an aspiring young folklorist from Australia who had been killed in a car accident. For several years the JEMF remained a shared personal preoccupation among the group. Then, in 1964, they succeeded in formalizing an affiliation with the University of California, Los Angeles, and moved into UCLA's Folklore and Mythology Center. The foundation began to publish the JEMF Newsletter to share archival materials from the collection and present and encourage scholarship related to early commercial hillbilly. A year later, D. K. Wilgus, the record review editor for the *Journal of American Folklore*, gathered a collection of the group's work to be published in the *Journal*'s seminal "Hillbilly Issue." The urban folk revivalists seemed to believe intuitively that commercialization did not determine the meaning of cultural products; the writings collected in the "Hillbilly Issue" explicitly theorized the relationship between folk and popular culture, between commercialism and authenticity.[37]

In his introduction to the issue, Wilgus proposed that a full understanding of American folk music required "more careful distinctions" than any that could be made through a binary opposition between "commercial" and "folk." He and other contributors emphasized the extent to which the folk culture of late-nineteenth-century rural America was based on continual interaction with urban commercial culture, and he noted the enduring influence of pre-commercial forms and styles on commercial popular music. Wilgus also issued a call specifically for study of the business of country music, writing, "The most significant study of hillbilly music will reach beyond the normal domain of the folklorist, examining [the hillbilly] section of the music business as one aspect of American popular culture." A number of contributors noted the paucity of original materials and the factual errors that had already been introduced into the historical record through excessive reliance on oral history and popular press accounts. They expressed the hope that the JEMF would become a central repository for important materials that would alleviate some of these distortions.[38]

In spite of a theoretical embrace of commercial country music on its own terms, though, the majority of the scholarship produced by folklorists continued to reflect a preoccupation with the aspects of the business that were historically distant enough to be "excessively dead." Scholarly study of contemporary country music would not take shape for several more years, with Bill Malone's *Country Music USA*, a book originating as a dissertation under the purview of business history rather than folklore, comparative literature, or American studies. Careful attention to commercial culture in its own right would develop through somewhat independent channels, such as the soon-to-be-formed Popular Culture Association. Still, even if the revivalists and folklorists of the early 1960s were animated primarily by their concern for a folk tradition that only occasionally intersected with commercial country music, they were willing to accept that commercial music could express more complex phenomena than just the cupidity of its makers. The mutually reinforcing movements in popular and intellectual culture brought together the cultural power of the entertainment industries and the cultural authority of the academy to promote a new popular understanding of commercial country music that industry figures like John Lair and Art Satherly had been advancing for decades with only marginal success.[39]

In Nashville, the value of this realization was perhaps less important than the simple fact that the well-educated scions of the East Coast cultural oligarchy had not only embraced commercial country music but gravitated to the most discordant, nasal, and twangy of its styles. Jack Hurst, a columnist for the *Nashville Tennessean*, informed readers that country music had finally become culturally acceptable because the folk revival "put an emphasis on authenticity and history, always a major stock in trade in country music's big store of material." Joe Allison later offered a similar explanation to *Billboard*. An academic presentation of country music as history, he said, "gives the college kids something they can apply an intellectual approach to and study." The reporter to whom he spoke agreed, observing that "digging country music is the in thing with the college kids, who enjoy anything which gives them a chance for intellectual discussion."[40]

The idea of supplementing the Hall of Fame with a museum that could popularize the history of country music had emerged early in discussions of the new building. But with the upsurge in formal academic attention to country music, some members of the CMA began to see the enormous cultural value of stimulating intellectual inquiry into the genre's history. Nonetheless, the idea of supporting a popular museum by developing a research library and archive met with some resistance from the CMA board initially. Joe Allison contacted the JEMF for help in selling the concept, and Ed Kahn, the executive secretary, enthusiastically offered his assistance. Kahn and others on the JEMF board felt that corporate involvement in the preservation and popularization of the history of folk and country music was critical not only to the academic project but also to the value, or lack of it, that was popularly attached to country as a cultural form. Kahn may have betrayed his own ignorance of earlier historicizing efforts by people like Lair and Satherly, but his admonition to the industry that it should take a leading role in supporting and popularizing its own history was timely nonetheless. "The public image of country music certainly will not change until the self-image of the industry itself changes. Not even the first step has been taken to bring respect to this large segment of the music business. There is probably no equally large segment of the American economy that has existed for so long without attempting in some way to understand or explain itself. . . . Area after area of popular culture has seen to it that popular histories are written, but country music has not even managed to encourage one good article!"[41]

In August 1965, Kahn was invited to meet with the CMA board in San Francisco to discuss the founding and mission of the JEMF. Shortly thereafter, he guided several board members on a tour of the foundation's facilities at UCLA and explained some of the organization's projects: the newsletter, record reissues, and other scholarship that had emerged from the materials in the collection. The board began to warm to the idea of creating a similar repository in Nashville. *Close-Up* explained the importance of such cultural work to CMA members, describing the JEMF's mission as "educating the public to the value of [country] music as a part of its cultural heritage." Kahn and the other directors of the JEMF "made it clear the [JEMF] serves its purpose best at UCLA" but offered their assistance to the CMA as it set up the museum and library. In September, the CMA voted to provide the JEMF with a $2,500 annual scholarship for a research assistant whose immediate task would be to photocopy the holdings of the archive to serve as the basis for the CMA's own collection. Archie Green indirectly made possible the donation of an important personal collection of memorabilia and correspondence amassed by a country music aficionado who had been killed in Vietnam. The CMA contacted trade publications to solicit donations of back issues. By the time its space was ready, the library had already begun to accumulate an important collection.[42]

As building plans progressed, space for the new library was allocated in a mezzanine loft, and within two years of the building's opening, expansion was under way to make more room for the archive. In formulating the library's mission statement, the CMA addressed not only the importance of historical research for improving the cultural status of country music but also the issue of self-respect that Ed Kahn had raised in his call for corporate historymaking. On the one hand, the Country Music Foundation Library would "enhance the cultural and educational values of country and western music as a genuine and dynamic folk expression" by "mak[ing] available the materials of various media for learning and research." But the library was also to serve as a resource for improving the self-esteem of the industry. By becoming "a research center for all people concerned with country and western music . . . recording artists, their agents, musicians, composers, disc jockeys, radio and television personnel, music publishers, trade publications, and the recording industry," the library would offer those in the industry an opportunity to celebrate their achievements and tradition.[43]

In spite of their intertwined historical origins, though, the fates of the Country Music Foundation Library and the JEMF collection diverged, in large part because of the different relationships each institution cultivated with the country business and academe. The scholars attached to the JEMF did not draw the traditional bright line between commercial and folk, but they tended nonetheless to focus on past artists whose lack of commercial value in the present returned them to a kind of folk status. The JEMF maintained a healthy, though far from antagonistic, distance from the Country Music Foundation and from the influence of the industry. It continued to function exclusively as a traditional scholarly archive and suffered as a result from the financial uncertainty that so often plagues academic institutions. By the late 1960s, the JEMF was consistently running deficits. A group of supporters organized a series of benefits during the early 1970s that kept the organization afloat, but by 1983 the JEMF was too far in debt to UCLA to recover. The JEMF holdings were sold to the University of North Carolina and became part of the Southern Folklife Collection.[44]

The Country Music Foundation Library, by contrast, celebrated contemporary commercialism without reservation. Indeed, the library and the Hall of Fame became another way in which the industry and fans mobilized commercial success in the pursuit of respectability and cultural legitimacy. The library's proximity to the artists and businesspeople of Music Row gave archivists and oral historians unparalleled access to sources. Sustained corporate support and income from the museum itself made for a generous income flow that allowed the library to assemble one of the most sweeping collections of popular music artifacts and documents in the world. Once the material was available, it stimulated scholarly as well as popular interest. A WSM promotion director noted in 1967 the sudden "unusual interest on the part of college students . . . from the Ivy League to the western junior colleges." By decade's end, the seedy commercialism of country music had spawned a thoroughly dignified center for cultural research.[45]

Perhaps because of its institutional ties to the entertainment industries, the library also became a more important resource than the JEMF in the creation of a popular history of country music. No sooner had the archive been installed in the new Hall of Fame building than the CMA began to collaborate with NBC for the first comprehensive network television documentary history of country, *Music from the Land*, narrated by Eddy Arnold. In the mid-1970s, the archivist Danny Hatcher estimated that about half of the library's inquiries came from scholars but that the other half came from "various segments of the entertainment world: national journalists, television and film producers and the recording industry itself, coming to us to obtain information they can find nowhere else." If folkloric accounts of the industry tended toward narratives of decline, the history preserved by the library promoted the commercial expansion of country music as a tale of progress and triumph, and the means for telling this story were the commercial media themselves. This was nowhere more evident than in the library's public face, the Hall of Fame and Museum.[46]

Like the genre it honored, the Hall of Fame and Museum building was a thoroughly modern design suffused with symbolic references to the rural past. The central section was built in the shape of a barn and finished on either end with a wall of glass panels evoking the stained glass of a church. On either side, the barn was flanked by low brick wings in the unadorned straight-line ranch style of small office buildings of the day. Visitors approached the building by way of the "Walkway of the Stars," a Grumman's Theatre–style sidewalk inlaid with bronze stars commemorating country artists. The walkway had been yet another fundraising vehicle for the building. Each artist represented there had donated $1,000 or more toward construction, though the program aroused some dismay when the horn player Al Hirt donated enough to be included. The grounds of the museum were symmetrically and sparely landscaped with two reflect-

Commercialism and Tradition   195

7   The original Country Music Hall of Fame was completed in 1967 and combined modern ranch-style architecture with allusions to traditional barns and churches. Inside, visitors learned about country's transformation from a rural vernacular style into a multimillion-dollar industry. *Photo courtesy of Country Music Hall of Fame and Museum.*

ing pools decorated by simple fountains. The *New York Times,* apparently without irony, described the overall effect as "large, modern, barnlike." The building became a physical symbol of country's success to which fans responded with approval. The museum's director, Dorothy Gable, explained to a reporter that the opulence of the building attracted commentary from many visitors. "They feel we did the right thing, whatever it cost. It's a building everyone can point to with pride, and country music fans do that. They all express gratitude that we didn't do a half-way job, that we went all-out and got something with dignity."[47]

Once inside, visitors were reminded again and again of the commerce of country music. The first stop was a theater featuring a loop film about the music's history. The film initially shown to introduce visitors to the genre was a 1966 history of country music called *What's This Country Coming To?* Narrated by Tex Ritter, the movie had been designed originally for inclusion in the CMA's radio promotion campaign. Like the other materials the CMA aimed at broadcasters and advertisers, the film focused on the genre's growth from a regional phenomenon to a national commercial power. The narrative began with the early field recordings of pioneers like Ralph Peer and moved to footage of Dottie West in a modern Nashville recording studio. Its final minutes focused on the success of country format radio, particularly on its appeal for sponsors, and closed by pronouncing, "Country music has become money music. . . . [It] has been around for a long, long time, the Smiths and the Jones have discovered it, and country music has 'come of age.'" Perhaps because the museum's managers decided fans found statistics about the penetration and demographics of country format radio boring—though patrons regularly sat through more than one showing—the film had been replaced by 1969 with *The Country Music Story*, also narrated by Ritter. The new film featured more discussion of the social history of country music and less testimony by happy broadcasters, but it continued to celebrate the commercial achievements of the Nashville Sound and the country industry.[48]

After viewing the film, visitors moved into an exhibit that demonstrated a Nashville recording session, "complete with advice from the engineering room," and the manufacture and pressing of records. It was peculiarly fitting that, although the song being recorded in the studio exhibit—a cover version of Arlie Duff's 1954 hit "Y'All Come"—was not originally a commercial recording, the museum received so many inquiries about where it could be purchased that copies were eventually pressed and made available in the gift shop. The north wing also included a light and sound display that matched the song being played with a lit photo of the artist. Uncle Dave Macon's portrait glowed to the tune of "I'll Keep My Skillet Good and Greasy," Hank Williams's to "Your Cheatin' Heart." Having had a chance to hear the music and reflect on the mastery of technology that it represented, visitors moved next into the Hall of Fame itself. The Hall now honored fourteen members, three of whom were not artists but executives in various phases of the business. Their bronzed portraits lined the walls of a room that contained a glass case of artifacts relating to their careers. The following room contained another case of artifacts, which museum managers said garnered the most attention. Here, visitors could see Patsy Cline's mascara case, Jim Reeves's clothes, and a floorboard of the plane in which Hawkshaw Hawkins, Cowboy Copas, and Cline had been killed. "People associate the artifacts with the artists, and thus associate the artists with themselves," one description of the museum reported. The museum's director noted that the display moved some visitors to tears.[49]

The final section of the museum featured a "series of western store fronts" including a country store complete with "a bale of hay, a liquor jug, and the big, leather-upholstered chair used by Jimmy Davis when he was governor of Louisiana." Through one of the store windows, patrons could watch early footage of the Grand Ole Opry. Amid all the rusticity were several maps and charts, all of which emphasized "the economic growth and evolution of the music." One showed its roots in European and African folk music, and its subsequent spread from a regional "into a nationwide and even worldwide phenomenon." Another depicted its relative contemporary popularity in various areas of the country, and still another, the growth of the industry "from $30,000 a year to more than $100-million." Throughout the museum, then, the stories of commercial success and cultural value were intertwined. Far from seeing the commercialism of the music or the museum as an impeachment of the authenticity of either, fans responded emotionally and positively to the story of the genre's triumph in the sophisticated world of modern entertainment. In praising the museum, they embraced the same story the CMA had presented in its sales shows—the successful modernization of country music and its audience.[50]

The historical project undertaken by the Country Music Foundation was successful on many levels. The activities of the library and archive elevated the cultural status of the music by encouraging academic interest in it and helped to popularize the history of country through a variety of media. The museum was enormously popular among fans and other tourists, and its receipts far exceeded the hopes of the CMA. But the most important success was in presenting a history-as-definition of country music that embraced commercialism and change as a tradition in itself. In addition to imposing a greater retrospective continuity on styles than contemporaries might have been able to discern, this process substituted historical fiat for aural characteristics in marking the boundaries of the genre. As a result, nearly anything the industry and its marketing apparatus wanted to claim could now become a valid part of the country music tradition. Like any good history, this story was both changeable and usable. Styles that were rejected by the industry and its fans at the time could be written back into the canon to emphasize stylistic continuities that had been broken by institutional or audience barriers, as in the case of 1970s California country-rock, or to highlight country's influence on mainstream popular music, as in the case of rock-abilly. Conversely, contemporary styles that might not otherwise be acceptable to fans could be legitimated by reference to a professed historical pedigree or loyalty to "the country tradition."

Although wrangling over authenticity and commercial contamination continued to ebb and flow in response to stylistic changes, the historical work of the Country Music Foundation synthesized the genre's commercial and folk expressions in a way that ensured the independence of country music, in marketing terms if not in stylistic ones. Country music listeners absorbed the story of the industry's commercial success and responded in contradictory ways. The centralization of production and the subsequent trend toward a more uniform sound alienated some listeners, who argued that commercialism itself was responsible for the unwelcome changes. Others simply accepted the logic of commercial production and encouraged like-minded listeners to exercise their purchasing franchise in the consumer democracy of popular culture. And for many listeners, the story of the industry's commercial development became a symbol of their own material success.

6

Silent Majorities

THE COUNTRY AUDIENCE AS COMMODITY,

CONSTITUENCY, AND METAPHOR, 1961–1975

Although it continued to regard its traditional fans as its greatest asset, the industry's intensified focus on the consumer identities of its audience dramatically affected the position of those who had become most invested in the genre's commercial success: the officers and activists of the fan club world. Fan clubbers frequently complained that the industry was abandoning its most dedicated listeners and that format radio was ruining country music. Many in the industry sought to dismiss such dissatisfaction as one more manifestation of a timeless and simplistic impulse to decry all change as decline. In fact, although many fans certainly objected to the stylistic changes of the Nashville Sound, their complaints of betrayal developed from a remarkably accurate assessment of how changes in the scope and structure of the country music business were affecting the nature of fan activity. As the CMA's efforts to expand and thoroughly professionalize the country business bore fruit, the part-time, nonprofessional women who had all along struggled to balance family and club work were systematically marginalized within the industry and pushed into exclusively consumer roles. These activists continued to embrace commercialism, both as a democratic process and as a symbol of cultural and social value, but they increasingly chafed at their own exclusion from the commercial apparatus of the industry.

Contemporary observers demonstrated little interest in this slice of audience experience, gravitating instead to the compelling image of the gullible crowd that had dominated popular representations since the 1950s. In the late 1960s, country music was increasingly imagined by outsiders as the unalloyed cultural expression of a phantasmal "silent majority" of disaffected white, working-class Americans. Cast by the left in the image of *A Face in the Crowd*'s menacing mass and by the right in the guise of the noble common man, the country music audience, and the country industry's commercialism, emerged as a dominant metaphor for the appeal of American consumer democracy and the collapse of the New Deal order.

FAN DANCE: GENDER, COMMERCIALISM, AND FAN CLUBS

Casual country listeners and devoted fans alike made sense of country music's commercialism in the context of overlapping conversations about cultural hierarchies, class and regional identities, and individual memories and emotions. In each of these discourses, the countrypolitan sound and the commercial aspirations it represented became touchstones for larger negotiations of cultural value. For the fans who were most actively involved in promoting country music, though, the debate about commercialism and aesthetic worth intersected with a more prosaic struggle for influence within the industry. Though they have often been imagined as a blanket critique of smoother sounds, fan club activists' complaints about the Nashville Sound were a reasoned response to specific changes in the industry that limited their ability to participate in the business of country music: the repetitiveness of country format radio, the implementation of tight playlists and with them the foreclosure of opportunities for the local artists many fan clubs supported, and the progressive professionalization of artists' public relations functions. The most powerful symbol of this shift to a less permeable border between audience and industry was the exclusion, in 1970, of fans from the field's most important professional event, the WSM Disc Jockey Festival.

Throughout the 1950s, fans had been developing networks of acquaintances and correspondence that allowed them to trade information and expertise. Some had become part of the larger constellation of popular culture fan clubs through participation in club monitoring organizations such as the Fan Club League and the Canadian Club Council (later the International Council of Fan Clubs). These umbrella organizations provided consumer information on the quality and activity of individual clubs, shared tips on how to run a club, and developed community standards about the proper roles and responsibilities of fan club officers, honorees, and members. Both groups organized clubs in various media and musical styles, including country, but it was not until 1960 that a monitoring organization devoted exclusively to country music was formed by a Pueblo, Colorado, housewife named Blanche Trinajstick.[1]

Blanche became involved in boosting country music during the 1950s, and her experience as a country fan was typical of that era. A native of Texas, she met her husband while he was stationed there during World War II and moved to Colorado with him at the end of the war. As she later wrote in an autobiography for her magazine, *K-Bar-T Country Roundup*, she found herself culturally ill at ease as a rural Southerner in the urban North, a discomfort she encapsulated by reference to attitudes toward country music. "The people in Colorado, unlike the people Blanche had known before, looked down their noses at you if you mentioned country music," she told her readers. Like many of the correspondents in *Country & Western Jamboree's* Crusade for Country Music, Blanche—or Trina, as she was more often called—was frustrated at the lack of country music broadcasting in her area and took direct action to try to influence the media executives who determined the content of local radio programming, writing hundreds of letters to local stations to request more country music and launching "a personal crusade to not only create interest in her kind of music, but to convince the radio stations that people *did* want to hear country music!"[2]

In 1960, just as the CMA was inaugurating its campaign to help stations switch to full-time country radio, Trina and a friend decided to start the *K-Bar-T Country Roundup*, a journal and fan club registry that would review club publications, serve as a clearinghouse for publicity on country music artists, and provide contact information for active clubs.

Over the next decade, *K-Bar-T* became a forum for fan club organizers and members to talk about their activities, to identify what they liked about clubbing and the kind of coverage fan club journals offered, and to reflect on the relationship between fans and the industry. Though she would never directly answer questions on the number of members in K-Bar-T, Trina told one inquirer in 1966 that the quarterly magazine and supplemental newsletters were mailed to "more than 300 and less than 1,000 members."[3]

Each issue of *K-Bar-T* included a list of upcoming personal appearances by country artists along with news about upcoming releases and recording plans, fan reviews of concerts and records, and artist interviews and biographies. Such material paralleled the content and reporting style of commercially produced fanzines, but, like the journals generated by individual fan clubs, *K-Bar-T* attracted readers as much for its departures from commercial press coverage as for its commonalities. Fans particularly valued direct communication from the artists and embraced a continued sense of regionalism in the face of the increasingly national sweep of the country industry. When asked what they liked to see in fan journals, readers overwhelmingly agreed that a "newsy letter" from the honored star was the feature they turned to first, but they also emphasized the important role clubbing played in giving exposure to new and regional artists who had not attracted Nashville's attention. "I enjoy reading about *new* artists, and not the same old favorites all the time," wrote one respondent, while others asked for "new stars stories," "news of up-coming new artists," and "stories on artists and DJ's—if they're different."[4]

In addition to providing an alternative to the commercial fan press that brought attention to lesser-known artists, *K-Bar-T* provided far more expansive coverage of what one reader called "fans or others connected with the business" than did commercial magazines. Each issue featured several pages of news about the fan clubs, with notes on management changes, membership drives, and awards from umbrella organizations. In "Loco Weeds," another regular column, presidents of member clubs answered questions on club management such as "How far in advance do you plan your publications?" and "How long should a prexy wait after a journal deadline for her honoree's letter before she sends the journal out anyway?" By the mid-1960s, one of the magazine's most popular features was a regular column called "Ask Trina," in which Trina responded to reader mail on a variety of subjects. Though their honoree stars were the explicit focus of attention, members often appeared to be more interested in their relationships with each other. They frequently asked for advice on how to handle difficult issues such as how to "deal with people who write letters and continually run down artists, fan clubs, and fan club presidents," how to "prove your club is reliable," or how to deal with a state club representative who did not discharge her duties properly.[5]

But the most contentious issue discussed in *K-Bar-T* was the changing relationship between fan clubs and the industry, particularly as it was shaped by the advent of format radio. Deejays were not alone in harboring resentment at having the influence of their own preferences gradually eliminated by the implementation of tight, chart-driven playlists. As champions of undiscovered new talent, fan club activists viewed the clubs as "the only medium whereby the worth of artists who do not have their records placed on sale, and on a nation-wide scale, can be determined." But format radio hopelessly curtailed the promise that even the most active fans could influence the decisions of program directors in favor of their stars. "How do the disc jockeys expect a new artist's song to be in the charts if no one will play his records?" one editorial complained. The idiosyncrasies of individual deejays had been replaced by a far more centralized decision-making process, and fans felt suddenly and unaccountably disconnected from the industry's star-making machinery. "Isn't there anything that we, the fans and friends of these artists, and the country fans in general, can do to help these new, deserving artists?" the editorial despaired. In another issue, a deejay offered a careful analysis of the advertising pressures that guided programming at large regional stations and suggested that fan clubs would do better to focus their efforts on smaller stations that carried equal reporting weight in the creation of the charts but were likely to be underserved with promotional records from the major labels and more amenable to taking risks on unknowns. As they had during the 1950s, fans during the Nashville Sound era continued to educate themselves about the intricacies of broadcasting, advertising, and the record business. But where their exasperation had once been focused on outsiders who discriminated against country music, now country radio itself increasingly drew their ire.[6]

Fan club activists were careful to distinguish between the structure of format radio and the content it delivered. Contributors to *K-Bar-T* felt free to defend modern country music in impassioned terms. "There is no place today for Country Music as we knew it yesterday, except on your phonograph or radio's 'golden oldies,' " wrote one contributor. "Today's country music is for the most part modern, with an up-tempo beat. . . . The majority of people agree with this." Another piece in the same issue reflected on the "age old subject of regression, status quo, or progression or whatever you call it," concluding that all kinds of change and variation were acceptable "if the record has the basic country sound that is the most important thing." These and similar defenses of newer sounds appeared alongside harsh criticism of format radio. "The present day format in radio is strictly for the birds!" proclaimed yet another article in the same issue. "They think country music fans are nitwits, or idiots. . . . We do not like to listen to the same thing around the clock every day." Another fan more succinctly addressed the charge that those who complained about new country radio were simply resisting healthy and inevitable change, arguing instead that the restrictiveness of the format, rather than its specific content, created discontent. "We are not now, nor have we ever been, against country music modernizing itself," he wrote. "We are against forcing it on the public and programming it to the exclusion of everything else."[7]

The rise of format radio symbolized for many fans the increasingly centralized control of the country industry's promotional institutions and the erosion of fans' traditional roles in promoting their favorite music. However annoyed some fans were at the repetitive and insular nature of format radio, though, their deepest indignation was reserved for the organizers of the WSM Disc Jockey Festival. Fans and fan club presidents had been attending the festival almost since its inception in 1952, but in the early 1960s their presence became problematic in a way it had not been before. At the 1962 convention, eighteen fan club presidents met with the head of the country-western section of the Canadian Club Council to discuss a range of club issues, including "the 'UN-welcome Mat' of the convention." Offended that the official publicity released by WSM "definitely did NOT include a welcome to the fan clubs at the convention," club presidents organized to respond. Much of the problem, one president in attendance speculated, lay with imposters. "Fan clubs are snubbed by WSM personnel because at one time they *were* welcome. This produced much havoc, for people who had ne'er an idea of what a fan club is, claimed to be such, and were registered as such. Then the fun began! Those un-associated outsiders gave honest-to-goodness fan clubbers the black mark. This, however, was partly the fault of WSM, for not requiring positive proof of identification." For legitimate presidents and club members, she stressed, the convention was an important opportunity to conduct business, to meet with honorees who lived in distant parts of the country, and to share expertise among presidents. "The prexies at the 1962 convention had their artists behind them 100%," she observed. "The clubs should be given a chance to prove they help the artists." Those in attendance decided to rent a suite at the following year's convention to "exhibit club publications, etc., so that all present might have a chance to see what our purpose is."[8]

The following year, *Music City News* enthusiastically, though erroneously, reported that Blanche Trinajstick had organized the "first Fan Club Convention ever held" in conjunction with the WSM Disc Jockey Festival. In keeping with the proposal made at the previous year's meeting, the K-Bar-T convention included a room to display club publications as well as "a business discussion of fan club topics, plus a club banquet, which was followed by entertainment by attending artists." On the final day, the group availed themselves of George Hamilton IV's bus tour of Nashville, passing by such landmarks as the WSM studios, the Ryman Auditorium, Music Row, and the prosperous suburb of Brentwood, home to many country stars. In honor of the occasion Trina published a special issue of the *K-Bar-T Country Roundup* featuring a welcome to everyone attending the fan club convention and a reflection on why clubs should be included in the most important industry gathering for the country field. Her description of fan club presidents established her vision of clubs not simply as consumer confederations but as integral components of the industry. "Why not fan clubs at the Country Music Festival?" she asked. "Are they not an active, important part of the country music field? . . . Fan club presidents are many things rolled into one—she promotes, she publishes, she distributes records, she handles publicity. . . . So how come she isn't considered an important enough part of her artist's career to be included in country music activities?"[9]

By the time the fan club convention was established, many clubbers, including Norma Barthel, Cora Rea Haning, and Chaw Mank, had been attending the deejay festival for almost a decade. But unlike sporadic individual participation, the fan club convention provided a forum for celebrating the work that fans put into their clubs and for demonstrating the value of their efforts to the industry. Clubs were invited to set up tables to display their journals and other materials, and for the duration of the convention the fan club room served as a focal point for fans to meet and greet one another. The annual business meeting provided an opportunity for fans and artists to talk to one another about trends in clubbing and the industry. The highlight of the week was the K-Bar-T awards banquet, which featured performances by dozens of artists, including stars like Ernest Tubb and Bill Anderson. K-Bar-T members voted on awards for artists in categories that mirrored industry awards— best songwriter, best band, and best song, among others—and, in keeping with the assertion that the fans themselves were part of the industry, they also voted on awards for club activists—most active member, best fan club journal, best new fan club. But, as Trina's co-organizer, Ruth Slack, pointed out, the most rewarding part of the convention was the opportunity to see other fans, friends, and correspondents from around the country. "Many of these people only get to see each other once a year," she observed, "and it is just wonderful to see the greetings of one to another." Before long, the K-Bar-T convention was joined by fan events sponsored by other organizations. In 1967, former K-Bar-T member Loudilla Johnson and her sisters Loretta and Kay founded a new monitoring organization, the International Fan Club Organization (IFCO), and in 1968 they began sponsoring their own reception and autograph session at the Hermitage Hotel.[10]

In spite of their sense of themselves as a vital part of the country industry, the women involved in fan club activity had always recognized their second-class status within it. Ernest Tubb's club president, Norma Barthel, noted as much in her account of an exchange between two deejays overheard at the 1955 Disc Jockey Convention: "I hadn't been down [in the lobby of the Andrew Jackson Hotel] two minutes before I overheard someone saying, 'Isn't that one of the fan club presidents?' His buddy said, rather disgustedly, 'I'm sure I don't know.' And he walked away!" The deejay who had first recognized Norma subsequently came over to introduce himself, but in spite of the fact that she had been a columnist and freelance contributor to fan magazines since the 1940s and headed one of the most successful clubs in the country field, Barthel clearly faced condescension and worse from some in the business. Though their contributions to the industry had always been trivialized to some degree, the image of fan club activists was further tainted during the 1960s by new discourses about gender and popular music. As women, they were easily assimilated to negative stereotypes about teeny-boppers and groupies that were making their way from the music trade press into the emerging critical rock press and the popular imagination. Among pop industry professionals, the adoration of female fans, especially teenagers,

8 Blanche Trinajstick (right) opens the doors for fans
waiting to attend the K-Bar-T awards banquet in 1969.
The banquet was the culminating event of the annual fan
club convention held in conjunction with the Disc Jockey
Festival. Though fans viewed themselves as an integral
part of the industry, WSM progressively excluded them
from the industry's major convention. *Photo courtesy of
Country Music Hall of Fame and Museum.*

was widely equated with bad, "schmaltzy" music produced by commercially constructed idols—the very characterizations that the country music industry had struggled against for decades.[11]

Country fan club members were well aware that they were as vulner-
able as female pop fans to being typecast as groupies, and they explicitly
combated both the image and behaviors that might invoke it. One club
president wrote that, while it was understandable for fans to want to
meet a star for an interview or other publication material, or "just to size
[him or her] up . . . before jumping on the bandwagon for him or her,"
club activists had to take special care not to create the wrong impression.
"Usually, when I leave my seat I take an indirect route to the stage door,"
she wrote. "And when having pictures made with any of the stars, I kind

of stand to the side, instead of standing real close, which makes a better picture . . . and can't cause any mistaken ideas on anyone's part." Another lamented, "There are times when I'm almost ashamed to admit that I am a fan club president, because I know what people are thinking of me." Though most fan clubbers were willing to concede that the image of fans as "out and out tramps, whose only interest in country music is to 'make out' with the artists" might represent the disgraceful conduct of a few bad apples, they objected to the industry's willingness to paint all fans with the same broad brush. One deejay who expressed his support of the promotional work the clubs performed recognized the discrimination clubbers faced as a result of the sexualized groupie image. He suggested that they would never be taken seriously so long as they were perceived merely as fans. "Come to think of it, why call it a fan club?" he asked. "One's first impression is a bunch of girls, giggling and screaming at their favorite artist. Why don't they call it a promotion club? It has a more business like sound to it than fan club."[12]

Though the activities of the one were frequently indistinguishable from those of the other, the distinction between businesswoman and fan was significant. As volunteers, fan club organizers undermined the Nashville music community's effort to present itself as a thoroughly professional, businesslike entertainment center rather than a collection of naïve backwoods amateurs. Female executives in the industry, including the CMA's executive director, Jo Walker, and BMI executive Frances Preston, were embraced as symbols of Nashville's sophistication and progressivism. Fan clubbers represented an altogether different set of associations. Particularly at the WSM Disc Jockey Festival, the industry was not anxious to be represented by what many considered a pack of rural housewives untutored in the social graces required for corporate networking. Fans were acutely aware that some artists and businesspeople viewed them as "just plain country hicks with no class, as one of them came right out and said," and the motives behind such denigrating stereotypes seemed fairly transparent to many. "Could it be they are inwardly ashamed of their country music background, and feel insecure that they won't be accepted in the new field they are hoping to enter into?" asked one clubber, perhaps hitting uncomfortably close to the mark.[13]

But even as the distinction between industry and fans was thrown into sharper relief, the elaboration of the field's business infrastructure created a growing recognition of how important the clubs' public relations functions could be. Norma Barthel reported that many in the industry were beginning to appreciate the potential value of a well-run club. One star, she wrote, had recently told her that "it would have cost him thousands of dollars if he'd have hired someone to put out all the publicity and be the help that his fan club had been." "So many times we [fan clubs] are left out," she noted, "but the situation is certainly getting better all of the time. Being a fan club president for the past 19 years it makes me so happy to know that we are finally being recognized as a vital part of the country music field." IFCO co-founder Loudilla Johnson agreed with Barthel's assertion that those within the industry finally recognized the value of fan clubs in the 1960s. Years later she recalled that it was around the time IFCO was established that record labels and artists finally began to understand fully the marketing value of fan clubs.[14]

Ironically, though, recognition of the business importance of clubs ultimately contributed to the decline of widespread participation and fan control. By the early 1970s, many artists were shifting promotional responsibilities from unpaid fan club organizers to professional publicists who, as employees, could be held to a different standard of accountability, and fans found themselves displaced from what they viewed as their position within the industry. Trina particularly admonished stars against abandoning their fan clubs for more professional publicity staff. "The main purpose of a fan club *is* publicity on the artist. It is promotion and support for his records, his shows, his every activity. . . . But what is the result when someone else is commissioned to 'promote' the artist, and in doing so, takes away some of the responsibilities, *and privileges,* that normally belong to a fan club?" she asked, emphasizing the exchange of work and rewards that underpinned the relationship between presidents and their honorees. Rather than hiring a professional publicist, she urged artists to recognize the role of fan club presidents and perhaps even to give them some long overdue compensation for their work. "Why not have a little more faith in your fan club prexy, and if you have money to buy this sort of thing, give it to your fan club prexy, who does all these things for you anyway?"[15]

Some argued that professional publicists could not produce the benefits of the fan clubs' grassroots approach. One deejay described the unique publicity functions that fan clubs served "in areas sometimes overlooked by others who make promotion their business." Smaller stations often had trouble obtaining news and recent releases from record labels, he pointed out, and fan clubs were willing to service stations that otherwise could not gain the industry's attention. "The disc jockey who works on a small town station . . . has to constantly beg for records," he wrote. "The fan club prexy does much to alleviate this problem by keeping in contact with various deejays."[16]

In keeping with their goals as boosters of the genre, club activists welcomed greater sales, more radio exposure, and larger audiences; they accepted commercialism and consumer democracy as reasonably fair mechanisms for determining popular standards of aesthetic value; and, as they had during the late 1950s, they continued to present themselves as an important part of the industry, not only in what they understood to be their critical roles as consumers but also as active participants in the promotion, distribution, and public relations functions that supported the country field. By the late 1960s, though, fan club organizers found themselves increasingly at odds with Nashville's effort to craft a thoroughly professional image for the field by drawing ever stricter boundaries between producers and consumers.

FAN FAIR AS CONSUMER SPECTACLE

WSM and industry sentiment against fan participation in the deejay convention intensified in direct proportion to the growth in fans' numerical and institutional presence there. By 1969 the occasional derogatory comment had become more or less open hostility. Fans defended their position all the more vociferously and were particularly outraged by the charge that they were a threat to the professionalism of the convention. "The general complaint about the fans is that they have no business at the conventions, that they are just there to 'rub elbows' with the artists, and generally make a nuisance of themselves," Trina wrote in *K-Bar-T.* "May I ask if any of you who voice these complaints have ever visited the Noel Hotel, which is more or less the 'fan' headquarters during convention, and compared the goings on there with the 'action' at the Andrew Jackson, where most of the DJ's and trade hang out? If you did, you might have cause to wonder just WHO it is that creates all the nuisance in Nashville at convention time." Another fan echoed her complaint. "I have never drank, hank-pankied around or in any way, I hope, offended anyone in the music business while attending the convention. . . . I wish I could say the same for some business people, DJ's and artists!!" In response to a reader's question about how best to "break down the barrier between WSM and the country music fans," Trina noted that even some deejays and promoters had begun to worry about "the attitude toward the 'fans' in Nashville," but she optimistically predicted that such concern was the first step toward solving the problem.[17]

As fans prepared for the 1970 convention, they faced more than the usual frustrations. The Andrew Jackson Hotel, where most of the industry participants traditionally stayed, had closed and was to be demolished, leaving the convention with an acute shortage of hotel rooms. At the same time, WSM seemed to be handling registration differently than it had in the past, to the exasperation of many fans. "Always before you could send in your registration money after mid-summer," Trina complained. "But several have told me that their checks were returned with the information that registrations were not being accepted until mid-September!! It seems that Nashville is always coming up with new ideas to discourage 'fans' from attending the convention." However resigned fans were to being treated as second-class citizens at the convention, they were obviously taken aback when they learned upon arriving that they would not be permitted to register at all. Not surprisingly, the litmus test for separating legitimate from illegitimate registrants was whether or not they were paid professionals, "gainfully employed in the field," a definition that, as Trina pointed out, "just naturally excluded fans, fan club presidents, etc."[18]

Fans were at first incredulous that WSM management really meant to exclude them on a permanent basis. The "Ask Trina" column in the wake of the convention was peppered with their confusion and hurt. "Why does the CMA try to keep fans and club presidents from attending the convention?" asked one member. "This question was asked by several ... and we can not answer it, yet," Trina responded. "The only reason I've heard was shortage of space and this was WSM, not CMA. I hope to have some definite answers when our meetings with WSM are over, and until such time, I won't try to answer this question." Another asked whether fans would be permitted to register in 1971. Again, Trina could only offer that she was to meet with Bud Wendell of WSM after the first of the year to discuss the matter. But by the time spring rolled around, it was clear that the CMA was proceeding with a different plan altogether. *K-Bar-T* reprinted a press release from *Billboard* announcing that the board had decided at its January meeting in Houston to hold a spring festival beginning in 1972. Repeating again the industry-audience dualism that fan clubbers found entirely illogical, the release described the event as a gathering "geared for the fan rather than the industry."[19]

By midyear even the most optimistic fans had accepted the obvious: the decision to exclude clubs from the deejay convention was deliberate and final. An anonymous fan wrote a scathing letter in *K-Bar-T* expressing her frustration that fans were being limited exclusively to a consumer role. Recent reports of a slump in the country music business, she said, had been blamed on the economic recession, but she felt there were other forces at work. "Could it possibly be that the 'fans' resent the unfair treatment they've received from the country music industry lately?" she speculated. "The straw that really broke the camel's back was the slamming of doors in the fans' face in Nashville last year. No reasonable explanation, no thought of trying to work things out so fans could be included, just a closed door, which may as well have carried a bold sign reading, 'YOU ARE NOT WANTED HERE!' In essence, they were saying, 'Support us with your money but don't bug us.' I'm sure the fans got the message!"[20]

Trina continued to articulate a conception of fan clubs as a vital component of the industry's promotion and distribution apparatus and complained that the Nashville establishment was creating a false distinction between segments of the industry. "It is a 'split' in the country music field, a separation of the fans from the rest of the industry," she told readers of *K-Bar-T*. For Trina, the expulsion of fans from the convention demonstrated an appalling lack of respect, but even more pernicious was the fundamental revision of the relationship between audience and industry that the decision seemed to call for. Suddenly, the very mission of K-Bar-T seemed hopelessly out of synch with the structure of the industry. Members began to ask for clarification of the organization's goals, its audience, and the purpose of the fan convention. Asked whether the magazine was for fans, clubs, or the industry, Trina once again resisted the distinction, presenting the three groups as co-equal parts of a single entity. "As for K-T being for any *one* branch of the industry—how do you separate one from the other?? Seems to me this is what Nashville is trying to do, and I don't think it's possible. What is one, without the other?"[21]

As the members of K-Bar-T sorted out the implications of their exclusion from the Disc Jockey Convention, the CMA launched headlong into preparations for its spring fan celebration. The event itself was modeled in part on the International Country Music Festival that had been taking place for several years in Wembley, England. Jo Walker and Hubert Long, a talent agent who chaired the organizing committee for the new fan celebration, had attended the first Wembley festival in 1969, and in April 1971 the CMA board and officers held their quarterly meeting there. (Since board members and their companies paid for their own travel, the CMA, with its usual promotional flair, had encouraged them to take on the extra expense by chartering a bona fide double-decker bus to transport the board from airport to hotel for their January 1971 meeting in Houston.) The festival plans announced after the January meeting had been quite vague, but by the time the board returned from Wembley, the CMA newsletter brimmed with excitement over what it now called the First Annual International Country Music Fan Fair. At least eight labels had committed to staging showcases for their artists, who would include Bill Anderson, Loretta Lynn, and Conway Twitty, all of whom had played at Wembley, as well as Johnny Cash, Merle Haggard, Porter Wagoner, Dolly Parton, and Buck Owens. In addition to the label showcases and a bluegrass spectacular, one morning would be set aside for fan clubs to conduct their business meetings, and a second was designated for club executives to meet with representatives of WSM and the CMA.[22]

The Disc Jockey Convention continued to cast its shadow over even the most enthusiastic pronouncements about the new event. "The Fan Fair is the result of natural growth and will be born as a fully mature offspring of the Opry Birthday Celebration," *Close-Up* explained to its readers, a number of whom, like Ruth Slack, were also connected to the fan clubs. "The Opry Birthday Celebration evolved from a small industry affair for DJ's and Country Music Broadcasters . . . [and] grew into its present massive meeting of Country Music industry interests," the statement continued, verging on an apology. "The growth was so swift that there is no longer capability to accommodate anyone other than the industry. Thus, the new born Fan Fair will start life as a giant with all the major facets of activity similar to the Opry Birthday Celebration of today."[23]

The CMA invested a great deal of effort in creating a festival that fans would appreciate and enjoy, but Fan Fair's organizers missed the central point that animated the criticisms leveled by Blanche and others like her. The club convention had been an opportunity for fans to create their own spectacle, not simply to serve as spectators to someone else's performance. Fan Fair, though it offered an opportunity to meet the stars, collect autographs, attend concerts, and revel in the bustle and hype of Nashville, undermined the autonomy of the clubs and cast them as consumers rather than active participants in the industry.

The CMA's decision to meet in Denver in the summer of 1971, a critical juncture in the preparations, was undoubtedly linked to the fact that both IFCO and K-Bar-T were headquartered in Colorado, and it can be read as an indication of the association's earnest desire to include clubs in the planning of Fan Fair and to continue to build support for the event among both industry and audience constituencies. But the fact that the structure of Fan Fair had already been determined undermined the gesture, as did the wording of the announcement that the board would meet with representatives of the two major club-monitoring organizations. According to *Close-Up*, the directors hoped the meeting would help them "get the feeling of the record market consumer," with the result that fans found themselves once again defined by consumerism rather than creativity. The denigration of fan clubs was based in part on their organizers' part-time status and identity as mothers and homemakers, and club organizers like Trina called attention to the injustice of such attitudes by defiantly embracing their multiple roles. Trina peevishly declined the invitation to attend the CMA board meeting with a pointed reminder of the complex web of obligations into which fan clubbers incorporated their work and a jibe at what she considered to be the CMA's condescending attitude. "The CMA printed the information about meeting with me without waiting to hear from me about it. I had previous commitments with the Camp Fire group my daughter belongs to on that day and would not cancel them to attend the meeting."[24]

Though the CMA's intentions appear to have been magnanimous, the plans for Fan Fair only reinforced fans' exclusion from the production side of country's official cultural economy. Still, not all fan clubbers responded with defensiveness and resentment. The organizers of IFCO found the official explanation for excluding fans from the Disc Jockey Convention somewhat empty, but they also thought the CMA plan held a good deal of promise for fans. Loudilla Johnson recalled later that industry complaints about fans at the deejay meeting seemed overblown, particularly because, once they were no longer allowed to register, there was no way for fans to interfere in the business of the convention. Her own conclusion was that, in light of the Wembley Festival and the increasing fan presence at the deejay meeting, the CMA had recognized an "untapped market" for a major festival. Properly organized, such a festival could not only satisfy fan curiosity about the inner workings of Nashville but also capture trade headlines and demonstrate the size and devotion of the country audience. In any case, Loudilla later reasoned, if

IFCO was to represent the fans in any capacity, she owed it to them to explore the possibilities whether she supported the idea personally or not. Her efforts were not entirely in vain, as the rhetoric surrounding Fan Fair shifted noticeably after the meeting to emphasize the search for ways the clubs and unaffiliated fans could "most effectively realize their importance and a direct involvement in the Country Music Fair." "WSM and CMA officials have long been aware of the vital role the fan plays in the music business," the CMA noted, "and various methods whereby fans can be informed of this were discussed." After the Colorado meeting, the IFCO membership voted to move their annual convention and dinner to coincide with Fan Fair.[25]

Trina, meanwhile, was steadfast in her refusal to accept the concert and autograph extravaganza as a substitute for the fan convention and announced that K-Bar-T would not participate. In her view, the proposals for the event continued to suggest a disturbing disjuncture between industry understandings of fan clubs and fans' own view of their work. Again positioning the clubs as part of the industry, she complained that Fan Fair did "not include plans for any activities by the fan club organizations, but [was] completely under WSM and CMA control." "I understand a meeting was held with a representative from CMA during convention to discuss the Fan Fair, and those present came away more confused and angry than before, because no satisfaction was gained in regards to the FAN CLUBS being recognized," Trina reported after the 1971 Disc Jockey Convention. "It would be good if they'd have the Fan Fair in April, as planned," she wrote, "and include the FAN CLUBS in October." Until Fan Fair made room for fans to organize events themselves, it could not be considered an acceptable substitute for the fan convention. And in any case, she wrote, again reminding all concerned that fan clubbers might have better things to do, "There is no way I can get away from home for a trip at that time of year."[26]

Some five thousand fans and more than a hundred artists did, however, get to Nashville for the first annual Fan Fair in April 1972, and the event was judged a tremendous success. In addition to attending showcase concerts, the bluegrass spectacular, and an old-time fiddling contest, fans could also indulge their interest in the more modern trappings of the country industry. In between the IFCO business meeting, touring the hall housing the club and industry display booths, and seeking out autographs, fans were invited to attend live tapings of television shows and could choose from a variety of activities such as taking a bus tour of the stars' homes or visiting the new Country Music Hall of Fame and Museum, both of which presented the story of Nashville's commercial success as a narrative that could unite fans, artists, and businesspeople in celebration of the genre's material progress and that of its audience.[27]

After several more years of hosting the K-Bar-T fan convention in October in defiance of WSM's wishes, Trina turned her attention away from country music, though not from fan clubbing. In 1977, she turned K-Bar-T into the National Association of Fan Clubs, a monitoring organization for clubs of all kinds around the world. As K-Bar-T waned as a force in the country music fan club world, IFCO became the voice of the country fan, in part because the CMA promoted it in that capacity. *Country Song Roundup*, which had eliminated both its "Pickin' on the Pen Pals" column and its regular section of press announcements from club presidents in the mid-1960s, revived its coverage of clubs in 1972 with a feature column by the Johnson sisters.

"I see a lot of things happening in country music that disappoint me greatly," Trina wrote as the plans for Fan Fair became more concrete and elaborate. "If we let it happen, without a fight, we can look forward to having the fan clubs pushed even farther back, and maybe even eliminated." The establishment of Fan Fair symbolized a new relationship between the country industry and its fans. Fans like the Johnson sisters who were able to function more like full-time professionals, whether they were paid or not, continued to limn the border between industry and audience, providing promotional and public relations support to their honorees and maintaining the social networks that had always proven one of the most rewarding aspects of club work. But they were fewer and farther between and were generally replaced or supplemented by professional publicists. Those like Trina, who had to balance their club work with family and employment commitments, were relegated to spectatorial, consumer roles. For them, it was not the stylistic changes and commercial success of the Nashville Sound, nor even the naked pursuit of profit, that rankled but the fact that their role in that pursuit had, as Trina predicted, been largely eliminated.[28]

Still, fans' struggles to transcend isolated spectatorship, whether expressed through Trina's boycotting or through the Johnson sisters' cooperative but insistently autonomous position, forced the country field to acknowledge their presence to a greater degree than any other popular music genre did its fans. Today, Fan Fair is an annual pilgrimage for many country devotees, a ritual unique in popular music that celebrates the genre's vibrant fan culture. The rounds of autograph tables, star-sponsored picnics, and Opry celebrations are orchestrated events in need of an audience rather than participants; but whatever the losses associated with the redefinition of country fandom, Fan Fair remains a testament to the unusually powerful role country music fans had carved out for themselves by 1970. Like the intensive, semi-professional club activities of an earlier era, Fan Fair is, as Curtis Ellison has argued, an opportunity for fans to identify with country music's enactment of "popular mythology about American commercial success." It is also an artifact of the unique way the industry developed, and of the critical part fan clubs played in providing a public relations and promotional structure during Music Row's formative decades.[29]

FROM MARKET TO MAJORITY

While country fans resisted some of the practical implications of their identity as a marketing demographic, they were less acutely sensitive to others. By the late 1960s, the CMA's efforts to communicate both the size and cultural uniqueness of its audience attracted the attention not only of advertisers but of political strategists as well. Country music had long been implicated in Southern politics, but its partisan leanings had always been ambiguous. Country artists campaigned for Democrats, Republicans, and Populists throughout the twentieth century, and musicians-turned-candidates like Jimmie Davis, Lee "Pappy" O'Daniel, and Stuart Hamblen emphasized their populist credentials and wit by performing themselves on the campaign trail. But it was not until George Wallace consistently mobilized country music and its stars in support of his gubernatorial and presidential runs that the music began to be perceived as inherently conservative. In part, the popular construction of country music during this period simply echoed the role the genre had played in midcentury debates about the impact of mass media. One might easily imagine George Wallace as Lonesome Rhodes made flesh: the left's nightmare of a pop culture demagogue rallying modern backwoods primitives with plain-folks minstrelsy and earthy anti-intellectualism. But the brand of conservatism to which mainstream country was ultimately harnessed, and its utility to the politics of Richard Nixon and the New Majority in particular, was more in line with the upwardly mobile suburban poetics of Spiro Agnew than the overtly racist populism of Wallace.[30]

In practice, country music did not so much shift to the right as the right shifted to country, consciously seeking to transform an established marketing demographic into a political one. A *Washington Post* op-ed piece written by Kevin P. Phillips—the leading theorist of the "emerging Republican majority" coalition of traditional conservatives, populist-conservatives, and new suburban wealth—suggested that if Nixon aides wanted to understand "the swing voters who will renew—or terminate—[his] White House lease in 1972," they would do well to tune in to the nation's country and ethnic radio stations. "Politically, economically, and culturally," Phillips argued, the 30 percent of the population that listened to such music were "the forgotten Americans"—"those who drive the trucks, plow the farms, man the factories, and police the streets." The description could have been penned by the CMA itself, and it testified to the organization's success in marketing its audience as an important and powerful segment of the public, at once the great American mainstream and a special, largely neglected group. Embracing country music, Phillips argued, would allow the Republican Party to "use the emotional issues of culture and race to achieve . . . a 'positive polarization' of American politics" without attacking civil rights, actively opposing integration, or resorting to the kind of overt racism that would alienate moderates.[31]

For nearly two decades, the country music press had attacked the holders of cultural power who denigrated the genre: the media executives who ignored it, the academics and preservationists who dismissed it as commercial drivel, the urban sophisticates who sneered at rural hicks. The country audience's antipathy for what the conservative movement now dubbed the New Class had only to be transformed into a political impulse. But while traditional conservatives recognized the value of country's cultural antagonisms, their assessments of the music still awkwardly juxtaposed a newfound admiration with the traditional tone of condescension. One *National Review* columnist excoriated conservatives for accepting the condemnations of early preservationists (whom he described, in grand populist style, as "an effete corps of impudent academic snobs") and for "believing without further thought that singers of Country Music are yahoos whose only concession to civilization is the wearing of red suspenders to keep their homespun britches up." In spite of this enthusiastic elevation of country's worth, however, more than a trace of allegiance to traditional social and cultural hierarchies persisted. "The nation and its better classes (if we are still permitted to speak of such people)," he concluded, "rest upon the shoulders of the yeomanry; if their expression cannot be appreciated, it should not be rubbished."[32]

By the spring of 1970, after careful consideration of Phillips's analysis, Nixon determined that his 1972 reelection bid would focus on blue-collar workers and Southern whites, and the use of country music as political symbolism was an obvious component of this strategy. He invited Johnny Cash and Merle Haggard to the White House to perform and, in September, issued a national proclamation designating October as Country Music Month. The latter gesture in particular indicated a canny sensitivity to the rituals of political courtship. The CMA had worked since its inception to cultivate relationships with politicians of all stripes, from Democratic senator Albert Gore Sr. to governors Buford Ellington and Frank Clement, but with limited success. Jo Walker's own organizational skills had been honed first in the arena of state political campaigning, and she recognized from the outset the political dimension of the CMA's mission. "Politics is part of living, I guess," she later reflected. "You're trying to win friends and influence people to your side whether you're in a political campaign or whether you're promoting a type of music." The industry had already relied once on Gore and Clement to defend its interests before Congress, so it was not surprising that the CMA looked immediately to political alliances to gain exposure for country music and establish Music Row as a serious industry.[33]

The organization's strategy was characterized by a combination of cultural, political, and economic aspirations. As Walker later explained, the CMA sought the support of politicians originally out of its longstanding sense of cultural inferiority, "to kind of have the prestige in the eyes of some people." This was almost certainly the intention of CMA president Connie B. Gay when, in 1959, he mobilized his considerable Washington connections to organize a "stag barbecue" for congressmen to meet Gene Autry and the members of the newly established CMA board. But most initiatives also aimed at pragmatic benefits such as lobbying for specific legislation and business interests, or using media coverage of politics or government-mandated public service broadcasting time to advertise country music. An early, and innovative, CMA promotional idea evinced this combination of commercialism and politics. Harry

Stone conceived a series of televised public service announcements that would use country music stars to promote tourism spots in the state of Tennessee—an idea that would have simultaneously generated a steady stream of free television appearances for country luminaries and emphasized the industry's importance to the state's economy—but the sitting governor, Buford Ellington, refused to meet with him to discuss the proposition.[34]

The CMA's overtures reflected an ideological bent no deeper than a businesslike investment in cultivating power. "You always need some clout with politicians," Jo Walker sagely observed. But so long as the industry offered politicians only the traditional tokens of barter, corporate support and perhaps a patina of celebrity, it wielded relatively little bargaining power. When the Nixon campaign became interested in wooing the country audience, however, the CMA found itself awash in media-friendly political events and official enthusiasm for the music that "reflects the joys, the sorrows and the ideals of our people." After years of unsuccessfully pursuing Lyndon Johnson's imprimatur for Country Music Month, the industry warmly returned the Nixon administration's embrace. To Jo Walker, the motives behind Nixon's sudden interest in country music were opaque, and largely irrelevant. "California was always a pretty good state for country music," she later speculated. "I don't know if he knew some people in the business or—I just don't know why he was interested in it. But I know that we were mighty thrilled when he proclaimed October as country music month."[35]

Much of the conservative analysis of country music focused on the promise of the traditionalist and patriotic themes represented in songs like "The Fightin' Side of Me," "Welfare Cadilac," or "Day of Decision." Echoing older validations of country as the voice of the pioneers, hopeful conservatives issued declarations that "our strength and the strength of this troubled country ultimately resides with these maligned people." One editorialist alluded, consciously or unconsciously, to the reactionary post–Civil War compromise that produced Jim Crow when he observed in the wake of the Watergate scandal that country was the "music of reconstruction. The nation certifying basic premises—home, job, faith—after a dangerous and anarchic decade when music was preeminently the tool of radicals. It's good. The trend that gave Nixon his mandate." For many, though, the ultimate argument for taking country seriously lay in its commercial power rather than its musical quality or its ability to represent the folk. Just as commercialism had been mobilized to represent the respectability of country and its audience, it could also be used to demonstrate the music's potential political value. "If crass conservatism cannot be moved by matters of quality or popularity, perhaps Country Music's commercial success will catch its attention," one author editorialized, before providing a litany of sales figures and business triumphs enjoyed by country stars and entrepreneurs. "The important point of all this is that our Country Music is the healthiest nucleus for the expression of American traditional virtues."[36]

Like conservatives, liberal critics attributed to country music an almost mystical ability to speak to and for white working-class America. One went so far as to accuse country music of "creating, encouraging, and isolating a rootless proletariat." Another contended that "the rural and lower classes" had always been "hotbeds of conservatism and reaction" and advanced the curious claim that "country music's distinctive 'sound' reflects its conservative and discriminatory make-up, even when a given song has no overt political or religious message." *Esquire* argued more circumspectly that country music was simply a more effective vehicle for expounding conservatism than traditional politics. The average visitor to the Opry had come 450 miles one way to see the show, the magazine observed before asking, "Who would come that far to listen to Spiro Agnew's message to Middle America?"[37]

For a number of critics, the most disturbing aspect of the nexus between country and conservatism was what they perceived as the commercial exploitation of political reaction. Harkening back to Richard Hofstadter's analysis of the longstanding illiberal rural majority and its pernicious bent for nostalgia over history, the folklorist Jens Lund charged the country industry with peddling a " 'nostalgic cast' [that] has proved to be one of the most profitable traits of American society from the entertainment industry's point of view. The 'good old days' are always marketable, whether on Currier and Ives prints or on grooved discs of celluloid." Similarly, in his review of Paul Hemphill's 1970 exposé, *The Nashville Sound*, John Seelye interpreted country's newfound popularity neither as a product of smoother pop sounds nor of Southern migration to Northern urban centers—both of which, he noted, took place at least a decade before the country boom of the late 1960s—but rather attributed it to "the tendency of Country and Western singers (and disc jockeys) to push a rightwing, reactionary political line." Rather than exploiting a cultural demographic, Seelye and Lund suggested, the Southern Strategy had created one: "the emergence of Middle America is bringing with it Middle American sentiments and music, and the music of Blue Collar America is the twangy, whangy, jingoistic jingles of Nashville and the Grand Ole Opry."[38]

A bemused rumination on the surprising popularity of the hillbilly variety show *Hee Haw* also suggested the parallels between the reduction of politics to a form of candidate advertising based on cultural style and the reduction of commercial culture, especially country music, to a profitable form of political pandering. Contrasting the heartland humor of *Hee Haw* with the "sophistication and dissent-oriented sense of political irony" that had characterized the *Smothers Brothers Comedy Hour*, which CBS cancelled in 1969, one critic accused the networks of "adapting to the climate of the Nixon era" and "pursuing their own version—conscious or unconscious—of a Southern strategy. And *Hee Haw* is a key element. One might call it the Spiro Agnew of the CBS line-up, the key to the heart of the 'silent majority.'" The shift was driven only incidentally by political cowardice; far more important, the critic concluded, was the desire to capture middle-American conservatives as a lucrative audience: "In the Age of Aquarius, the big money is evidently on the 'silent majority.'"[39]

In spite of the consensus that pervaded the popular press by 1970, the genre's conservatism had seemed anything but inevitable only a few years earlier, and more than one commentator noted, even during the flush of Nixon's plain-folks cultural offensive, that country music's populism could as easily turn to economic liberalism as social conservatism. As late as 1968, an article in *Harper's* observed that even heartland Nashville showed signs of tumbling into rebellion: "There are beards in town, and mini-skirts; not all the home-rolled cigarettes come from Prince Albert cans. Grand Ole Opry artists do not yet sing of LSD trips or blood donations to the Vietcong; even so, the Opry style and sound are changing." *Newsweek* questioned the depth of country's conservatism, pointing out that in spite of the "glib generalization" of "amateur sociologists" who ascribed country's popularity to "a ground swell of right-wing sentiment," much of it was actually attributable to the work of "free-thinking, modern songwriters like Kris Kristofferson and Tom T. Hall." Others were considerably less sanguine about country's potential for progressiveness but found the spectacle of liberals trying to "rescu[e] country music from the racists and restor[e] its natural affinity for the alienated and oppressed" to be an important feature of the culture landscape, even if it revealed only the dangerous consequences of "the assumption that you can actually divorce style from its content."[40]

Old Right conservatives, too, were wary of the potential consequences of celebrating cultural populism. Writing in the pages of the *National Review*, Chilton Williamson Jr. observed of Kevin Phillips's "resentful proletariat" that "it does not appear that economic resentments lie at the root of [their] dissatisfaction" but rather "socio-cultural grievances." Nonetheless, he warned, "Cultural animosities reflect, just as surely as do economic resentments, class hostility." Cultural populism had allowed conservatism to "divest itself of its lounge-lizard intellectualism ... slough off its country club image and make itself appealing to a grassroots constituency," but the ties binding that populism to the economic conservatism of the upper class were tenuous, and the politics of low culture like country music, he cautioned, "can go either way—right or left." The New Majoritarians, "willing to inflame [lower middle-class] prejudices by flattering their customs and tastes," might well find themselves presiding over what Williamson called "country & western Marxism," while old-line conservatives would be forced to renounce their own cultural authority for fear of "offending the people who, though they are part of the cultural problem—Joe Sixpack, the Neiman-Marcus vulgarians—are also part of the political solution."[41]

Fans themselves seemed no more certain than cultural critics or political theorists about the political implications of listening to country music. Politics was seldom mentioned in *K-Bar-T*, for example, and then only obliquely, often in the context of fans updating readers about sons serving in Vietnam. One notable exception occurred when Ruth Wood wrote in to describe a Merle Haggard show she attended in Los Angeles, where she saw the first standing ovation in her fifteen years of country concertgoing in the city. As Haggard played "Okie from Muskogee," the crowd became progressively more enthusiastic, she wrote. "After *each* line, the audience applauded. And when he sang, 'We still fly Old Glory down at the Court House' people began to cheer—and by the time he had finished, the whole audience, something like 5,000 people, was on its feet!!!! Cheering and clapping!!" This communal demonstration of patriotism translated directly into political identity for Wood: "The grass roots, or 'silent majority' were certainly not silent that night in the Shrine Auditorium." But Wood also perceived membership in the Silent Majority as a moderate position consisting primarily of patriotism. Assuming what she imagined to be the voice of the crowd that night, Wood summed up their sentiments this way: "We are Americans, and proud of it. We love and respect our flag and our servicemen in Viet Nam. We know this country has its faults and we'll try to correct them, but even with all its faults, *this is our country!* Land of the free, and we will not shame or defile it or its flag." The *New York Times* correspondent Roy Reed observed a compelling demonstration of the elasticity of this kind of Americanism at a Tommy Cash concert in New Orleans. There, he reported, the audience "apparently saw nothing contradictory in applauding both 'Six White Horses,'" a lament for the deaths of the Kennedys and Martin Luther King Jr., and Merle Haggard's anti-protest song, "'The Fightin' Side of Me.' Tommy Cash sang both within five minutes."[42]

The problematic nature of country music's politics was nowhere more evident than in the industry's approach to race. The popular imagination consistently equated country music with racism. When the Marine Corps sought to ease racial tensions at Camp Lejeune, where a Marine had been beaten to death during a racially motivated brawl, it instituted a series of policies that included a firm commitment to investigating claims of discrimination, a prohibition on racially exclusive meetings, and a decree that "disciplinary action must be taken against blacks who play excessively loud 'soul' music and whites who play excessively loud 'country' music." But while some underground country labels released aggressively racist material, the mainstream industry, like the Nixon administration, was guilty mainly of downplaying the significance of race altogether. Publicity agent and future CMA president Tandy Rice explained country's appeal as white escapism. Country, he told a reporter, "is stable, like the backbone of this great country. The lyrics are simple, and sincere, not about civil rights and such. . . . The lyrics are about what concerns everyday folks." Writing in the *Nation*, Paul Dickson similarly argued that, while "the casual listener might conclude that the content of [country music] has shifted to the right; actually it has stayed where it was. It has not changed in a changing world and it tells us a lot about people of the same description."[43]

To the country industry and its fans, stereotypes of retrograde racist hicks were simply an extension of the accusations of cultural and economic backwardness that had so long stigmatized the genre. This connection was aptly summarized by Merle Haggard—touted as the personification of working-class traditionalism more often than almost any other country entertainer—when he repudiated Wallacite racism. Asked why he had refused to campaign for Wallace, Haggard replied, "Wallace is unrefined and uncontemporary. He's strictly against the black man. He wants to keep 'em niggers." More than one reader must have wondered whether the racism or the failure to be contemporary repulsed Haggard most. By the early 1970s—partially in spite of and partially because of the presence of black artists such as Charley Pride, Linda Martell, and O. B. McClinton—country was resoundingly white without being expressly anti-black, and indeed, this was precisely why the New Majority theorists found it so useful. No other cultural form allowed for a clear embrace of Southern traditions and values while still hewing to a moderate position on civil rights. And, like those theorists, the country industry pointedly ignored racism in favor of the class politics of the American Dream.[44]

SELLING THE AMERICAN DREAM

In 1974, the Grand Ole Opry followed in the footsteps of many of its listeners by moving from a run-down neighborhood in the heart of downtown Nashville to a spacious suburban park. Opryland U.S.A. was a 369-acre attraction "designed to be the home of American music," with a new Grand Ole Opry building, which one reporter tartly described as "a $15 million testament in red brick to the fact that country music is both a national habit and a thriving industry." Opryland combined animal rides, concessions, gift shops, and eating areas in a family-friendly, tourist-oriented country music theme park that already welcomed more than two million people a year by the time the new auditorium itself was opened. The Opry's new home had a number of advantages over the old Ryman Auditorium, including air conditioning, ample dressing-room space, and over a thousand more seats, every one of them cushioned. Like the Country Music Hall of Fame, it was quickly perceived as a statement of country's respectability and commercial power, for good and ill. While *U.S. News & World Report* attributed much of Nashville's tourism and construction boom to the new park, some fans warned that "it is only natural for people to resent success" and cautioned that Opryland might well suffer from its association with the commercialism of the Nashville Sound.[45]

The mainstream popular press covered the move with nostalgia, fretting that the Opry was betraying its hallowed tradition for a little material comfort. "Swivel seats and air conditioning. That doesn't seem right," wrote Nashville chronicler Paul Hemphill. Another report warned that the move threatened the very source of the Opry's genius. "Dropouts and dreamers . . . will not gravitate to an amusement park that serves only soft drinks, and they will never again shape their talents and goals in the imposing shadow of the Opry House," the article predicted. No one noted the irony in the notion that the Grand Ole Opry, which had been the symbol of "the crass commercialization of country music, once rooted in folksong" during the 1930s and 1940s, could now be portrayed as the authentic cultural expression of the modern industrial folk. But even these stories recognized the attraction of country's narrative of success and commercialism. Underlying the aspirations of the dropouts and dreamers, of course, was the possibility of stardom and wealth. As *Esquire* magazine explained, the way "wealth is pursued and used [there] makes Nashville not simply *another* version of the American Dream, but today—in the America of the Seventies—the funkiest dream of all."[46]

It was perhaps in this regard that country music most clearly resonated with Nixon's Southern Strategy, and it was thus particularly fitting that on its opening night in its new quarters the Opry welcomed Nixon as the first president of the United States ever to grace its stage. Fifteen years earlier, Vice-President Nixon had faced off against Nikita Khrushchev in the famous Moscow "kitchen debate." Standing next to the kitchen of a model suburban home, which he pointed out was readily available to the average American worker, Nixon had equated the post-war profusion of consumer goods and choices with democracy, freedom, and diversity. As a cultural text, the business of country music offered its listeners a similar account of the promise of the American Way, even when the songs it produced focused on the trials of ordinary people and proclaimed a money-can't-buy-happiness anti-materialist ethic. As Bill Malone later remarked, the commercial history of country music described "a phenomenon that had evolved from southern regional roots into an industry with international implications. . . . [A] rags-to-riches story" in the greatest Horatio Alger tradition. In this sense, country's commercialism became a symbol of a second-wave New South and of the successful Southern and Western migrants who were as likely as anyone to enjoy the fruits of American abundance in Nixon's modest suburban ranch house.[47]

As it did for many of its audience members, Nashville's commercialism served Nixon as a metaphor for the validity of the American Dream; for other observers, however, it continued to embody corrupt materialism and cheap, disposable culture, and it was in this latter incarnation that Music City was most forcefully presented in the 1970s. A few weeks after President Nixon opened the new Opry house, Robert Altman began shooting *Nashville*, which he described as "a metaphor for my personal view of our society." Following twenty-four main characters whose lives intersected over the course of five days in Nashville, the film continually emphasized the intertwined themes of material success and culture-as-commodity that the country industry had come to represent in popular discourse. "Today, Nashville is a city of instant success," Altman told an interviewer, echoing the assessment of *Esquire*'s reporters. "You get off the bus carrying a guitar, and, with luck, in two years you have a guitar-shaped swimming pool."[48]

Ironically, the movie itself had its origins in United Artists executives' efforts to exploit country's commercial success. The original project, called *The Great Southern Amusement Company*, was intended as a country-based star vehicle for the company's record division, little more than a filmic advertisement for the soundtrack. The notion underlined the extent to which country's success as an industry had itself been recycled as a saleable storyline. United Artists ultimately passed on an early treatment of the *Nashville* script, undoubtedly because its take on Music City's triumph was less than entirely celebratory.[49]

Though it was generally received as a stark, even vicious, attack on American materialism and the incurable shortcomings of consumer democracy, *Nashville* contains a multiplicity of contradictory perspectives. Like other Altman films, it is, as Leo Braudy would describe it, an "open" film, in which "the attitude of the film toward the objects it contains" is ultimately ambiguous and never "exhaust[s] the meaning of what it contains." All of the characters are flawed or ridiculous in some way. Some, like Sueleen Gay and Albuquerque, invest in Nashville's illusions blindly; others, like Tommy Brown and Haven Hamilton, do so more knowingly. Some, like Brown, Hamilton, and Connie White, successfully manipulate those illusions, while others, particularly Barbara Jean, are lost to their unreality. The camera appears to observe whatever comes within its frame without privileging the position of one character over any other. Perhaps because its form echoes the country industry's self-conscious presentation as a commodity and thereby similarly makes space for a variety of identifications with and rejections of the commodification of everyday life, the finished film became one of the most influential portrayals of country music in popular culture, reifying commercialism in the form of the country industry.[50]

Though many critics castigated the film for its condescension toward both its own characters and the fans and makers of country music, *Nashville* tacitly acknowledges country's power as a positive embodiment of consumer democracy for its fans. One of the film's befuddled celebrity hopefuls, Albuquerque, trudging down the side of the road into Nashville with her newfound friend Kenny, explains that she plans to become "a country-western singer, or star." Then she adds, in a matter-of-fact tone underscoring the interchangeability of the two professions, that if stardom doesn't work out, "I could always go into sales." Later, as she tries to get someone to listen to her demo, she declines a convivial offer of a beer with a terse, "No thanks, this is business." Albuquerque recognizes the business of commercial music and embraces it with joy and naïveté rather than cynicism—"It's the new one! It's the new one, alright!," she enthuses as she ascends the walk to the new Opry building —and, as a testament to the occasional benediction of success that makes the Nashville dream so alluring, she actually does get her big chance at the end of the film.[51]

Much of the film's exploration of the impact of commercialism on American life is delivered in the quirky, impressionistic monologue of Hal Phillip Walker, the phantom presidential candidate whose campaign rally provides the film's narrative continuity and climax. Walker never appears on screen; he is entirely a chimera of the media that expound his message, but his voice blares throughout the film from a roving campaign sound truck, always emphasizing the reduction of citizenship to consumerism. As the truck emerges from campaign headquarters at the beginning of the film, Walker pleads for the attention of his "fellow taxpayers and stock holders in America," and thenceforth the truck never appears without invoking the language of business and money. Walker compares the government to a corporation in need of a change of management, issues a warning that "it's time to pause and do some accounting," and admonishes his listeners that "we have some problems that money alone cannot solve."[52]

But, just as Albuquerque can be viewed simultaneously as pathetically deluded and as possessed of a surprisingly incisive conception of commercialism as a path to personal fulfillment, the Walker message juxtaposes the emptiness of politics as commercial hucksterism with repeated gestures to the underlying moral dimensions of market exchange. "There's no such thing as a free lunch," Walker's disembodied voice intones during an unusual caesura in the film's continually jostling multitrack soundscape, a reminder that Americans are not entirely innocent of the cultural and political bargain that consumer democracy required. Even the justice Walker promises is represented as a process of exchange and accounting. "If the books are to be balanced," he counsels, "we're going to have to do the balancing."

The compassion Altman shows for Albuquerque's boundless faith in the promise of commercialism is heightened by contrast with the cruelty of his portrayal of Opal, an obnoxious and potentially fraudulent reporter from the BBC. The parallel between Opal's documentary-in-the-making and the project of the film itself is not accidental. The screenwriter, Joan Tewkesbury, created Opal as an ambivalent reflection on her own and Altman's roles as social critics. Opal was, as Altman put it, "supposed to represent us . . . outsiders full of bullshit." Throughout the film, she busily engages in her own effort to turn Nashville into an overblown metaphor for American consumerism, a process that reaches its zenith as she wanders through an auto junkyard dictating a hilariously melodramatic eulogy to the cars' "rotting, decaying, rusty heaps, their innards ripped out by greedy, vultures' hands." While she pleads with the cars to tell her their stories ("O, Cars! Are you trying to tell me something? Are you trying to convey to me some secret?"), she spends the rest of the film incessantly talking over everyone else, "too busy gushing and oozing to take her foot out of her mouth," or to listen to what anyone else has to say. By identifying themselves with Opal and her "pseudo-compassionate intellectualized comments about the American wasteland," Altman and Tewkesbury call into question the very critique *Nashville* was perceived as mounting.[53]

Though Altman positioned himself as an observer rather than a critic through this distancing, the film nevertheless insists on the overpowering presence of commerce both within its own frame and beyond. Nothing is free in Nashville, a point made even before the opening credits have run, with a sequence—perhaps in reference to the project's origins, perhaps to the commercials that had funded the Country Music Hall of Fame—that positions the film as an advertisement for it own soundtrack through a campy parody of "those late-night, hard-sell TV commercials that urge us to buy cut-rate record albums containing all 106 of our all-time favorite golden oldies." Advertising similarly frames the film's vignette of the Grand Ole Opry as both performance and sales pitch. The opening shots of the sequence are dominated by an announcer's voiceover for Goo Goo Clusters candy, and the billboard-style ad that hangs from the Opry's stage set is an ever-present reminder of what the per-

Silent Majorities

formers are really there for. The performers are all cast members, with varying degrees of musical talent, whom Altman and his musical director intended as representatives of sincere effort more than quality. The real country industry is represented by the only widely recognizable Opry figure onstage: the show's real announcer, who both directs audience applause and delivers commercials from his lectern.[54]

Such devices remark relatively indulgently on the omnipresence of consumerism in American culture and even offer a good-natured gesture to the film's own position as a product of the commercial entertainment industry. *Nashville* both ridicules Opal's superficial parrotings of the standard condemnation of American materialism and, in Walker's speeches, alludes to the way the language and symbolism of money represent notions of morality, justice, and value. In doing so, it recognizes the possibilities of commercialism's multiple meanings. At the same time, however, *Nashville* condemns the commingling of politics, culture, and commercialism. As one reviewer noted, "the ever present truck is itself a commercial, announcing each time it appears another item in the populist dream it is selling." The parallels between the sometimes vicious manipulations of Walker's advance man, John Triplette, and the opportunism of the New Majority cultural initiative are obvious. "The thing with these country people is, they have a real grassroots appeal," Triplette tells his Nashville host. "And they're the people that elect the president." But when it suits his purposes, he also denigrates the music as "country crapola" and its artists as "local yokels," explaining to the folk singers he is trying to recruit that the rally will feature country simply because "this redneck music is very popular right now." There was thus a deep irony at work when observers later interpreted *Nashville* as a prophetic foreshadowing of Jimmy Carter's political style, and especially when the architect of Nixon's cultural strategy, Kevin Phillips, castigated Carter for running "a *Nashville* candidacy," "all vagueness, posturing, packaging."[55]

The subordination of all other values to commercialism figures as a personally brutalizing process, as well. As Barbara Ching has argued, the film "mourns America's enslavement to commercial interests," particularly through the character of Barbara Jean. One early scene is organized around an airport homecoming reception for the fragile, ailing singer. When one of the assembled fans voices her hope that the star will grace the audience with a song, her companion—a black waiter and busboy who serves throughout the film as the one regular Joe who recognizes and rejects the politics of country's commercialism—acidly points out that Barbara Jean "don't sing unless she gets paid." Barbara Jean later confirms that her singing has always been both a commodity and a livelihood when, during an onstage breakdown, she delivers to a paying audience a bewildered ramble about the time she and her mama got fifty cents from the Fridgidaire man for learning to sing not one but two of his promotional jingles. "I think ever since then I been workin,' . . . supportin' myself," she mumbles as reason disintegrates. Barbara Jean is escorted offstage, and her husband-manager, facing an improbably angry crowd demanding what they paid for, is pressured into offering a free performance at Hal Phillip Walker's rally the following day. Only a Sunday morning hymn offering "free grace" to sinners provides a respite from the relentless pursuit of and demand for payment.[56]

Nashville was greeted with a storm of critical praise that overflowed movie review columns and spilled onto editorial pages, even commanding the cover of *Newsweek*. Critics, especially those on the left, particularly applauded Altman's choice of Nashville as a metaphor for the American condition. "Could there be a city with wilder metaphoric overtones than Nashville, the Hollywood of the c. & w. recording industry, the center of fundamentalist music and pop success?" asked Pauline Kael in her pre-release review. "It was a brilliant notion to use Nashville, the capital of Middle America's music, as the scene for a melodramatic operetta on the theme of the country's disarray," the critic Robert Hatch wrote in the *Nation*. The critic for the *New Republic* suggested that Nashville was a particularly apt setting for the movie because it could justly be imagined as a microcosm of the nation, "not only because Nashville is the capital of a culture—the huge country-music business—but because that culture cuts right across the U.S., geographically and socially." *New York Times* editor Tom Wicker passionately embraced the film's metaphorical treatment of country, describing it as "a two-and-a-half hour cascade of minutely detailed vulgarity, greed, deceit, cruelty, barely contained hysteria, and the frantic lack of root and grace into which American life has been driven by its own heedless vitality." Apparently ignoring the fact that Opal is among the few characters in the film who Altman allows to remain laughably detestable, Wicker's condemnatory list of country's disposable culture echoed her junkyard monologue in the movie: "autos obsolete and crunchable the day they're sold, its fast-food parlors, plastic motel rooms, take-out orders, transient sex and junk music."[57]

Wicker was not the only critic to miss the satire of leftist cultural critique embodied in Opal's character, or to reduce the film's multiple perspectives and complex commentary to a simple polemic against consumer culture and commercialized politics. Like its supporters, the film's detractors generally assumed *Nashville*'s authorial perspective to be that of the urban intellectual, and they responded accordingly. "Now that blacks are sacrosanct," one particularly acid review ran, "rednecks and hillbillies are the only real butts that hip northerners have left. Niggers of the seventies, they can be parodied, mocked in absolute chic safety." Frustrated at serving once again as the backdrop for someone else's morality play, the country music industry roundly condemned the film. "When you show the anatomy of a man, you should show something besides his rear end," the producer Billy Sherrill complained. One defender of country music and popular culture more generally remarked that *Nashville* "looks down on the people" with embarrassment, in the tradition of mid-fifties mass cultural critics "who don't have and don't really want an understanding of the lives of common people."[58]

The most troublesome issue for many observers, especially those aligned with the industry, was Altman's apparent lack of respect for the country audience. Minnie Pearl told a reporter that the shots of the audience during the Opry sequence had "a plastic look about the fans that turned me off. They took a group of regular Opry fans who were scared about bein' in a movie, and they had them do the scene over and over. It showed in their faces. Also, they left out the most important part of Nashville: the fellowship and love that exists between country singers and their fans." In later interviews, Altman did appear mildly flummoxed by the audience of Opryland visitors he recruited. "Those are the faces of the audience," he commented of the audience shots with an incredulous laugh. "This was a real audience. . . . They just came in their campers and trailers." Indeed, he seemed unsure about the degree to which the audience accepted the performances as real and the degree to which they were consciously participating in those performances. "They came in to see Lily Tomlin and Henry Gibson and to see a movie being made. And they brought their Instamatic cameras and they took pictures," Altman told an interviewer, acknowledging the audience's understanding of the nature of the performance. But a moment later, he emphasized the audience's experiences of theater and reality as apparently seamless. "At one point when Henry Gibson was on he said, 'Now, Barbara Jean, she's in Vanderbilt Hospital,' and he gave that address. In the film you'll see a woman take out a piece of paper and write it down."[59]

9 Shelley Duvall and Scott Glenn watch the Grand Ole Opry in a scene from Robert Altman's 1975 film *Nashville*. The audience extras surrounding them focus their attention on the cameras filming them, revealing country fans' ongoing fascination with the mechanics of the entertainment industries.

Yet, particularly when compared with the shots of the mindless, hysterical mobs in *A Face in the Crowd*, a film to which some critics compared *Nashville*, Altman's quest for verisimilitude yielded an uncomfortably astute portrait of the audience and its self-conscious participation in country's commercial enterprise. "Those people come in, they aren't there to be entertained, nor *are* they entertained," he said of the regular Opry crowd, returning again to an emphasis on audience awareness of the artifice and mechanics of the entertainment business. In sustained shots of *Nashville*'s Opry crowd, Altman allows audience members' eyes to drift from the stage and fasten instead on the real show: the cameras that are filming them. Looking into the lens, their staring eyes reveal both an awareness of their position as a part of the entertainment commodity and a fascination, not with the down-home artifice of the performers, but with the spectacle of the commercial industry that provided so much of country's fan appeal.[60]

Reporting on Nixon's appearance at the new suburban Opry, a *New York Times* correspondent contrasted the earthy urban grit of Tootsie's Orchid Lounge with the theme park polish of the new venue. "But this is what country has come to in America. No longer stigmatized—even

Silent Majorities

New Yorkers are discovering it—it has gained the sort of respectability that leads to commercialism." The architects of the CMA's marketing strategy might have suggested that the reverse more closely approximated the truth: only through commercialism had the industry and its audience gained respectability, and even a measure of political importance. But while commercialism had advanced the claim of respectability, it remained a troublesome feature of the genre's image. Perhaps to a greater degree than ever before, especially for those on the left, the industry figured as a key metaphor for the corrosive effects of capitalism and the venality of populist politics. The practical consequences of commodifying the country audience also included a fundamental revision of the relationship between the industry and its fans in a way that potentially threatened listener loyalties. And, ironically, the utility of class resentments and obligations in shaping the industry's claim to cultural legitimacy would decrease over the coming decades in any case, replaced by criteria of multiculturalism, diversity, and hybridity that the cultural politics of commercialism did not address.[61]

Nashville is . . . its tawdriness, its triumphs, its money-greed, its racism, its smash-ups and pillheads and ego-trips, and the painful spectacle of genuinely creative, sensitive semi-"folk" artists ripping themselves apart in pursuit of a Cadillac-and-ranch-house success. That's what commercialism means.—CRAIG MCGREGOR, "The Nashville Sound"

To me, commercial is a beautiful word. It means people will like it.

—HARLAN HOWARD

Conclusion

MONEY MUSIC

Although *Nashville* was almost universally perceived as a harsh condemnation of the country music industry and the commercialization it represented, the film shared much in common with the genre it examined. Altman insistently represented his film as a commodity that could allow audiences simultaneously to criticize and take pleasure in its commercialism. Through gestures both emphatic and subtle, from the opening title sequence to the Opry audience's knowing gaze through the camera's lens, the film revealed and reveled in its own status as a cultural commodity of the very kind it so archly criticized. The same self-conscious awareness of inescapable commodity fetishism was reinforced by Opal's presence as an avatar for the filmmaker: a critic of the trashiness of consumer culture who is nonetheless enthralled by the celebrities Nashville and Hollywood's eminently disposable cultural commodities produce. Indeed, this ironic stance was a commonly noted and widely praised feature of the film.[1]

But this self-referential awareness of being embedded in commodity exchange might as easily be understood as having been borrowed from country music as having been bestowed upon it by the film. As Aaron Fox has suggested, one of country's most compelling characteristics as a genre has been its "poetic self-regard as a commodity," its continual references to its own position as cheap goods, and its stylistic insistence on the speaking object—the bottle, the empty house, the half-smoked cigarette in the ashtray—which remind listeners constantly of their own investments in the cultural texts that commercialism and commodities convey.[2]

Gretchen Wilson's 2004 paean to the redneck women who "keep it country"—a traditionalist hard-core honky-tonk anthem that also revitalized country's sagging market fortunes—serves as one example of the way country's fixation on the commodity exposes, accepts, and criticizes the meanings of commercialism. As she describes what exactly makes her a redneck, Wilson neatly captures the connection between economic and cultural value that has shaped perceptions of country music since its emergence as a commercial genre. "Victoria's Secret, well their stuff's real nice, but I can buy the same damn thing on a Wal-Mart shelf half-price," she drawls, suggesting that it's not what she wears but its location in the retail hierarchy that marks her as "trashy, a little too hard core." Rejoicing in her lowness, Wilson defiantly embraces the stereotypes that mingle white poverty, country music, and Wal-Mart wares, thereby highlighting mass culture's matching of "social differences with cultural differences with product differences." By simultaneously embracing and challenging the validity of such mapping, Wilson reiterates the commercial conundrum that suffuses and helps to define country.[3]

The centrality of commercialism as both an indictment of bad taste and a marker of social identity became the basis for the CMA's tremendously successful campaign to reprogram the sound of country radio and recast the image of the country audience in the 1960s. It remained implicit in the organization's controversial 2001 marketing slogan—"Country. Admit it. You love it."—which both drew attention to and mocked the popular imagination of the country audience as lowbrow and low-class. But the particular mapping of cultural to social and economic differences that underpins such constructions did not originate within the country industry. Instead, the beginnings of the music's class identity can more clearly be located in the cultural politics of middle-class reformers and preservationists, who sought to dismiss the genre as appealing only to the lower classes or to suggest that the educational power of broadcasting could minimize the public taste for hillbilly and other music of poor quality. As thousands of rural migrants joined the urban working class, carrying their cultural preferences with them, the music's lowbrow status was confirmed. Far from being able to establish through advertising or any other means a popularly understood correspondence between class status and cultural choice, the producers of country music struggled against such equations for decades, finally adopting affluent blue-collar America as a marketing niche only in the 1960s.

The implications of this mapping project, the impact of specific commercial structures, and the meaning of commercial success itself were as contested among the professionals as they were among fans. Diverse elements of the business responded differently to the dangers and possible rewards of producing country as mass commercial culture, though they were united in their personal sensitivity to country's lower-class reputation. The artists and entrepreneurs of the 1930s framed country's cultural value in terms of citizens and pioneers, but this image increasingly gave way during the 1950s to industry rationales of worth that emphasized the genre's economic power and the wealth it produced for professionals. For those in the country industry, as for their audience, the commercialism of country music became as important as its sincerity or authenticity in defining the music's appeal.

Commercialism's complex role in shaping country's generic meanings continues to be embodied in Country Music Hall of Fame and Museum. In 2001, the museum moved from the north end of Music Row to the city's burgeoning new SoBro district, just south of the slightly seedy lower Broadway strip where Tootsie's Orchid Lounge sheltered the dropouts and dreamers of country's honky-tonk mythos. The $37 million building joined newly constructed indoor and outdoor sports arenas, a public library, the Frist Center for the Visual Arts, and the Tennessee Performing Arts Center in a tourist-friendly "cultural crossroads" that for the first time placed the city's "musical heritage front and center in the new show area of downtown." Its location and high-concept postmodern design aptly synthesized the city's longstanding ambitions as a center of high culture with its far more popular image as Music City USA and repositioned country music as a core element of both. The "sweetly nostalgic" old building was quietly bulldozed to expand employee parking for the BMI offices next door.[4]

Where the structure of the old building had been modeled on the barns and churches of rural America, albeit in modern materials, the structure of the new museum refers not only to piano keys, bass clefs, and musical notes but also to symbols of commercial and consumer

10 The new Country Music Hall of Fame and Museum, completed in 2002, embodies the confluence of tradition and commercialism in both its architecture and its exhibits. A sweeping Cadillac tailfin overlaid with piano-key windows dominates the exterior, while visitors inside stroll through the spaces of commercial production, from barn dance backstages to recording studios. *Photo courtesy of Country Music Hall of Fame and Museum.*

culture: radio towers, Cadillac tailfins, LPs and CDs. Its postmodern eclecticism is "homespun in a large, high-style, and clearly contemporary package." Inside, the exhibitions are housed in reconstructions of the industrial spaces where the music is produced. The story of the music's early commercial successes unfolds amid exposed cables, pulleys, and a catwalk designed to evoke the backstage wings of a theater. By the time the chronology reachs the 1970s, visitors find themselves walking vinyl floors past walls lined with acoustical tile that gesture to the studios of Music Row.[5]

The move, like that of the Opry nearly thirty years earlier, occasioned a good deal of reflection on country music's legacies of authenticity and commercialism. For many, particularly within the industry, the new museum represented a belated recognition of country's importance to the city's economy and its hard-won legitimacy as a cultural form. "Whoever named Nashville 'Music City USA' hit it right on the head, but there was no darned thing to show for it," the bluegrass banjoist Earl Scruggs told a reporter. "But this new building, well, I'd say it sure is a fine, fine place." "This just makes me so proud. . . . We've come a long way," Brenda Lee told another. The public relations campaign that accompanied the museum's opening emphasized the themes of modernity, expense, and respectability that had become some of country's most enduring tropes. "Our fans expect high tech, they expect state-of-the-art, and that's what this is," Trisha Yearwood explained in the museum's press release, while the museum's director, Kyle Young, enthused that the new building "almost puts us in landmark territory." In a formulation that both contrasted and conflated the spaces of culture and commerce, the release concluded that, upon leaving the building, "museum guests return to a new kind of town square, now less a center of commerce and government and more a seat of Southern culture."[6]

Others interpreted the move as a sign of the genre's drift away from its moorings in cultural simplicity and populism. Such fears were amplified when, shortly after arriving at the new location, the museum fired several senior staff members in its special projects division. The decision provoked a storm of protest among scholars of country music, who viewed it as the culmination of a decades-old battle within the Hall of Fame between the forces of self-serving corporate hagiography and the forces of serious historical inquiry. The longstanding suspicion that, in spite of its pretensions as a research center, the Hall of Fame was nothing but a public-relations "spin job" created to stroke the egos of the industry leapt to the fore in much of this commentary. In a letter of protest to the board of trustees of the Country Music Foundation, the historian Charles Wolfe warned that the *Journal of Country Music* would be "turned into a slick, Garthian fan magazine full of eye candy for the high rollers who contribute to the Hall of Fame." A fan-based website suggested that the foundation's announcement of a possible new "vision statement" for the Hall of Fame must refer to the staff there "seeing visions of more money from special interest donors." Bill Monroe's biographer fretted that "under the command of the persons responsible for these firings—the CMF will abandon its world-renowned commitment to country music history and scholarship."[7]

Such concerns rested implicitly on a sharp, and largely spurious, dichotomy between the museum's historical and commercial missions and neglected the way in which the museum itself had been conceived in part as a marketing strategy targeted to the desires of a middle-class, intellectual audience that had traditionally disdained the music precisely for its crass marketing extravagance. Moreover, these charges emerged at a moment when the distinction between the curatorial and the commercial was dissolving, as scholars in the field of museum studies increasingly turned their attention to the similarities between the aesthetics of display in retail and curatorial environments, to the role of museums in the tourism industry, and to the interpenetration of commercial and display spaces within museum buildings themselves. With museums mounting shows of consumer products from pearls to motorcycles, the line between exhibition and advertising blurred further, making the Country Music Hall of Fame's commercial entanglements far more conventional than they had once been. Like the music it honors, the new museum is neither merely a commercial marketing strategy nor simply an expression of cultural preservation, but an intricate mixture of both.[8]

The museum's curatorial direction in its new location, however, also points to the limitations of country's traditional politics of class and commercialism. As the discussion of commercialism within traditional museum studies suggests, by the time of the Hall of Fame's move, postmodern sensibilities had thoroughly transformed the notion of cultural hierarchy, exposing the ways cultural distinctions, particularly those rooted in critiques of commercialism, serve to enforce social difference and distance. As culture and commerce became largely indistinguishable from one another, and as the lack of distinction ceased to be a compelling cause for intellectual concern, the importance of country's longstanding commercial taint lost much of its potency as a mark of inferiority. Instead, country's badness, and the backwardness of its audience, were increasingly figured through charges of racism and an unsavory whiteness. External critics had once pronounced country bad because of its position in a central conflict in American culture, that between class hierarchy and the mythology of consumer democracy. But beginning in the late 1950s, as Aaron Fox argues, country became " 'bad' music precisely because it is widely understood to signify an explicit claim to whiteness, not as an unmarked, neutral condition of lacking (or trying to shed) race, but as a marked, foregrounded claim of cultural identity—a bad whiteness."[9]

The shift from class to race as the central terrain of country's lowness perhaps underpins the Country Music Hall of Fame and Museum's recent interest in reclaiming the connections between country and R&B and soul. In its new home, the museum expanded on an earlier box set dedicated to "the black experience in country music" and a special issue of the *Journal of Country Music* on African Americans in country by mounting several commercially and critically successful exhibits that explicitly addressed race in country music. "Night Train to Nashville" and two accompanying CD box sets explored the city's rhythm-and-blues recording industry after World War II. The exhibit's segment on collaborations between country and R&B artists bore the title "Reconsider Me," a label that seemed to allude fairly directly to the cultural reevaluation of country the museum hoped to elicit. The title of the subsequent exhibit on Ray Charles, "I Can't Stop Loving You: Ray Charles and Country Music," likewise invoked the racial taboo surrounding country (a black R&B artist ought not to have loved racist country) and at the same time suggested an enduring connection with African American audiences (Ray Charles loved country enough to risk his career on a record that, against the odds, became a tremendous commercial success).

Though such efforts offer a healthy corrective to superficial popular evaluations of country's whiteness and racism, they ignore the ways the genre's central dynamics of commercialism and consumer democracy elided race during the 1950s and 1960s. Nashville aggressively staked its claims to both marketability and cultural respectability during those years on a conception of commercialization that emphasized the democratic, egalitarian function of consumerism. On the one hand, the industry's pursuit of respectability through consumerism was consciously presented as a pluralist philosophy. It was aimed at overcoming what both the industry and the audience perceived as regional and class discriminations. On the other, it presented a vision of social and individual progress that obscured the presence and effects of persistent racism. The commodity and class politics of country's marketing and consumption, though they emerged independently of New Right politics, easily aligned the music with "Silent Majority" cultural populism and with the superficially color-blind narratives of class mobility and meritocracy that characterized the Agnew-Nixon revolution. Though the politics of commercialism served its purpose in revising the image of country's audience, the genre's cultural worth, and the business itself, the legacy of this erasure continues to bedevil the industry's search for respectability.

On the occasion of its grand opening, a local reporter observed that the Country Music Hall of Fame and Museum not only "literally tells the history of country music, it *enshrines* that history." Part venal pursuit of

tourist and entertainment dollars, part lofty commitment to cultural
preservation and reflection, and no less effective in either pursuit as a
result of its commitment to the other, the new museum recapitulated
the country industry's role as a vehicle for exploring the impact of commercialism and commodification on American cultural life and reflected
the decline of the commercial narrative as the central problematic in
understandings of the genre. Its imposing, self-consciously elaborate
edifice and its internal gestures to the spaces of industrial cultural production continue to remind us that commercialism has been no less
powerful a cultural discourse than authenticity, and that it has equally
profoundly shaped the social narratives country music offers.[10]

Notes

INTRODUCTION

1 Davidson, *The Big Ballad Jamboree*, 13–14.

2 Ibid., 41–42.

3 Peterson, *Creating Country Music*; Jensen, *The Nashville Sound*, 7; Daley, *Nashville's Unwritten Rules*, 11, 12.

4 Sanjek, "They Work Hard for Their Money," 10. This viewpoint was expressed most influentially by Theodor Adorno beginning in the 1930s. See Adorno, "On the Fetish Character in Music and the Regression of Listening," and Horkheimer and Adorno, *Dialectic of Enlightenment*.

5 Neil Strauss, "The Country Music Country Radio Ignores," *New York Times*, March 24, 2002, sec. 2, 1, 31.

6 Cross, *An All-Consuming Century*, 12; Twitchell, *Lead Us into Temptation*, 17–49; Donahue, *Freedom from Want*; Cohen, *A Consumers' Republic*; Kammen, *American Culture, American Tastes*, 95–161; Denning, *The Cultural Front*, 466–72.

7 Sanjek, "Institutions," 48–49; Negus, *Music Genres and Corporate Cultures*. Studies of the resistant cultural economies of popular music audiences are too numerous to cite, but among the most influential have been Fiske, *Reading the Popular*; Jenkins, *Textual Poachers*, 24–28; and Radway, *Reading the Romance*.

8 For an understanding of the financial and cultural economies of popular culture, I am indebted to Fiske, *Understanding Popular Culture*, 23–47; and Fiske, *Reading the Popular*.

9 Tichi, *High Lonesome*.

10 Peterson, *Creating Country Music*, 129–30. Similar ambiguities surrounding the nature of audience response and influence appear in Peterson's discussion of "Blind Jilson" Setters and his explanation of the popular appeal of radio barn dance (see pp. 63, 70). See also Peterson and Beal, "Alternative Country."

11 Jensen, *Nashville Sound*, 160, 84. Several scholars have recently called for a more nuanced understanding of audience participation in the culture industries and in the circulation of commercial culture. Matt Hills suggests that we should focus on "the significance of consumption and commodification within fan cultures" and work to incorporate both consumption and production into a single narrative. Richard Peterson similarly argues that we must pay more attention to the process by which "fans actively participate in fabricating authenticity." See Hills, *Fan Cultures*; Peterson and Anand, "The Production of Culture Perspective," 326.

1 COMMERCIALISM AND COUNTRY MUSIC

1 "Cowboy Bill Johnson Gets World's Largest Fan Letter—30 Foot," *National Hillbilly News*, September 1941, 1; Barfield, *Listening to Radio*, 19, 7; Douglas, *Inventing American Broadcasting*, 304.

2 Peterson, *Creating Country Music*; Kyriakoudes, "The Grand Ole Opry and the Urban South." For an exception, see Mancini, "'Messin' with the Furniture Man.'"

3 Barn dance was not the only form of hillbilly broadcasting. Border superstations and the farmer stations from which they developed aired a steady stream of hillbilly music without the vaudeville trappings of the barn dance. However, the development of the country industry relied, as Richard Peterson has argued, on the broadcasting of hillbilly under a recognizable generic heading. Doerksen, *American Babel*, 71–92; Hagerty, "WNAX"; Barnouw, *A Tower in Babel*, 168–72, 258–59; Peterson, *Creating Country Music*, 29, 97–118.

4 Malone, *Country Music USA*, 33–34. Bill quoted in Biggar, "The WLS National Barn Dance Story," 106. Like Bill, the programmer for Atlanta radio station WSB, Lambdin Kay was said to program by desperation as much as reason. According to one witness, Kaye would air "anybody who could sing, whistle, play a musical instrument, or even breathe heavily." Wolfe, "The Triumph of the Hills," 59.

5   Peterson, *Creating Country Music*, 77, 102–5; Cantril and Allport, *The Psychology of Radio*, 82; Wolfe, *A Good-Natured Riot*, 15–20; Kingsbury, ed., *Encyclopedia of Country Music*, 244, 519–20; Patterson, "Hillbilly among the Flatlanders." A particularly eloquent description of the syncretic role of the Depression-era barn dance can be found in Cantwell, *Bluegrass Breakdown*, 43–46.

6   Smyth, "Early Knoxville Radio (1921–1941)," 111. It is unclear what station the two worked for, but both would certainly have been familiar with WHO's barn dance, whose sizeable audience extended into the South and Northeast. Patterson, "Hillbilly Music among the Flatlanders," 15.

7   Rice, "Renfro Valley on the Radio, 1937–1941," 17; Smyth, "Early Knoxville Radio," 113; Joe Allison interview by John Rumble, May 26, 1994, audiotape, tape 1, side 1.

8   Hagerty, "WNAX," 178; Barnouw, *Tower in Babel*, 168–72, 258–59.

9   Hettinger, *A Decade of Radio Advertising*, 228, 242; Cantril and Allport, *Psychology of Radio*, 76. Susan Smulyan argues that the network system severely curtailed broadcasting of specialized material such as hillbilly but, judging from programming statistics, her case may be somewhat overstated. Smulyan, *Selling Radio*, 30–31.

10   Doerksen, *American Babel*, 17, 71–91.

11   Hettinger, *Decade of Radio Advertising*, 250.

12   Killian, "Southern White Laborers in Chicago's Local Communities," 17–60; Biggar, "The WLS National Barn Dance Story," 106; Danbom, "Romantic Agrarianism in the Twentieth Century," 2; Martin L. Davey, "Secrets of a Successful Radio Program," *Broadcasting*, July 1, 1932, 9.

13   Kenney, *Recorded Music in American Life*, 8, 17; Wilgus, "An Introduction to the Study of Hillbilly Music," 198, 200; "What the Popularity of Hill-Billy Songs Means in Retail Profit Possibilities," 177.

14   Atherton, *Main Street on the Middle Border*, 296; Evans, *Prairie Farmer and WLS*, 228–29; Peterson, *Creating Country Music*, 48–55; Asbel, "The National Barn Dance"; Green, "Hillbilly Music," 222; Traver and Maring, "*Stand By*," 158; McCusker, "'Dear Radio Friend,'" 181; McCusker, "'Bury Me Beneath the Willow,'" 223–25.

15   *WLS at the Fair* (Chicago: Prairie Farmer Publishing Company, 1933), 26, 28; Steele, "The Inside Story of the Hillbilly Business," 21.

16   Smith, "'Hill Billy,'" 154, 208; Hettinger and Neff, *Practical Radio Advertising*, 113. Similar marketing assumptions, based on race rather than class, about what music would be appropriate for what audiences contributed to the widening distinction between hillbilly and country blues. See Peterson, *Creating Country Music*, 195–96.

17   Crawford, *America's Musical Life*, 471–78.

18   "What the Popularity of Hill-Billy Songs Means in Retail Profit Possibilities."

19 Ryan, *The Production of Culture in the Music Industry*; Peterson, *Creating Country Music*, 70–75; Leamy, "Now Come All You Good People."

20 "Bull Market in Corn"; Peterson, *Creating Country Music*, 41–42, 45–47.

21 Suisman, "The Sound of Money," 50–63; Peterson, *Creating Country Music*, 47; Ryan, *Production of Culture in the Music Industry*, 53.

22 Ennis, *Seventh Stream*, 100.

23 "Hill-Billy Music," *Variety*, December 29, 1926, 1, quoted in Peterson, *Creating Country Music*, 68–69; Barnouw, *Tower in Babel*, 236–37.

24 Miles, "Some Real American Music."

25 Ibid., 3, 7, 13; Green, "Hillbilly Music," 223; Malone, *Country Music USA*, 40–42.

26 Cantwell, *When We Were Good*, 32; Whisnant, *All That Is Native and Fine*, 207–15.

27 Cantwell, *When We Were Good*, 32; Whisnant, *All That Is Native and Fine*, 226–36, 197.

28 Douglas, *Listening In*, 136–37; Lazarsfeld, *Radio and the Printed Page*, 15–17.

29 Evans, Prairie Farmer *and* WLS, 181. See Smulyan, *Selling Radio*, 60, 144.

30 Smulyan, *Selling Radio*, 39, 60–61; National Broadcasting Company, *Broadcasting*, vol. 2, 4–6.

31 Cantril and Allport, *Psychology of Radio*, 95; Hettinger, "What We Know about the Listening Audience"; Lazarsfeld, *Radio and the Printed Page*, 22.

32 Lazarsfeld, *Radio and the Printed Page*, 22; see also Douglas, *Listening In*, 143.

33 Lazarsfeld, *The People Look at Radio*, 49, 140–41.

34 Lazarsfeld and Kendall, *Radio Listening in America*, 19–25, 33, 135–36.

35 Wilgus, "Country-Western Music and the Urban Hillbilly," 162.

36 Conkin, *Tomorrow a New World*, 140; Pescatello, *Charles Seeger*, 140–43.

37 Valiant, "Journal of a Field Representative."

38 Ibid., 186; Pescatello, *Charles Seeger*, 143.

39 Pescatello, *Charles Seeger*, 144; Valiant, "Journal of a Field Representative," 196, 200–201.

40 Gregory, *American Exodus*, 230, 322.

41 McCusker, " 'Dear Radio Friend,' " 179–80; "Ever Have a Saturday Night Barn Dance Party in Your House?" *Rural Radio*, March 1938, 19; Hugh and Ann MacNabb, letter to the editor, *Rural Radio*, March 1938, 25.

42 Green, "Early Country Music Journals"; Traver and Maring, "*Stand By*," 149–61; McCusker, " 'Dear Radio Friend,' " 173–95.

43 Fuller, *At the Picture Show*, 133–69.

44 Mrs. Ed Dalton, letter to the editor, *Rural Radio*, January 1939, 24; scrapbook, Kevin Parks Collection (Chicago, Ill.); McCusker, "'Dear Radio Friend,'" 173, 180; Lois Almy, letter to the editor, *Stand By!*, August 24, 1935, 2.

45 "Family Gossip," *Rural Radio*, August 1938, 28; "WLS at the Fair"; *Rural Radio*, May 1938, 22; "Ever Have a Saturday Night Barn Dance Party?" 19; *Rural Radio*, October 1938, 4–5.

46 "Cracker Barrel," *Rural Radio*, September 1938, 12; Nora F. McCormick, letter to the editor, *Rural Radio*, October 1938, 29; Tressa Bierma, letter to the editor, *Rural Radio*, October 1938, 29; Frances Webb, letter to the editor, *Rural Radio*, April 1938, 29; Mrs. Ruth Williams, letter to the editor, *Rural Radio*, July 1938, 29.

47 "Cracker Barrel," *Rural Radio*, November 1938, 29; "An Open Letter from the Publisher," *Rural Radio*, February 1939, 12.

48 Barbas, *Movie Crazy*, 59–85.

49 Peterson and Di Maggio, "From Region to Class, the Changing Locus of Country Music," 503; Lazarsfeld and Kendall, *Radio Listening in America*, 136.

50 Berry, *Southern Migrants, Northern Exiles*; Gregory, *American Exodus*; Cohen, *Making a New Deal*; Killian, "Southern White Laborers in Chicago's Local Communities," 123, 126.

51 Peterson, *Creating Country Music*, 131.

52 Berry, "Social Highways, 353–54; McCusker, "'Dear Radio Friend,'" 184.

53 McCusker, "'Dear Radio Friend,'" 188.

54 Evans, Prairie Farmer *and* WLS, 228–29.

55 Grundy, "'We Always Tried to Be Good People,'" 1614, 1604.

56 Criesler, "Little Oklahoma," 94, 55, 100.

57 Tosches, *Country*, 27.

58 Killian, "Southern White Laborers in Chicago's Local Communities," 300, 303; Hoekstra, "The Three Decade Night of the Sundowners," 31. See also Wilgus, "Country-Western Music and the Urban Hillbilly"; Malone, "Honky Tonk."

59 Killian, "Southern White Laborers in Chicago's Local Communities," 302–3, 309–10; Berry, "Social Highways," 249.

60 Killian, "Southern White Laborers in Chicago's Local Communities," 321–22; Bill Bailey, "Small Talk," *Down Beat*, March 24, 1954, 20.

61 Asbel, "National Barn Dance," 21, 23; Gregory, "Southernizing the American Working Class"; Guy, "Down Home."

1 Malone, *Country Music USA*, 200–213; Pugh, "Country Music Is Here to Stay?"; Peterson, *Creating Country Music*, 185–201.

2 Hearings before the Subcommittee on Communications of the Committee on Interstate and Foreign Commerce, U.S. Senate, 85th Congress, 2d Session, S. 2834 (March 11–July 23, 1958), 447–56, 488–526.

3 Ryan, *Production of Culture in the Music Industry*, 83.

4 Barnouw, *The Golden Web*, 218; Ennis, *Seventh Stream*, 107; Rumble, "Fred Rose and the Development of the Nashville Music Industry," 85.

5 Sanjek, *Pennies from Heaven*, 179–82; Ennis, *Seventh Stream*, 99–128; Peterson, *Creating Country Music*, 185–92.

6 Rumble, "Fred Rose and the Development of the Nashville Music Industry," 68–115; John Rumble, "Acuff-Rose Publications," in *Encyclopedia of Country Music*, ed. Kingsbury, 5.

7 Ivey, "The Bottom Line," 420.

8 Brackett, *Interpreting Popular Music*, 103; Ryan, *The Production of Culture in the Music Industry*, 116–17.

9 Pugh, "Country Music Is Here to Stay?," 35; Peterson, *Creating Country Music*, 191.

10 Brackett, *Interpreting Popular Music*, 104; Pugh, "Country Music Is Here to Stay?," 35; Ennis, *The Seventh Stream*, 124–28, 168–71, 182–92; "Pistol Packin' Mama," *Life*, October 11, 1943; Morris, "New, Improved, Homogenized," 99–100.

11 *Billboard* articles quoted in Brackett, *Interpreting Popular Music*, 104.

12 Rumble, "Fred Rose and the Development of the Nashville Music Industry," 1–68.

13 *Billboard*, August 3, 1946, 123; Pugh, "Country Music Is Here to Stay?," 34–35.

14 Maurice Zolotow, "Hillbilly Boom," *Saturday Evening Post*, February 12, 1944, reprinted in *A History and Encyclopedia of Country, Western, and Gospel Music*, ed. Gentry, 58–60; *Billboard*, August 3, 1946, 123.

15 Rumble, "Fred Rose and the Development of the Nashville Music Industry," 123–39, 228.

16 Escott, *Hank Williams*, 142–44.

17 Rumble, "Fred Rose and the Development of the Nashville Music Industry," 243–48, 252–60; *Billboard*, September 15, 1951.

18 Jensen, *The Nashville Sound*.

19 Lomax, *Nashville*, 81; Sanjek, *Pennies from Heaven*, 355; Ennis, *Seventh Stream*, 137; Johnny Sippel, "Hillbilly Deejay Prime Asset to Country & Western Music," *Billboard*, September 15, 1951, 61.

20 Sanjek, *From Print to Plastic*, 38–39.

21 Ennis, *Seventh Stream,* 131–60; Douglas, *Listening In,* 229–41; Passman, *The Deejays,* 121–27; Biff Collie interview by Douglas B. Green, October 30, 1974, audiotape, tape 2, side 1.

22 Sanjek, *From Print to Plastic,* 37; Sanjek, *Pennies from Heaven,* 228; Sippel, "Hillbilly Deejay Prime Asset," 61.

23 Sippel, "Hillbilly Deejay Prime Asset," 61; Ronnie Pugh, "Biff Collie," in *Encyclopedia of Country Music,* ed. Kingsbury, 103.

24 Biff Collie, quoted in Stockdell, "The Development of the Country Music Radio Format," 38.

25 Joe Allison interview by John Rumble, March 15, 1994, audiotape, tape 1, side 1; Biff Collie interview by Douglas B. Green, October 30, 1974, audiotape, tape 1, side 1; Joe Allison interview by Diane Pecknold, March 26, 1999, audiotape, tape 1, side 1; Haslam, *Workin' Man Blues,* 141; Johnny Sippel, "Folk Talent and Tunes," *Billboard,* November 3, 1951, 40.

26 Sippel, "Folk Talent and Tunes," *Billboard,* June 26, 1948, 110; *Billboard,* issues of January 28, 1950, 107; June 26, 1948, 31; July 10, 1948, 30; July 17, 1948, 33.

27 Joel Friedman, "Radio, Country Music, Like Twins, Grow Big Together," *Billboard,* May 24, 1954, 17; Joe Allison, "Country Music Fans Not Easy to Fool," *Pickin' and Singin' News,* February 15, 1954, 2.

28 Allison interview by Rumble, March 15, 1994, tape 1, side 1; Allison interview by Pecknold, March 26, 1999, tape 1, side 2; Stockdell, "Development of the Country Music Radio Format," 38.

29 Portis, "That New Sound from Nashville," 270.

30 Bill McDaniel quoted in "Madness, Mayhem, and Music," *Billboard,* October 28, 1967, 64.

31 Sanjek, *From Print to Plastic,* 37; Sanjek, *Pennies from Heaven,* 228; "Madness, Mayhem, and Music," 65; Wolfe, *A Good Natured Riot,* 4–9; John Rumble, "DJ Convention," in *Encyclopedia of Country Music,* ed. Kingsbury, 149.

32 Peterson, *Creating Country Music,* 182–83; Escott, *Hank Williams,* 251.

33 Peterson, *Creating Country Music,* 184; "Our Little Sunbonnet Girl," handbill, box 1, Kevin Parks Collection, Chicago, Ill.; "Listener's Mike," *Stand By!,* August 24, 1935, 2; Porterfield, *Jimmie Rodgers,* 355–57.

34 Pugh, *Ernest Tubb,* 185–86.

35 Ibid., 186–87; Porterfield, *Jimmie Rodgers,* 363; *Billboard,* May 16, 1953, 20.

36 Pugh, *Ernest Tubb,* 132–33; "Congressman Wants 'Day' for Country Music," *Pickin' and Singin' News,* Audition Issue, n.d. [1953], 5; "25,000 Fans Attend Rodgers Dedication," *Pickin' and Singin' News,* June 13, 1953, 1, 6.

37 Pugh, *Ernest Tubb,* 185–87; Ellison, *Country Music Culture,* 47–49; "Rodgers Remembered," *Newsweek,* June 8, 1953.

38 "600 Leaders Attend Music City Disc Jockey Festival," *Pickin' and Singin' News*, December 14, 1953, 1–2; "Wiser Presents Stars' Awards," *Pickin' and Singin' News*, December 14, 1953; Paul Ackerman, "WSM DJ Festival Public Relations Coup," *Billboard*, November 28, 1953, 1.

39 Ackerman, "WSM DJ Festival Public Relations Coup," 42; "Editorial," *Billboard*, December 5, 1953, 41; Cliffie Stone, "Big C&W Boom on Coast," *Down Beat*, November 18, 1953, 5, 16-S; Hank Thompson, "Here's What It Takes to Organize a Western Band," *Down Beat*, May 6, 1953, 19.

40 "C & W Deejays Organize," *Down Beat*, December 30, 1953, 17; "Disc Jockeys Begin National Organization of Mutual Aid," *Pickin' and Singin' News*, December 14, 1953, 2; Allison interview by Rumble, March 15, 1994, tape 1, side 1.

41 Ebby McCord, "New Paper Dedicated to Country Music" and "Opry Mopp'ry," *Pickin' and Singin' News*, Audition Issue, n.d. [1953], 1, 4, and 2; Letters to the Editor, *Pickin' and Singin' News*, August 1953, 9; Allison, "Country Music Fans Not Easy to Fool," 2; "Uncle Joe's Country Capers," *Pickin' and Singin' News*, February 26, 1954, 2.

42 "Disc Jockeys Begin National Organization of Mutual Aid," 2; "Bon Voyage," *Pickin' and Singin' News*, December 14, 1953, 2.

43 McCord, "New Paper Dedicated to Country Music," 4; "Guard Well," *Pickin' and Singin' News*, June 13, 1953, 2; "About Our Ratings," *Pickin' and Singin' News*, Audition Issue, n.d. [1953], 2.

44 "To the Artists: Proceed Slowly," *Pickin' and Singin' News*, October 10, 1953, 2.

45 Allison, "Country Music Fans Not Easy to Fool," 2.

46 Mrs. D. N. Barnett, letter to the editor, *Rural Radio*, October 1938, 25; Peterson, *Creating Country Music*, 48–50; Porterfield, *Jimmie Rodgers*, 8–9.

47 "Stevenson Scores G.O.P. for Crisis," *New York Times*, May 27, 1954, 39; Joe Martin, "Politicians Descend on Meridian Fete," *Billboard*, June 5, 1954, 14; "Politics Not Needed," *Billboard*, June 5, 1954.

48 Russell Baker, "Stevenson Back for Florida Bid," *New York Times*, May 19, 1956, 10; Martin, "Politicians Descend on Meridian Fete," 14, 26.

49 Pugh, *Ernest Tubb*, 190; "Congress to Go Hillbilly? Invite House Members to Meridian Festival," *Billboard*, May 22, 1954, 41; "Country and Western Jubilee Section," *Billboard*, May 22, 1954, 17; Logan, *Elvis, Hank, and Me*, 160.

50 "Agenda Set Up for Jimmie Rodgers Fete," *Billboard*, May 21, 1955, 16, 23, 36; Guralnick, *Last Train to Memphis*, 190–91; Logan, *Elvis, Hank, and Me*, 123–34, 160.

51 "Agenda Set Up for Jimmie Rodgers Fete," 16; Bill Sachs, "Honor Jimmie Rodgers; Talk Nat'l C&W Days," *Billboard*, June 4, 1955, 15, 24.

52 Paul Ackerman, "CMDJA Confab OK's Plan for Annual Country Music Fete," *Billboard*, November 19, 1955, 11; Allison interview by Pecknold, March 26, 1999, tape 1, side 1.

53 "WSM Country Fest Pulls Record Crowd," *Billboard*, November 27, 1954, 11, 16; "Country Music Jocks Build for the Future," *Billboard*, November 27, 1954, 11; Paul Ackerman and Bill Sachs, "Gratis Disks Snare D. J. Meet Spotlight," *Billboard*, November 19, 1955, 11, 13.

54 Douglas, *Listening In*, 246–48; Chapple and Garofalo, *Rock 'n' Roll Is Here to Pay*, 57–64; "Who Picks Disks? D.J.s Say They Do: Stations Say No," *Billboard*, November 10, 1956, 21, 70; Jensen, *Nashville Sound*, 43.

55 Bill Sachs, "Fracas Mars Peace of C&W Music Field," *Billboard*, February 11, 1956, 14; Bill Sachs, "Country D. J. Music Fest to Springfield," *Billboard*, May 19, 1956, 13, 15; "Drop Petty Bickering," *Billboard*, March 3, 1956, 53; Bill Sachs, "Rodgers' Day Event Pulls Big Turnout," *Billboard*, June 2, 1956, 12.

56 Bill Sachs, "C&W Deejays Kick Off First Annual," *Billboard*, June 23, 1956, 29, 40; "DJ Association Parts Company with Festival," *Country Music Reporter*, November 24, 1956, 1, 6; "C&W Deejays Vote to Go Independent," *Billboard*, November 17, 1956, 18; Bill Sachs, "CMDJA Registers Solid Progress," *Billboard*, March 23, 1957, 79; Nelson King, "C&W Parley Supports Action to Combat Blue Lyrics," *Down Beat*, December 29, 1954, 16; "40 Sign in for CMDJA Meet in K.C.," *Billboard*, June 17, 1957, 32; "CMDJA Board Quits to Form New C&W Org," *Billboard*, June 30, 1958, 9; "CMA Formed at Miami Confab; 5 Named to Plans Committee," *Music Reporter*, July 7, 1958, 13; Jo Walker-Meador interview by John Rumble, June 18, 1996, audiotape, tape 1, side 2.

57 Allison interview by Pecknold, March 26, 1999, tape 2, side 1; Jo Walker-Meador interview by Diane Pecknold, August 2, 1999, audiotape, tape 1, side 1; Stockdell, "Development of the Country Music Radio Format," 40.

58 Walker-Meador interview by Pecknold, August 2, 1999, tape 1, side 1; Allison, "Country Music Fans Not Easy to Fool," 2.

59 Chapple and Garofalo, *Rock 'n' Roll Is Here to Pay*, xiii; Ennis, *Seventh Stream*, 259–83; Lipsitz, *Rainbow at Midnight*, 301–33; Jensen, *Nashville Sound*, 38, 64–67.

60 Nelson King, "Who's to Blame for Dip in Country Music Field?," *Down Beat*, October 20, 1954, 18; Barlow, *Voice Over*, 98–99; Tosches, *Country*, 120–56; Kennedy and McNutt, *Little Labels—Big Sound*, 60–67; Jon Hartley Fox, "Nelson King," in *Encyclopedia of Country Music*, ed. Kingsbury, 283.

61 Randy Blake, "Disc Jockey Urges Return to Spinning Only Country Music," *Down Beat*, January 26, 1955, 1, 19; King, "Who's to Blame for Dip in Country Music Field?," 18; Nelson King, "True C&W Music Called Key to Return of Hits," *Down Beat*, November 3, 1954, 16; Barlow, *Voice Over*, 57, 99; Daniel, *Lost Revolutions*, 166–67.

62   "Drop Petty Bickering," 53; "Diskeries Scorn Anti-Pop Bias of Some DJ's," *Billboard*, March 3, 1956, 54; "Don't Lose That Kid," *Billboard*, March 17, 1956, 18; King, "Who's to Blame for Dip in Country Music Field?," 18; King, "True C&W Music Called Key to Return of Hits," 16.

63   Malone, *Country Music USA*, 247–49; Malone, "Elvis, Country Music, and the South"; Tosches, *Country*, 35–38.

64   Guralnick, *Last Train to Memphis*, 225–36.

65   "Folk Music Fireball—Elvis Presley," *Country Song Roundup*, September 1955, 14; Guralnick, *Last Train to Memphis*, 123, 222–23.

66   Ennis, *Seventh Stream*, 238–40; Paul Ackerman, "Pop Is Dipping Fingers Into C&W Water to Heat Up Hits," *Billboard*, August 13, 1955, 1, 25; Bill Sachs, "Growth of C&W Field an Industry Phenomenon," *Billboard*, March 3, 1956, 53; Joel Friedman, "C&W Big Factor in 1955 Record Sales," *Billboard*, March 3, 1956, 68; Ren Grevatt, "Country & Western Field Hops Fences, Covering the Nation," *Billboard*, March 23, 1957, 1, 24.

67   " 'The Reporter' Knocks on Every Door," *Country Music Reporter*, March 30, 1957, 1; "Sticks Grab Domination in Music Biz Spurt," *Country Music Reporter*, October 13, 1958, 6.

68   Logan, *Elvis, Hank, and Me*, 134, 167; Escott, *Hank Williams*, 105; Guralnick, *Last Train to Memphis*, 215–16, 279; Ivey, "The Bottom Line," 433–34.

69   John Rumble, "The Emergence of Nashville as a Recording Center: Logbooks from the Castle Studio, 1952–1953," *Journal of Country Music*, December 1978; Robert K. Oermann, "Owen Bradley," typescript biography, n.d., Owen Bradley folder, CMFL; William Ivey, "Chet Atkins," in *Stars of Country Music*, ed. Bill C. Malone and Judith McCulloh (Urbana: University of Illinois Press, 1975), 284.

70   Malone, *Country Music USA*, 256; " 'Where Do We Go from Here?' Is A. & R. Question," *Billboard*, August 12, 1957, 1, 51; Cohen, "The Class Experience of Mass Consumption," 158–60; Tedlow, "The Fourth Phase of Marketing: Marketing History and the Business World Today," 15–19; Cohen, *A Consumers' Republic*, 292–344.

71   Malone, *Country Music USA*, 256; "Music Trade Paper Snobbery 'For Birds': Sales Show Difference," *Music Reporter*, August 3, 1957, 1, 3; "Labels Ride Country Talent 'Gravy Train,' " *Music Reporter*, September 14, 1957, 1.

72   "Air Play, Improved Distrib Could Speed Fall Country Boom," *Music Reporter*, August 25, 1958, 1; "Music Trade Paper Snobbery 'For Birds,' " 8; " 'The Reporter' Knocks on Every Door," 1; "MR's First Survey Report Shows C&W Treasure Waiting," *Music Reporter*, November 17, 1958, n.p.

73   "New MR Charts Tag Tunes Right," *Music Reporter*, March 24, 1958, 6; "Confused Charts—Two-Headed Evil in Trade Press," *Music Reporter*,

June 16, 1958, 1, 15; "Charlie's Column," *Music Reporter*, April 21, 1958, 2; "Country Clippin's," *Music Reporter*, June 30, 1958, 14; "Charlie's Column," *Music Reporter*, August 3, 1957, 2.

3 COUNTRY AUDIENCES AND MASS CULTURE

1 Gregory, "Southernizing the American Working Class," 148; Jackson Lears, "A Matter of Taste," 45–46; Rieder, "The Rise of the 'Silent Majority,'" 248.

2 Denning, *The Cultural Front*, 469–70; Bertrand, *Race, Rock, and Elvis*, 125–57.

3 Gregory, "Southernizing the American Working Class," 151.

4 Lipsitz, *Rainbow at Midnight*, 326.

5 Fox, *Madison Avenue Goes to War*; Marchand, *Advertising the American Dream*.

6 Filene, *Romancing the Folk*, 133–64; Bodnar, *Remaking America*, 138–66.

7 Hofstadter, *The American Political Tradition and the Men Who Made It*, v; Hofstadter, *The Age of Reform*, 12, 19–20.

8 Filene, *Romancing the Folk*, 163–76.

9 Kammen, *American Culture, American Tastes*, 95–101, 147–48; Packard, *The Status Seekers*; Riesman, *The Lonely Crowd*, 217–24;

10 Votaw, "The Hillbillies Invade Chicago"; Berry, *Southern Migrants, Northern Exiles*, 176; Harkins, *Hillbilly*, 173–77.

11 McPartland, *No Down Payment*; Levy, *Small-Town America in Film*, 111–15. Anthony Harkins notes that the emergence of nonthreatening, domesticated images of the hillbilly on television during the late 1950s similarly challenged the hegemony of the suburban middle-class ideal. Harkins, *Hillbilly*, 173–204.

12 *A Face in the Crowd*, dir. Elia Kazan (Newtown, 1957); Denning, *Cultural Front*, 469.

13 Williamson, *Hillbillyland*, 168–69.

14 Lipsitz, *Time Passages*, 39–76; Berry, *Southern Migrants, Northern Exiles*, 172–80.

15 Sanjek, *Pennies from Heaven*, 328, 330.

16 "Celler Hearings Provide Pros with Yocks!," *Billboard*, September 22, 1956, 1; "Celler Committee Winds Up Hearings," *Billboard*, October 6, 1956, 39; "Hearings Provoke Some Censure but More Laughs," *Billboard*, September 29, 1956, 30.

17 Sanjek, *Pennies from Heaven*, 402, 405, 423–24; "BMI Charged with B'dcast Monopoly," *Billboard*, September 22, 1956, 69.

18 "Governor Ready to Fight for BMI before Congress," *Country Music Reporter*, November 24, 1956, 1, 3.

19 U.S. Congress, Senate, Subcommittee on Communications of the Committee on Interstate and Foreign Commerce, Hearings on S. 2834, 24–29.

20 Sanjek, *Pennies from Heaven*, 405; " 'Payola' Hit at BMI Inquiry: Chairman Calls for Proof," *Billboard*, March 24, 1958, 8; Subcommittee on Communications of the Committee on Interstate and Foreign Commerce, Hearings on S. 2834, 106.

21 Subcommittee on Communications of the Committee on Interstate and Foreign Commerce, Hearings on S. 2834, 107; Horowitz, ed., *American Social Classes in the 1950s*, 16.

22 Subcommittee on Communications of the Committee on Interstate and Foreign Commerce, Hearings on S. 2834, 118–19, 141–42; Sanjek, *Pennies from Heaven*, 427; "He Likes Country Music," *Chicago Daily News*, March 13, 1958, 4; "Hillbilly Tunes Praised in House," *New York Times*, March 13, 1958, 59.

23 Subcommittee on Communications of the Committee on Interstate and Foreign Commerce, Hearings on S. 2834, 447–56, 477–98, 520–26, 456, 485.

24 Ibid., 479–81, 487, 489.

25 Ibid., 490, 524.

26 Smulyan, *Selling Radio*; "ASCAP Songsmiths Punch Up Case for Smathers' Bill in D.C. Hearings: Cuffo 'BMI Disks,' D.J. Payola in Focus," *Variety*, March 26, 1958, 59; Sanjek, *Pennies from Heaven*, 430; "D.C. Solons Face the Music," *Variety*, March 19, 1958, 75.

27 Lears, "A Matter of Taste," 46–54.

28 "Sons of the Pioneer," *Pickin' and Singin' News*, May 23, 1953, 2; "Crying, Dying, or Going Away," *Pickin' and Singin' News*, August 1953, 2.

29 "Why Wouldn't Them-'Ere Highbrows Let Our Tex Play-Act, Too?" *Pickin' and Singin' News*, Audition Issue, n.d. [1953], 5.

30 Ralph J. Gleason, "Ralph's Yellin' for Helen over Sting from Bing," *Down Beat*, November 4, 1953, 6.

31 "Grand Opera Star on Grand Ole Opry," *Pickin' and Singin' News*, January 30, 1954, 1; "Fans Sample Country Music as Sung by Helen Traubel on the WSM Grand Ole Opry," *Pickin' and Singin' News*, April 9, 1954, 1, 5.

32 "An Open Letter to the U.S. Congress," *Pickin' and Singin' News*, February 26, 1954, 2; Levine, *Highbrow/Lowbrow*, 211–31.

33 "An Open Letter to the U.S. Congress," 2.

34 "Maryville, Near Smokies, Plans 'Homecoming,' " *Pickin' and Singin' News*, June 13, 1953, 1; "Home of Stars Ready for Big Hillbilly Day," *Pickin' and Singin' News*, October 8, 1954, 1; "Uncle Joe's Country Capers," *Pickin'*

and Singin' News, February 26, 1954, 2; "Casey Strong Opens New 'Hill-William' Show in Texarkana," *Pickin' and Singin' News,* February 26, 1954, 12; Pugh, "Country Music Is Here to Stay?," 37.

35 Harkins, "The Significance of 'Hillbilly' in Early Country Music, 1924–1945," 318–19; Fred G. Hoeptner, "'Country' or 'Western'—It's a Choice of Words," *Country & Western Jamboree,* summer 1958, 37.

36 "Our Secret: 'A Crusade for Country Music,'" *Country & Western Jamboree,* June 1957, 5; "You Can Help Get More C&W Music on the Air," *Country & Western Jamboree,* August 1957, 29.

37 "Country Music Is Good Business for Martha White Mills," *Country & Western Jamboree,* July 1957, 14; "You Can Help Get More C&W Music on the Air," 29.

38 Ben A. Green, "Country Music Sweeps the Way to Happiness," *Country & Western Jamboree,* winter 1957, 14; "Perryman's Procedures for Profitable Promotions," *Country & Western Jamboree,* summer 1958, 34–35.

39 "Country Music Crusade in Phase 2—And You Have a Job to Do Now," *Country & Western Jamboree,* summer 1958, 17; "You—the Fans—Guide Country Music and Its People," *Country & Western Jamboree,* September 1957, 5, 23.

40 McCusker, "'Dear Radio Friend'"; Newman, "Critical Mass"; Fox, *The Mirror Makers,* 199–210; Kammen, *American Culture, American Tastes,* 133–61.

41 Kammen, *American Culture, American Tastes,* 146; Janice Kelly, letter to the editor, *Country & Western Jamboree,* summer 1958, 6.

42 Millie Anthony, letter to the editor, *Country & Western Jamboree,* September 1957, 21; Jim Seafeldt, letter to the editor, *Country & Western Jamboree,* February 1957, 4; Margaret Mock, letter to the editor, *Country & Western Jamboree,* winter 1957, 6; "The Mail Bag," *Country & Western Jamboree Yearbook,* 1959, 94.

43 Jim Evans, "The Jimmie Rodgers Fan Club," *America's Blue Yodeler,* summer 1953, 3; Norman Lee Nelson to Connie B. Gay, April 27, 1960, Correspondence, Incoming, 1960: WGAY Radio Station, box 1, Connie B. Gay Papers; Billy and Buddy to Connie B. Gay, March 22, 1960.

44 R. H. Compton, letter to the editor, *Country & Western Jamboree,* July 1957, 7; August J. Urchota, letter to the editor, *Country & Western Jamboree,* August 1957, 28.

45 Billie LaFerney, letter to the editor, *Counry & Western Jamboree Yearbook,* 1959, 83; George Middleton, letter to the editor, *Country & Western Jamboree Yearbook,* 1959, 83–84; Steve Goldbloom to Connie B. Gay, June 8, 1959, Correspondence, Incoming, 1959: WGAY Radio Station, box 1, Connie B. Gay Papers.

46 Lipsitz, *Time Passages,* 123; Bob Caroll, letter to the editor, *Country & Western Jamboree,* August 1957, 4.

47 W. B. Williams Jr. to Connie B. Gay, October 25, 1959, Correspondence, Incoming, 1959: WGAY Radio Station; Harland Anderson to Connie B. Gay, September 28, 1959, Connie B. Gay Papers; Mock, letter to the editor, 6.

48 Dave Connor, Dorothy Paul, and Rosie Lang, letters to the editor, *Country & Western Jamboree,* August 1957, 6, 26, 27, 7; Hazen and Freeman, *Love Always, Patsy,* xi.

49 Eunice Van Stone, letter to the editor, *Country & Western Jamboree,* winter 1957, 27; Raymond Cook, letter to the editor, *Country Song Roundup,* September 1958, 22.

50 *Song Exchange News,* summer 1940, n.p.; *Hill Country Messenger,* June 8, 1946, Fan Club papers, Country Music Foundation Library and Media Center, Nashville, Tenn.; Jim Evans to Curley, June 5, 1962, Correspondence: Incoming T-Z folder, Evans Correspondence, Outgoing, 1946–1971 box, Jim Evans Papers; Barbas, *Movie Crazy,* 109–34; Pugh, *Ernest Tubb,* 145; Blanche Trinajstik, "Ask Trina," *K-Bar-T Country Roundup,* August 1972, 14.

51 Pugh, *Ernest Tubb,* 103, 110. In private correspondence, Norma Barthel later estimated membership to have been nearly 2,000 at its peak in the late 1940s. Norma Barthel to Jim Evans, July 16, 1954, Norma Barthel folder, Evans Correspondence, Incoming, box 1, Jim Evans Papers.

52 Willis Glenn, "Birth of the Roy Acuff Fan Club," *Dunbar Digest,* n.d. (c. 1957), 14.

53 "Fan Clubs Are 'Unheralded Publicity Agents,'" *Hank Snow Fan Club Newsletter* (n.d. [1953]), 5, Fan Club papers; Jack Howard, "My Visit to Nashville," *Hank Snow Fan Club Newsletter* (n.d. [1955]), 2; Norma Winton Barthel, "We had a Time at the D.J. Festival Again!" *Melody Trails,* January 1956, 9–11. In fact, the same barriers that most likely prevented club women from organizing—their geographical diffusion, their lack of money, and their limited power in the structure of the industry—ultimately contributed to the demise of the Country Music Disc Jockey Association; Jo Walker-Meador interview by Diane Pecknold, August 2, 1999, audiotape, tape 1, side 1.

54 Barbas, *Movie Crazy,* 109–34.

55 Hazen and Freeman, *Love Always, Patsy,* 100–101, 121.

56 Evans, "The Jimmie Rodgers Fan Club," 3; Evans Correspondence, Incoming T-Z, Outgoing box, Outgoing, 1946–1971 folder, Jim Evans Papers; Jim Evans to Brad McCuen, September 3, 1961; Roy Horton to Jim Evans, July 26, 1948, Evans Correspondence, Incoming, Roy Horton, 1948–1955, ; Horton to Evans, November 22, 1948.

57 Hazen and Freeman, *Love Always, Patsy,* 39, 12, 17.

58 Blanche Trinajstick, "Trailblazin'," *K-Bar-T Country Roundup,* April 1961, 4; Fran Anderlohr, "Spotlighting a Fan Club President: Fran Anderlohr,

President, Billy Glenn Fan Club," *K-Bar-T Country Roundup*, June 1970, 43; Blanche Trinajstick, "The Story of Trina," *K-Bar-T Country Roundup*, March 1967, 40; Mary Lou Bergau, "Highlighting a Fan Club President: Mary Lou Bergau, President, Gary Williams Fan Club," *K-Bar-T Country Roundup*, September 1969, 39; Blanche Trinajstick, "The Fan Club President," *K-Bar-T Country Roundup*, August 1972, 26; Blanche Trinajstick, "Ask Trina," *K-Bar-T Country Roundup*, October 1972, 16.

59 Blanche Trinajstick, "Why Not Fan Clubs?," *K-Bar-T Country Roundup*, November 1964, 34.

60 Blanche Trinajstick, "Ask Trina," *K-Bar-T Country Roundup*, November 1965, 11, and March 1971, 39; Evans to McCuen, September 3, 1961.

61 Trinajstick, "Story of Trina," 40; Ruth Slack, "To the Passing Years," *K-Bar-T Country Roundup*, June 1967, 38; Norma Barthel to Jim Evans, May 25, 1963, Norma Barthel folder, Evans Correspondence, Incoming, box 1, Jim Evans Papers.

62 Gregory, "Southernizing the American Working Class," 149; Lipsitz, *Time Passages*, 39–75; Haslam, *Workin' Man Blues*, 141.

4 MASSES TO CLASSES

1 Lieberson, "'Country Sweeps the Country," 165.

2 Stockdell, "The Development of the Country Music Radio Format," 50; Jensen, *The Nashville Sound*, 38–89.

3 "A Prophetic View of CMA," *Billboard*, March 18, 1978, 18, 20; "CMA Organizes for C&W's Biggest Era: Directors Elected," *Music Reporter*, November 24, 1958, 1, 4; Jack Stapp, typescript speech, pp. 4, 9, 11, Country Music Association Sales and Marketing Programs (microfiche: fiche 2 of 3), Country Music Association Papers.

4 Stapp, typescript speech, 3; Stockdell, "Development of the Country Music Radio Format," 24, 50; "36% of U.S. AM Stations Carry C&W," *Billboard*, September 4, 1961, 2. The 1961 figures probably represent an improvement over 1958, since the development of the country format was already under way and a number of stations had increased the amount of time they devoted to country music in 1960 and early 1961. See "All Country," *Close-Up*, January 21, 1960, 2; "60 Stations Expand C&W Output," *Music Reporter*, October 31, 1961, 18; and Bill Sachs, "21 More Stations Add More Country Music or Go 100% Country Music in One Month," *Close-Up*, March 1961, 2.

5 New categories have since been added to this original configuration, as have officer positions. Stapp, typescript speech, 2, 4, 6; Bill Sachs, "Honor Jimmie Rodgers; Talk Nat'l C&W Days," *Billboard*, June 4, 1955, 15, 24; "CMA to Crash New Frontiers under Gay," *Music Reporter*, December 1, 1958, 1, 19.

6   Stapp, typescript speech, 1.

7   "CMA Formed at Miami Confab," *Music Reporter*, July 7, 1958, 13; "DJ Hall of Fame Reunion," n.d., 1999 (videocassette), tape 1, Country Music Foundation Library and Media Center; "Country Music Assn. Gets State Charter" *Music Reporter*, September 29, 1958, 14.

8   Wolfe, *A Good-Natured Riot*, 179–80, 261–65; John Rumble, "Harry Stone," in *Encyclopedia of Country Music*, ed. Kingsbury, 511; "CMA Taps Stone to Lead C&W into Greatest Era," *Music Reporter*, January 19, 1959, 15.

9   Jo Walker-Meador interview by Diane Pecknold, August 2, 1999, audiotape, tape 1, side 1; "Stone Floods Ky.-Ind. with Come-Ons for CMA Spec," *Music Reporter*, February 9, 1959, 16; "CMA Spec Grosses $8,100—'Bigness' Potential Seen," *Music Reporter*, March 16, 1959, 16, 18; "Impressive Jimmie Rodgers Fete Re-Stresses C&W Power," *Music Reporter*, June 22, 1959, 16–17; *Country Music Association Special Newsletter*, July 2, 1959.

10 "C&W Personal Appearances Cure 1957 Gold Bonanza," *Billboard*, March 23, 1957, 79, 86.

11 *Close-Up*, issues of July 2, 1959, 1; August 24, 1959, 1; October 7, 1959, 2; Minutes of the CMA Board of Directors, November 11, 1959 (microfilm: reel 1), Joe Allison Papers; "CMA Sponsors First Anniversary Banquet, Salutes Grand Ole Opry 34th Birthday," *Music Reporter*, October 17, 1959, 16; "CMA Stresses Need for $$, New Members," *Billboard*, November 16, 1959, 2, 14; "Harry Stone Leaves CMA Executive Post," *Billboard*, November 23, 1959, 4; "Jo Walker: CMA's Lucky Accident," *Billboard*, March 18, 1978, 8.

12 "Just Plain Jo Is a Dynamo," *Billboard*, October 28, 1967, 74; Walker-Meador interview by Pecknold, August 2, 1999, tape 1, side 2; *Close-Up*, February 26, 1960, 1.

13 "Optimism Pervades C&W Music Fete," *Billboard*, August 22, 1960, 2; *Close-Up*, February 26, 1960, 1–2; June 10, 1960, 2; August 11, 1960, 4; "CMA Committee Works on Second Mailing," *Music Reporter*, October 31, 1960, 40.

14 "CMA Committee Works on Second Mailing," 40; "Country Music: A Gold Mine for City Broadcasters," *Sponsor*, August 8, 1960, 76; Charles Bernard, "The Madison Avenue Report," *Close-Up*, July 1961, 1, 3.

15 Douglas, *Listening In*, 219–56.

16 Stockdell, "Development of the Country Music Radio Format," 41–42.

17 Joe Allison interview by Diane Pecknold, March 26, 1999, audiotape, tape 1, side 1.

18 Ibid.; Stockdell, "Development of the Country Music Radio Format," 43.

19 Allison interview by Pecknold, March 26, 1999, tape 1, side 2; Jo Walker-Meador interview by Diane Pecknold, August 5, 1999, audiotape, tape 1, side 1.

20 Joe Allison interview by John Rumble, May 26, 1994, audiotape, tape 1, side 2; "New C&W Format over KRKD Has Wide Appeal," *Music Reporter*, September 30, 1957, 7; Stockdell, "Development of the Country Music Radio Format," 57.

21 "Sincerity No. 1 'Must' for C&W Show, Says CMA," *Music Reporter*, October 31, 1960, 26; "Play C&W Straight—Not as a Novelty, Is Bob Staton's View," *Music Reporter*, December 22, 1962, 26.

22 "It Pays to Play Country Music," typescript, n.d., Country Music Association Promotions and Advertising (microfiche: fiche 1 of 1), Country Music Association Papers; Walker-Meador interview by Pecknold, August 5, 1999, tape 1, side 1; "Guidelines for Country Music Radio Format," pamphlet, n.d., CMA Guidelines–Country Music Programming (microfiche: fiche 7 of 12), Country Music Association Papers; "Air Checks Available," *Close-Up*, November 1965, 6.

23 John Rumble, "Joe Allison," in *Encyclopedia of Country Music*, ed. Kingsbury, 11; "Rose, Gay Renamed to Top CMA Posts," *Music Reporter*, November 16, 1959, 12; Allison interview by Pecknold, March 26, 1999, tape 1, side 1.

24 Allison interview by Pecknold, March 26, 1999, tape 1, side 2; Charlie Williams, "A Fable," *Close-Up*, June 1961, 4; *Sponsor*, August 8, 1966, 72.

25 Stockdell, "Development of the Country Music Radio Format," 66; Allison interview by Rumble, May 26, 1994, tape 2, side 1; "Radio Profile: KRAK Radio, Sacramento, California," *Close-Up*, April 1965, 4, 8.

26 Allison interview by Pecknold, March 26, 1999, tape 2, side 1.

27 "Change to C&W Boosts Audience, Profit," *Broadcasting*, October 18, 1965, 74; Allison interview by Pecknold, March 26, 1999, tape 1, side 1; Stockdell, "Development of the Country Music Radio Format," 77.

28 "Country Stations: Fatter and Happier," *Sponsor*, August 8, 1966, 43; "CMA Broadcasters Meeting Huge Success," *Close-Up*, November 1965, 6; Stockdell, "Development of the Country Music Radio Format," 85; Walker-Meador interview by Pecknold, August 5, 1999, tape 1, side 1.

29 *Broadcasting*, October 18, 1965, 79, 82, 87; "Country Is Spelled with '$' not 'Cents,'" *Sponsor*, August 8, 1966, 40.

30 "Country Stations: Fatter and Happier," 43.

31 "Sponsor Crash-Plan Held Country Music 1st Need," *Music Reporter*, November 7, 1960, 16; *Close-Up*, February 6, 1961, 1.

32 "Crum vs. Husky? Audiences Won't Decide in Advance," *(Country) Music Reporter*, October 20, 1956, 6; Williamson, *Hillbillyland*, 50–51; "C&W Salute Wins N.Y. Radio Execs," *Music Reporter*, March 31, 1962, 37.

33 "C&W Salute Wins N.Y. Radio Execs," 37; "C&W Crashes Air Time in Sophisticated New York," *Music Reporter*, July 28, 1962, 24; "CMA Sets Museum & Show," *Music Vendor*, December 1, 1962.

34 "CMA Steps Up Bid for Status," *Billboard,* April 6, 1963, 8; Hal B. Cook, "CMA Sings a Message," *Billboard,* May 18, 1963; Rumble, "Joe Allison," 11; "Allison: Sincerity, Simplicity—Acceptance," *Billboard,* November 4, 1965, 112; "Allison Sees C&W as Source of Today's Music," *Billboard,* November 2, 1963, 133.

35 Allison interview by Pecknold, March 26, 1999, tape 2, side 1; Joe Allison, "Presentation to the Sales Executives Club of New York," Country Music Association Sales and Marketing Programs (microfiche: fiche 1).

36 Joe Allison, "The Sound of Country Music, Presented for the Adcraft Club of Detroit on Friday, April 17, 1964," 4, 11, 14, 15, Country Music Association Sales and Marketing Programs (microfiche: fiche 1).

37 "C&W Pulse Published for 24 U.S. Markets," *Close-Up,* September 1965, 1; "CMA's 'The Sound of Country Music'—Smash!" *Music City News,* July 1965, 1, 6; Hal Cook to Frances Preston et al., November 12, 1964, Chicago Show 1965 (microfiche: 1 of 1), Country Music Association Papers.

38 Joe Allison, "The Sound of Country Music, Presented for the Sales-Marketing Executives of Chicago, Monday, June 7, 1965," 8, 13–17, Country Music Association Sales and Marketing Programs (microfiche: fiche 1, 2).

39 Rieder, "The Rise of the 'Silent Majority,'" 248; Allison interview by Pecknold, March 26, 1999, tape 1, side 1; "Country Stations: Fatter and Happier," 42.

40 "The C&W Sound Captures U.S. Heart & Purse," *Sponsor,* May 20, 1963, 32.

41 "Switch to C&W Format Seems to Forecast Higher Ratings," *Broadcasting,* August 1, 1966, 55; "Trade Eyes WJJD's Switch to C&W as Barometer of Nashville Climate," *Variety,* March 3, 1965, 58; Stockdell, "Development of the Country Music Radio Format," 73–74.

42 "Radio Profile: WJJD Radio, Chicago, Illinois," *Close-Up,* October 1965), 5; WJJD Aircheck, May 13, 1965, 8:00 a.m.–9:00 a.m. (audiocassette), master 1326, Marvin Bensman Collection, University of Memphis Library, Memphis, Tenn.; WJJD Aircheck, May 7, 1965, 1:00 p.m.–2:00 p.m. (audiocassette), master 1325; WJJD Aircheck, February 15, 1965, 10:00 a.m.–11:00 a.m. (audiocassette), master 1438; "Switch to C&W Puts KRAK in Top 3," *Billboard,* May 23, 1964, 14.

43 "Trade Eyes WJJD's Switch to C&W," 55, 58.

44 "C&W Pulse Published," 1; "Radio's New Sound Golden, but Shocks Adults," *Chicago American,* March 7, 1965, sec. 3, p. 4; "On Radio," *Chicago American,* March 14, 1965, sec. 6, p. 5.

45 "Yahoo! They Brought Mountains to Chicago," *Chicago American,* June 8, 1965, sec. 1, p. 20; "600 Executives Hear Country, Western Stars," *Chicago Tribune,* June 8, 1965, sec. 2, p. 1; "Change to C&W Boosts Audience, Profit," *Broadcasting,* October 18, 1965, 74; Stockdell, "Development of the Country Music Radio Format," 80, 84; "Country Is Spelled with '$' not 'Cents,'" 40.

46 "Country A M's Go to Town," *Variety*, January 19, 1966, 43; "Country Is Spelled with '$' not 'Cents,'" 41; "Radio's New Sound Golden," 4; "Numbers Mean Dollars on Madison Avenue," *Sponsor*, August 8, 1966, 45–46, 47; "The New Appeal of Country Music," *Broadcasting*, August 1, 1966, 53.

47 Jensen, *Nashville Sound*, 16; "N.Y. 'Discovers' Nashville's Opry," *Music Reporter*, December 4, 1961, 2; "C&W Crashes Air Time in Sophisticated New York," 24; "New Appeal of Country Music," 53.

48 Joe Allison to Lazar Emanuel, August 10, 1965, 1, and Allison to Emanuel, September 17, 1965, 1, W J R Z folder, Joe Allison Papers.

49 Allison to Emanuel, August 10, 1965, 1; Ed Nielson to All Announcers, November 1, 1965, both in W J R Z folder, Joe Allison Papers.

50 Sy Levy to All P G W Colonels & W J R Z Local Sales Staff, August 5, 1965; "Random Sales Points Re: Country Music," typescript, August 5, 1965; Allison to Emanuel, September 17, 1965, 1. All in W J R Z folder, Joe Allison Papers.

51 "Country Music Comes to Town 24 Hours a Day on W J R Z Radio!," typescript, n.d. [September 1965], 2, W J R Z folder, Joe Allison Papers; Allison interview by Pecknold, March 26, 1999, tape 2, side 1; Allison to Emanuel, September 17, 1965, 1.

52 Claude Hall, "More Powerhouse Outlets Make Theirs Country Style," *Billboard*, January 8, 1966, 39; Charles Portis, "That New Sound from Nashville," *Saturday Evening Post*, February 12, 1966, reprinted in Linnell Gentry, ed., *A History and Encyclopedia of Country, Western, and Gospel Music* (Nashville, Tenn.: Clairmont, 1969), 272–73.

53 "Growing Sound of Country Music," *Broadcasting*, October 18, 1965, 70, 75; "Numbers Mean Dollars on Madison Avenue," 44, 45; "New Appeal of Country Music," 56.

54 Cohen, *A Consumers' Republic*, 403; Cross, *An All-Consuming Century*; May, "Cold War—Warm Hearth"; Marling, *As Seen on T V*, 243–83; Newman, "Critical Mass."

5 COMMERCIALISM AND TRADITION

1 Nick Barone, letter to the editor, *Music City News*, September 1964, 2; Lynn Nickless, letter to the editor, *Music City News*, November 1964, 2.

2 Frankie Rodgers, letter to the editor, *Music City News*, August 1966, 3; Flora Johns, letter to the editor, *Music City News*, August 1965, 2; Norma J. Agans, letter to the editor, *Music City News*, February 1965, 2.

3 Sandra McCallister, "How the Fans Are Failing Country Music," *K-Bar-T Country Roundup*, June 1970, 50.

4 Nancy Ann Krotec, letter to the editor, *Music City News*, January 1965, 2; Barbara J. Huss, letter to the editor, *Music City News*, December 1964, 2.

5 Esther Wood, "What Country Music Means to Me," *K-Bar-T Country Roundup*, September 1971, 26.

6 Mrs. Charlie Siclari, letter to the editor, *Country Song Roundup*, August 1967, 27; Judy Wilson, letter to the editor, *Music City News*, October 1965, 2; A. D. "Red" Suiter, letter to the editor, *Music City News*, October 1965, 2.

7 "What's All This Jazz," *Music City News*, April 1964, 2.

8 Ibid., anonymous letter to the editor, *Music City News*, June 1964, 11; Howard Claude, letter to the editor, *Music City News*, January 1965, 2; Bruce Hubbard, letter to the editor, *Music City News*, September 1964, 2; James Kennison, letter to the editor, *Music City News*, October 1965, 2.

9 James Kennison, letter to the editor, *Music City News*, November 1965, 38.

10 Vernon Scott, "Twang, Twang, Twang," *Stars and Stripes*, September 15, 1961, 16; T. Sgt. Paul J. Graupp, letter to the editors, *Stars and Stripes*, October 5, 1961, 14.

11 Sp5 Arthur L. Ellis, letter to the editors, *Stars and Stripes*, October 5, 1961, 14; ATC Division, Rota, Spain, letter to the editors, *Stars and Stripes*, October 5, 1961; "Sparks Fly in Country Feud in Stars & Stripes," *Billboard*, October 30, 1961, 22.

12 "Country Music Association, Inc., Membership Application," *Billboard*, November 17, 1962, n. p.

13 Paul Ackerman, "Optimism Pervades C&W Music Fete," *Billboard*, August 22, 1960, 32; Minutes of the CMA Board of Directors, November 11, 1959 (microfilm: reel 1), Joe Allison Papers.

14 Ackerman, "Optimism Pervades C&W Music Fete," 32; Minutes of the CMA Board of Directors, reel 1; Jo Walker-Meador interview by Diane Pecknold, August 5, 1999, audiotape, tape 1, side 1; Joe Allison interview by Diane Pecknold, March 26, 1999, audiotape, tape 2, side 2.

15 Walker-Meador interview by Pecknold, August 5, 1999, side 1, tape 1; Cecil Whaley, "Synopsis of Important Events," 16; "Step Up Hero with New Name for Country Music," *Music Reporter*, October 31, 1960, 13, 16.

16 Allison interview by Pecknold, March 26, 1999, tape 2, side 2.

17 Paul Ackerman, "CMDJA Confab OK's Plan for Annual Country Music Fete," *Billboard*, November 19, 1955, 11; Ackerman, "Optimism Pervades C&W Music Fete," 32; "Board Meeting," *Close-Up*, February 6, 1961, 1; Walker-Meador interview by Pecknold, August 5, 1999, tape 1, side 1.

18 "Time to Rejoice," *Billboard*, October 31, 1960, 23; "Board of Directors and Officers Meet," *Close-Up*, May 1961, 1; "Country Music Hall of Fame," *Close-Up*, June 1961, 1; "News from CMA Office," *Close-Up*, July 1961, 3.

19 "CMA Banquet Features Talent, C&W Hall of Fame Unveiling," *Close-Up*, November 1961, 3; "Association Lists Gains, New Plans," *Billboard*, November 6, 1961, 1, 52; "Rodgers, Williams, Rose 1st in CMA Hall of Fame," *Music Reporter*, November 6, 1961, 4; "National Country Music Week," *Country Song Roundup*, February 1962, 19; "The CMA Country Music Hall of Fame . . . A New Landmark of Distinction," *Close-Up*, December 1961, 4.

20 "Music in November: Extension of Remarks of Hon. Otis G. Pike of New York in the House of Representatives, Friday, June 15, 1962," in *A History and Encyclopedia of Country, Western, and Gospel Music*, ed. Gentry, 153; "CMA's Country Week Getting Lift from Many Sources," *Cash Box*, October 20, 1962, n.p.; "Eyes of Nation Swing to National CM Week," *Billboard*, October 7, 1962, 50.

21 John Lomax III, "The Center of Music City: Nashville's Music Row," in *Encyclopedia of Country Music*, ed. Kingsbury, 386–87; Carr, "Will the Circle Be Unbroken," 507.

22 Jo Walker-Meador interview by Pecknold, August 2, 1999, audiotape, tape 1, side 2; Jo Walker interview by Rumble, July 30, 1997, audiotape, tape 3, side 1.

23 Walker interview by Rumble, July 30, 1997, tape 2, side 2; "Music City, U.S.A. . . . The New Frontier of Sound" and "Music City's Booming Land Rush," *Music Reporter*, June 29, 1963, n.p.

24 Walker interview by Rumble, July 30, 1997, tape 3, side 1, and tape 2, side 2; "Eyes of Nation Swing to National CM Week," 50.

25 "CMA Meet Sets Museum & Show," *Music Vendor*, December 1, 1962, n.p.; "CMA Execs to Meet in N.Y. Jan. 24–25," *Music Reporter*, January 19, 1963, 19; "Autry, Rose Helm Fast Growing CMA," *Music Reporter*, June 29, 1963, n.p.

26 "CMA Will Have Permanent Home Thanks to Nashville Land Grant" and "Metro Mayor Hails C&W Industry; Appoints Tradesmen Ambassadors," *Close-Up*, November 1963, 4, 3.

27 Walker interview by Rumble, July 30, 1997, tape 3, side 1.

28 "Country Music Capitol Is Target for Classy CMA C&W Sales Pitch," *Close-Up*, February 1964, 1; Joe Allison, "Presentation to the Nashville Chamber of Commerce, Country Music Association Sales and Marketing Programs" (microfiche: fiche 2), Country Music Association Papers.

29 Allison, "Presentation to the Nashville Chamber of Commerce" (fiche 2).

30 "Proposed CMA Building Is One Step Closer to Reality," *Close-Up*, March 1964, 4; "First Donation for Proposed Country Music Hall of Fame," *Close-Up*, April 1964, 1; "New York Drive Slated May 21st," *Close-Up*, May 1964, 1; "CMA Building Fund Passes Mid-Point," *Close-Up*, June 1964, 1; "CMA Museum to Be Built," *Billboard*, November 7, 1964, 1.

31 "CMA Museum to Be Built," 1; Walker interview by Rumble, July 30, 1997, tape 2, side 1.

32 Walker interview by Rumble, July 30, 1997, side 1, tape 2; "CMA's 'Performance' a Giddyup Go-Album," *Billboard,* January 8, 1966, 39–40; "CMA Completes Historic 6th Year," *Close-Up,* October 1965, 7.

33 "CMA's 'Performance' a Giddyup Go-Album," 39–40; Whaley, "Synopsis of Important Events," 15–16.

34 Warren, "The Story of the Country Music Association," 9–10; Hemphill, *The Nashville Sound,* 32–35.

35 "Hoedown on a Harpsichord," *Time,* November 1, 1960, 52; Marek, "Country Music Nashville Style"; "Country Music: The Nashville Sound," *Time,* November 17, 1964, 76, 79; John Rumble, "CMF," in *Encyclopedia of Country Music,* ed. Kingsbury, 100; "CMA Completes Historic 6th Year," 4; Walker-Meador interview by Pecknold, August 5, 1999, tape 1, side 1.

36 Cantwell, *When We Were Good,* 32, 331–34.

37 Cohen, "The John Edwards Memorial Foundation," 113–19.

38 Wilgus, "An Introduction to the Study of Hillbilly Music," 201–3, 199; Kahn, "Hillbilly Music."

39 Wilgus, "An Introduction to the Study of Hillbilly Music," 196; Malone, "Country Music and the Academy," 42.

40 Hurst, "Nashville's Country Music Brings Cultural Turnabout"; "Allison: Sincerity, Simplicity—Acceptance," *Billboard,* November 4, 1965, 112.

41 Joe Allison interview by John Rumble, March 15, 1994, tape 1, side 1; Kahn, "Hillbilly Music," 264.

42 "CMA Provides Scholarship Fund," *Close-Up,* October 1965, 3; "A Niche in the Ivory Tower," *Billboard,* October 28, 1967, sec. 2, p. 24; Walker-Meador interview by Pecknold, August 5, 1999, tape 1, side 1.

43 Warren, "Country Music Foundation in Brief," 6.

44 Cohen, "John Edwards Memorial Foundation," 120–21.

45 "Niche in the Ivory Tower," 42.

46 Whaley, "Synopsis of Important Events," 16; "Hall of Fame Home: Country Music's Solid Foundation," *Billboard,* March 18, 1978, CMA-12, CMA-42.

47 Travis, "A Barn-Style Museum for Country-Style Music"; Walker-Meador interview by Rumble, July 30, 1997, tape 2, side 1; "Guardian of the Hall of Fame Gates," *Billboard,* October 28, 1967, sec. 2, p. 76.

48 For uncertainty about the early films run in the theater, see Fryd, "'The Sad Twang of Mountain Voices,'" 303, 325, 334; Whaley, "Synopsis of Important Events," 15; *What's This Country Coming To?,* audio visuals (microfiche: fiche 6 of 12), Country Music Association Papers; "Guardian of Hall of Fame Gates," 77; Warren, "Country Music Foundation in Brief," 5.

49 Travis, "Barn-Style Museum," 15; "Country Music Hall of Fame Mem-

bers and Their Years of Election," in *Encyclopedia of Country Music,* ed. Kingsbury, 617; "Guardian of the Hall of Fame Gates," 76–77.

50 Warren, "Country Music Foundation in Brief," 6; Travis, "Barn-Style Museum," 15.

6 SILENT MAJORITIES

1 Alice Meyers, "Looking Back," *K-Bar-T Country Roundup,* June 1970, 12.

2 Blanche Trinajstick, "The Story of Trina," *K-Bar-T Country Roundup,* March 1967, 36.

3 "Ask Trina," *K-Bar-T Country Roundup,* February 1966, 21.

4 "Loco Weeds," *K-Bar-T Country Roundup,* February 1963, 29–30.

5 "Ask Trina," *K-Bar-T Country Roundup,* May 1964, 21.

6 "Editorial," *K-Bar-T Country Roundup,* May 1964, 17; Red Wilcox, "Behind the Mike," *K-Bar-T Country Roundup,* February 1966, 13–14.

7 In the December 1969 issue of *K-Bar-T Country Roundup:* Billy Glenn, "Country Music Blows Its Cool," 13; Sherwin Linton, "More on the Current Trend in Country Music," 15; Philip Urgola, "Country Music at Its Crossroads," 36. Johnny Henderson, "On Radio & Records," *K-Bar-T Country Roundup,* June 1971, 22.

8 Marty Surprise, "Fan Clubs at the Convention," *K-Bar-T Country Roundup,* February 1963, 31. ·

9 *Music City News,* January 1965, 4; Fred Travis, "'Music City USA' Theme of Nashville Tours," *New York Times,* June 27, 1965, XX15; Blanche Trinajstick, "Why Not Fan Clubs?," *K-Bar-T Country Roundup,* November 1964, 34.

10 Blanche Trinajstick, "Convention Highlights," *K-Bar-T Country Roundup,* December 1966, 16–18; "Convention Report," *K-Bar-T Country Roundup,* November 1967, n.p.; Ruth Slack, "My Visit to Country Music Land," *K-Bar-T Country Roundup,* December 1967, 39–44; Loudilla Johnson telephone interview by Diane Pecknold, June 20, 2001.

11 Norma Winton Barthel, "We Had a Time at the D.J. Festival Again!," *Melody Trails,* January 1956, 9–11; Coates, "Teenyboppers, Groupies, and Other Grotesques"; Rhodes, *Electric Ladyland.*

12 "How Do You Impress People?," *K-Bar-T Country Roundup,* May 1964, 31; "Open Letter to C/M Artists, or: A Fan's View Point," *K-Bar-T Country Roundup,* June 1971, 15; Mike Hoyer, "A Disc Jockey's Opinion," *K-Bar-T Country Roundup,* February 1963, 32.

13 Pecknold, "'I Wanna Play House'"; "Are C-W Fans Being Used?" *K-Bar-T Country Roundup,* March 1967, 30.

14   Norma Barthel, letter to the editor, *Music City News*, August 1963, 15; Johnson interview by Pecknold, June 20, 2001; Marjie McGraw, "Johnson Sisters: The First Ladies of Fan Clubs Share Their Story," IFCO website, http://www.ifco.org (accessed June 16, 2001); Ellison, *Country Music Culture*, 183–86.

15   "Ask Trina," *K-Bar-T Country Roundup*, February 1966, 24.

16   Ibid.

17   Blanche Trinajstick, "An Editorial," *K-Bar-T Country Roundup*, December 1968, 33; Betty Carson, "Who Said 'Too Many Fans in Nashville'?" *K-Bar-T Country Roundup*, December 1969, 24; "Ask Trina," *K-Bar-T Country Roundup*, December 1969, 17.

18   "Ask Trina," *K-Bar-T Country Roundup*, September 1970, 47, and December 1970, 15.

19   "Ask Trina," *K-Bar-T Country Roundup*, December 1970, 15; "Convention Plans—1971," *K-Bar-T Country Roundup*, March 1971, 5.

20   "Open Letter to C/M Artists."

21   "Ask Trina," *K-Bar-T Country Roundup*, December 1970, 15.

22   Anderson, "Bill Anderson Writes on Wembley '69"; "Arrival in Houston Preview of London Meet" and "CMA Board to Attend Wembley Festival," *Close-Up*, March 1971, 1; "CMA/WSM Sets 1st Int'l CM Fan Fair," *Close-Up*, July 1971, 1–2.

23   "CMA/WSM Sets 1st Int'l CM Fan Fair," 1–2.

24   "CMA Board Meeting July 8–9 in Denver," *Close-Up*, July 1971, 7; "Ask Trina," *K-Bar-T Country Roundup*, September 1971, 27.

25   Loudilla Johnson telephone interview by Diane Pecknold, August 16, 2004; "Fan Fair Committee Meets with Fan Club Officials," *Close-Up*, August 1971, 2.

26   "Ask Trina," *K-Bar-T Country Roundup*, February 1972, 9; December 1971, 31–32; June 1972, 27.

27   "Thanks!," *Close-Up*, May 1972, 2, 9; "Fan Fair Excites Fans in Spectacular Activities," *Music City News*, May 1972, n.p.

28   "Ask Trina," *K-Bar-T Roundup*, December 1971, 32.

29   Ellison, *Country Music Culture*, 171.

30   Malone, *Don't Get Above Your Raisin'*, 210–53; Don Cusic, "Politics and Country Music, 1963–1974," in *Country Music Annual 2002*, ed. Charles K. Wolfe and James E. Akenson (Lexington: University Press of Kentucky, 2002), 161–85; Van Sickel, "A World without Citizenship."

31   Phillips, *The Emerging Republican Majority*; Phillips, "Revolutionary Music"; Carter, *The Politics of Rage*, 379–81.

32   Greenway, "No Talk That God Is Dead."

33   "Country Music Month, 1971," *Weekly Compilation of Presidential Documents*, September 28, 1970, 1407; Jo Walker-Meador interview by John

Rumble, June 18, 1996, audiotape, tape 1, side 1; Jo Walker-Meador interview by Diane Pecknold, August 2, 1999, audiotape, tape 1, side 2.

34 *Country Music Association Newsletter,* June 15 and July 7, 1959; Walker-Meador interview by Pecknold, August 2, 1999, tape 1, side 2. Gay was an ardent supporter of both Kennedy and Johnson and served on a number of presidential commissions in both administrations.

35 "County Music Month, October 1972," *Weekly Compilation of Presidential Documents,* October 16, 1972, 1509; Walker-Meador interview by Pecknold, August 2, 1999, tape 1, side 2.

36 Greenway, "No Talk That God is Dead," 842, 857; Mano, "Going Country."

37 King, "Red Necks, White Socks, and Blue Ribbon Fear," 34; Lund, "Fundamentalism, Racism, and Political Reaction in Country Music," 91; "Another Version of the Dream," 139.

38 Lund, "Fundamentalism," 91; Seelye, "The Sound of Money."

39 Stephanie Harrington, "Who's Got the Last Hee Haw Now?" *New York Times,* January 4, 1970, 97.

40 King, "The Grand Ole Opry," 46–47; Axthelm, "Lookin' at Country with Loretta Lynn"; Goldstein, "My Country Music Problem—and Yours."

41 Williamson, "Country & Western Marxism."

42 Esther Wood, "Country Music & Americanism," *K-Bar-T Country Roundup,* December 1969, 25; Roy Reed, "Country Music Becomes Concerned," *New York Times,* April 19, 1970, 49.

43 Homer Bigart, "Marines to Step Up Campaign to Ease Racial Tensions," *New York Times,* February 28, 1970, 11; Donald Henahan, "Grand Old Nashville Sounds: They're Achangin,'" *New York Times,* October 22, 1967, 82; Paul Dickson, "Singing to Silent America," *Nation,* February 23, 1970, 212.

44 Wren, "The Great White Soul Sound: Country Music," 12.

45 Keillor, "At the Opry," 51; Osborne, "The Nixon Watch," 9; Axthelm, "The Dream on the Barroom Floor"; "The Boom that Music Brought to Nashville," *U.S. News & World Report,* July 29, 1974, 60; Johnny Henderson, "The Nashville Paradox," *K-Bar-T Country Roundup,* February 1972, 22.

46 Hemphill, *The Nashville Sound,* 240; Axthelm, "The Dream on the Barroom Floor," 69; Danker, "Country Music," 393; "Another Version of the Dream," 147, 137.

47 Marling, *As Seen on TV,* 275–79; DiMaggio, Peterson, and Esco, "Country Music," 43–44; Malone, *Singing Cowboys and Musical Mountaineers,* xi.

48 Vincent Canby, "A Satire, a Melodrama, a Celebration," *New York Times,* June 15, 1975, D1.

49 Stuart, *The Nashville Chronicles,* 39–41, 48.

50 Braudy, *The World in a Frame*, 45.

51 Paul Gardner, "Altman Surveys Nashville and Sees 'Instant' America," *New York Times*, June 13, 1975, 26.

52 Boyum, "Just Plain Populist Folks"; Gilliatt, "'Love and Death and 'Nashville,'" 107.

53 Viertal and Walker, "The Long Road to Nashville," *New Times*, June 13, 1975, 56; Byrne and Lopez, "Nashville," 17.

54 Ching, "Sounding the American Heart," 209.

55 Stuart, *Nashville Chronicles*, 22.

56 Ibid.

57 Kael, "Coming: 'Nashville,'" 80; Hatch, "Nashville"; Kauffmann, "Nashville," *New Republic*; Wicker, "'Nashville'—Dark Perceptions in a Country Music Comedy."

58 Nik Cohn, quoted in Richard A. Peterson, "Nashville and America in One Dimension," *Society*, January 1976, 94; Patrick Anderson, "The Real Nashville," *New York Times Magazine*, August 31, 1975, 42; John Yates, "Smart Man's Burden: *Nashville, A Face in the Crowd*, and Popular Culture," *Journal of Popular Film* 5, no. 1 (1976): 23, 27.

59 Minnie Pearl quoted in Stuart, *Nashville Chronicles*, 292; commentary by director Robert Altman in *Nashville* (DVD), directed by Robert Altman (1975; Hollywood, Calif.: Paramount Home Video, 2000); Byrne and Lopez, "Nashville," 16.

60 Byrne and Lopez, "Nashville," 16.

61 B. Drummond Ayers, "Nixon Plays Piano on Wife's Birthday at Grand Ole Opry," *New York Times*, March 17, 1974, 53; Fox, "White Trash Alchemies of the Abject Sublime," 39–61.

CONCLUSION

1 Kael, "Coming: 'Nashville,'" 79; Robert T. Self, "Invention and Death: The Commodities of Robert Altman's *Nashville*," *Journal of Popular Film* 5, no. 3/4 (1976): 281–84.

2 Fox, "White Trash Alchemies of the Abject Sublime," 52.

3 Fiske, *Understanding Popular Culture*, 28–29.

4 Country Music Foundation, "Introduction to the New Country Music Hall of Fame and Museum," press release, May 2002, in Diane Pecknold's possession; Miriam Pace Longino, "Country Music's Treasures Get a Stunning New Home," *Atlanta Constitution*, May 11, 2001, E1.

5 Kreyling, "Country Comes to Town."

6 Heim, "It's a Twang Thang"; Longino, "Country Music's Treasures";

Country Music Foundation, "Introduction to the New Country Music Hall of Fame."

7 Edward Morris, "The Battle of Nashville," February 20, 2002, *Salon.com*, http://www.salon.com/ent/music/feature/2002/02/20/country_war/index .html (accessed February 1, 2006); Charles Wolfe, letter to the editor, *Nashville Tennessean*, September 18, 2001.

8 Gerard Corsane, ed., *Heritage, Museums, and Galleries: An Introductory Reader* (New York: Routledge, 2005).

9 Pierre Bourdieu, *Distinction: A Social Critique of the Judgment of Taste* (Cambridge, Mass.: Harvard University Press, 1984); Fox, "White Trash Alchemies of the Abject Sublime," 44.

10 Randy Fox, "Hallowed Hall," *Nashville Scene*, May 10, 2001.

Selective Bibliography

ARCHIVES AND MANUSCRIPTS

Connie B. Gay Papers, Country Music Foundation Library, Nashville,
    Tennessee
Country Music Association Papers, Country Music Foundation Library,
    Nashville, Tennessee
Hoosier Hop Collection, Archives of Traditional Music, Bloomington,
    Indiana
Jim Evans Papers, Country Music Foundation Library, Nashville, Tennessee
Joe Allison Papers, Country Music Foundation Library, Nashville,
    Tennessee
Kevin Parks Collection, Chicago, Illinois

NEWSPAPERS AND PERIODICALS

America's Blue Yodeler
Billboard
Broadcasting
Chicago American
Chicago Daily News
Close-Up
Country & Western Jamboree

(Country) Music Reporter
Country Song Roundup
Down Beat
Hill Country Messenger
K-Bar-T Country Roundup
Melody Trails
Music City News
Pickin' and Singin' News
Rural Radio
Songwriter's Exchange News
Sponsor
Stand By!
Variety

INTERVIEWS

Allison, Joe. By John Rumble. March 15, 1994. Country Music Foundation
   Library and Media Center, Nashville, Tennessee (CMFL).
——. By John Rumble. May 26, 1994. CMFL.
——. By John Rumble. June 3, 1994. CMFL.
——. By Diane Pecknold. March 26, 1999. In the interviewer's possession.
Collie, Biff. By Douglas B. Green. October 30, 1974. CMFL.
——. By John Rumble. October 26, 1982. CMFL.
Johnson, Loudilla. By Diane Pecknold. July 18, 2001. Telephone interview.
——. By Diane Pecknold. August 16, 2004. Telephone interview.
Walker-Meador, Jo. By John Rumble. June 18, 1996. CMFL.
——. By John Rumble. July 30, 1997. CMFL.
——. By Diane Pecknold. August 2, 1999. In the interviewer's possession.
——. By Diane Pecknold. August 5, 1999. In the interviewer's possession.

PUBLISHED SOURCES

Adorno, Theodor. "On the Fetish Character in Music and the Regression of
   Listening." In *The Culture Industry: Selected Essays on Mass Culture*,
   edited by J. M. Bernstein. New York: Routledge, 1991. 47–54.
Anderson, Bill. "Bill Anderson Writes on Wembley '69." *Opry: The Journal
   of Country Music, Yearbook Issue* (1969): 14–15.
"Another Version of the Dream." *Esquire*, November 1971, 137–47.
Asbel, Bernard L. "The National Barn Dance." *Chicago*, October 1954, 23.
Atherton, Lewis. *Main Street on the Middle Border.* Bloomington: Indiana
   University Press, 1954.

Axthelm, Pete. "The Dream on the Barroom Floor." *Newsweek*, March 25, 1974, 69.

———. "Lookin' at Country with Loretta Lynn." *Newsweek*, June 18, 1972, 66, 71–72.

Barbas, Samantha. *Movie Crazy: Fans, Stars, and the Cult of Celebrity.* New York: Palgrave, 2001.

Barfield, Ray. *Listening to Radio, 1920–1950.* Westport, Conn.: Praeger, 1996.

Barlow, William. *Voice Over: The Making of Black Radio.* Philadelphia: Temple University Press, 1999.

Barnouw, Erik. *A Tower in Babel: A History of Broadcasting in the United States.* Vol. 1: *To 1933.* New York: Oxford University Press, 1966.

———. *The Golden Web: A History of Broadcasting in the United States.* Vol. 2: *1933 to 1953.* New York: Oxford University Press, 1968.

Berry, Chad. *Southern Migrants, Northern Exiles.* Urbana: University of Illinois Press, 2000.

———. "Social Highways: Southern White Migration to the Midwest, 1910–1990." Ph.D. diss., Indiana University, 1995.

Bertrand, Michael. *Race, Rock, and Elvis.* Urbana: University of Illinois Press, 2000.

Biggar, George C. "The WLS National Barn Dance Story: The Early Years." *JEMF Quarterly* 7 (autumn 1971): 106.

Bodnar, John. *Remaking America: Public Memory, Commemoration, and Patriotism in the Twentieth Century.* Princeton, N.J.: Princeton University Press, 1992.

"The Boom that Music Brought to Nashville." *U. S. News & World Report*, July 29, 1974, 60.

Boyum, Joy Gould. "Just Plain Populist Folks," *Wall Street Journal*, June 9, 1975, 13.

Brackett, David. *Interpreting Popular Music.* New York: Cambridge University Press, 1995.

Braudy, Leo. *The World in a Frame: What We See in Films.* Chicago: University of Chicago Press, 2002 [1977].

"Bull Market in Corn." *Time*, October 4, 1943, 33–34.

Byrne, Connie, and William O. Lopez. "Nashville." *Film Quarterly* 29 (winter 1975): 13–25.

Cantril, Hadley, and Gordon W. Allport. *The Psychology of Radio.* New York: Harper and Brothers, 1935.

Cantwell, Robert. *Bluegrass Breakdown: The Making of the Old Southern Sound.* Urbana: University of Illinois Press, 1984.

———. *When We Were Good: The Folk Revival.* Cambridge, Mass.: Harvard University Press, 1996.

Carney, George O. "Spatial Diffusion of the All-Country Radio Stations in the United States, 1971–1974." *JEMF Quarterly* 8 (summer 1977): 58–65.

Carr, Patrick. "Will the Circle Be Unbroken: The Changing Image of Country Music." In *Country: The Music and the Musicians,* edited by Paul Kingsbury. New York: Abbeville Press, 1988. 476–523.

Carter, Dan T. *The Politics of Rage: George Wallace, the Origins of the New Conservatism, and the Transformation of American Politics.* Baton Rouge: Louisiana State University Press, 2000.

Cavicchi, Daniel. *Tramps Like Us: Music and Meaning among Springsteen Fans.* New York: Oxford University Press, 1998.

Chapple, Steve, and Reebee Garofalo. *Rock 'n' Roll Is Here to Pay: The History and Politics of the Music Industry.* Chicago: Nelson-Hall, 1977.

Ching, Barbara. "Sounding the American Heart: Cultural Politics, Country Music, and Contemporary American Film." In *Soundtrack Available: Essays on Film and Popular Music,* edited by Pamela Robertson Wojcik and Arthur Knight. Durham, N.C.: Duke University Press, 2001. 202–25.

———. *Wrong's What I Do Best: Hard Country Music and Contemporary Culture.* New York: Oxford University Press, 2001.

Ching, Barbara, and Gerald W. Creed, eds. *Knowing Your Place: Rural Identity and Cultural Hierarchy.* New York: Routledge, 1996.

Coates, Norma. "Teenyboppers, Groupies, and Other Grotesques: Girls and Women and Rock Culture in the 1960s and Early 1970s." *Journal of Popular Music Studies* 15, no. 1 (2003): 65–94.

Cohen, Lizabeth. *Making a New Deal: Industrial Workers in Chicago, 1919–1939.* New York: Cambridge University Press, 1990.

———. "The Class Experience of Mass Consumption." In *The Power of Culture: Critical Essays in American History,* edited by Richard Wightman Fox and T. J. Jackson Lears. Chicago: University of Chicago Press, 1993.

———. *A Consumers' Republic: The Politics of Mass Consumption in Postwar America.* New York: Alfred A. Knopf, 2003.

Cohen, Norm. "The John Edwards Memorial Foundation: Its History and Significance." In *Sounds of the South,* edited by Daniel W. Patterson. Durham, N.C.: Duke University Press, 1991. 113–26.

Conkin, Paul. *Tomorrow a New World: The New Deal Community Program.* Ithaca, N.Y.: Cornell University Press, 1959.

"Country Music: The Nashville Sound." *Time,* November 17, 1964, 76, 79.

Crawford, Richard. *America's Musical Life: A History.* New York: Norton, 2001.

Criesler, Lillian. "Little Oklahoma: A Study of the Social and Economic Adjustment of Refugees in the Beard Tract, Modesto, Stanislaus County, California." M.A. thesis, University of California, 1935.

Cross, Gary. *An All-Consuming Century: Why Commercialism Won in Modern America.* New York: Columbia University Press, 2000.

Daley, Dan. *Nashville's Unwritten Rules: Inside the Business of Country Music.* New York: Overlook, 1999.

Danbom, David B. "Romantic Agrarianism in the Twentieth Century." *Agricultural History* 65 (fall 1991): 1–12.

Daniel, Pete. *Lost Revolutions: The South in the 1950s.* Chapel Hill: University of North Carolina Press, 2000.

Danker, Frederick. "Country Music." *Yale Review* 63 (spring 1974): 392–404.

Davidson, Donald. *The Big Ballad Jamboree.* Jackson: University Press of Mississippi, 1996.

Denning, Michael. *The Cultural Front: The Laboring of American Culture in the Twentieth Century.* New York: Verso, 1997.

Dickson, Paul. "Singing to Silent America." *Nation,* February 23, 1970, 211–13.

DiMaggio, Paul, Richard A. Peterson, and Jack Esco Jr. "Country Music: Ballad of the Silent Majority." In *The Sounds of Social Change: Studies in Popular Culture,* edited by Serge Denisoff and Richard A. Peterson. Chicago: Rand McNally, 1972. 38–55.

Doerksen, Clifford J. *American Babel: Rogue Radio Broadcasters of the Jazz Age.* Philadelphia: University of Pennsylvania Press, 2005.

Donahue, Kathleen G. *Freedom from Want: American Liberalism and the Idea of the Consumer.* Baltimore: Johns Hopkins University Press, 2004.

Douglas, Susan J. *Listening In: Radio and the American Imagination, from Amos 'n' Andy and Edward R. Murrow to Wolfman Jack and Howard Stern.* New York: Random House, 1999.

Ellison, Curtis W. *Country Music Culture: From Hard Times to Heaven.* Jackson: University Press of Mississippi, 1995.

Ennis, Philip H. *The Seventh Stream: The Emergence of Rock 'n' Roll in American Popular Music.* Hanover, N.H.: Wesleyan University Press, 1992.

Escott, Colin. *Hank Williams: The Biography.* Boston: Little, Brown, 1994.

Evans, James F. *Prairie Farmer and WLS: The Burridge D. Butler Years.* Urbana: University of Illinois Press, 1969.

Filene, Benjamin. *Romancing the Folk: Public Memory and American Roots Music.* Chapel Hill: University of North Carolina Press, 2000.

Fiske, John. *Understanding Popular Culture.* New York: Routledge, 1989.

———. *Reading the Popular.* New York: Routledge, 1989.

Fox, Aaron A. "White Trash Alchemies of the Abject Sublime: Country as 'Bad' Music." In *Bad Music: The Music We Love to Hate,* edited by Christopher J. Washburne and Maiken Derno. New York: Routledge, 2004. 39–61.

Fox, Frank. *Madison Avenue Goes to War: The Strange Military Career of*

American Advertising, 1941–1945. Provo, Utah: Brigham Young University Press, 1975.

Fox, Stephen. *The Mirror Makers: A History of American Advertising and Its Creators.* New York: Vintage, 1984.

Frank, Thomas. *The Conquest of Cool: Business Culture, Counterculture, and the Rise of Hip Consumerism.* Chicago: University of Chicago Press, 1997.

Fryd, Vivien Green. " 'The Sad Twang of Mountain Voices': Thomas Hart Benton's *Sources of Country Music.*" *South Atlantic Quarterly* 94 (winter 1995): 301–35.

Fuller, Kathryn H. *At the Picture Show: Small-Town Audiences and the Creation of Movie Fan Culture.* Washington: Smithsonian Institution Press, 1996.

Gentry, Linnell, ed. *A History and Encyclopedia of Country, Western, and Gospel Music.* Rev. ed. Nashville, Tenn.: Clairmont, 1969.

Gilliatt, Penelope. " 'Love and Death and 'Nashville.' " *New Yorker,* June 16, 1975, 107–9.

Goist, Park Dixon. *From Main Street to State Street: Town, City, and Community in America.* Port Washington, N.Y.: National University Press, 1977.

Goldstein, Richard. "My Country Music Problem—and Yours." *Mademoiselle,* June 1973, 115.

Green, Archie. "Hillbilly Music: Source and Symbol." *Journal of American Folklore* 78 (July–September 1965): 223.

——. "Early Country Music Journals." *JEMF Quarterly* 16 (fall 1980): 140–46.

Greenway, John. "No Talk That God Is Dead." *National Review,* August 11, 1970, 842, 857.

Gregory, James N. *American Exodus: The Dust Bowl Migration and Okie Culture in California.* New York: Oxford University Press, 1989.

——. "Southernizing the American Working Class: Post-War Episodes of Regional and Class Transformation." *Labor History* 39, no. 2 (1998): 135–54.

Grundy, Pamela. " 'We Always Tried to Be Good People': Respectability, Crazy Water Crystals, and Hillbilly Music on the Air, 1933–1935." *Journal of American History* 81 (March 1995): 1591–1620.

Guralnick, Peter. *Last Train to Memphis: The Rise of Elvis Presley.* Boston: Little, Brown, 1994.

Guy, Roger. "Down Home: Perception and Reality among Southern White Migrants in Post World War II Chicago." *Oral History Review* 24 (winter 1997): 35–52.

Hagerty, Bernard G. "WNAX: Country Music on a Rural Radio Station, 1927–1955." *JEMF Quarterly* 11 (winter 1975): 177–82.

Harkins, Anthony. "The Significance of 'Hillbilly' in Early Country Music, 1924–1945." *Journal of Appalachian Studies* 2 (fall 1996): 311–22.

———. *Hillbilly: A Cultural History of an American Icon.* New York: Oxford University Press, 2004.

Haslam, Gerald W. *Workin' Man Blues: Country Music in California.* Berkeley: University of California Press, 1999.

Hatch, Robert. "Nashville." *Nation,* July 5, 1975, 28.

Hazen, Cindy, and Mike Freeman, eds. *Love Always, Patsy: Patsy Cline's Letters to a Friend.* New York: Berkley, 1999.

Heim, Joe. "It's a Twang Thang." *Washington Post,* May 12, 2002, E1.

Hemphill, Paul. *The Nashville Sound: Bright Lights and Country Music.* New York: Simon and Schuster, 1970.

Hettinger, Herman S. *A Decade of Radio Advertising.* Chicago: University of Chicago Press, 1933.

———. "What We Know about the Listening Audience." In *Radio and Education,* edited by L. Tyson. Chicago: University of Chicago Press, 1933.

Hettinger, Herman S., and Walter J. Neff. *Practical Radio Advertising.* New York: Prentice-Hall, 1938.

Hills, Matt. *Fan Cultures.* New York: Routledge, 2002.

"Hoedown on a Harpsichord." *Time,* November 1, 1960, 52.

Hoekstra, Dave. "The Three Decade Night of the Sundowners." *Journal of Country Music* 20, no. 1 (1998): 31.

Hofstadter, Richard. *The American Political Tradition and the Men Who Made It.* New York: Vintage, 1959.

Hofstadter, Richard. *The Age of Reform.* New York: Vintage, 1955.

———. *The American Political Tradition and the Men Who Made It.* New York: Vintage, 1959.

Horkheimer, Max, and Theodor Adorno, *Dialectic of Enlightenment.* New York: Continuum, 2002.

Horowitz, Daniel. *Vance Packard and American Social Criticism.* Chapel Hill: University of North Carolina Press, 1994.

———, ed. *American Social Classes in the 1950s: Selections from Vance Packard's* The Status Seekers. Boston: Bedford Books, 1995.

Horstman, Dorothy. *Sing Your Heart Out, Country Boy.* Nashville, Tenn.: Country Music Foundation Press, 1986.

Hurst, Jack. "Nashville's Country Music Brings Cultural Turnabout." *Nashville Tennessean,* January 9, 1966, 14.

Ivey, Bill. "The Bottom Line: Business Practices That Shaped Country Music." In *Country: The Music and the Musicians,* edited by Paul Kingsbury and Alan Axelrod. New York: Abbeville Press, 1988. 406–51.

Jenkins, Henry. *Textual Poachers: Television Fans and Participant Culture.* New York: Routledge, 1992.

Jensen, Joli. "Genre and Recalcitrance: Country Music's Move Uptown." *Tracking* 1, no. 1 (1988): 37.

——. *The Nashville Sound: Authenticity, Commercialization, and Country Music.* Nashville, Tenn.: Country Music Foundation and Vanderbilt University Press, 1998.

Kael, Pauline. "Coming: 'Nashville.'" *New Yorker,* March 3, 1975, 79–83.

Kahn, Ed. "Hillbilly Music: Source and Resource." *Journal of American Folklore* (July–September 1965): 257–64.

Kammen, Michael. *American Culture, American Tastes: Social Change and the Twentieth Century.* New York: Alfred A. Knopf, 1999.

Kauffmann, Stanley. "Nashville." *New Republic,* June 28, 1975, 22.

Keillor, Garrison. "At the Opry." *New Yorker,* May 6, 1974, 46–70.

Kennedy, Rick, and Randy McNutt. *Little Labels—Big Sound: Small Record Companies and the Rise of American Music.* Bloomington: Indiana University Press, 1999.

Kenney, William Howland. *Recorded Music in American Life: The Phonograph and Popular Memory, 1890–1945.* New York: Oxford University Press, 1999.

Killian, Lewis M. "Southern White Laborers in Chicago's Local Communities." Ph.D. diss., University of Chicago, 1949.

King, Florence. "Rednecks, White Socks, and Blue Ribbon Fear." *Harper's,* July 1974, 30–34.

King, Larry L. "The Grand Ole Opry." *Harper's,* July 1968, 43–50.

Kingsbury, Paul, ed. *The Encyclopedia of Country Music.* New York: Oxford University Press, 1998.

Kirby, Jack. *Media-Made Dixie: The South in the American Imagination.* Baton Rouge: Louisiana University Press, 1978.

Kreyling, Christine. "Country Comes to Town." *Nashville Scene,* May 10, 2001, 26.

Kyriakoudes, Louis M. "The Grand Ole Opry and the Urban South." *Southern Cultures* 10, no. 1 (2004): 67–84.

Lazarsfeld, Paul F. *Radio and the Printed Page: An Introduction to the Study of Radio and Its Role in the Communication of Ideas.* New York: Duell, Sloan, and Pearce, 1940.

——. *The People Look at Radio.* Chapel Hill: University of North Carolina Press, 1946.

Lazarsfeld, Paul F., and Patricia Kendall. *Radio Listening in America.* New York: Prentice-Hall, 1948.

Leamy, Hugh. "Now Come All You Good People." *Collier's,* November 2, 1929, 58.

Lears, Jackson. "A Matter of Taste: Corporate Cultural Hegemony in a Mass-Consumption Society." In *Recasting America: Culture and Politics in the Age of the Cold War,* edited by Lary May. Chicago: University of Chicago Press, 1989. 38–61.

Levine, Lawrence. *Highbrow/Lowbrow: The Emergence of Cultural Hierarchy in America.* Cambridge, Mass.: Harvard University Press, 1988.

Levy, Emanuel. *Small-Town America in Film.* New York: Continuum, 1991.

Lewis, Lisa A., ed. *The Adoring Audience: Fan Culture and Popular Media.* New York: Routledge, 1992.

Lieberson, Goddard, "Country Sweeps the Country." *New York Times Magazine,* July 28, 1957, 13, 48.

Lipsitz, George. *Time Passages: Collective Memory and American Popular Culture.* Minneapolis: University of Minnesota Press, 1990.

——. *Rainbow at Midnight: Labor and Culture in the 1940s.* Urbana: University of Illinois Press, 1994.

Logan, Horace, with Bill Sloan. *Elvis, Hank, and Me: Making Musical History on the Louisiana Hayride.* New York: St. Martin's Press, 1998.

Lomax, John III. *Nashville: Music City, USA.* New York: Harry N. Abrams, 1985.

Longino, Miriam Pace. "Country Music's Treasures Get a Stunning New Home." *Atlanta Constitution,* May 11, 2001, E1.

Lund, Jens. "Fundamentalism, Racism, and Political Reaction in Country Music." In *The Sounds of Social Change: Studies in Popular Culture,* edited by Serge Denisoff and Richard A. Peterson. Chicago: Rand McNally, 1972.

Malone, Bill C. "Honky Tonk: The Music of the Southern Working Class." In *Folk Music and the Modern Sound,* edited by William Ferris and Mary L. Hart. Jackson: University Press of Mississippi, 1982. 119–28.

——. *Country Music USA.* Austin: University of Texas Press, 1985.

——. "Country Music and the Academy: A Thirty Year Professional Odyssey." In *Sounds of the South,* edited by Daniel W. Patterson. Durham, N.C.: Duke University Press, 1991. 41–56.

——. "Elvis, Country Music, and the South." In *All That Glitters: Country Music in America,* edited by George H. Lewis. Bowling Green, Ohio: Bowling Green State University Popular Press, 1993. 51–58.

——. *Singing Cowboys and Musical Mountaineers: Southern Culture and the Roots of Country Music.* Athens: University of Georgia Press, 1993.

——. *Don't Get above Your Raisin': Country Music and the Southern Working Class.* Urbana: University of Illinois Press, 2002.

Mancini, J. M. "'Messin' with the Furniture Man': Early Country Music, Regional Culture, and the Search for an Anthological Modernism." *American Literary History* 16, no. 2 (2004): 208–37.

Mano, D. Keith. "Going Country." *National Review,* January 18, 1974, 90.

Marchand, Roland. *Advertising the American Dream.* Berkeley: University of California Press, 1986.

Marek, Richard. "Country Music Nashville Style." *McCall's*, April 1961, 92–93, 168–70.

Marling, Karal Ann. *As Seen on TV: The Visual Culture of Everyday Life in the 1950s.* Cambridge, Mass.: Harvard University Press, 1994.

May, Elaine Tyler. "Cold War—Warm Hearth: Politics and the Family in Postwar America." In *The Rise and Fall of the New Deal Order, 1930–1980,* edited by Steve Fraser and Gary Gerstle. Princeton: Princeton University Press, 1989. 153–81.

McCusker, Kristine M. " 'Dear Radio Friend': Listener Mail and the National Barn Dance, 1931–1941." *American Studies* 39 (summer 1998): 173–95.

——. " 'Bury Me beneath the Willow': Linda Parker and Definitions of Tradition on the National Barn Dance." *Southern Folklore* 56, no. 3 (1999): 223–43.

McPartland, John. *No Down Payment.* New York: Simon and Schuster, 1957.

Miles, Emma Bell. "Some Real American Music." *Harper's*, June 1904, 118–23.

Morris, Edward. "New, Improved, Homogenized: Country Radio since 1950." In *Country: The Music and the Musicians,* edited by Paul Kingsbury and Alan Axelrod. New York: Abbeville Press, 1988. 88–107.

National Broadcasting Company. *Broadcasting.* Vol. 2. New York: National Broadcasting Company, 1933.

Negus, Keith. *Producing Pop: Culture and Conflict in the Popular Music Industry.* London: Arnold, 1992.

——. *Music Genres and Corporate Cultures.* New York: Routledge, 1999.

Newman, Kathleen Michelle. "Critical Mass: Advertising, Audiences, and Consumer Activism in the Age of Radio." Ph.D. diss., Yale University, 1997.

Osborne, John. "The Nixon Watch: Having Fun." *New Republic,* March 30, 1974, 8–10.

Packard, Vance. *The Hidden Persuaders.* New York: Pocket Books, 1958.

——. *The Status Seekers.* New York: David McKay, 1959.

Passman, Arnold. *The Deejays.* New York: Macmillan, 1971.

Patterson, Timothy A. "Hillbilly among the Flatlanders: Early Midwestern Radio Barn Dances." *Journal of Country Music* 6 (spring 1975): 12–18.

Pecknold, Diane. " 'I Wanna Play House': Configurations of Masculinity in the Nashville Sound Era." In *A Boy Named Sue: Gender and Country Music,* edited by Kristine M. McCusker and Diane Pecknold. Jackson: University Press of Mississippi, 2004. 86–106.

Pescatello, Ann M. *Charles Seeger: A Life in American Music.* Pittsburgh: University of Pittsburgh Press, 1992.

Peterson, Richard A. "Class Unconsciousness in Country Music." In *You Wrote My Life: Lyrical Themes in Country Music,* edited by Melton A.

McLauren and Richard A. Peterson. Philadelphia: Gordon and Breach, 1992. 35–62.

——. *Creating Country Music: Fabricating Authenticity.* Chicago: University of Chicago Press, 1997.

Peterson, Richard A., and N. Anand. "The Production of Culture Perspective." *Annual Review of Sociology* 30 (2004): 311–34.

Peterson, Richard, and Bruce Beal. "Alternative Country: Origins, Music, Worldview, Fans, and Taste in Genre Formation—A Discographic Essay." *Popular Music and Society* 25 (spring/summer 2001): 233–49.

Peterson, Richard A., and Paul DiMaggio. "From Region to Class, the Changing Locus of Country Music: A Test of the Massification Hypothesis." *Social Forces* 53 (March 1975): 497–506.

Phillips, Kevin P. *The Emerging Republican Majority.* New Rochelle, N.Y.: Arlington House, 1969.

——. "Revolutionary Music." *Washington Post,* May 6, 1971, A19.

"Pistol Packin' Mama." *Life,* October 11, 1943, 43–44.

Porterfield, Nolan. *Jimmie Rodgers: The Life and Times of America's Blue Yodeler.* Urbana: University of Illinois Press, 1979.

Portis, Charles. "That New Sound from Nashville." *Saturday Evening Post,* February 12, 1966, 30–38.

Pugh, Ronnie. *Ernest Tubb: The Texas Troubadour.* Durham, N.C.: Duke University Press, 1996.

——. "Country Music Is Here to Stay?" *Journal of Country Music* 19, no. 1 (1997): 32–38.

Radway, Janice A. *Reading the Romance: Women, Patriarchy, and Popular Culture.* Chapel Hill: University of North Carolina Press, 1984.

Rhodes, Lisa L. *Electric Ladyland: Women and Rock Culture.* Philadelphia: University of Pennsylvania Press, 2005.

Rice, Harry S. "Renfro Valley on the Radio, 1937–1941." *Journal of Country Music* 19, no. 2 (1997): 19–20.

Rieder, Jonathan. "The Rise of the 'Silent Majority.'" In *The Rise and Fall of the New Deal Order, 1930–1980,* edited by Steve Fraser and Gary Gerstle. Princeton, N.J.: Princeton University Press, 1989. 243–68.

Riesman, David. *The Lonely Crowd: A Study of the Changing American Character.* New Haven, Conn.: Yale University Press, 1971.

"Rodgers Remembered." *Newsweek,* June 8, 1953, 62.

Rumble, John. "Fred Rose and the Development of the Nashville Music Industry, 1942–1954." Ph.D. diss., Vanderbilt University, 1980.

Ryan, John. *The Production of Culture in the Music Industry: The ASCAP-BMI Controversy.* Lanham, Md.: University Press of America, 1985.

Sanjek, David. "Institutions." In *Key Terms in Popular Music and Culture,* edited by Bruce Horner and Thomas Swiss. Malden, Mass.: Blackwell, 1999. 46–56.

———. "They Work Hard for Their Money: The Business of Popular Music." In *American Popular Music: New Approaches to the Twentieth Century,* edited by Rachel Rubin and Jeffrey Melnick. Amherst: University of Massachusetts Press, 2001. 9–28.

Sanjek, Russell. *From Print to Plastic: Publishing and Promoting America's Popular Music (1900–1980).* Brooklyn: Institute for Studies in American Music, 1983.

———. *Pennies from Heaven: The American Popular Music Business in the Twentieth Century.* New York: Da Capo Press, 1996.

Scott, Derek B., ed. *Music, Culture, and Society: A Reader.* New York: Oxford University Press, 2000.

Seeger, Charles. "Music and Class Structure in the United States." *American Quarterly* 9 (fall 1957): 281–94.

Seelye, John. "The Sound of Money." *New Republic,* June 27, 1970, 21.

Shortridge, James R. *The Middle West: Its Meaning in American Culture.* Lawrence: University Press of Kansas, 1989.

Smith, Arthur. " 'Hill Billy' Folk Music: A Little-Known American Type." *Etude Music Magazine,* March 1933, 154, 208.

Smulyan, Susan. *Selling Radio: The Commercialization of American Broadcasting, 1920–1934.* Washington: Smithsonian Institution Press, 1994.

Smyth, Willie J. "Early Knoxville Radio (1921–1941): WNOX and the 'Midday Merry Go-Round.' " *JEMF Quarterly* 18 (fall/winter 1982): 109–15.

Stamp, Shelley. *Movie-Struck Girls: Women and Motion Picture Culture after the Nickelodeon.* Princeton, N.J.: Princeton University Press, 2000.

Steele, Harry. "The Inside Story of the Hillbilly Business." *JEMF Quarterly* 10 (summer 1974): 20.

Stockdell, Richard Price. "The Development of the Country Music Radio Format." M.A. thesis, Kansas State University, 1973.

Stuart, Jan. *The Nashville Chronicles: The Making of Robert Altman's Masterpiece.* New York: Simon and Schuster, 2000.

Sugrue, Thomas J. "The Incredible Disappearing Southerner?" *Labor History* 39, no. 2 (1998): 161–66.

Suisman, David. "The Sound of Money: Music, Machines and Markets, 1890–1925." Ph.D. diss., Columbia University, 2002.

Tedlow, Richard S. "The Fourth Phase of Marketing: Marketing History and the Business World Today." In *The Rise and Fall of Mass Marketing,* edited by Richard S. Tedlow and Geoffrey Jones. London: Routledge, 1993.

Tichi, Cecelia. *High Lonesome: The American Culture of Country Music.* Chapel Hill: University of North Carolina Press, 1994.

——, ed. *Readin' Country Music: Steel Guitars, Opry Stars, and Honky Tonk Bars.* Durham, N.C.: Duke University Press, 1995.

Tosches, Nick. *Country: The Twisted Roots of Rock 'n' Roll.* New York: Da Capo Press, 1996.

Traver, Jerome D., and Joel M. Maring. "*Stand By:* Journalistic Response to a Country Music Radio Audience." *JEMF Quarterly* 19 (autumn 1983): 150.

Travis, Fred. "A Barn-Style Museum for Country-Style Music." *New York Times,* January 7, 1968, sec. 10, p. 15.

Tribe, Ivan M. "The Economics of Hillbilly Radio: A Preliminary Investigation of the 'P.I.' System in the Depression Decade and Afterward." *JEMF Quarterly* 20 (fall/winter 1984): 80.

Twitchell, James. *Lead Us into Temptation: The Triumph of American Materialism.* New York: Columbia University Press, 1999.

Valiant, Margaret. "Journal of a Field Representative." *Ethnomusicology* 24 (May 1980): 182.

Van Sickel, Robert W. "A World without Citizenship: On the (Absence of) Politics and Ideology in Country Music Lyrics, 1960–2000." *Popular Music and Society* 28 (July 2005): 313–31.

Votaw, Albert N. "The Hillbillies Invade Chicago." *Harper's,* February 1958, 64–67.

Warren, Thomas D. "Country Music Foundation in Brief." *Ralph Stanley International Fan Club Journal* 4, no. 1 (1969?): 5–6.

——. "The Story of the Country Music Association." *Ralph Stanley International Fan Club Journal* 4, no. 1 (1969?): 7–13.

Whaley, Cecil. "Synopsis of Important Events." *Ralph Stanley International Fan Club Journal* 4, no. 1 (1969?): 13–17.

"What the Popularity of Hill-Billy Songs Means in Retail Profit Possibilities." *Talking Machine World,* December 15, 1925, 177.

Whisnant, David E. *All That Is Native and Fine: The Politics of Culture in an American Region.* Chapel Hill: University of North Carolina Press, 1983.

Whyte, William. *The Organization Man.* New York: Simon and Schuster, 1956.

Wicker, Tom. "'Nashville'—Dark Perceptions in a Country Music Comedy." *New York Times,* June 15, 1975, D1.

Wilgus, D. K. "An Introduction to the Study of Hillbilly Music." *Journal of American Folklore* 78 (July–September 1965): 195–203.

——. "Country-Western Music and the Urban Hillbilly." *Journal of American Folklore* 83 (April–June 1970): 157–79.

Williamson, Chilton, Jr. "Country and Western Marxism: To the Nashville Station." *National Review,* June 9, 1978, 711–16.

Williamson, J. W. *Hillbillyland: What the Movies Did to the Mountains and*

What the Mountains Did to the Movies. Chapel Hill: University of North
  Carolina Press, 1995.
Wilson, Charles Morrow. *Money at the Crossroads: An Intimate Study of
  Radio's Influence upon a Great Market of 60,000,000 People.* New York:
  National Broadcasting Company, 1937.
Wolfe, Charles. "The Triumph of the Hills: Country Radio, 1920–1950." In
  Country, the Music and the Musicians, edited by Paul Kingsbury and
  Alan Axelrod. New York: Abbeville Press, 1988. 52–87.
———. *A Good-Natured Riot: The Birth of the Grand Ole Opry.* Nashville,
  Tenn.: Country Music Foundation and Vanderbilt University Press,
  1999.
Wray, Matt, and Annalee Newitz, eds. *White Trash: Race and Class in
  America.* New York: Routledge, 1997.
Wren, Christopher S. "The Great White Soul Sound: Country Music." *Look,*
  July 13, 1971, 11–13.

Index

Autry, Gene: ASCAP and, 27, 109; CMA and, 220; fan clubs, 39, 125; listener response to, 49; Fred Rose and, 57, 60

Bare, Bobby, 188

Barn dance radio: audience for, 19–20, 38–39, 48; diverse content of, 16–17, 52; early development of, 15–16; independent radio stations and, 18–19, 52; middle-class imagery of, 21–23; relationship to broadcast advertising, 17–19; relationship to jazz, 20; revival of format, 53; theatricality of, 41–42, 52

Barthel, Norma, 126–27, 131, 206–7, 209–10

Benson, Al, 86

Bernard, Charles, 142–43, 153–54

Bill, Edgar L., 15, 19

Billboard: country music charts, 58–59, 63, 93; coverage of country disc jockeys, 83–84, 67; coverage of Jimmie Rodgers Memorial Day, 79–80; coverage of WSM Disc Jockey Festival, 73–74, 80; hillbilly stereotyping, 60, 73–74; role in revising image of country music, 60–61, 70–71, 90

Blake, Randy, 66, 86, 159

Boone, Pat, 89

Botkin, B. A., 99

Bradley, Owen, 91, 93, 134

Briley, Beverly, 184–85

Broadcast advertising: association with early country radio, 8, 14, 17–19 55, 58; CMA campaign for, 152–59, 161–62; country format radio and, 3–4, 92, 94; fan awareness of, 118, 122

Broadcast Music, Inc. (BMI): Acuff-Rose Publications and, 57–58; conflict with ASCAP, 54, 103–11;

defense by country industry, 105–6, 108–10; formation and structure, 32, 55–56; role in development of Music Row, 53, 56–58, 74; support of CMA, 187

Brooker, "Cracker" Jim, 76, 179, 180

Buchanan, Annabel Morris, 29–30, 38, 190

Burton, Robert Jay, 187

Butler, Burridge D., 21, 31, 36, 47, 51

Campbell, Glenn, 151

Carter, Jimmy, 231

Carter Family, 190

Cash, Johnny, 139, 214, 220

Castle Studios, 91

Celler, Emanuel, 104–6

Charles, Ray, 155

Cherry, Hugh, 67

Clement, Frank: CMA and, 220; Jimmie Rodgers Memorial Day and, 72, 80; testimony to Congress, 105–6, 108–10, 183

Cline, Patsy: correspondence with Treva Miller, 128–30; in Country Music Hall of Fame and Museum, 197; early career, 129–30; fan club, 127–28

Cohen, Paul, 91

Collie, Biff, 67, 81, 144

Coolidge, Arlan, 106–7

Cooper, Jack, 87

Country & Western Jamboree: "Crusade for Country Music," 116–19, 132; fan letters to, 121–25; role in explaining country industry, 118–19

Country Music Association (CMA): commercialism and, 5, 6; development of country format radio and, 132, 146–49, 151, 160, 163; efforts to define country music, 174–75, 178–80; Fan Fair and, 10, 212–18; history initiatives of, 6, 10, 177–

Fan Fair: as alternative to fan conventions, 212, 214; fan response to, 10, 215–17; organization and founding of, 213–14, 216–17; role in redefining fan-industry relations, 217–18

Fan magazines: class identity and, 44, 96–97; coverage of barn dance radio, 40–42; as promotional organs, 126; promotion of rural-urban distinctions, 42–43. See also *Country & Western Jamboree; K-Bar-T Country Round-Up*

Flatt and Scruggs, 155, 185, 190

Foley, Red, 22, 71, 89, 188

Folklorists: conceptions of folk culture, 97–99; cultural functions of country music and, 36–38; early rejection of commercial country music, 2, 14, 28–30, 178, 237; research on country music, 6, 191–92, 195

Folk music: distinguished from country music, 2, 28–29, 80, 190; festivals, 29–30; portrayal of country music as, 21, 61, 113, 190–91

Ford, "Tennessee" Ernie, 144

Gable, Dorothy, 196

Gay, Connie B.: definition of country music by, 174, 179; as disc jockey, 66; role in CMA radio marketing, 153; role in formation of CMA, 137, 141, 159, 220; support of Country Music Hall of Fame and Museum, 187

Gershwin, Ira, 104

Gibson, Don, 155, 185, 188

Gilbert, Martin, 187–88

Glenn, Willis, 126, 130

Goldwater, Barry, 105

Gore, Albert, Sr., 108, 220

Grand Ole Opry: anniversary celebration, 67, 69–70; at Carnegie Hall, 163; in Country Music Hall of Fame and Museum, 198; at Jimmie Rodgers Memorial Day, 81; listener response to, 13; move to Opryland, 226, 239; musical content of, 16, 49 52; in *Nashville*, 229–31, 233–34; Richard Nixon's appearance on, 227–28; response to rock and roll, 90; role in development of Music Row, 53, 57, 66, 184; Harry Stone and, 138; as symbol of conservatism, 222–23, 227; Helen Traubel's appearance on, 114. *See also* WSM; WSM Disc Jockey Festival

Green, Archie, 191, 193

Green, Ben, 117–19

Griffith, Andy, 101–2

Haggard, Merle, 214, 220, 224–26

Hall, Tom T., 223

Hamblen, Stuart, 218

Haning, Cora Rea, 206

Haverlin, Carl, 74, 104

Hay, George D., 16, 41, 69

Haynes, Dick, 67

Hee Haw, 223

Hidden Persuaders, The, 107–8. *See also* Packard, Vance

Hill, Eddie, 67

Hill & Range, 91, 187

Hillbilly stereotype: audience responses to, 46–49, 150, 160–62, 164–65, 116, 124, 135; barn dance portrayal of, 25, 41–42; barn dance rejection of, 21–22; country music industry and, 5–6, 72, 114–16, 133–35, 137, 144, 146, 153, 158, 183; in popular culture, 95, 100–103, 133; in sociological assessments, 100, 103, 134; U.S. Army and, 176

Hoeptner, Fred, 191

Riesman, David, 100
Ritter, Tex, 113, 155–57, 161, 186, 196
Robbins, Marty, 91, 188
Rock and roll: audience responses to, 96–97, 105, 170; disc jockey responses to, 84, 86–88; emergence of, 54, 85, 88; race and, 86–87, 97, 122–23, 132; role in development of country industry, 2, 89–94, 134; Smathers Bill and, 105, 107–8; as threat to country music, 78, 86, 90–93. *See also* Presley, Elvis
Rodgers, Jimmie: in Country Music Hall of Fame, 181; death, 70–71, 75; fan club, 39, 128–29; Memorial Day celebration, 71–74, 78–84, 88, 137, 139–40
Rogers, Roy, 125
Rose, Fred: business practices, 62–63; in Country Music Hall of Fame, 181; cultural status of country music and, 61–62, 72, 94; formation of Acuff-Rose Publications and, 57; as songwriter, 60–62, 70
Rose, Wesley, 62, 93, 137–38, 186

Satherly, Art, 60–61, 72, 94, 192
Schofield, Dick, 143–45, 147, 188
Schwartz v. BMI, 104. *See also* Broadcast Music, Inc.
Seeger, Charles, 36, 37, 99
Sherrill, Billy, 233
Sholes, Steve, 88, 91, 141, 180
Silent majority, 201, 223–24, 242
Sippel, Johnny, 59, 67, 68
Slack, Ruth, 131, 207, 214
Slater, Manning, 150
Smathers, George, 106, 111
Smathers Bill (S. 2834), 106–11, 182
Snow, Hank: fan club, 126–27; Jimmie Rodgers Memorial Day and,

71–73, 79, 81; popularity of, 70; Elvis Presley and, 91
Song Exchange Club, 40
Stallard, Dal, 68
Stapp, Jack, 93, 135–37
Stevenson, Adlai, 79–80, 84
Stone, Cliffie, 67, 74, 144
Stone, Harry: as CMA executive director, 138–40, 187, 220–21; departure from CMA, 141; as WSM station manager, 138. *See also* Country Music Association

Thompson, Hank, 74
Tin Pan Alley: defined, 24; parallels with Music Row, 55, 66, 113–14; *Schwartz v. BMI* and, 103; transformation of publishers' functions and, 64–65, 104; view of hillbilly music, 5–6, 24–27, 58–60
Traubel, Helen, 113–14
Trinajstick, Blanche "Trina": on class identity of country fans, 130; family and, 131, 215, 217; fan club convention and, 206, 208, 211, 217; formation of K-Bar-T and, 202–3; on relationship between industry and fan clubs, 206, 210–14, 217; response to Fan Fair, 210–17
Tubb, Ernest: CMA and, 80–82, 137, 139, 188; fan club, 125–26, 207; fan club convention and, 207; hillbilly stereotype and, 72; Jimmie Rodgers Memorial Day and, 71–73, 79, 80–82
Twitty, Conway, 214

Vagabonds, The, 16, 60
Valiant, Margaret, 36–38

Wagoner, Porter, 214
Walker-Meador, Jo: country format radio and, 147; Country Music Hall of Fame and Museum and,

DIANE PECKNOLD

is a postdoctoral teaching scholar at the Commonwealth

Center for the Humanities and Society at the University of

Louisville. She is the coeditor of *A Boy Named Sue:*

Gender and Country Music (2004).

Library of Congress Cataloging-in-Publication Data
Pecknold, Diane.
The selling sound : the rise of the country music industry
/ Diane Pecknold.
p. cm. — (Refiguring American music)
Includes bibliographical references (p.   ) and index.
ISBN-13: 978-0-8223-4059-1 (cloth : alk. paper)
ISBN-13: 978-0-8223-4080-5 (pbk. : alk. paper)
1. Country music—History and criticism. 2. Music
trade—United States. 3. Country music—Social aspects.
I. Title.
ML3524.P43 2007
781.642'09—dc22
2007021235

MUSIC
OF THE
HEART

The printer's symbol on the cover and title page is from the cover of John Wesley's first tune book, *A Collection of Tunes, Set to Music, As They are commonly sung at the Foundery*, 1742,